Masquerades in African Society

Masquerades in African Society

Gender, Power, and Identity

Walter E.A. van Beek and Harrie M. Leyten

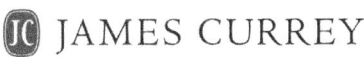

JC JAMES CURREY

First published 2023
Paperback edition 2025
James Currey

ISBN 978-1-84701-343-9 (Hardback)
ISBN 978-1-84701-388-0 (Paperback)

James Currey is an imprint of Boydell & Brewer Ltd
PO Box 9, Woodbridge, Suffolk IP12 3DF, UK
www.jamescurrey.com
and of Boydell & Brewer Inc.
668 Mt Hope Avenue
Rochester, NY 14620–2731, USA
www.boydellandbrewer.com

A CIP catalogue record for this book is available from the British Library

Contents

Illustrations

Maps

Figures

Tables

Full credit details are provided in the captions to the images in the text and at the end of this volume. The authors and publisher are grateful to all the institutions and individuals for permission to reproduce the materials in which they hold copyright. Every effort has been made to trace the copyright holders; apologies are offered for any omission, and the publisher will be pleased to add any necessary acknowledgement in subsequent editions.

Acknowledgements

There are many people we would like to thank for the role they have played in this endeavour. First the African Studies Centre at Leiden University for its generous support and its great library, the Museum of World Cultures in the Netherlands[1] for its invaluable collections in objects and books, and the use of their ethnic thesaurus; the Rietberg Museum in Zürich with the wealth of information from Eberhard Fischer and Lorenz Homberger; the supporting criticism of Arie de Ruyter from Utrecht University and Michael Rowlands from University College London; the comments by Jan-Bart Gewald, Jan Jansen, Rogier Bedaux, Catrin Finkenauer, Ian Fowler, Anne-Marie Bouttiaux and Saskia Brand, and the invaluable assistance of Joris Leyten. Special thanks go to the anonymous reviewers engaged by James Currey for their incisive comments on an earlier, partial version, which induced a thorough rewrite, as well as the reviewers of the present edition thanks to whom this book is not a hundred pages longer. In this process the editorial assistance of Jaqueline Mitchell has been crucial and we are very grateful for her continuous support and constructive comments. The enthusiasm of our colleagues who full-heartedly gave permission to use their photos for the illustrations in the book provided a great stimulus for the book, and we particularly thank Simon Ottenberg for his generous donation of video material from his personal archives. The cooperation between the two authors themselves rests on a long-term friendship and professional relation, which has been solidified at Tilburg University with the help of Paul Post. As always, the deepest gratitude is to our partners in life, Martina van Beek-Bom and Clémence Leyten-Thoman, for their patience and long-suffering when the book took longer than expected.

Walter E.A. van Beek
† Harrie M. Leyten

---

1   A merger of the Tropical Museum of Amsterdam, the Royal Museum of Ethnology in Leiden, the Africa Museum in Berg en Dal, and the World Museum in Rotterdam.

Introduction

Enter the mask

In the late afternoon the compound of Oulai Théodore is filling up with spectators eager to see the gegbadë *mask, which is renowned in the Ivorian city of Man, the capital of the Dan peoples. The courtyard is lined with benches facing the raffia wall that hides the house from view, and the men, women, and children from the village gradually find their places. At sunset, three musicians move in with drums, and a singer uses a gourd rattle to set the tempo. Their first task is to call the spirits, for without their inspiration the mask cannot work. The audience appreciates this as well, clapping and singing along while they start to dance; in Africa music means movement. A small chorus of young men and girls gathers around the singer, just next to the raffia wall, singing the response lines while dancing and clapping to the rhythm. The call for the mask is followed by the* getan, *the music of the mask. This music is more joyful and intense, and the dancing picks up. The atmosphere grows livelier and more animated, to prepare the audience but mainly to persuade the spirits to join the performance. At this point a voice is heard from the inside, and a woman intones the song 'The* ge *has arrived';* ge *is the general word for the masked figure. Gegbadë is not yet in sight, but the people can hear it respond to the singer, using a variety of voices, muffled, shrill, even screeching — an entrancing range of voices. The chorus shouts out cries of encouragement into the enclosure, and* gegbadë *starts directing the music with its voice, singing and speaking in proverbs, while on the outside an interpreter repeats what the mask has said in a loud voice.*

Benedictions flow from the house, with all present answering 'amina' (amen), and while the music and the singing are going full throttle, the masked figure slowly comes out of the house. First offering a view of its large striking beak, gegbadë *lingers in the opening, a tantalising half-view for the crowd, invoking in song and speech its own spirits but also those of other houses. The master drummer enters the house and, walking backwards, guides the masked apparition into the courtyard. Responding to the swift rhythms of the spirits' song,* gegbadë *spreads its arms, its body undulating to the pulse of the drums, and at long last dances into full view: it is huge. Its large mantle is spread out widely over the thick, heavy raffia skirts that billow over the ground; the cone-shaped leather hat on its head renders it taller than life. Cloth strips, hanging from the hat, frame the wooden headpiece, a striking face with an enormous beak lined with dark hair. Now the mask commands the dance, dominating the grounds in majestic moves and pointed gestures; attendants follow in its wake, watching its every move.* Gegbadë *has arrived.*

Daniel Reed reported this event in Dan territory in 1998,[1] followed by a description of the divination session that the mask entered into, which we will address in a later chapter. But here our main subject matter comes into full view: a mask ritual. Among the many kinds of ritual, those with masks stand out: the mask is an apparition that is highly orchestrated, with a great sense of drama, and wrapped into layers of meaning. In more than one sense the mask *is* the ritual, so masquerades form a ritual category that can profitably be singled out and analysed as such. This study concentrates on the roster of rituals that feature masks, analysing these performances in their social setting,[2] in those societies in Africa that have such rituals. Our guiding questions will be two-tiered: Which societies form the eco-sociological context for masquerades? What internal dynamics do the various types of mask rituals address in these societies, and how do they do this?

The study of masking

Our answers bridge two disciplines. Though for early anthropologists, indigenous art forms – called 'primitive' at that time – were objects of intensive studies, for their successors this was less the case.[3] During most of the twentieth century, cultural anthropology and art history studied African culture along parallel lines that hardly ever crossed, deriving only occasional inspiration from each other without seriously engaging in a quest for joint understanding. Africanist anthropology developed a fascination for power systems on the ground, and for kinship and lineage dynamics, as well as for ritual and witchcraft, and later focused on development and macropolitical issues, whereas art history found its primary topic inside museum collections, in the cultural object as such. While for instance British social anthropology

1   Reed 2003: 18–29.
2   Lewis 2013.
3   Forge 1973: xiii. Anthony Forge's expectation that in the following decade the anthropological study of art would take an important place in social and cultural anthropology (ibid.: xvii) has not been borne out, since that is nowhere near the case.

tended to stay aloof from the materiality of culture, museum curators were relatively late to enter the field to study objects in their socio-cultural setting.[4] Anthropology studied social dynamics and the effects of modernity, and when confronted with objects spoke about material culture; museum curators used the object as an informant, as art, and discovered the artist as an individual creator.[5] This historic divide has been unfortunate, but towards the end of the millennium some focused academic conferences[6] triggered a number of border crossings that reduced the distance between the two disciplines. In the meantime anthropology had grown out of its structural-functionalist paradigm, and regained an appreciation of history on the one hand, and of performance, materiality,[7] and aesthetics on the other. Art history, from its side, had developed a fascination for the terrain, unveiled the relevance of the person of the local artist within his social context,[8] and explored the contrasts between art-historical and indigenous interpretations.[9] In fact, these cross-over studies have made this book possible, written as it is by an anthropologist and a museum curator.

The study of masks forms a good example of this disciplinary divide. As the pride and glory of ethnographic museums, masks were claimed by art history, while anthropologists had neglected them to a surprising degree. For quite a few groups that have masquerades, their solid and extensive ethnographies mention masks only in passing, sometimes even just in a single footnote; listing these authors would look like anthropological patricide. Thus, our extensive knowledge about how masks look is not matched by a

4   Notable trail blazers were, among others, Marcel Griaule 1938, Dominique Zahan 1960, 1980, Guy le Moal 1980, Robert Thompson 1974, Christopher Roy 1987b, Susan Vogel 1997a, Zoë S. Strother 1998.

5   For instance D'Azevedo 1979; Abiodun et al. 1994; Fischer 2008; Lamp 2014. Both disciplines found each other, to some extent, in archival studies: Willis 2017.

6   For example, the 1965 symposium 'The aristocratic traditions in African art' at Columbia University, resulting in Fraser and Cole 1972, and the 1967 Wenner Gren conference 'Primitive art & society', resulting in Forge 1973.

7   Schechner and Turner 1985; Arweck 2004.

8   Major inspirations that we mention include Anne-Marie Bouttiaux's two major publications on masks (2009b, 2013a) and the seminal articles of Patrick McNaughton 1991, 1992. Other authors to whom we pledge scholarly allegiance will be mentioned in the text.

9   '"Art" in our sense does not exist in Baule villages' (Vogel 1997a: 80), and 'Conventional art-historical concerns […] are relatively unimportant to the Baule', ibid.: 89. See also Bouquet 2001.

similar insight into their use, function, social context, or political dynamics,[10] a gap we aim to fill with this anthropological study of masquerades.

In this book we use 'mask ritual' and 'masquerade' as alternate expressions. They are not exactly synonyms; a distinction has been made between the internal view (masking) and the external view (masquerade),[11] and not all masquerades function within the religious context that the term 'ritual' evokes. But for us these distinctions are less germane, since we question the total phenomenon of mask performances, ranging from ritual to entertainment, from the perspectives of both the masker and the audience.[12] Therefore in the text the two terms, mask ritual and masquerade, are used interchangeably.

Our fascination with masks has developed both inside the museum and in the field. As an anthropologist Walter van Beek has done extensive fieldwork, first among the Kapsiki of North Cameroon, and second among the Dogon of Mali, two groups that are quite comparable in ecology and history but definitely not in masking; the former culture has no masks, whereas the latter has them in abundance. Harrie Leyten has personal experience with a Ghanaian culture where masquerades are significantly absent, but has worked extensively with masks in his capacity as Africa curator of the Tropical Museum in Amsterdam, now part of the Museum of World Cultures.

Our specific angle was triggered by books on African art, for the maps indicating where masks are found on the continent[13] showed a pattern that aroused our curiosity. The distribution of art objects in these maps, including masks, raised the spectre of the African forest zone, so the question rose whether African masquerades correlated with ecology, and thus with specific social structures or historic dynamics. However, these maps were very general and lacked detail, so we started an inventory of all groups reported to have mask rituals and, plotting these on a map of the continent, came up with a

---

10   For an attempt to fill this gap, see Hersak 2010, 2012 and 2020 on Songye masks, and from a more technical standpoint, O'Hern et al. 2016.

11   See for instance Picton 1988b: 185–186.

12   The word 'masquerade' is also used in puppet theatre, for instance in Mali, but that kind of theatre falls outside our scope – even if it does show links with mask rituals. See Arnoldi et al. 1996, and Arnoldi and Den Otter 2008.

13   For instance Bacquart 2004, Blackmun, Poynor and Cole 2000, Bleakley 1978, Bouttiaux 2009b, 2013b, Brain 1980, Bravmann 1973, 1974, H.M. Cole 1989, Coquet 1996. Holbeke 1966, Homberger 2008, De Heusch 1995, Huet 1995, Kasfir 1988b, Kerchache et al. 2008, Kecskési and Vajda 2007, Martin and Féau 1997, McClusky and Massaquoi 2015, Napier 1986, 1988, Neyt 2010, T. Phillips 1995, Segy 1976, Stepan 2005, R. Thompson 1974, Wassing 1970, Weinhold and Cook 2000, and Wittmer and Arnett 1978.

more precise distribution of masking which proved both complicated and peculiar. We give these detailed maps at the end of this introduction.

Masking has been described as an 'old trick of the human race',[14] but appears less common than hitherto supposed, at least in Africa. Our thesis is that the peculiar distribution of mask rituals on the continent is neither haphazard nor an artefact of fieldwork or collecting, but is informed by specific ecological, historical, and sociological factors that form the conditions for masquerades. This is the central issue in Chapter 1: What ecological, historical, and socio-cultural factors lie behind the presence or absence of masquerades in African societies, and how do these conditions explain the specific distribution we found? Triggered by the distribution of masking in three distinct zones, we developed a theoretical model to explain why the groups within masking zones tend to have mask rituals, and why social formations in other areas have neither developed nor adopted them. In order to explain this difference, the model focuses on the cultural dynamics by which mask rituals impact on local social formations: we analyse both the conditions under which masquerades are present, and how masquerades interact with their host societies; the two issues belong together. Highlighting internal societal dynamics, the model identifies the three social fields we found to be essential to our explanation: gender, power, and identity. Using the parameters of the model, the empirical chapters examine the roster of mask rituals and masquerades in Africa, and analyse how each of these ritual types interacts with social processes inside African masking societies.

The methodological starting point of this book, therefore, combines an anthropological approach to rituals with art history, a discipline characterised by meticulous and insightful descriptions of objects and performances.[15] The theoretical basis of the book stems from comparative anthropological insights. We are aware that in recent decades anthropology has generally moved away from comparison and theory formation, and that the kind of questions we ask ourselves might be considered out of fashion, yet we consider them indispensable to understanding the masking phenomenon. In our chapters we use the numerous studies in African art to furnish the data on masking, and anthropological field studies for the social setting; the model itself provides the encompassing framework to link the two.

In order to avoid confirmation bias – by looking mainly at corroborating examples – in the chapters that follow we include some case studies that

---

14 Roberts 1980.
15 Though art history is turning increasingly to more theoretical approaches: Rea 2019.

seem to run counter to our thesis. We continue to be open to anomalous cases, but any social scientific theory is probabilistic, so it will not be falsified by a single counter-example.

As the Nigerian scholar Umar Danfulani remarked, speaking about indigenous religion in general: 'A masquerade is not watched from one spot.'[16] Any attempt at explanation is part of a more general quest for meaning. And in a ritual as complex and multifaceted as a masquerade, the term 'meaning' has many dimensions.[17] One may look at the signification of the object, for instance the sculpted head, or at the whole mask-apparition, in terms of how it was made, what it represents, and how this relates to religious notions; art history has pursued this angle with virtuosity. A second approach focuses on how the dancer 'inhabits' his own mask and experiences the dance, plus how his public judges him, the sociology of performance. A third group of meanings regards the aim and message of the mask rites, and what people get out of the mask ritual – the cultural signification of masking. The fourth meaning looks at the impact of these rituals on society: their relation to the social dynamics of their host cultures. All of these will be mentioned, but our main angles are the third and the fourth, the interaction between masking ritual and society. Finally, the very same ritual can have divergent meanings for different participants; Audrey Richards observed:

> The Archbishop of Canterbury does not give the same account of the meaning of the Holy Eucharist as the verger who watches at the church door, the worshipper in his Church or the young boy or girl who has just been confirmed.[18]

The crucial difference is that the archbishop has the institutionalised authority to explain his interpretation in detail from the pulpit and impose it on others, an authority that is absent in indigenous African religions.[19] To avoid confusion, the term 'meaning' will be used sparingly and with caution.

Structure of the book

In Chapter 1 we develop a theory of why masquerades fit into certain societies and not in others: we delineate the parameters for a 'masking society', define the notion of 'arena' as a special characteristic of the relevant social fields, and formulate our hypothesis on how mask rituals interact

---

16 Danfulani 1999a: 43.
17 Kapferer 2004.
18 A. Richards 1982: 113–114.
19 See Whitehouse 2004 for an analysis of two contrasting kinds of religiosity.

with the local arenas of gender and power, and with identity construction. Chapter 2 defines masks and develops a typology, researches the emic grounds for the attribution of power to masks, and scans what types of rituals involve masks.

Building on this framework, Chapters 3–8 peruse these various types of mask rituals in order to analyse how masquerades address gender, power, and identity. Masks are deeply gendered, and three chapters focus on gender dynamics in the rites of passage featuring masquerades: male initiation (Chapter 3), secret societies (Chapter 4), and funerals (Chapter 5). The pivotal Chapter 6 looks at the complex relation between masks and women, which in our view forms a key to understanding masks, highlighted by the rare occasions where women wear masks.

Power is the second major social field and arena that masks address, and in politics, the subject of Chapter 7, masks appear as a separate power base interacting in complex ways with political structures. Chapter 8 addresses the interaction of masquerades with the processes of social order: law, healing, divination, and anti-witchcraft actions; the Dan example mentioned above fits in here.

Increasingly, masking has become important in collective identity formation at various echelons, so Chapter 9 elaborates on how masquerades have become focal points of modern identity constructions. Chapter 10 describes the encounter of the modern African state with masks, explores historical connections between masking and slavery, and traces global extensions of African masks. In conclusion, Chapter 11 subsumes our argument for the socio-cultural niche of mask rituals, and speculates on the past and the future of masking.

The Mask Crescent: Distribution of Masks and Masking in Africa

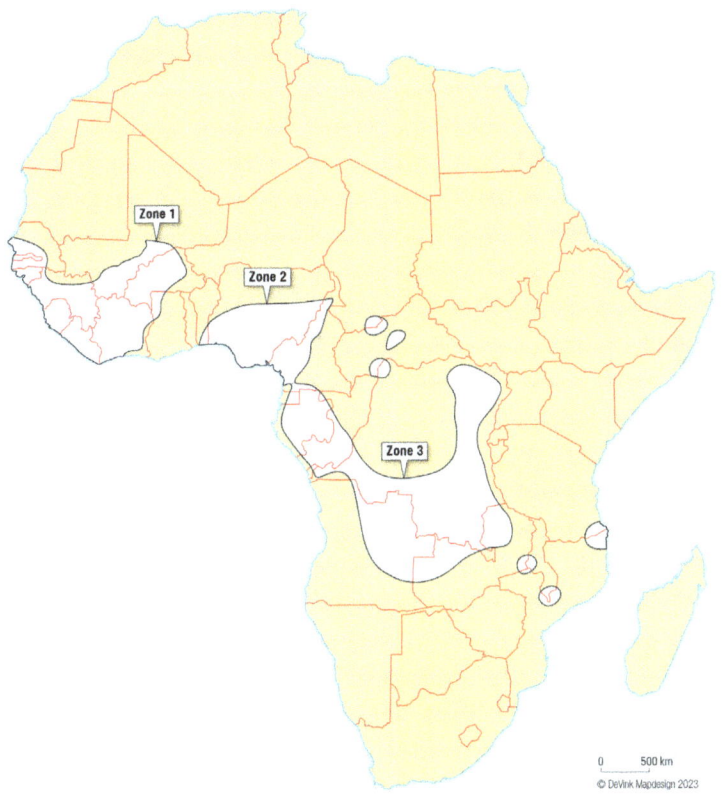

Map 1. Distribution of masking in Africa, indicating the three masking zones.

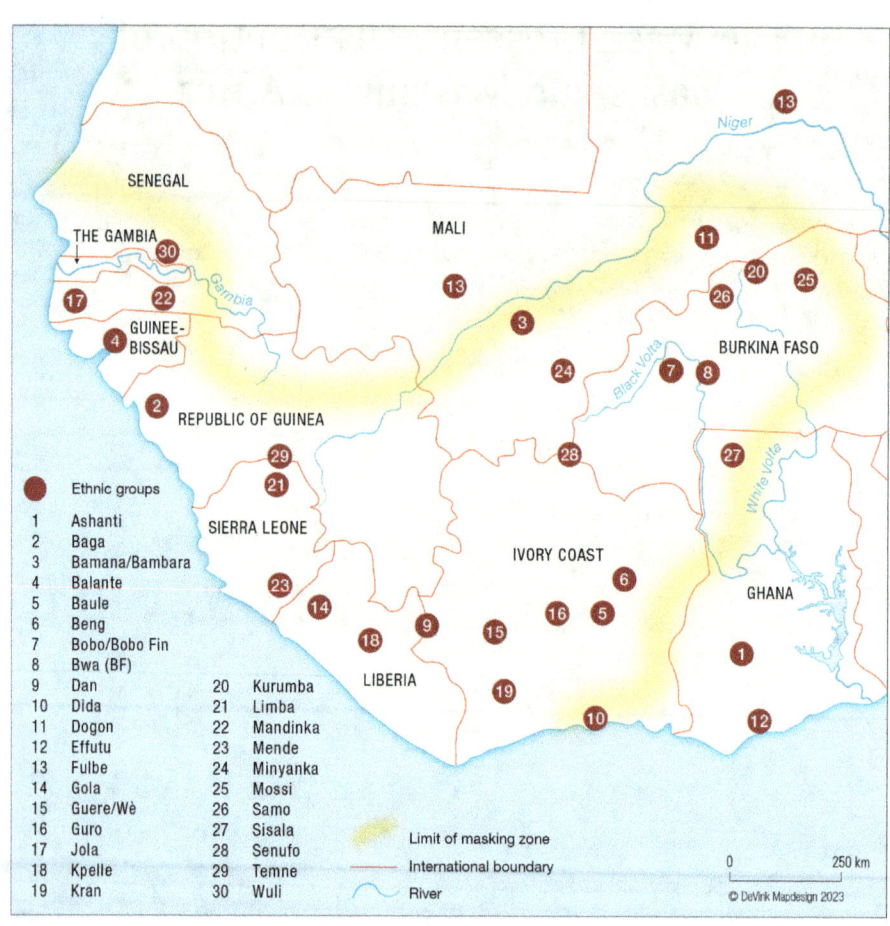

Map 2. Zone 1: West Africa.

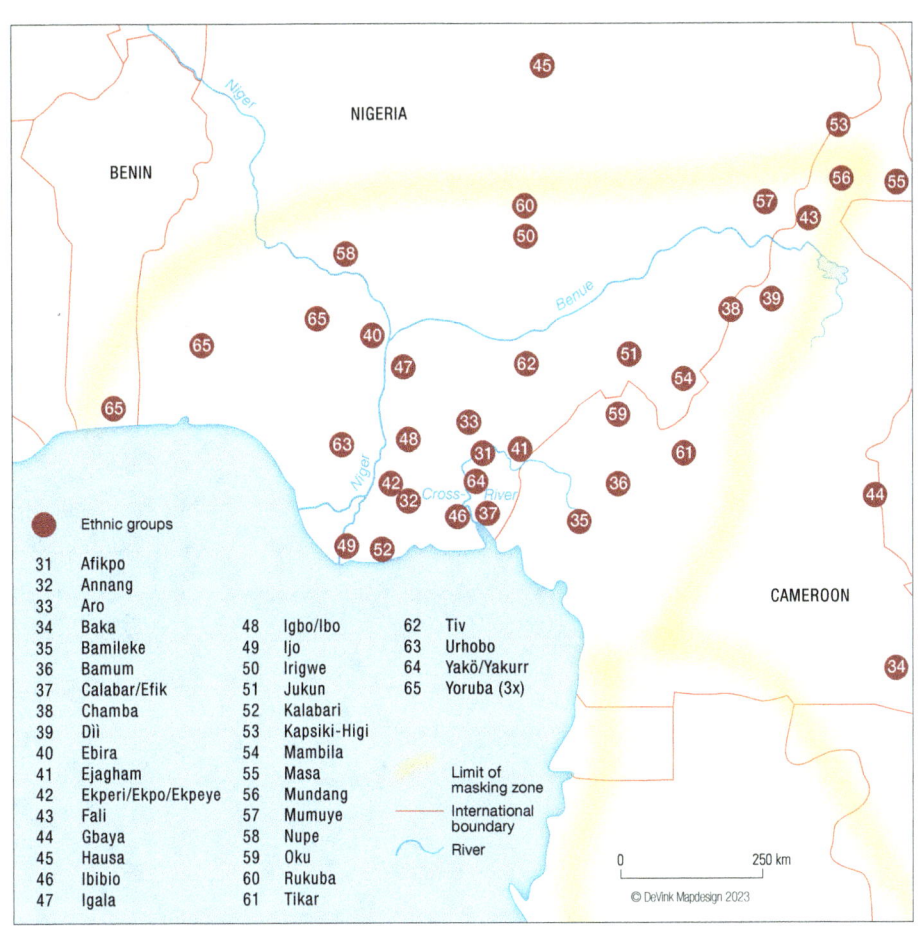

Map 3. Zone 2: West–Central Africa.

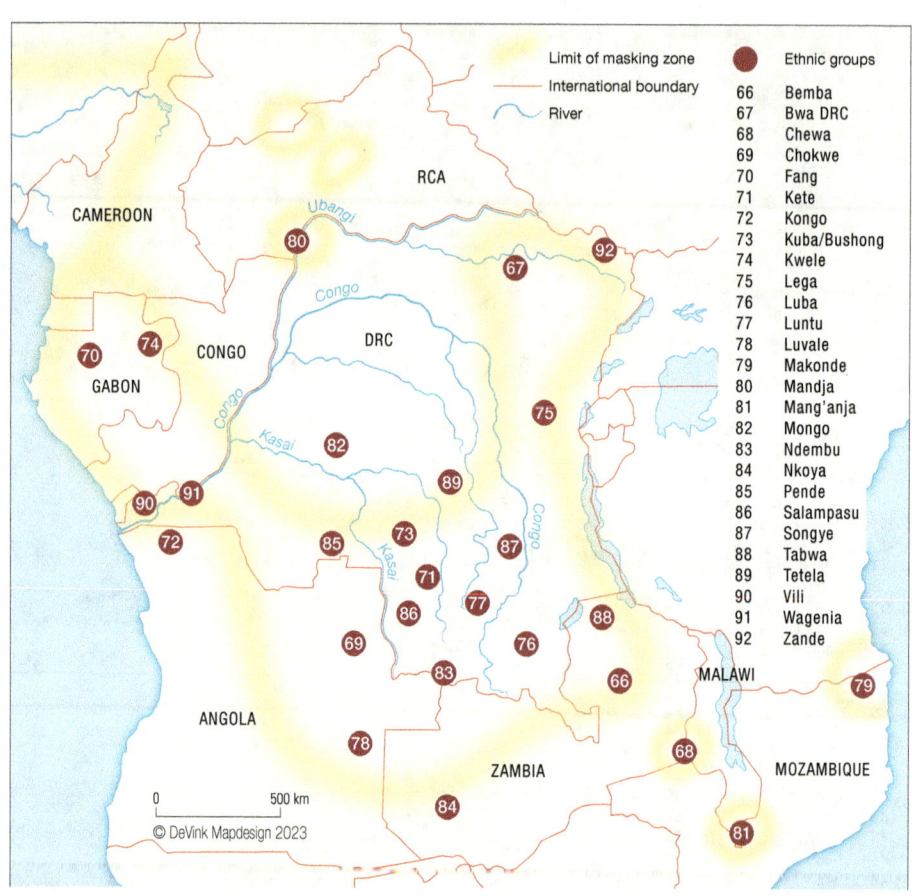

Map 4. Zone 3: Central and East Africa.

1

Mask Distribution and Theory

Masking zones

The incidence of masks and masquerades across the contininent, as shown in the maps in the previous section, highlighted a surprising pattern in masking activity: although few objects are as 'African' as masks, most African cultures do not have masks at all, just as most African countries do not house masquerade traditions. Mask rituals are found in what we shall call the 'Mask Crescent', a broad, band-like area running from Senegal eastwards over the whole width of the subcontinent, and then curling downward around the Bight of Biafra, as far as the eastern limits of the Congo Basin,[1] plus a sprinkling in East Africa. The Crescent is not continuous and consists of three distinct zones: West Africa (Zone 1), West-Central Africa (Zone 2) and Central-East Africa (Zone 3), each with its own characteristics. Our theory addresses all three zones, yet each of them shows its own configuration of explanatory factors and particular masking habitus, while the interruptions in the Crescent are crucial elements in our explanation. Occasionally these interruptions have been noted in the literature, especially their absence in the Ghanaian region, which has been dubbed the 'Akan Gap'.[2]

In 1988 Sidney Kasfir remarked: 'There have been unsuccessful theories to correlate African masking with language, ecology, and with ancestral forms of religion.'[3] In our quest to solve that quandary we need both the general overview map and the precise distribution maps for each of the masking zones, but this entails some methodological considerations. Plotting

---

1   North of that basin there is a sprinkling of masking cultures – the northern rim of the Democratic Republic of the Congo (DRC), and the southern part of the Central African Republic (CAR) – which we have indicated provisionally, mainly owing to ethnographical uncertainty.
2   McNaughton 1992.
3   Kasfir 1988b: 4.

societies on maps inevitably implies a yes–no answer to the question of whether mask rituals are present, which tends to efface internal variation. For instance, mapping does not account for the relative importance of masks on the ground, since the position of masking in societies that have masquerades can vary widely. In practice the relative importance of masks in rituals forms a continuum: from marginal masking, where a few rituals feature a single mask, to intense masking where most rituals revolve around a host of masks, with all intermediate positions. Also the individual histories of specific masking types fall beyond the scope of our map.[4] The same holds for the difference between fully functioning masquerades and extinct ones; in quite a few cases, masks are on the verge of disappearance, or have now disappeared, while even in ethnic groups that do have mask rituals, not all villages may have them. All these are counted as masking groups.

Distribution maps must be based upon some sort of ethnic identification. Anthropology started out as a science of 'tribal cultures', but has long disengaged itself from that notion, as too many of these socio-cultural 'entities' proved to be of recent formation, often triggered by colonial intervention.[5] In addition, cultural boundaries were shown to be permeable, cultural variation inside one group larger than expected, and the borders with adjoining groups gradual and vague, so the notion of a homogeneous, territorial, and linguistic unit with a definite expressive culture – the so-called 'tribe' – has been laid to rest quite some time ago. Similarly, in art history the old idea of 'one tribe, one style' has given way to the notion of a multiplicity of styles inside one cultural tradition, and of visual elements easily crossing ethnic borders, however defined.[6] So the maps of the zones use a broad, vague line between the areas where masks can be found, and those where they are absent.

While fully recognising that such socio-cultural units are usually constructs of both history and research, one does need some label to indicate

4   However fascinating these may be as a mirror for societal transformations, as in the case of the Igala: Kasfir 2019, Sargent 1988, Boston 1968.
5   See van Binsbergen 1992, and De Heusch 1995. Jan Vansina reports that the Vili and Nunu of Cabinda and Gabon became distinct social units only after the abolition of the slave trade. Together with the Bobangi, Okande, and Aduma they developed from caravaneer and merchant groups: Vansina 1990: 202, 206.
6   The *bedu* mask of Zone 1 is an example. Originally belonging to the Nafana group, this mask genre has spread over adjoining groups (Arnaut 2013: 150). See Sidney Kasfir 1984 for a thorough critique of the 'one tribe, one style' notion, and, for Zone 3, Vansina 1990: 18–19. See also Bravmann 1973, 1974, and 1979. For a historical overview see Ravenhill 1996b.

a group.[7] In museum circles the plural 'peoples' instead of 'people' has gained acceptance to indicate a particular strain of cultural heritage: the Yoruba peoples, the Mumuye peoples.[8] This has the advantage of allowing variation within the cultural group, and when appropriate will be used. But the humbler notion 'ethnic group' has largely replaced earlier terms. An ethnic group is neither a fixed cultural unit, nor indivisible, and while referring to a series of nesting identities, the term has the advantage of also being a self-referent, a way people identity themselves; we use ethnic identification primarily as self-definition by the participants. For instance, a 'Baule mask ritual' is a performance featuring masks by people who identify themselves as Baule in contrast to other groups.[9] In the words of Sandra Green:

> Ethnicity is defined here as a system of social classification embraced by groups or individuals who identify themselves and are identified by others, as distinct on the basis of their shared putative or real cultural, ancestral, regional, and/or linguistic origins and practices, and where the identities of groups and individuals so classified are also subject to periodic reinvention.[10]

The map indicates in what areas mask rituals are found, but this does not imply that all groups inside this region have masks; quite a few peoples inside the Crescent have no mask rituals at all, not so much because they have lost the tradition, but simply because they never had it. Since our theory tries to explain why people have masquerades, it also should make plausible why other societies do not, so these cases are important. The three zones simply indicate where one might find ethnic groups with mask rituals, somehow, somewhere, sometime.

Our sources are scholarly publications on masks, from whatever discipline, mostly from the history of art and museum publications; the reticence among anthropologists to write about masks is being redressed only recently. Of course, there is a thriving market in African art, including masks, but art dealers are not always overly informed or forthcoming about the provenance

---

7   For reference beyond the ethnographic literature, we used the Museum Thesaurus for ethnic labels, and thank Annette Schmidt for this. We checked these names with the language maps of the site Ethnologue.org, consulted many times over the project.
8   For instance, Berns and Fardon 2011.
9   At least nowadays. Susan Vogel notes that the cover term 'Baule' is of quite recent use (Vogel 1997a: 34), which is by no means exceptional. But, whatever the historic depth of ethnic groups, they do function in present-day interaction in Africa, and are increasingly important in self-definition.
10   Green 1996: 12.

of their objects. But some dealers are well informed, especially when they specialise in one region, and their information was useful to cover some lacunae in the ethnographic reporting. Clearly the ethnographical project of describing the whole gamut of cultural variety on the continent is far from completed; the number of groups without specific information is surprisingly large, but the information density varies between the three zones.[11] All in all we are confident that the bulk of all masking cultures in Africa falls within the indicated zones.

In our analysis of masking, a three-way distinction in the timeline of history is expedient: the past, the past-in-the-present, and the present. This distinction, derived from linguistics, is helpful in situating mask rituals inside the dynamics of local histories. In this parlance, the past as such is what is no longer there; it may be remembered but it is hardly relevant to present social life. Society has moved on and has relegated the custom in question to the cultural archives of collective memory. We will see in quite a few cases that mask rituals have been completely abandoned, for instance when a society has turned to Christianity or Islam and no longer performs any of the rites involving masks, at times even distancing itself from such a past. But in most of our cases the mask rituals still persevere, either as a cherished past which might be reenacted at will, or − even more relevant − as a valued element of their cultural heritage that they want to retain, even if it might have lost some of its cultural poignancy. Boys' initiations with masks are still held, adapted these days to school holidays. Secret societies might have lost most of their political power − although they are are often surprisingly resilient in changing political climates − while death celebrations have included masking performances as part of a large repertoire of festivities; all these are clearly the past-in-the-present. Yet masks also feature in the present. Mask rituals are still being performed, not only in quite a few indigenous religions even today, but also in cultural festivals and tourist performances, and as icons of nascent nationalism, masks and their spectacular dances increasingly function in a fully modern setting. Most of the masquerades in this book can be seen as past-in-the-present, though, and that is the way we will describe them in the case descriptions and analyses: the present as inheritance.[12]

11 Especially in Zone 3; the regions east and north of the Congo Basin are sparsely described.
12 Picton 2009: 298.

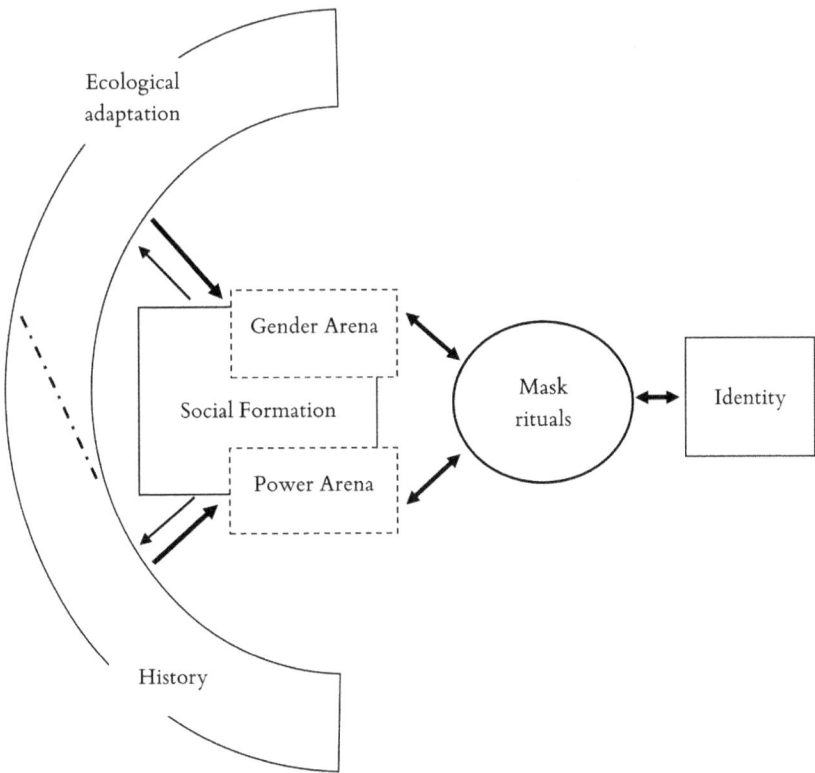

Figure 1.1. Theoretical schema.

Theoretical approach

Our theoretical vantage point is that masking is not an independent phenomenon, but is consonant with specific social and political configurations that belong to particular types of societies; these societies, in turn, are informed by ecological conditions and historic processes. Our theory addresses neither mask origins nor diffusion, but stipulates which kinds of society are conducive to rituals with masks and how masquerades address crucial issues in those societies. The focus is not on the artistic creations or visual expressions of the individual masks themselves, but on the presence or absence of mask rituals as such, and on social fields or arenas through which the masquerades impact on society. The chain of reasoning is schematised in Figure 1.1.

The schema reads as follows. Each social formation or local society is largely informed by two general factors: its ecological adaptation and its history; the enveloping semi-circle highlights their status as important background factors. Within the social formation, two fields are hypothesised as crucial for masking, namely gender and power. In our view, the status of these fields is critical to the presence or absence of masking rituals; the bold circle indicates mask rituals as the central topic of the book. In turn, the mask rituals inform local and ethnic dynamics of identity construction. The arrows point in both directions, since the relations are reciprocal, but – as indicated by their thickness – not always in equal measure.

The ecological adaptation is the way a community has adapted to its physical environment in extracting resources and making a living; the choices and options the society has for acting within the context of its physical setting shape many aspects of the socio-cultural habitus of the group.[13] This relation with its environment is interactive, for any society also influences its habitat to some extent. The factor of history implies both the large-scale and long-term dynamics of the larger region, and the local pathways into the present; the causal arrow points into both directions since any group is at the same time a result of its history and history-in-the-making.

This is a book on mask rituals, and our guiding notion is that their presence must be explained from what they 'do'. Any high-investment ritual like masking needs a solid rationale behind it, addressing important issues in its home society; we share this point of view with a large body of literature on masks, which has informed this study. In our analysis we position the *fons et origo* of mask rituals inside local communities, with a crucial emphasis on both the relationship between the genders, and the different ways of male bonding: masquerades appear to fit in, feed upon, and feed back into, the social fields of gender and power, and the way they do so forms the mainstay of this book; in turn, the dynamics inside those fields inform the ways of constructing identity. We characterise these fields as 'arenas'. Any social field characterised by contestation, competition, or at least a noted indeterminacy, we define as an arena, meaning that the relations between the various actors or groups in the social field are not completely crystallised, and are subject to negotiation and diverging definitions; in short, the outcome of strife in the arena is open. The fields

---

13   This is the approach of cultural materialism, a paradigm that has solved puzzles like ours by following analogous reasoning (Harris 1981). However, we see little reason to burden our analysis with the theoretical meta-structure Marvin Harris used. A major inspiration has been Ingold 2000 and 2011.

of gender and power are not necessarily arenas in all societies, but only in certain social formations and under specific conditions. Our thesis is that masquerades tend to function in societies where one or both these fields have the characteristics of an arena – usually both, since they are related.

The first field is gender, which in local communities in Africa means the socio-cultural definition of being either male or female. Gender is important anywhere, but constitutes an arena if the relations between men and women are under negotiation, occasional redefinition, or contestation. That is not the case in all cultures, for in societies with either gender symmetry or rigorous gender asymmetry there is no indeterminacy. Masquerades appear when gender is an arena, and show this clearly since the masks are consistently gendered themselves. Mask dancers are, almost to a fault, male, for even if a mask portrays a woman, it is a man who dances with it. Not only are mask rituals a masculine domain, but masking rules exclude women, performances aim to frighten women, and on the face of it the ritual world of masks appears to be definitely women-unfriendly; numerous studies have highlighted this male dominance in masquerades, even in cases where they highlight the role of women inside the masking complex.[14] This fundamental gendering does not mean that women have no import in masks and mask rituals; on the contrary, they are in many ways crucial, a major angle in our volume, and we will see gender tables turned as well. But anyway, we show how the gender arena lies at the basis of masking, and how mask rituals feed back into that arena.

The second arena is power. Two meanings of the term are important here: the sociological concept that marks asymmetric relations among people, and the more religious one implying the force inherent in the otherworld, the power of gods, spirits, ritual, and magic. These two kinds of power are very closely related in African thought,[15] and masking is one major way in which the sociological power system merges with the otherworldly force. Power is a function of all social relations, but the main issue in African local communities is the manner of male bonding, both locally and at higher echelons. Again, the field of male power is considered an arena if the relations between men are under negotiation and periodic redefinition, or contestation. Political systems with rigorous hierarchies, fixed positions, and clear inheritance rules appear much less prone to masking than polities in which different sources of power are in competition, and where power positions shift with personality, age, and wealth. Mask rituals are seen to

14 For example, Glaze 1981; Langeveld 2003.
15 See Ellis and Ter Haar 2004 for a major elaboration on the relation between religion and politics; for art and politics see Fraser and Cole 1972.

operate in political configurations with a degree of indeterminacy, so open power arenas, and in our view this indeterminacy is one of the factors underlying the masking phenomenon.

In their worldwide study of reproductive rituals Karen and Jeffery Paige[16] take the relation between ritual and power even further: 'Ritual is not simply an alternative to politics; it is a continuation of politics by another means.'[17] They see preindustrial societies wrestling with potential crises, which they term 'dilemmas', to be solved by ritual means since no other tools are available. Mask rituals are closer to reproductive rituals than they would seem at first glance, and their link with power is indeed important. However, in our view power describes only part of the picture, because, as Ronald Grimes remarked, there is much more to ritual than just politics: 'The politics of ritual do not preclude its very real psychological, religious, and imaginative aspects. Religion and psychology are not mere cover-ups for politics, but real domains in themselves.'[18] Raphael Njoku warned that 'the study of an element of custom like the masquerade institution cannot be reduced to a single story'.[19] Though politics and social organisation do form a crucial field of operation for mask rituals, the phenomenon of masking requires weaving together of multiple stories. So we combine a series of related factors: the background elements of history and ecology, the types of social formation, and the configurations of the fields of gender and power.

Once established, masquerades feed into the dynamics of identity construction, with the performance as a focal point, as our first vignette shows. People love their masquerades and identify with them, and variations in performance may distinguish between villages, just as mask types may distinguish between ethnic groups. In modern times, tourism exploits the appeal of masquerades, and in many African countries inside the Crescent, mask dances have become regular features of guided tours. In this way the masquerades themselves morph into identification points, and – the flipside of identity – ways to construct difference. Since few rituals are as public and impressive as large masquerades, this form of theatre is a prime tool for modern politics, and politicians readily use this appeal to promote their own goals, using masks as political billboards. Also, mask shows are used increasingly for national and even continent-wide representations of collective identity.

16   Paige and Paige 1981.
17   Ibid.: 43. Rephrasing the classic remark by Von Clausewitz, who defined war as 'the continuation of diplomacy by other means'.
18   Grimes 2000: 48.
19   Njoku 2020: 36.

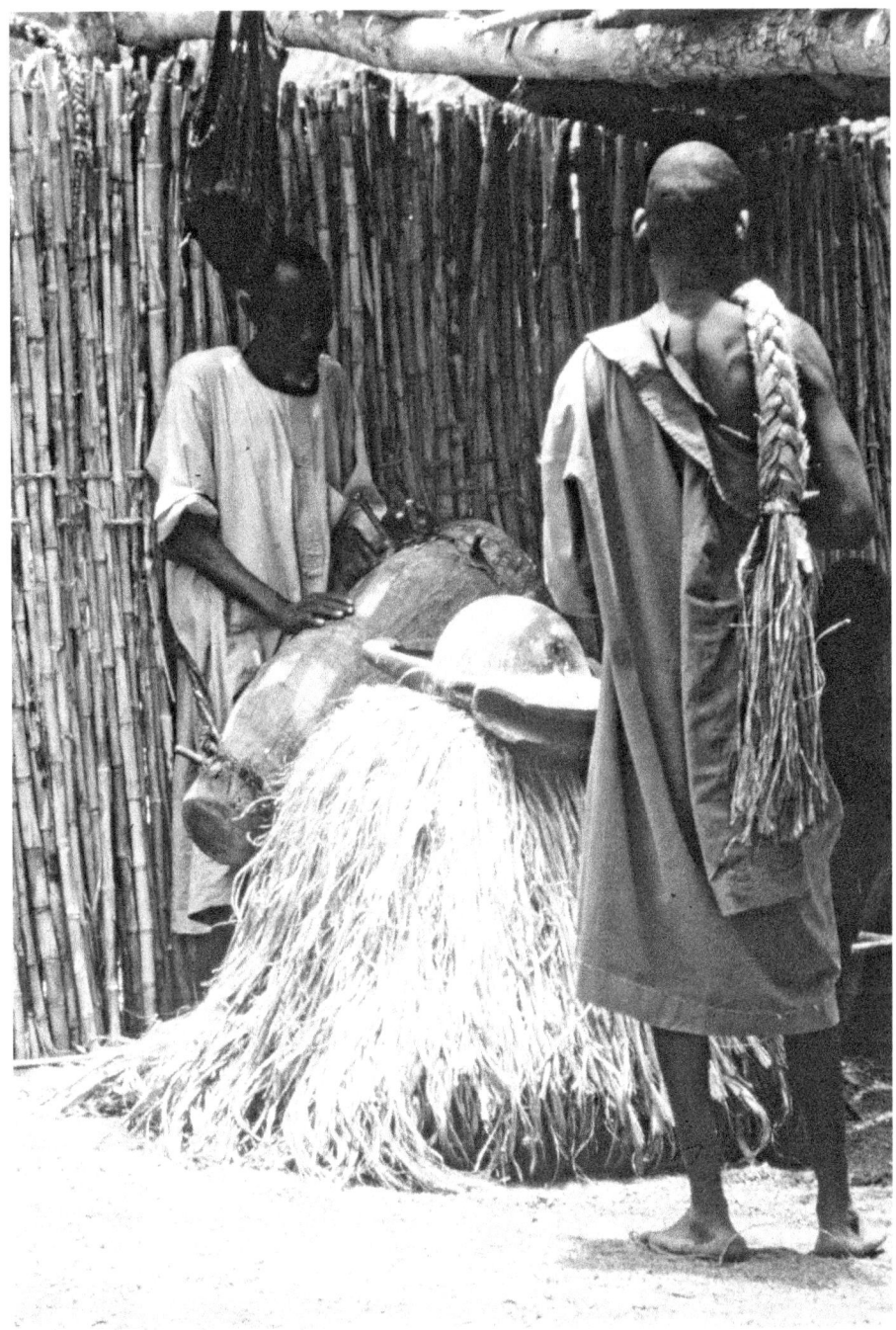

Figure 1.2. Not all masks are always an imposing presence: two elders try to prod a truculent mask into action. Chamba, Cameroon 1980. Photo: Richard Fardon.

Parameters of masking

What are the commonalities of the societies in the three zones that could make them a plausible haven for masquerades? We identify five major parameters that in combination characterise the communities of the Crescent in contrast with other areas in Africa:

1.   an ecological adaptation in which women have a large share in food production; labour as the major capital; no cattle husbandry;

2.   a history of slavery, slave raiding, and general political insecurity;

3.   recognisable communities with a tendency toward matrilineal descent, a prenatal attitude, and low bride wealth;

4.   a political organisation with competing power bases, therefore an open power arena;

5.   no inheritable wealth: an orientation to symbolic capital and visual aesthetics.

First, we will look at the two background factors: ecological adaptation and history. As Map 1 shows, the forested areas of Africa form the core of the Crescent, with extensions into dryer ecotopes. The ecologies of the zones are characterised by a versatile horticulture, based on a slash–and–burn system or one of crop rotation and fallowing. Women play a large part in the production of food, particularly of root crops such as cassava and yams, plus some rice, sorghum, and millet. This subsistence economy is supplemented by a wide variety of cash crops such as cocoa, palm oil, nuts, or pineapple, or in the dryer areas: cotton, tobacco, and peanuts. Generally, in the Crescent the women are responsible for the food crops, while the men grow the cash crops. That division of labour can be found in most of Africa, but the forest band is characterised by women taking a large responsibility for nourishing the whole family. In the Crescent we encounter societies where women shoulder many of the daily responsibilities for the running of the farm, and do the lion's share of the work in the fields, upon which the well-being of the family ultimately depends. Usually men own the land that women cultivate. Phyllis Kaberry's classic study makes this perfectly clear: after the men have reclaimed the bush fields, the women do all the sowing, weeding, and harvesting, and they are proud of it;[20] a saying in this area goes: 'The men own the land; the women own the crops.'

[20]   Kaberry 2005: 35.

These wetter parts of Africa house the tsetse fly, *Glossina palpalis*, the host for *Trypanosoma brucei*, the vector for sleeping sickness, an affliction that attacks not only wild animals, but also cattle and humans. The fly transmits the vector from animal to humans, but it needs shade, and therefore thrives in dense vegetation. Before the present tsetse eradication campaigns, this illness made cattle husbandry impossible in the broad forest band in which the Crescent is situated; as we shall see, the contours of the Mask Crescent are for a large part defined by the absence of *Bos taurus indicus*,[21] the zebu, the bovine subspecies that is dominant in African cattle husbandry and lacks resistance against the vector. We shall follow the ramifications of this 'zebu exclusion' further on.

The second factor, history, refers mainly to slavery, for these are the areas scourged by the slave[22] trade. The map could be read as an aftermath of the Atlantic slave trade, but on closer inspection the relation is more complex, for the three zones do not really coincide with the historical area of major slave trading. Zone 1 was not central in slave trading, while the gap between Zone 1 and 2, on the other hand, was a major slaving centre. In contrast in the Bight of Benin, at the centre of Zone 2, Calabar and Douala were major slaving ports. On the other hand the coast of Gabon consists largely of mangrove forest with few ports, and Angolan slaves were transported by the Portuguese to Brazil both from Cabinda and Luanda, and from Benguela, which is far to the south, outside the Mask Crescent. The masking cases in Zone 3 are found mostly far inland, with the coast being actually devoid of them.

So masking is not a coastal phenomenon. It was not the presence of European slave traders on the coast that triggered masking in Africa; the impact was more indirect. In our analysis it is the system of slave trading and raiding that further inland generated the conditions mentioned in factors 3 and 4, the local dynamics conducive to masking rituals. General insecurity was a major factor in the genesis of local communities, which until this day form a haven for mask rituals. Goody's classic analysis explains how as

21 We follow the standard taxonomy in which all kinds of cattle are variants of one species, *Bos taurus*, since they all interbreed easily; in Africa the two subspecies are *Bos taurus indicus* and *Bos taurus taurus*. *Bos taurus taurus* is more resistant to trypanosomiasis and has a different relation with masking.
22 We realise that the terminology on slavery is under scrutiny, and is shifting from 'slave' to 'enslaved' to highlight the fact that this was a condition forced upon them. We do recognise this fact, even when considering inherited slavery, pawnship, or debt slavery, so whenever we speak of 'slave' we imply people enslaved by physical force, descent, social pressure, or economic need.

a result of the slave trade the coastal polities acquired specific characteristics in the form of small, clearly defined centralised realms that depended on European weapons and locally organised trade networks and slave raids, carrying the shock waves of the slave trade far into the interior of the continent.[23] However, some of the masking societies historically were active in slave raiding as partners in the Atlantic trade. Not only coastal people like the population of Calabar, but also inland groups like the Luvale[24] gained a reputation for commercialising human lives; and they both mask. Masking is not just for the victims.

About the same time as the Atlantic trade, in the savannah belt far to the north a string of jihads marked the establishment of Fulbe emirates throughout the West African Sahel, until the end of the nineteenth century.[25] These cavalry-based Sahel states were organised according to wide kinship networks and alliances, and were of longer duration than the rebellion-prone states of the coast. Still, these states also depended on a 'slave mode of production',[26] leading to ever larger numbers of slaves being extracted, and to the genesis of slave-run plantations. Slave raiding and trading was stock in trade for these revivalist Muslim movements, which have dominated the West African Sudanic zone for half of the second millennium. Both the Atlantic trade and the Muslim slaving system continued to grow, the Atlantic one until the end of the eighteenth century, the Muslim one until well into the nineteenth century.

For the local communities this pincer movement increased the pressure in this vast region and made it highly insecure. Many masking cases in this book were the target populations for slave raiders, forming, as Eric Wolf called them, the 'people without history'.[27] These groups had to cope with a continuous threat of enslavement, both from the Atlantic south and from the Sahelian north, and some of the regions in between were severely depopulated. The slave trade relied both on actual raids and on internal warfare in and between target populations with their own forms of slavery, so the insecurity of the larger area was internalised into local political systems.

This dual threat held mainly for Zones 1 and 2. In the wide swathe of Zone 3, slave raiding was even more an inland affair. Good ports are scarce, and large stretches of coast are swampland covered with mangrove, with very

---

23   Goody 1971.
24   Sangambo, Hansen and Papstein 1979.
25   Last 1974.
26   Lovejoy 2012.
27   Wolf 1997.

few people living on the coastline. So in Zone 3 the great rivers, such as the Congo River, formed the actual axis of the slave raiding and trading, and the impact of the Atlantic trade depended on having access to these trade arteries.[28] Trade first came here – with ivory as a major commodity – with the arrival of the Portuguese in the sixteenth century. With a growing demand for slaves in the Americas, the extraction area for slaves moved further inland, leaving aside those areas closer to the coast that were hard to reach. Owing to the large distances, an elaborate transport system emerged, with stopping places at nodal points along the route and caravans, porters, and farms furnishing the trade with food in a trade network that branched ever deeper into the interior. Internally this trade created great differences in wealth, with rich traders on the coast, caravaneers and intermediaries in the interior, and a target population that kept withdrawing. In some areas plantations based on slave labour were established, especially after 1830 when the Atlantic trade halted, for the internal production mode went on much longer. Some new polities developed in the vicinity of the ports through the stream of imported goods, guns, iron, and copper, but also luxury goods.

How did the local people cope with this slaving threat? In Zone 3, with its low population densities and migratory subsistence, they moved, opening new frontiers of forest and establishing isolated settlements with little centralisation and few external contacts, developing the secret societies and healing associations that furnished the links between them. In areas outside the reach of the trading system, the internal political dynamics prevailed.

In Zones 1 and 2, with their much higher population density, that option was not available, and the local people had to defend themselves. Some could organise themselves in a military way, like the Mundang of Cameroon,[29] but that demanded a cavalry and only happened occasionally. The general reaction to endemic insecurity was forming communities of defence in fortified villages, settling on inaccessible terrains, or using other possibilities of defence provided by the habitat. These are what Eric Wolf calls the 'shatter zones',[30] recognisable on the maps of Zone 1 and 2: regions with an inaccessible terrain where villages could defend themselves, with many small ethnic groups huddled together; much of the density in the maps of these zones reflects this dynamic. Mountains and hillsides form a prime location for such defensive settlements, such as the Bandiagara cliff in Mali and the Jos Plateau in Nigeria, or the hills on the border between Nigeria

---

28 This analysis is based on Vansina 1990, 1992b.
29 Adler 1982.
30 Wolf 1997.

and Cameroon from Mount Cameroon up to the Mandara Mountains near Lake Chad; flood plains were another option. But West Africa has few mountain ranges or major rivers, so many of the villages relied on architecture, developing fortified settlements. Whatever the layout, the social reaction was one of ethnic splintering in the form of closed village communities, and thus local isolation. The defensive villages had to become self-sufficient entities, without intensive links to other settlements.

As David Pratten points out, for some regions like southern Nigeria defence was just the first phase of the local reaction to the slaving threat. A second phase saw a reduction in actual slave raiding, and an increase in kidnapping and individual abductions; finally 'the third phase saw the expansion of the internal market for slaves in which decentralised peoples not only sold but absorbed slaves, and in which commercial transactions were increasingly based on the pawning or sale of descendants'.[31] Internal commerce in humans replaced slaving expeditions; people had grown accustomed to imported foreign goods and the need for income out of this trade prevailed over considerations of physical security.

Whatever the penetration of the slaving system locally, important keys to masking are to be found right inside the kinship relations in the village, and factor 3 points to a crucial social element related to the forest ecology: that of matrilineal descent. Although many patrilineal cultures live in the three zones, most matrilineal societies fall inside these areas[32] — as do almost all known African societies with double descent, which are much rarer. This option for matrilineal kinship reckoning is crucial for our explanatory model, since it is a major factor in both the gender balance and male organisation.[33]

Descent reckoning is not one single factor, but a cover term for an array of kinship relations. As Daryll Forde remarked, 'Any principle of [kinship] recruitment can itself be a matter of degree'.[34] For instance, the descent reckoning through women, or matriliny, forms the kinship logic underlying very different types of matriclan systems, ranging from small, nameless, and genealogically shallow mini-groupings to named, omnipresent social groups with clear leadership structures.[35] Crucially, these structures of matrilineal groups also vary along the rules of marital residence; when a new

---

31 Pratten 2007: 49.
32 Zone 3 is in fact almost identical to what has been called the matrilineal belt; Murdock 1959.
33 Ember and Ember 1971.
34 Forde 1964: 38. See for a curious mix of kinship tracing Muller 1997b.
35 Holy 1996.

couple lives with the bride's parents – matrilocal[36] – this leads to a different local group from when they take up residence with the groom's parents – patrilocal. These are not the only two possibilities, and we shall follow how other options for residence have their own impact on social formations, as on masking. Also, matriliny can undergird an array of political systems: all the zones, but especially Zone 3, show a wide range of centralised and decentralised political arrangements based on matrilineal descent. So there is matriliny and there is matriliny, and they can be miles apart.

Patriliny shows a similar variety, dependent on depth and segmentation of the lineages, the various corporate characteristics of the patri-groups, and their links with land. Some lineages are deep and branching, while others are shallow, and each of these may or may not be linked to land ownership; here too, there is a large diversity in political organisation, from acephalous societies to centralised kingdoms. So, again, there is patriliny and there is patriliny, and they can be miles apart. Descent systems can vary on a local scale as well: Susan Gagliardi notes how in the border region between Senufo and Bamana, both descent reckoning and marital residence shifted between neighbouring settlements;[37] they all had masks and secret societies. Or, as Simon Ottenberg puts it, 'Masks transcend the difference between patrilineal and matrilineal'.[38]

These two forms are not the only ways in which kinship can build lasting groups. A third way is called 'cognatic descent', which means descent lines in which both genders can be used in tracing descent. In this system, residence trumps genealogical descent: one counts as one's closest relatives the people one lives with – in fact, those one shares a village with, on either the father's or the mother's side. Thus a young couple can opt to take up residence with either the bride's parents or the husband's kin, and descent lines show both males and females, resulting in social groups called ramages.[39] Anthropological wisdom relates this cognatic descent to high population densities, because a couple may choose to settle where land is available. Ramages adapt well to land scarcity, but we will see them also appear when people are opening new territories; flexibility is the

36 We use the terms 'matrilocal' and 'patrilocal' to indicate a couple's marital residence with respectively the bride's mother and the bridegroom's father. In anthropological literature also the terms 'uxorilocal' (at the wife's) and 'virilocal' (at the husband's) are used.

37 Gagliardi 2010: 28–29. Our quotes are from the 2010 dissertation; the published version appeared recently: Gagliardi 2022.

38 Ottenberg 1975: 202.

39 Stone 2006.

hallmark of cognatic descent. Kinship and descent systems are not cast in stone, for societies shift their kinship systems when circumstances change or when they move into new territories.[40] Clearly, 'classifying societies as patrilineal, matrilineal or cognatic may hide as much as it reveals',[41] so in our parameters we just note a tendency for matrilineal kinship reckoning in the Crescent, a general notion that resonates well with the important role of woman in the ecosystem. In our analysis of the gender and power fields that tendency is crucial.

As for power, factor 4, in nearly all societies, be they of patrilineal, matrilineal, or cognatic descent, it is the men who occupy the positions of public representation and community power, with the women more confined to – and often dominant in – the domestic sphere. The manners of male bonding, however, show systematic differences between the types of descent. In patrilineal societies a local core of men share the same descent group, and thus easily form what Keesing[42] calls the 'board of directors'; they live with their paternal lineage members, their brides have moved over from their respective parental homes, and the men's lineages or clans provide the social and political skeleton for the village; as Holy stressed, this operates mainly at the local level, at the lower echelons of the lineage system: 'the content of every kinship relationship itself is dependent on the spatial proximity or distance between the participants in the relationship.'[43] And that is exactly where the local fields of gender and power are situated.

In matriliny on the other hand, the men are in a quandary as to how to organise themselves based on descent, since males of one matrilineage do not live together. This is called the 'matrilineal puzzle', and it is highly relevant to our explanation of masking. In the case of matrilocal residence a man lives with his in-laws, and in the patrilocal option he stays with his father, who belongs to another matrilineage (his mother's), while the man's main authority is his mother's brother, who lives elsewhere. So in both cases the man does not live with closely related males. Who are on the 'board of directors' of the local unit? One logical result of this quandary is that the male groups tend to be small and fleeting, dependent on the success of the individual man.

---

40 See for instance how the Kongo have adopted their kin system under the influence of the slave trade: MacGaffey 1983.
41 Edmund Leach, cited in Holy 1996: 123.
42 Keesing 1975; see Holy 1996 for a debate on this concept, and Schneider 1961 on what this means for kin relations.
43 Holy 1996: 115.

The Bemba case on the border between the Democratic Republic of the Congo (DRC) and Zambia is illustrative here. A man marries his bride and provides labour in the fields of his in-laws. His position depends on his work in their fields; if he is a hard worker, has success, begets children, and accrues wealth and prestige, he attempts to take his wife and children away to a newly built settlement, his own 'village'. There he is boss but has few men supporting him.[44]

An option that would concur with matriliny is marital residence with the husband's mother's brother, called avunculocal; thus the man lives with his male lineage mates after his marriage. However, in practice this means that both partners move to a new location where they did not grow up, and throughout the world one sees this only incidentally. In Africa it seems rare, but it is for instance the choice of the Kongo, a society that has historically adapted its kin system to the contingencies of history – meaning the slave trade – and on this basis has developed strong and lasting matriclans with clear political structures; and as our parameters would indicate, this group has indeed no masking tradition to speak of.[45] But it is not just local dynamics that are important: Central Africa offers a wide array of examples of how matrilineal descent reckoning functions at higher political echelons. Matriliny also underlies chieftaincies and centralised kingdoms, and in many instances the village as a geographical unit is not even evident.[46]

Variations abound and any system is dynamic, but the main trends are there. Whatever the rules of marital residence, the various forms of matriliny result in villages with a strong, independent position for women, a tight bond between a woman and her family, and a lack of self-evident bonding between males – the two arenas are closely linked. Genealogically, the lineages are shallow[47] and the male power structures are weak; the villages often split or move with the slash-and-burn agriculture of the forest. This means that the power balance between husband and wife is skewed toward the wife and is under continuous pressure, and the wife retains a strong bond with her brother; after all she furnishes his heirs. Male bonding can rely only to a small degree on close kinship between males, and this is meant

---

44   A. Richards 1982.
45   MacGaffey 1983, 1986, 2000. Instead, they are renowned for their *nkisi*, objects of power, such as statues full of nails and mirrors, which may well fullfil similar functions to masks: MacGaffey 1988.
46   For example among the Ndembu (V. Turner 1967, 1974) and the Nkoya (Van Binsbergen 1992 and 1981).
47   Van Binsbergen calls the Nkoya matrilineages 'kaleidoscopic' (1992: 90).

with an 'indeterminate' male position: it is under continuous redefinition; in short, it is an arena.

Not all masking societies are matrilineal – not by a long stretch; many are patrilineal and yet have masking rituals. The main factor is the same however, male political indeterminacy, showing as an open power arena. These societies are part of the same ecosystem in which female labour is important and where manual labour is the main asset. These patrilineal villages are deeply rooted in small territories and show a high village endogamy: most of the brides come from the village itself, just moving from one ward to another,[48] so the women remain in easy contact with their kith and kin. Although the husband holds more sway over her than he would in matrilineal cultures, the wife's position vis-à-vis her husband is strong because she has her own support group at hand.

The first part of factor 5, the absence of inheritable wealth, means that the patrilineal descent groups, clans or lineages, have a limited economic role, which does not lead to economic differentiation. These groups have little 'capital to work with' beyond labour. Access to fields is usually quite open, with cultural norms of sharing and distribution that ensure that all able-bodied men – and women – have the relevant resources at their disposal, meaning land. Hence, the patrilineal groups do not dominate the social scene and throughout the Crescent must compete with other types of male bonding, such as voluntary power associations and groups based on age, resulting in a meshwork of different types of boards of directors (factor 4). Thus, male bonding in these villages itself forms an internal arena. Lineages remain, but age shifts continuously, and these societies show structural tension not just between men, but also between old and young men; even if the old hold the reins of power, they depend on the young for labour; masks are a factor in this continuously shifting equation.

So in the patrilineal society that sports mask rituals, the strength of the lineage system is curtailed by principles other than descent.[49] Such a village tends to be a rather closed universe, with descent groups operating only within the village limits: another village, another set of clans. Although religious and economic ties may provide links between the villages, kinship seldom transcends the village border. Whenever power associations – also called secret societies – occupy this political vacuum, they serve as links between autonomous settlements. These societies have a prime link with

---

48 For instance, the patrilineal Jola of Senegal have a 90 per cent village endogamy (Langeveld 2003).

49 For the social dynamics between lineage and age group, see Memel-Foté 1980.

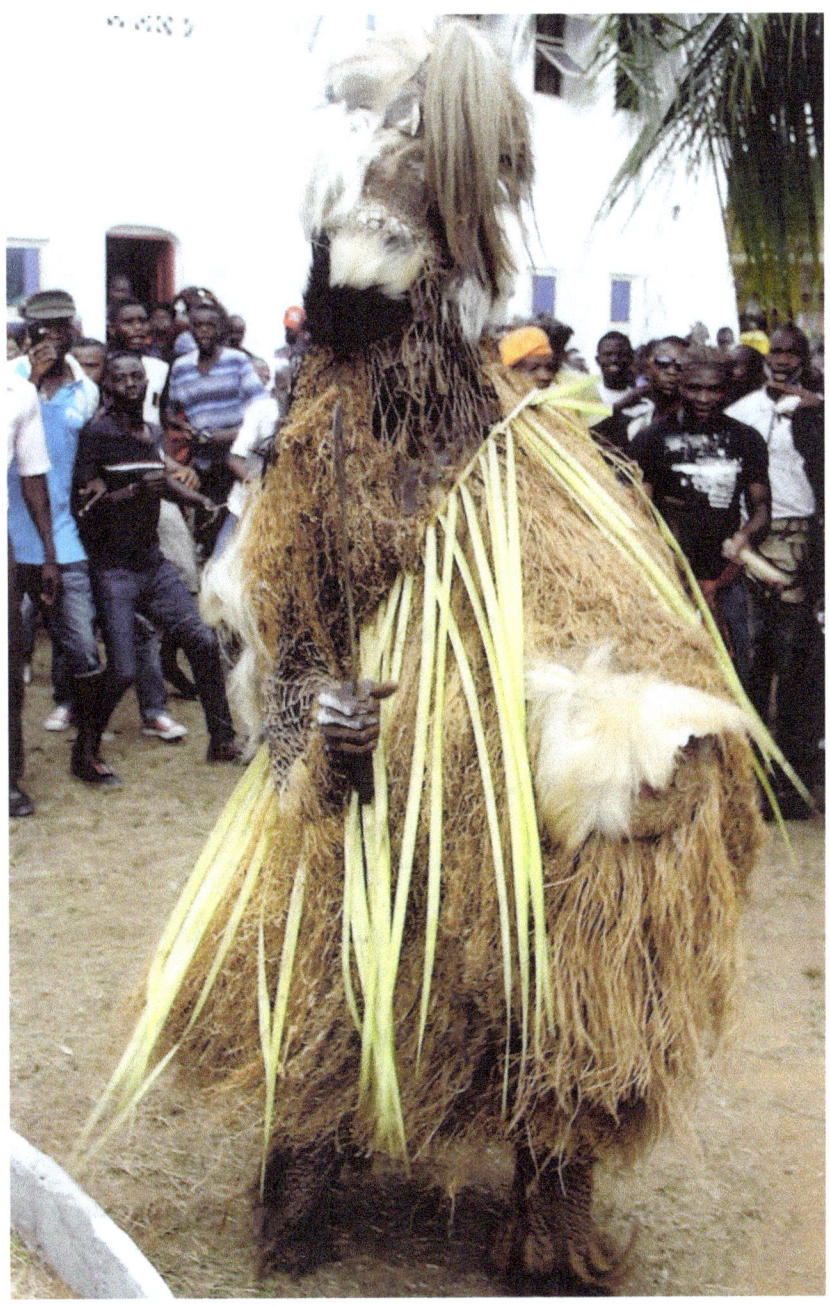

Figure 1.3. *Etangala* mask performance in Ugep, a town famous for its double descent. Yakö (Yakurr LGA), Cross River, Nigeria, 2016. Photo: Ivor Miller.

mask rituals: when power associations arrive on the scene, masks can never be far behind. Also in matrilineal societies with weak male bonding, there is ample social space for such power associations as an alternative way for males to organise, and they invariably command the masking rituals. In the larger political realms in the Crescent the power arena shows a complex meshwork of power configurations, not only between ruler and power association but also between the political centre and the hinterland.

The observation that the fields of gender and power form places of contestation holds *a fortiori* for double descent societies in which both patri- and matriclans function. The Cross River area of Nigeria harbours quite a number of these systems, the most famous being the Yakö. In these societies people are members of the patri-group of their father, but also of their mother's matriline. Usually marital residence is patrilocal, so the patri-lineage has a core of 'lineage-brothers' living together, while the matriclans are somewhat dispersed, even if they often manage much of whatever wealth there is. In these large villages spouses tend to stem from within the local community, so marital residence is not critical and the position of women is strong. The coexistence of both descent types means that lineage functions are divided between the two descent systems, which maintain each other in a tenuous balance, and these sizeable villages with their complex and crosscutting ties make for an inherent power arena with many players – and, indeed, almost all of them have mask rituals.[50]

Factor 3 points at a pronatal attitude as a fundamental feature, and this relates to bride wealth, meaning the goods that the groom hands over to his in-laws as a counter-gift to the bride he receives. This is neither a purchase nor a trade, but should be considered as part of a gift exchange, which compensates the bride's family for the loss of her labour, gives the husband exclusive sexual rights to the bride, and determines his fatherhood of her children.[51] All of this stresses the value of the bride, her work, and her children; consequently, the amount of bride wealth is an important sign of how far these rights are actually obtained by the husband: a large bride wealth means a serious transfer of rights to the husband – and a concomitant high valuation of a woman's work and progeny by the husband.[52]

Compared with other parts of Africa, the cultures in the Mask Crescent combine a pronatal attitude with low bride wealth, and often the groom

---

50   One exception is the Herero of Namibia, who as pastoralists never have masks (Gewald 1999); another is the Beng of Côte d'Ivoire, discussed in Chapter 7.
51   Stone 2006.
52   Goody and Tambiah 1973.

works for his in-laws to procure a bride – a practice called bride service.[53] Matrilineal systems transfer little bride wealth anyway, since few rights are actually transferred, but also the patrilineal cultures of the Mask Crescent feature a limited flow of goods from the groom to his in-laws. In quite a number of Zone 2 societies, bride wealth is 'a symbolic token in the form of services, goods or money, given to the bride's parents by the prospective groom'.[54] In some instances the idea of bride wealth is explicitly rejected – 'a bride should not cost anything' – and just a ritual exchange of minor gifts with symbolic value accompanies the bride's move to her groom's compound.[55] Or, as in some Zone 1 societies, the bride wealth consists of luxury goods and expensive consumables, not capital goods. Because people in the Crescent tend to marry within the village, both spouses can easily trace several kinship links between the two of them;[56] and as the major capital is labour, there is little other wealth to hand over. The marital residence may even depend on the amount of bride wealth, leading to another field of negotiation in the community.[57]

Factor 5 mentions the absence of inheritable wealth, which for a large part translates into the absence of cattle, a crucial issue that we examine below. Instead, these cultures develop elaborate systems of symbolic wealth, which in the case of centralised polities take the form of titles. The court issues a host of resounding titles, often conferred with prestige paraphernalia such as birds' feathers or special animal skins. These titles may or may not be inheritable, but anyway serve as a bond between individual males and the political centre, thus serving as an additional power base that relates well with masking.

Aesthetics, the final element of factor 5, is a notion well covered in art studies but underestimated in social explanation. In comparing Crescent cultures with non-masking societies in Africa, our impression is that visual aesthetics weigh heavier inside the Crescent than outside. Masquerades have a tremendous visual appeal, and whatever their sociological *raison d'être* – which we aim to explain here – rituals do have their intrinsic attraction, surely spectacular ones like masquerades. Cultural borrowing of masks is quite

---

53   See Goody 1973a.
54   See the Igbo of Nigeria, Njoku 2020: 83, or the Balante in Guinea-Bissau, Temudo 2019: 6, note 5.
55   As among the Mossi of Burkina Faso, who are both patrilineal and patrilocal: Luning 2010.
56   Cross-cousin marriage solves this quandary to some degree.
57   For example among the Kalabar, who grew rich on the slave trade: Horton 1993: 50.

common, often in the form of buying them from neighbours. Many stories in the Mask Crescent describe how in the past people bought a mask from their neighbours simply because they wanted to possess it.[58] The Mundang accredit their masks with a Dìì origin,[59] and Mende masks are reported to be sold to neighbouring groups.[60] Masks are even said to be captured or stolen, an appropriation of ritual mentioned only for masks, never for any other rite. Buying is an expression of value, but stealing is the ultimate appreciation: the Bwa in Burkina Faso stole their masks from the Gurunsi, for they thought these masks were more powerful. 'They tell of their ancestor, who raided a distant village to steal masks, which they felt embodied a great deal more magical power than their own.'[61] Just south of them, the Senufo make spare masks, in case of theft.[62] All of this implies that the probability of engaging in mask rituals increases with having masking cultures as neighbours; that old diffusionist argument holds, for even stealing a major ritual presupposes a niche for that complex inside the local ritual repertoire. And our theory focuses on exactly that niche.

Almost all societies with mask rituals have a sculptural tradition as well, with their own styles of visual expression.[63] In these cultures visuals count, and man-made material signs are both common and appreciated. That may hold for the costumes; it certainly holds for the headpieces. Carved tops bring in the dimension of woodcarving as a craft, which accounts for the close link between statues and masks; usually both are made by the same carvers. The masking cultures in the Crescent seem to revel in the 'thingness of things', in the materiality of their own culture, fabricating not just statues and headpieces, but also decorated utensils in all forms. In these cultures form is important and aesthetics matter – meaning, of course, their own aesthetics, which need not be the same as Western tastes. Already in 1974, Robert Thompson delved into the dynamics of African appreciation of their own art, highlighting the importance of the combination of form and motion, and visuals, music, and dance to generate a pleasing performance of mask dancing.[64] Susan Vogel's landmark study on the Baule elaborated on that approach,[65] showing that it was not just appreciation that differed, but also the relation between aesthetics and

---

58 The Banyang in Cameroon bought the masks from their neighbours; Nicklin 1979: 54.
59 Muller 2001.
60 Jedrej 1986: 74.
61 Roy 1987b: 42–44; see also Roy 1987a.
62 Richter 1979: 70.
63 For an example along the lines of gender, see Brent-Smith 1995.
64 R. Thompson 1974: 126 ff.
65 Vogel 1997b.

the objects' use: the more intricate the carving, the more the objects should be hidden from view – the Baule seem to cherish privacy with regard to their art.[66] Since a masquerade should be festive and pleasurable for the participants, the aesthetics of form and those of performance should reinforce each other.

Profiles of masking societies

Our core thesis is that masquerades primarily result from and reproduce dynamics in local arenas, both between the two genders and among men, and from there they influence the relations of these communties with the wider world. Even if masks are primarily male ritual tools, understanding their rituals needs continuous attention to the pivotal role of women. Not only are they habitually defined by masks as the 'other gender', which makes women the main reference group, but in some cases these tables are even turned. Figure 1.4 (p. 36) exemplifies the deep gendering of masks, though inversely as an exception that proves the rule. In Africa the seated party holds the reins of power, and – the Mende being one of the few cultures where women do wear masks themselves – here the seated wife shows the mask – her mask! – with her two men, husband and son, dutifully flanking her.

   We can now sketch a tentative profile of the community that forms the favourite local niche for masking rituals. Within a large region characterised by historical insecurity, the ethnic groups concerned practise a hoe horticulture that is not a priori expansive, but is situated in predominantly forested zones. The local organisation often comprises independent villages, at least settlements with a certain permanence that roughly coincide with the general African sphere of matriliny. The political centralisation may vary from acephalous societies to kingdoms, but local communities tend to be quite independent and form the main point of reference for individuals.[67] Women play a large role in food production. Localised descent groups have restricted corporate functions, and show a rather indeterminate 'board of directors', characterised by an open power arena with built-in tension between generations. The local kin groups do not manage major capital goods and have little wealth to inherit, while symbolic wealth consists mainly in the form of personal titles. Usually the descent system hardly surpasses the village boundaries and is in competition with alternative male bonding institutions, such as age grading and secret societies. Gender relations show a relatively strong position for the women. Couples marry 'just around the

---

66 See also Ravenhill 1996a.
67 Such villages are 'a social reality of their own', Förster 2019: 102.

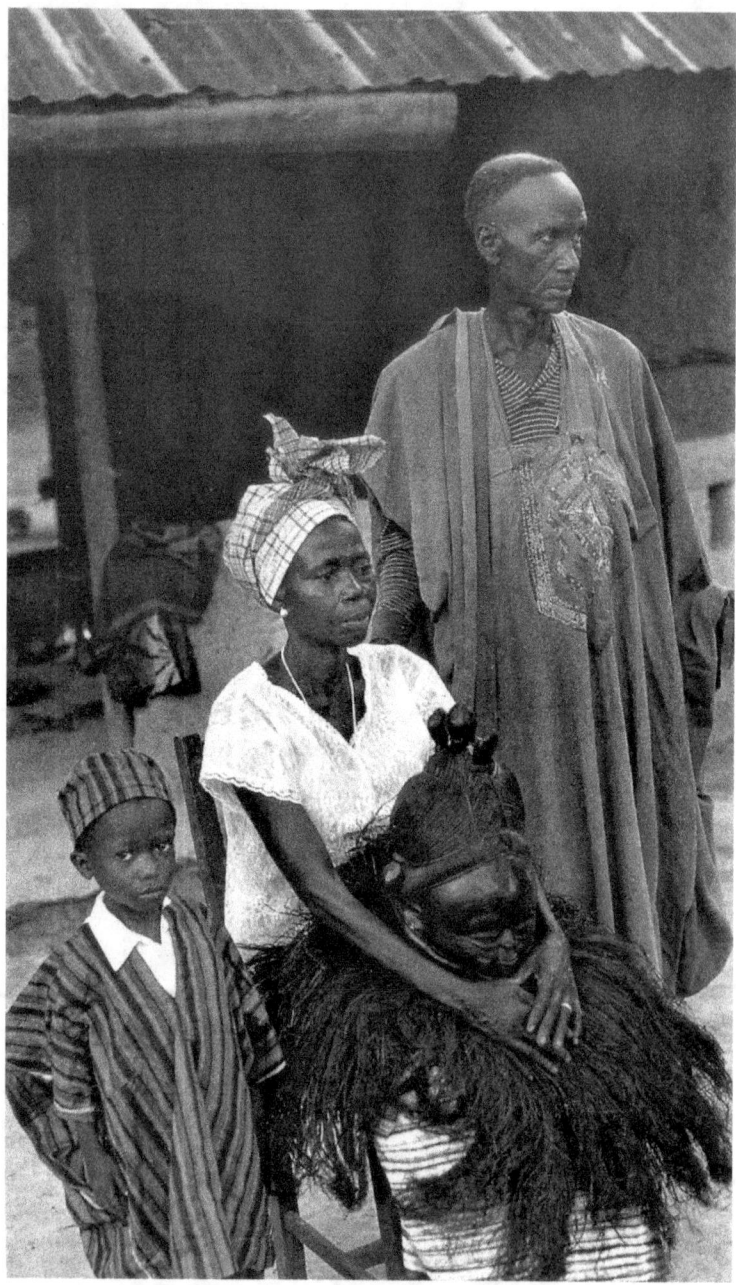

Figure 1.4. Pa McCarthy and his wife and child pose with the mask danced by Mama McCarthy during the season of *sande* initiations in Matru, Sierra Leone. Mende, Sierra Leone, 1974. Photo: Henrietta Cosentino.

corner' without substantial transactions, and wives remain in contact with their kin. Relations between villages are ambiguous due to the absence of an overarching descent authority.

The point of this study is that given these conditions, where both the gender balance and the male political system are under continuous debate and redefinition, mask rituals become a major player in redefining these relations. The forte of masks is that they form an additional power factor inside the community based upon their internal organisation, religious grounding, and aesthetic appeal. From their basis in this gentle tug-of-war between the genders and within the local political arena, mask rituals then branch out into power configurations and identity dynamics. And they do so in ways highly appreciated by the people in question, feeding into a sense of aesthetic that is hard to fulfil in other ways.

What concrete societies are we speaking about? In a classic overview, Robin Horton[68] posited three types of stateless societies in West Africa: Type A, the *segmentary lineage system*; Type B, the *layered community*;[69] and Type C, the *large compact village*.

Type A is formed by a series of patriclans, each consisting of a pyramid of ever smaller lineages tied together by patrilineal descent; together these clans and lineages make for an encompassing kinship-based social organisation. At various levels these lineages are tied to ecological resources, such as cattle and land; in field research on acephalous societies – a major occupation of classic anthropology – this was the prime social formation under study. Type B is characterised by a layering of the original occupants of the land and politically dominant newcomers: lineages are divided into 'landowners' and 'latecomers'. The main power source of the first is grounded in their ties with the land and earth spirits: they are the guardians of the earth altars, and are indispensable in rituals for crops and cultivation. The second category are the 'owners of the people', who command the labour force, and are politically ascendant.[70] This type is dominant in one region of West Africa, but is highly relevant for our overview. Type C is the large defensive village, the result of multiple insecurities including slavery and slave raiding. For this type, Horton

---

68 Horton 1976 (1971). We use letters instead of numbers to avoid confusion with the zones.

69 Horton called this the *dispersed territorially defined community*, but for the sake of brevity we use 'layered'.

70 The classic description stems from Fortes 1957, 1969. Whether this image of two different ethnic groups is actual history or political myth (MacGaffey 2013: 71) is not overly germane, since in both cases there is a power balance between earth chiefs and political rulers.

lists a complex arrangement of local lineages, age groups, and the presence of secret societies-*cum*-masks, thus prefiguring our analysis. This type is close to the profile we have sketched above.

Horton's overview comprises most of our first two Zones. For both Zone 3 and part of Zone 1 we add another constellation, Type D: the *frontier village*. This is the typical slash-and-burn forest village, moving with its swiddens, fissioning when needed, coalescing when expedient, in which the individual house can acquire positions of wealth and strength, depending on the house-holder's personal qualities. These mobile settlements are tied together in loose trade networks, or form part of warrior realms. Usually they are situated in areas with low population density. The name we have chosen stems from the work of Igor Kopytoff,[71] who identified the external frontier as an integral part of African communities. Type D derives from Zone 3, but is also applicable to the forested part of Zone 1.[72]

Mask rituals are found both in stateless societies and in states, but this distinction has been rendered less relevant by recent research, since it has become clear that many centralised realms in Africa that have been dubbed 'states' in fact were 'warrior states'[73] living on tributes, concerned less with governing than with reasserting their power through occasional military expeditions. These nodal points of periodic predation based themselves not on local production but on trade monopolies of luxury goods, often dominating the long-range trade routes that linked the African interior to the coast with its European traders. Exchanging the traditional wealth of the continent, such as ivory, gold, and slaves, the rulers focused on the accumulation of ostentatious riches, and then orchestrated public redistribution. Thus, trade furnished the realm with the wherewithal to generate clientele, as well as the theatrics of conspicuous ownership.

For many centralised polities in Africa, another characterisation is relevant. Clifford Geertz coined the term 'theatre state',[74] a polity held together by the performance of elaborate rituals in full public view, a realm defined by – and even grounded in – the ceremonial performance of the officeholders. All states have a theatrical aspect, but the issue is how dependent the state is on staged performances. Masquerades add to the theatricality of any state, so we will

---

71 Kopytoff 1987.

72 For an application of the 'frontier' concept to Côte d'Ivoire, see Grillo 2018: 123.

73 See Pratten 2007: 48 for a critique on the earlier concept of 'predatory state'.

74 Geertz 1980; his examples concerned kingdoms on Bali, Indonesia. For a critical reaction, see MacRae 2005. Several scholars held that state theatricals should rest on a solid political-economic basis, rather than just on a spectacle, as was Geertz's view; we side with these critics.

peruse in what way the so-called states inside the Crescent are recognisable as theatre states. As Pierre Bourdieu has made clear, any political formation must be based on a combination of various types of material, symbolic, cultural, or social capital, and for our explanation of the functioning of these 'states', the balance between material and symbolic capital is crucial.[75]

Within both egalitarian and centralised social formations mask rituals are rooted in local communities, and the forms of masking at the political centre depend on local masquerade traditions: court masquerades tend to reflect the mask rituals in the villages. So the four societal types mentioned, combined with the notions of warrior and theatre states, form a convenient starting point for characterising the conditions of grass roots communities in many societies of the Crescent. Since conceptual types are 'simplified, necessarily unfaithful, and theoretically tendentious'[76] compared with the varied, mixed situation in the field, we will use them as a shorthand for brief characterisations of the cases in question; as we shall see, these types mix and mingle, which allows us to discern their most relevant traits.

Types C and D, compact villages and frontier communities, represent societies in which gender and power are proper arenas; in these types mask rituals are functional, even to be expected, and together they characterise most of our cases; Type C is dominant in Zone 1 and Zone 2, whereas Type D dominates Zone 3. Type B, with one group having 'power over land' and another 'power over people', does not offer a ready haven for mask rituals, with notable exceptions.

However, it is Type A, the segmentary system, that gives the clearest and maybe most surprising view on masquerades: Type A societies harbour no masks, a hard and fast rule for which we have found no real exception yet. In these systems patriclans and lineages are organised along a pyramidical model, with each of the branches tied into inheritable wealth, which can take the form of land but often consists of cattle.

The zebu exclusion

Our profile, together with the four types, should explain both the outer borders of the Mask Crescent and its curious internal shape. We start with the latter: the wider Congo Basin shows up as a major interruption on the map. Here the main factor is demography. Part of this huge area is rainforest,[77] part forested

---

75 Bourdieu 1990.

76 Geertz 1980: 9–10.

77 The principal groups, such as the Mongo and the Tetela, are reported not to have masks, and these societies have few rituals anyway. For the Tetela, see the caption by

savannah,[78] but in both ecotypes subsistence is based upon a wide spectrum of food production, with foraging and fishing as prime activities, and a very flexible division of labour. Mobility is the rule, and is also a defensive strategy against slave raiders or other external threats; such groups can disappear into the forest. These societies consist of small groups, hamlets, and bands that coalesce, fission, and fuse again in a constant dynamic, and any leader depends largely on personal abilities.[79] In such a widely dispersed population the crucial dilemmas that mask rituals address are not present, so a low population density precludes mask rituals. In this basin the population density remains well below four per square kilometre; only beyond that 'historical watershed', as Jan Vansina calls it,[80] do processes of village formation and political centralisation set in. Beneath that limit, the gender and power arenas evaporate between the trees, and masks with them. Beyond that limit we arrive at Type D societies, which share some of their fluidity but have more complex social arrangements – and masks.[81]

But apart from the Akan Gap – which will be discussed in Chapter 7 – the shape of the Crescent is defined by its external borders, and these point to one glaring absence in the three zones: cattle. Masking cultures do not herd cattle; and wherever cows appear, masks tend to be absent. Zebu and mask do not mix, and the reasons are not hard to find. Cattle are capital, an asset that can be accumulated and requires management as well as organised transfer between generations, so cattle form the epitome of inheritable wealth. This has crucial social implications. Pastoral cultures are usually patrilineal, with wide-ranging clan and lineage systems, deep and segmented genealogies, and kinbased management systems that include vast tracts of land and a multitude of settlements and villages. Thus, cattle keeping leads to societal

---

De Heusch in T. Phillips 1995: 281: 'The myth of Tetela masks should now be laid to rest.' For the Mongo, see Bongango 2008.

78   The Gbaya occupy the enormous stretch of country in the heavily forested savannah between Cameroon, CAR, and DRC. They live in widely dispersed hamlets of up to 35 people, with small patrilineages that regroup continuously, and never develop a concise political or social leadership: Burnham 1975, 1980, Roulon-Doko 2017; Pilo Atta 2017.

79   A curious exception are the Baka, who operate fully within the rainforest as foragers, yet they do have a ritual that could be called a masquerade: see Joiris 1996; Tsuru 1998, 2001. This seeming anomaly depends on the fact that they live in an increasingly monetised environment while traditionally they have no notion of individual property: the spirits that these masks represent form the only form of – new – private property in this society.

80   Vansina 1990: 99.

81   Like, for instance, the Chokwe: Rodrigues de Areia 2003, Wastiau 2008.

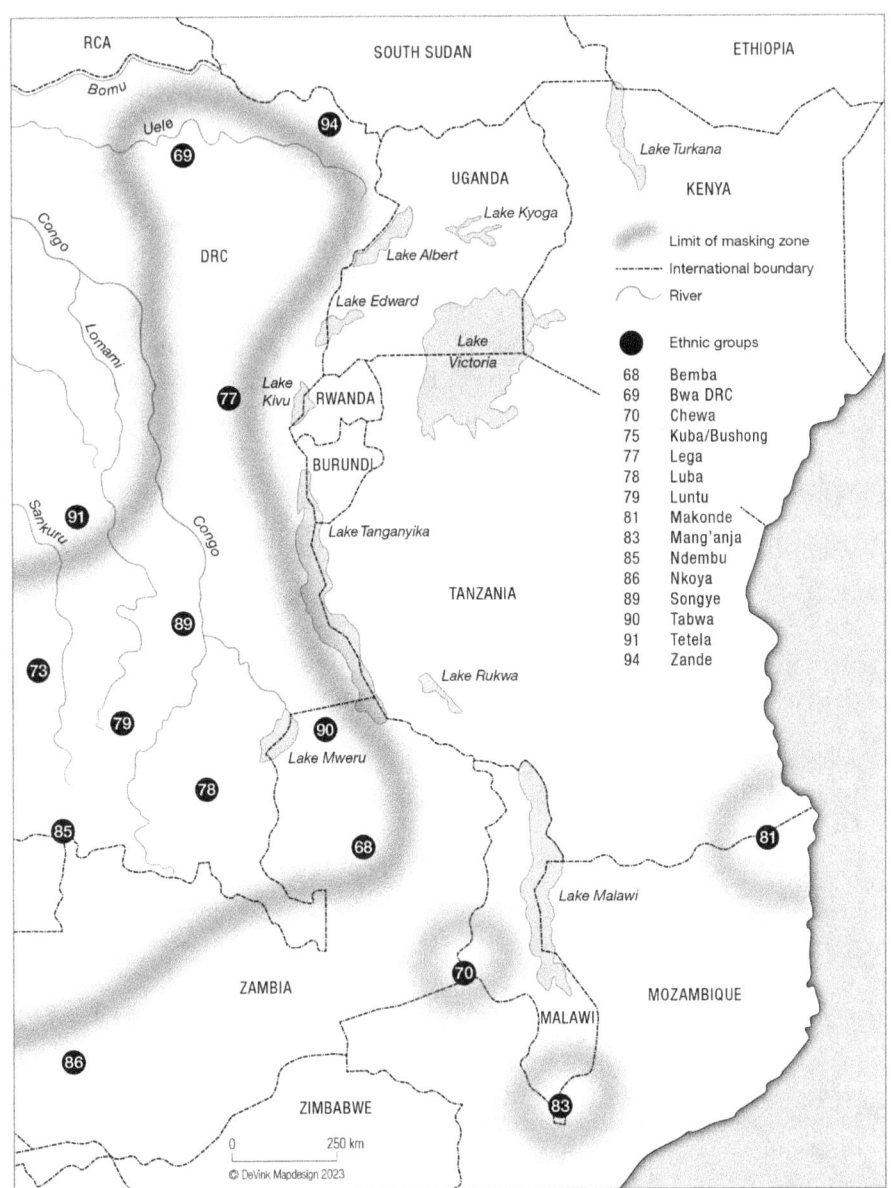

Map 5. East Africa and its masking cultures.

Type A, segmentary societies, with cattle playing a significant role not only as capital, but also as the focus of a pervading cultural fascination that leaves little room for mask rituals.[82] Since the situation varies with the zones, we will follow the zebu exclusion from east to west.[83]

Zone 3 shows a sharp eastern border, for the masks never seem to cross the western branch of the Great Rift, the mountain ranges that cradle the string of Great Lakes: Albert, Edward, Kivu, and Tanganyika, and to some extent also Lake Malawi.[84] This precise border is quite revealing. The eastern rim of the Congo Basin houses cultures that narrowly fit the masking profile, while the countries of Uganda, Rwanda, Burundi, and Tanzania have a completely different cultural habitus. East of the Rift one is in cattle country, with societies that both depend heavily on cattle for both ecology and in social organisation. The breed of cattle in question is predominantly the zebu (*Bos taurus indicus*), the humped, long-horned cattle. In these societies the zebu is all-important as the main source of livelihood, and as an icon of wealth. Cattle herding trumps horticulture, and the animals are milked; men herd, women milk. These people drink cow's milk, whereas people in most of the Mask Crescent cannot digest this well.[85] Herding means mobility, and even if full nomadism is rare, cattle husbandry demands movement for pasture over large spaces, since the African savannah is not nutrient-rich. Such a way of life generates societies with large lineages of considerable depth, and complex kinship systems that extend over vast distances, and thus cultures that are in constant interaction with surrounding groups – almost the opposite of the masking model.

These societies are strictly patrilineal and patrilocal, and their local patrilineages manage important capital.[86] Large bride wealth is required for marriage,

---

82 This has been dubbed the 'cattle complex', but any connotation with psychological afflictions is to be avoided. It is simply a societal type, also with considerable variations. In such a society, cattle are much more than providers of food. In daily life all major value is expressed in heads of cattle; bride wealth is paid in cattle, and all major transactions are in cattle. The indigenous religion is dominated by sacrifice of livestock.
83 See for a quantitative analysis Holden and Mace 2003.
84 Lake Mweru is part of the Congo River complex, fed by the Luapula River.
85 Owing to lactose intolerance – also called lactase deficiency – which in fact is a common condition in humans around the world.
86 Considerable debates surrounded the question whether patrilineal segmentary systems were actually found on the ground, or should be considered folk models. Starting from the prototypical Nuer social organisation, the emerging consensus was that patrilineal segmentation should be seen as a kind of ideology, a flexible grid that served as 'a representation of an enduring form of their society' (Holy 1996: 85).

implying the transfer of a substantial number of cattle, since each marriage involves a serious exchange of wealth for the rights in the bride and her offspring.[87] In these cultures the gender relations are more skewed and much less a matter of negotiation, and the dominion of men over women is considerably larger; many of the transactions between men concern payment and the restitution of bride wealth, and court cases are full of discussions on paternity. Inherited wealth and accumulated capital actually make masking pointless; their patrilineal structures have boards of directors that are simply too well-structured. In such systems masquerades as an independent force would be a highly disturbing factor, threatening the social fabric of male power.

Yet, there is a sprinkling of masking societies in East Africa. In the deep history of Africa, the region between the western and the eastern branches of the Great Rift has served as a corridor through which cattle herders have migrated from the north to the south,[88] often in the form of conquest. During their migration, these cattle herders intersected with the forested zone of the matrilineal belt, which runs all the way to the Indian Ocean,[89] thus forcing a patrilineal wedge between the Congo Basin and the matrilineal areas close to the Indian Ocean. South of Lake Malawi, the Chewa and Mang'anja of Zambia are such matrilineal groups, who, like the patrilineal Makonde on the border between Tanzania and Mozambique, were cut off from the rest of Zone 3 by people practising cattle husbandry. These three are among the East African enclaves of masking, a dynamic explained by the persistence of their secret societies.

The southern limit of Zone 3 follows the transition from open rain forest to dry forest, the vegetation where zebu can be kept.[90] This border area has a long history of internal wars, of political dominance of one group over another, each with their own specific rules of descent and political centralisation, and shows a gradual transition from 'masking territory' to 'cattle grounds',[91] with an in-between position of peoples who keep cattle but do not drink milk – and have no masks. All in all, also the southern limit of the Crescent is drawn by the zebu.[92]

87 Most bride wealth theory has been developed in this area; see Stone 2006.
88 See https://www.researchgate.net/publication/279222258_-_Invited_Review_-_ African_Indigenous_Cattle_Unique_Genetic_Resources_in_a_Rapidly_Changing_ World/figures?lo=1, consulted 16 August 2019.
89 Murdock 1959.
90 Alsan 2015.
91 As is the case among the Nkoya of Zambia, Van Binsbergen 1992: 229.
92 Not all cattle are zebu, for Africa houses another species as well, *Bos taurus taurus*, the West African shorthorn. Occurring in small numbers at isolated places, mainly in Zone

Cattle are absent in the forest zones owing to sleeping sickness, which means they are absent from most of Zone 3 and the coastal areas of the other two zones. Zones 1 and 2 extend well into the savannah, and at their northern rim people do have masks in a region where cattle thrive. But here the mixture of agriculture and pastoralism is different from that in East Africa, due to an ethnic division of labour. In the northern parts of Zones 1 and 2 sedentary groups practise horticulture, while specialised cattle holders have a different ethnic affiliation; the latter are dispersed over the whole area – in fact, throughout the Sahelian zone – and they are predominantly Fulbe. From Senegal to Chad, the Fulbe, or Fulani, herd their cattle in the areas of the Bamana, Bobo, Mumuye, and Fali, or of whatever other horticultural group – the list is long. These masking societies cultivate, and the Fulbe herd cattle and after the harvest let their cattle graze on the stubble of the sorghum and millet, fertilising the fields with their dung – in principle, an ecologically sound ecosystem. Some cultivators may own some cattle, and have the Fulbe herd them. Though the horticulturalists interact closely with the Fulbe in the economic sphere and their activities complement each other, their cultures do not mesh: they form two completely different types of societies on both sides of the ecological coin, and while one has masks, the other has certainly not.[93]

Socially and politically, this joint ecology is vulnerable and may lead to tensions, a precarious balance of power that may easily tip either way; at present (2023) the problems in the Sahel testify to this ecology's volatility. Such an ethnic specialisation means that, even if they are far removed from the forested areas, the local horticulturalists fit the pattern described above, that of the Type C society: independent patrilineal villages with

---

2, they probably stem from an earlier dispersion into Africa before the zebu invasion (Blench 1998). They resist tsetse better, and can subsist on a wider range of food and fodder. Most of these taurine populations are by now dwindling. Seignobos and Thys (1998: 9–14) show that these cattle had a limited role in the ecosystem, which never led to the so-called cattle complex. Shorthorns serve as a status symbol in the owner's lifetime, to be slaughtered at his funeral (Paarup-Laursen 1998). They are transient wealth, symbolic riches, and taurine-keeping does not seem to affect social dynamics much. They seem to have a dialectical relation with masks, for inasmuch as a taurine versus mask exclusion seems to hold, it has a symbolic logic. Fardon (2007) notes the strong symbolic resemblance between cowhide funerals of the Dowayo (taurines, no masks) and the mask-led burials of their Chamba neighbours (masks, no taurines). Thus, mask and bull seem to have similar positions in the symbolic repertoire, and there is little need to have both. See also Garine 1998 and Van Beek 1998.

93 De Bruijn and Van Dijk 1995.

some age organisation,[94] a high village endogamy, low bride wealth, and little inheritable wealth. Some of the most exuberant masking traditions are found precisely in this Sudanic–Sahelian belt, such as those of the Jola, Bamana, Senufo, Bobo, Bwa, Dogon, Mumuye, and Mundang. North of the masking border – which in Zone 1 follows the Niger Bend – rain-fed grain cultivation is no longer feasible; one is in the real Sahel, where the only ecological option is pastoralism – hence no masks. The dip on the northern border of Zone 1 is the Futa Highlands, where the Fulbe stem from: a cradle of pastoralism and a major pathway for Islam, for which masks are anathema.

Methodology

The theoretical model we employ necessitates a two-stepped examination of: (1) the historical and ecological conditions leading to societies with internal dynamics conducive for masquerades; and (2) the way in which mask rituals address – and are informed by – these dynamics. Since the chain of reasoning in our theoretical scheme runs from social formation to the arenas of gender and power, and from these to mask rituals, our testing must be two-tiered as well, and in reverse order, so must start from our core phenomenon, the masquerade. In the masking profile outlined above we have considered the first question. For an answer to the second question we need to review mask rituals themselves in order to relate them to processes inherent in the arenas in question: gender and power.

Ronald Grimes remarks: 'The study of ritual is closely intertwined with the swinging pendulum of power balances and imbalances' – which is precisely what we aim to look at – but continues: 'assuming that power *in* a ritual translates automatically into power *outside* a ritual is overly simple.'[95] The latter remark is the challenge we try to meet. The salient point here is that masks appear in a restricted number of ritual types, and that this limitation is most informative. For instance, masks only occasionally function in healing ceremonies, rarely in sacrifices, and hardly ever in cyclical, agricultural rites or rain rituals, while they are never present in marriage or birth rites. Instead, mask performances are crucial in initiation and death transitions – Chapters 3 to 6 – while also power holders such as kings and

---

94 For an in-depth analysis of the interplay of age and lineage in such a society, see Memet-Forté 1980.
95 Grimes 2014: 303, italics added by the author.

secret societies generate their masquerades, as does the maintenance of law and order – Chapters 7 and 8. For each of those ritual types we trace how mask performances impact gender and power balances. In all this the performative appeal of masquerades is crucial, and steers their central role in wider identity dynamics – Chapters 9 and 10.

In order to glean the relation between the rituals and internal societal dynamics, in each of the following chapters we analyse the interaction of mask ritual and society; in the conclusion to each chapter we assess how the specific societies we examine conform to the conceptual model proposed. In order to avoid repetitive ethnographical information, we use the typology developed above, while we also group these societies per culture area wherever feasible; thus, not all societies will be 'profiled' in the chapter where they first appear.

2

What is a Mask?

Explaining masks: The Magritte effect

A standard riddle of the Cameroonian Dìi questions whether the mask is an animal or a man. The correct answer is that it is neither: 'Below it is a man as an animal, but the upper part is a spirit.'[1] One could just as well answer that it is both, but the Dìi choice is that it is neither: so its own category. This particular Dìi mask covers only the upper part of the body, and the legs are naked; in some performances, the genitals of the dancer should be in sight, to prove he is a man, a circumcised one, and thus authorised to dance.[2] Such a riddle illustrates a kind of 'Magritte effect' that masks produce, using the felicitous expression of Jean-Pierre Warnier:[3] the masking apparition blends the thing and its representation, finding both its essence and its source of power in exactly that semantic confusion.

What do we mean by a 'mask'? In Western culture, what is called a 'mask' in a museum exhibition or art gallery is in fact a face covering.[4] In this book we call these 'headpieces', 'tops', or 'face covers', for we follow another definition of a mask, namely the African one. What informants call a mask is the entire costumed appearance, including the headpiece, the clothing or body cover, and the adornment on arms, legs, and feet, as well as the paraphernalia it holds in its hands: whips, whisks, sticks, adzes, or spears. In

1   Muller 2001: 61. See for this case also Muller 1997a, 1993, 2002, 2008.
2   Nudity underneath the mask is also known among the Nigerian Mumuye, who live in the same culture area.
3   Warnier 2007: 6–13, cited in Mohan and Douny 2021: 15. In the early 1920s the French surrealist René Magritte produced a painting of a pipe with on the painting the text '*Ceci n'est pas une pipe*' (This is not a pipe). He called this work '*Trahison des images*' (Treason of the images): the representation is not the same as the object. The painting became world famous.
4   For the relation between face and mask in Western artistic representations, see Belting 2013.

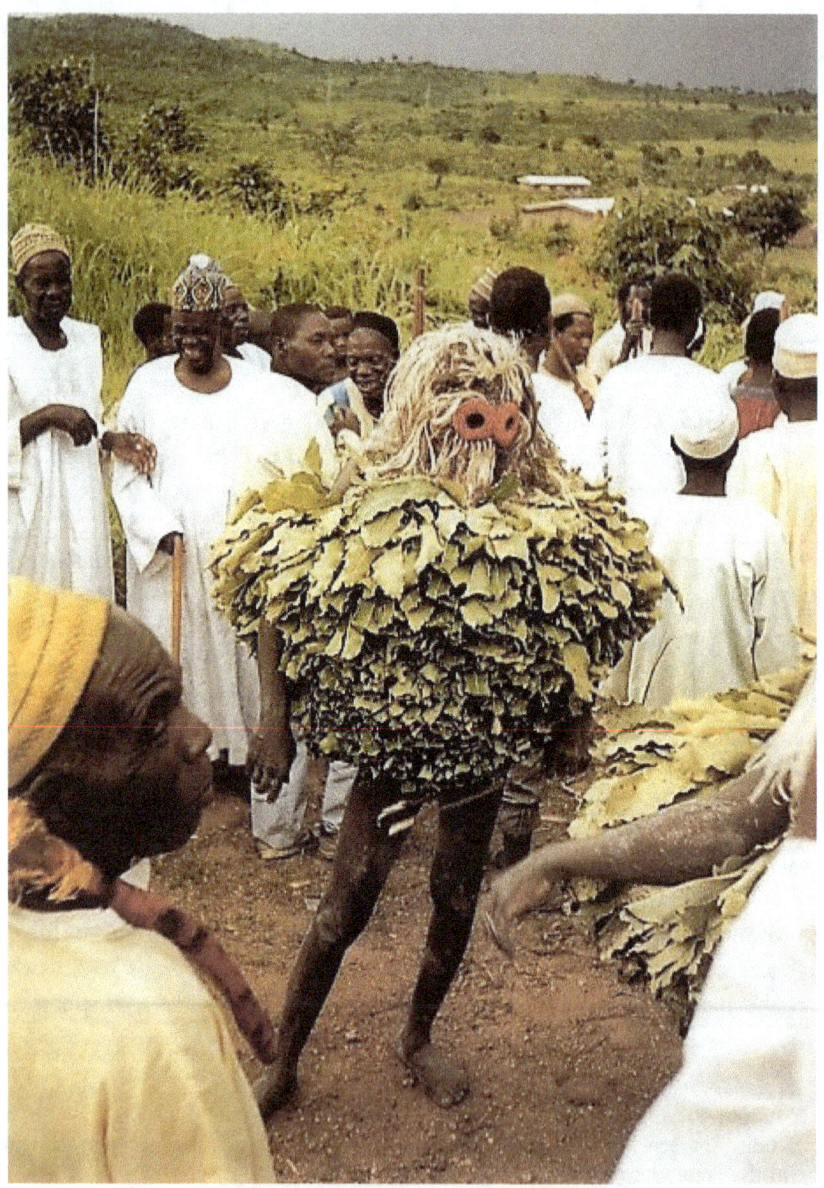

Figure 2.1. 'Half-man, half-spirit': the *geg* mask. Dìì, Cameroon. Photo: Jean-Claude Muller, c. 1992.

some cases, the same costume and headpiece may even become a different mask by simply changing the accessories and attributes. So we use the emic African definition: a 'mask' means costume + top + paraphernalia, coupled with, evidently, an invisible dancer inside; dance and music may be added to this definition. There are some cases where not all criteria apply, but together they cover the great majority of masks in Africa.[5] Though the hidden face is essential, in some instances the face is, very pointedly, in sight, while the apparition is still considered a mask; those exceptions occur within specific settings, depending on the occasion, and above all on the presence or absence of a non-initiated audience. In all our ethnographic cases there is a vernacular term for mask, and in all masking societies masks are defined as a total apparition characterised by anonymity.

The inclusion of the costume is crucial; a mask is much more than just a thing a man puts over his head or in front of his face; in fact, it amounts to a change in personality: one does not put on a mask, rather one *becomes* a mask. Studies on African art have noticed this notion of the mask as the whole costumed appearance time and again; Frederick Lamp illustrates this by a Guinean journal illustration of a Baga headpiece, with the caption: 'D'mba [mask] undressed'.[6] Yet most publications concentrate on these 'undressed masks', for the headpieces have a strong aesthetic appeal, and are available for study. However, recent approaches increasingly adopt the holistic view of masks, and since this book focuses on the rituals in which masks operate, we use the African definition.

This does not imply that the headpiece is unimportant; in fact it is crucial, but as part of the whole apparition. Only with a headpiece can a costumed figure be called a mask, and any definition of a mask is based on the principle that the face is covered. When a headpiece is worn in front of the face or as a helmet, that coverage is self-evident; but when the headpiece rests on top of the head, the face must be covered as well, usually with cloth or gauze. There are few exceptions to this rule, since the point of masking is that the dancer himself is unrecognisable – at least

5   Reviewing bodily adornment in Africa, Denise Paulme notes a continuum between body decoration and masking (Paulme 1973), showing the embeddedness of masks, which nonetheless retain their special character.

6   Lamp 2013: 82. Figure 2.2 on page 51 shows the dance of *d'mba*, Baga Sitemu. Since 1984, some villages have attempted to renew the pre-Islamic Baga ritual dance that was discontinued in the 1950s. Vincent Bangoura (centre) is one of the young leaders in this effort to learn the old dances, to carve and construct the Baga masquerades, to learn traditional songs and compose new ones, and to encourage the elders to pass down the traditional knowledge. Photo and information: Frederick Lamp.

the audience should be able to pretend not to recognise him. Since hiding the identity of the dancer is a crucial aspect of masking,[7] a mask without a headcovering is an incomplete mask. However, a headpiece on its own is not considered a mask – nowhere near so.

A basic mask typology

In order to solve the Dìì puzzle, we must first gain some overview of African masks. The variety of headpieces in Africa is dazzling and defies any easy categorisation; in fact, we have been stimulated in our endeavour by such attempts at pattern recognition.[8] The most common one is to distinguish between the ways the headpieces are worn, as a helmet, as a crest, as a face covering, or on top of the head; these are handy tools for description, but they become mingled throughout. An important study in this regard is Patrick McNaughton's attempt at a diffusionist history of horizontal headpieces.[9] Despite his impressive overview of literature, art-historical connections remain elusive, an important result that has stimulated our questioning into the phenomenon of masking along a different trajectory. Based on his Ebira material, John Picton devised a four-fold typology in performance, with the variables of distance between mask and audience on the one hand, and the human agency of the masker on the other.[10] Such a sophisticated typology is promising, but hard to implement when comparing cases, as it depends on emic interpretations for each case. Since our quest is to explain the presence of mask in local rituals, we use a more basic descriptive typology based on the costume, one that is also used by organisers of regional mask festivals.[11]

Whereas mask tops show an almost endless variation, the costumes are easier to classify. The definition of a mask as a costumed appearance with a headcovering, leads to four – admittedly quite basic – types: masks with costumes made of **leaves**, of **fibres**, of **cloth**, and of what we call **contraptions**. These types are merely tools for description, but they do show some correspondence with ritual, function, and historical development.

---

7   Hahner-Herzog et al. 1989.
8   Kasfir 1988b; Bouttiaux 2013a.
9   McNaughton 1991, 1992.
10   Following a lead of Jedrej 1980.
11   Such as the FESTIMA Festival International des Masques, in Burkina Faso. See Chapter 9.

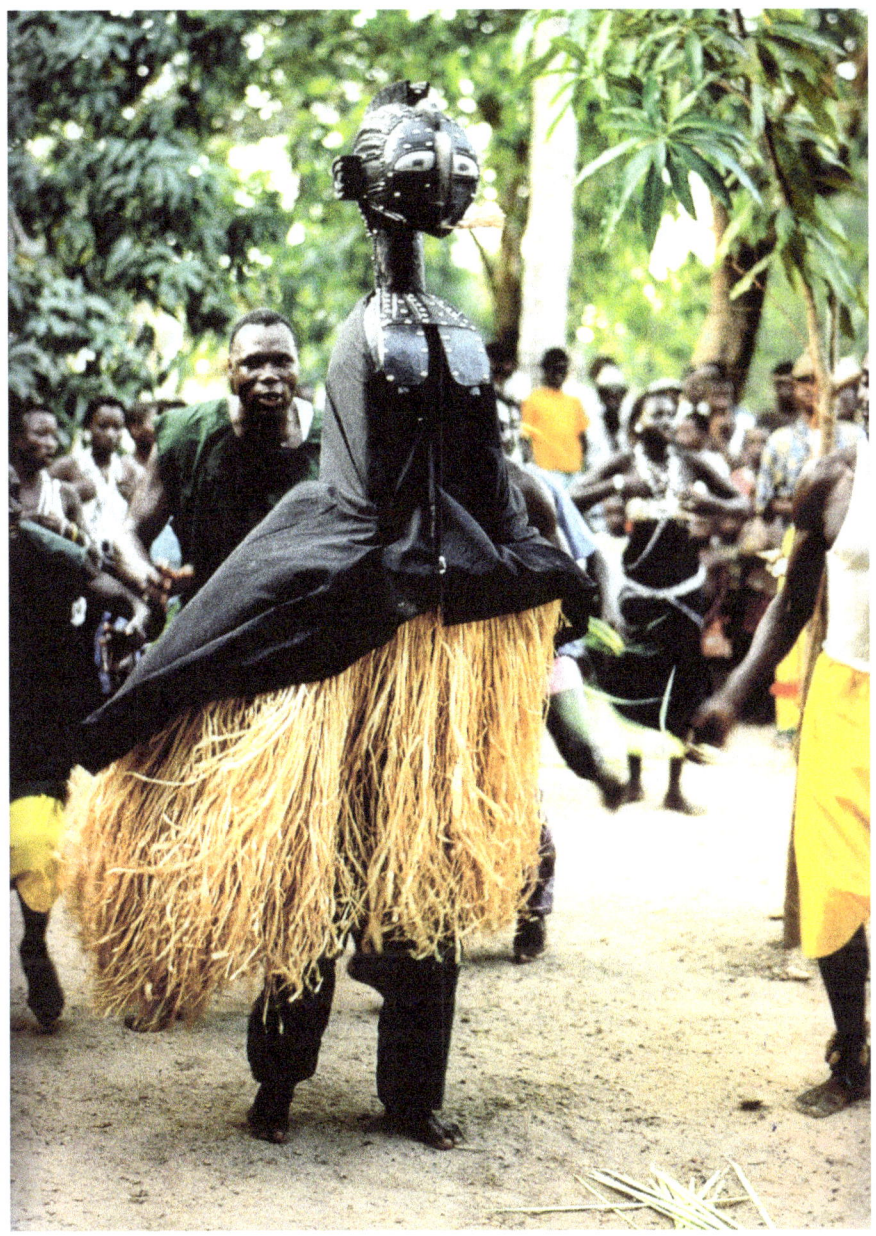

Figure 2.2. Only a fully clothed mask, such as this *d'mba*, is really a mask. Baga, Guinea. Photo: Frederick Lamp, c. 1990.

The first type is seldom encountered in museal collections,[12] but forms the basis of all masking: a costume made entirely out of leaves and twigs from the bush that also covers the head. With this type the disguise is striking since the human form easily disappears in the foliage, and it is also a mask that boys can make in their initiation camps. In all probability it is the oldest mask type, since wherever leaf masks function next to fibre or cloth, the leaf mask is always considered to be the most ancient. Some leaf masks are among the most spectacular the Crescent has to offer, like the *dwo* mask among the Bobo of Burkina Faso (Figure 2.3).

Leaf masks may have become play masks for boys, and may have been replaced by fibre masks for adults, viz. the Dogon.[13] Or newer types may have been added while the leaf masks remained, retaining considerable ritual weight, as among the Bobo and the Bwa peoples of Burkina Faso. The *bedik* masks in Senegal used for initiation are still made of leaves.[14] Many groups have consciously abandoned leaves in favour of more sophisticated costumes. On the Jos Plateau it was in the decade 1930–1940 that people shifted from leaf to fibre,[15] owing to internal trouble, and the Pende of DRC changed costume after political problems: 'people in Kwilu Pende lost faith in their spiritual denizens.'[16] Leaves linger, however, and are very often part of the fibre and cloth costumes as a gentle reminder of the bush.[17]

By far the most common type of costume consists of fibres. These masks may cover head and torso in one large heap of fibres, not too different from the leaf kind; the masks of the Cameroonian Mundang are an example. The classic fibre is raffia, the leaf-vein of the raffia palm, but also lianas, hemp, and strips of bark can furnish the material. Outside the forest zone, cultivars such as hibiscus and beans provide basic material for masks, and when large masquerades are due, the cultivation schedule is adapted to the needs of the ritual. For prospective dancers, working on the fibres is an integral part of mask preparations. In many initiations, after the boys have been introduced to the masks, they are taught how to make a fibre costume themselves.

---

12 Some museums collect and guard them if they belong to a carved headpiece: Museum für Völkerkunde Berlin (IIIC 721); Royal Museum for Central Africa, also called Afrika Museum Tervuren, EO.1960.39.154; and the Museu de Ethnologia do Ultramar (MLA: 268). We thank Rogier Bedaux for this information.
13 Van Beek 2006.
14 Ferry 2013.
15 Isichei 1988: 48.
16 Strother 2008.
17 Even among the *ékpè* masks of Calabar, which are materially far removed from bush, some foliage is indispensable: see Figure 10.6. Ivor Miller, personal communication.

Since fibres are more flexible and resilient than leaves, they can readily be made into a more structured design. Bark strips are usually not plaited, but raffia, hemp, and hibiscus fibres can be intricately knitted, plaited, and braided. An example is the way the Bobo plait a face-top as an integral part of the crown of a costume, a masterpiece of plaiting.[18] Fibres have one more advantage: they can be dyed, so colour enters the costumes. Dominant are the usual red, white, and black – the basic colours of the African palette – black often meaning indigo blue. In modern-day masks all colours are available, and are used with enthusiasm. Fibre costumes are often adorned with cloth items over the upper body, or with the dancers wearing trousers while their torsos are decked out with fibres. The first option can be witnessed in the *gegbadë* of our opening vignette, common in many initiation masks. The Dogon masking outfit follows the second option, where all masks whatever their type, wear wide, dark blue trousers as their basic clothing.

Fibre masks acquire their final shape and identity with the carved tops. The carved headpieces offer a flexible and detailed expression of individual mask types, and while the fibres define the apparition as a mask, the carved top indicates which one it is. So with the addition of wooden headpieces, the masks acquire individuality, and in their variety can become a theatrical troupe, performing in different roles. With carved tops, aesthetics and style become important; carvings can be either more or less accomplished and thus artesanal craftsmanship comes into the picture.[19]

The third major type of mask is made of cloth, usually large flowing robes hanging from the head down: in this type often both head and body are covered with one cloth. Fibre masks never have cloth tops, only cloth masks do. The Yoruba *egungun* is a splendid example of such a mask, very important in Yoruba culture, sophisticated and sometimes quite old (Figure 7.2). The face can be part of the cloth coverage itself, or covered with a head gauze. This kind of all-cloth mask is seldom used in boys' initiations; however, when women use masks in girls' initiations, like the Manding,[20] these tend to be made of cloth. With cloth as a material, other dynamics

---

18　Le Moal 2008.
19　Gagliardi 2018b.
20　Weil 1998. For this group, variant names are used. In the French literature they are called 'Manding', who speak 'Mandinka', while in English both 'Manding' and 'Mandinga' are common. De Jong uses 'Mandinko' and also 'Manding'. We use in the text, depending on the author cited, either 'Manding' or 'Mandinka'; for the map we use 'Mandinka'. We thank Menno Sypkens Smit for this information.

come to the fore. First, cloth patterns can distinguish between individuals and groups, but also express wealth and external trade connections, as the *egungun* does. The other association is with a burial shroud. Among the Ebira of Central Nigeria, one all-cloth mask with a specific construction and pattern signals the return of a recently deceased elder.[21]

The fourth type is the contraption, a structure that is worn by the dancer not as a costume but as a kind of edifice. Often, they are very complex, as with the *ijele* mask of Nigeria (Figure 9.3), a veritable building that the dancer carries around.[22] Light material is essential. Often constructed from basketry or wicker work, such masks can be colossal structures, borne on the shoulders and completely covering the person inside, or may require more than one dancer to support them: a multi-person mask. One Chewa mask called 'big stalk of bananas', or 'steama' (pidgin for train), requires four men to dance;[23] a recent version portrays a helicopter.[24] Similar tent-like constructions function in boys' rituals and the funerals of chiefs,[25] and they occur mainly in Zone 3.

In the form of a table:

Table 1. Overview of masking types.

Major material	Basic type	Headpieces	Additions
Leaves	leaf masks	leaf	
Fibres	all-fibre masks	fibre / wooden top	cloth, skins, cowries, beads
Cloth	all-cloth masks	cloth / wooden top	feathers, skins
Construction	contraption	no separate top	as many as possible

The great majority of masks in Africa fall into the second and third cells of the third column, a combination of fibre, cloth, and a wooden top, in whatever proportion. The reasons for this preference are clear: this type of mask is recognisable as having enough individual features to distinguish it

---

21 Picton 2009: 308. It would be interesting to compare Ebira masquerades with the *egungun* classification that the Drewals provide: Drewal and Drewal 1978.
22 Such a contraption can develop out of smaller ones, like the *afulele* masks of the Ekperi in Nigeria; Borgatti 2003: 54. Many new *mamiwata* headpieces show similar characteristics, as do specific Bamana masquerades; Imperato 1980: 54.
23 Birch 1988: 29; Curran 1999: 74.
24 Created by an inventive artist who also fabricated a python mask: Yoshida 2006: 228.
25 Blacmun and Schoffeleers 1972; Birch 1988: 30–31, 1996.

from others, is highly versatile, can interact well with audiences, and has enough vision to be mobile while strange enough to instil awe. But our classification might be more than a mere morphological sequence, for it also reads like a general evolution of masks. As said, many groups indicate that their oldest form was the leaf kind, and that the fibres came later,[26] while the cloth forms are restricted to complex, urbanised societies. An important caveat is that most masking societies possess not just one but many types of masks: fibres and leaves, or cloth and fibres, often in different genres of ritual. Thus, the typology is not restrictive; the main point is that different types of masks serve specific ritual purposes.

Masquerades are events, performances at a special time and place, so are in principle transient. The same holds, rather surprisingly, for the mask themselves, most of which exist for a short time only. Some have a short lifespan anyway: the leaf masks of the Bobo, despite their stunning appearance, wither away quickly, and after a performance are left behind in the very same bush they stemmed from. A fibre top is 'given back to the rivers from which it originally came', for example by the Niger Delta Urhobo.[27] Or, when specific masks are tied to chieftaincy, as is the case with the Dìì of Cameroon, they must be burned when a new chief is installed.[28] Pigments used to decorate carved headpieces fade and must be reapplied regularly. During initiation, novices wash existing wooden tops and repaint them for their coming-out ceremony:[29] they must appear new, not old. In principle, Africans guard their headpieces for as long as they have value for them and serve their ends, which often is just for one ritual or season, and all over the Mask Crescent carved tops are abandoned after use. Dogon headpieces are used for just one mask festival, and a new masking ritual demands new costumes and new tops. Although some should be retained for specific rituals, the bulk is discarded. Angolan disc-headpieces are thrown away in the bush, and elaborate Luntu face coverings with raffia, wood, and feathers are abandoned after the initiation.[30] Everything must be returned to nature.

Such ephemerality has long been ignored, and yet is fundamental. As Christine Kreamer formulated it, they are impermanent by design: 'Longevity [...] was not and is not the motivating factor for many of

26 The Dogon are one example (Van Beek 2006); the Bwa another (Roy 2003).
27 Foss 2003: 133.
28 Muller 2001: 65.
29 Colleyn 2002a, 2002b; Jespers 2011.
30 Petridis 2003: 140. For a regional comparison in this respect see Volper 2012.

Africa's tradition-based artists working in wood.'[31] It is Western culture that 'saves' them from perdition and displays them in museum vitrines – and a good thing that is – but becoming perennial is not their intended destiny.[32] Performance is an ephemeral art form par excellence, and so are the tops themselves; the very act of abandoning and especially destroying these power objects underscores their liminality.

The Nyau basketry frameworks of the Chewa in Malawi represent an enormous amount of work, performed by newly initiated boys. These large contraptions appear during a funeral, dance with a host of other masks, and at the next sunrise are burned to cinders: 'When the smoke disappears into the wind, it is said that the spirits of the deceased also disappear into the wind and become ancestral spirits.'[33] The ash is then mixed with food for the novices to protect them from the spirits of the deceased; masks serve to their very end. Zoë S. Strother relates how near the end of their initiation the eastern Pende boys used to burn their headpieces, as a farewell to their liminal period: at night the boys made a huge bonfire, 'enjoying the hiss and pop of the dried wood'.[34] On the *sigma* mask of northwestern Ghana, Césare Poppi reports how at the end of the initiation the acolytes must chop the headpiece and the bullroarer to pieces. And they go one step further, for they burn the wood, mix the ashes into water, and drink the mixture, thus accruing 'ability to speak' about the masks in a proper way. The outside form is ephemeral; what lasts is the experience.[35]

Some costumes are more perennial in nature, especially the cloth ones. In order to dance the *gelede* mask (Chapter 6), a dancer borrows clothes from his sister, mother, or girlfriend to complete the mask. Afterwards he will return them, and since the dance honours them as women, the use of their attire is apt and fitting. Each year demands its own new headpiece, however, and the old one is sold, especially now that the *gelede* has become a recognised cultural heritage. Some carved headpieces may last longer than just a few performances. After dancing as mask, a Dan performer asks an old woman to guard his headpiece, since the associated spirit no longer manifests itself. In that state the headpiece may lie dormant for a long time in the woman's house until a new spirit appears on the scene; with a

---

31 Kreamer 2010: 15.
32 Purpura 2010.
33 Yoshida 2006: 227; see Kreamer 2010: 21.
34 Strother 2008: 53.
35 Poppi 2013: 193.

new costume and a new spirit such a top acquires a second lease of life.[36] The portrait headpieces of the Baule, Susan Vogel reports, are often made or commissioned by the husband. He dances with it, and clearly pictures his wife, while she walks beside him, unmasked as the original inspiration: Figure 6.5. Such a top is tightly linked to her and will be discarded only at her death.[37] In fact, a lifespan is almost an eternity for a headpiece.[38]

Yet 'not everyone willingly accepts ephemerality',[39] and given the care with which Pende tops are carved, some owners of the headpieces may hang on to them. Strother witnessed works over ten years old, still in fine shape and with vibrant colours, being redone before each performance. In cases where a 'mask has died', a poignant expression for a damaged headpiece, it was repaired.[40] Ten years is long for the wet woodlands of DRC, but this stands in no relation to the ideas that white people have of the age of African art objects, where any trace of patina implies deep ancestral provenance. Senufo headpieces are carved of perishable light wood and painted in gaudy colours, intended to be used in the here and now. When the headpiece of Figure 2.4b arrived in the Metropolitan Museum of Art, during its pathway inside the art trade its bright paint had been scraped off to get the proper patina: it had been eternalised.[41]

Bush, spirits, ancestors, and other people

When we look at a mask, what are we looking at? Fundamentally, the African way of viewing them is not as a code – and therefore not as a symbolic representation of something else – but states that when one looks at a mask, that is what one sees, like the riddle on the Dìì mask.[42] This seems tautological, but it is not: the basic African interpretation of a mask is as an apparition that is *sui generis*, of its own kind. In 1992, Henry Pernet made the point that masks could not be reduced to what they were thought by

---

36 Personal information Eberhard Fischer.

37 Vogel 1997a.

38 The brass Senufo headpiece is one top that will remain forever: personal information from Till Förster.

39 Strother 2008: 53.

40 Ibid.: 54, and plate 8.

41 Information from Till Förster. Many museum pieces thus have their own histories in which the Western view is dominant; for the *epa* headpiece of Figure 6.3, see Leyten 2015, Chapter 1.

42 Anthony Forge: 'In primitive art, art objects are rarely representations *of* anything, rather they seem to be *about* relationships.' Forge 1973: xviii; italics in original.

Westerners to represent: masks should not be equated with spirits, ancestors, or for that matter, the bush, so a more emic approach is needed.[43] As Hans Koloss reported about the Oku of West Cameroon:

> When I asked my informants [...] whether the head of *Mabuh*, the still feared mask [...], is that of a human or of an animal, they looked at me with surprise and were confused. Their answer at last was that, regardless of any similarity, the head of *Mabuh* is neither that of a human or an animal: *Mabuh* is *Mabuh*.[44]

So for the performers, masks – viz. the complete apparitions – are themselves a distinct category of being.[45] Each particular language has its own generic term for a mask – again, for the entire costumed appearance – while the various types of masks, usually distinguished by specific headpieces, bear their own particular names, which are sometimes cryptic but often revealing.[46] Yet, whatever the specific name, any mask does not appear primarily as an *image* of another being but as its own presence – at the same time an object, an undefined being, and a presence, exactly what the Magritte effect implied. In short, a mask is a 'be-thing', an ambivalent apparition in a class of its own, neither a normal 'being' nor an object, neither an animal nor fully a spirit, but not fully human either; in our text we will refer to a mask in neutral terms as 'it'.

Being *sui generis* does not mean there are no interpretive connotations, for such an apparition is an invitation to sense giving and sense seeking. In line with the main notions in local religions, four associations of masks come to the fore: the wilderness, spirits, ancestors, and humans. As has been noted by many scholars of African art, a pervasive association of the masks is with the wilderness, the bush.[47] Masks are 'of the bush' – spirits or animals from the bush, but anyway be-things from the bush – so the notion of the wilderness is one major inspiration of masquerades, and the opposition of bush–village informs the basic worldview behind the masquerades.[48] The

---

43 Pernet 1992.

44 Koloss 2012: 43; *Mabuh* is a mask type that widely dispersed over the Grassfields.

45 Jean-Pierre Warnier uses the notion of the Moebius strip, with its inverted loop on which one encounters oneself: a nicely paradoxical image; see Warnier 2007: 142.

46 See for instance Mulinda 1995 for the Woyo. Individual masks may carry an individual name, but this is rare.

47 Even when associated with royalty, masks still refer to the bush; as for the Tikar: Abega 2000, Joseph 1974.

48 Schildkrout 1989. We use both terms, wilderness and bush, as synonyms, even if the latter is sometimes considered a colonial term.

wilderness is often seen as rich, endless, wise, fertile, and powerful, but at the same time dangerous, unknown, threatening, and deadly; the latter could for instance mean that sexual intercourse as an activity of the home may be forbidden[49] in the bush, but this is by no means universal.

The various masking cultures inhabit very different ecological systems, ranging from a Sahelian shrub to sumptuous forest, and from rich volcanic slopes to the ocean beach, yet the bush–village dichotomy runs quite parallel in all these cases, and seems to apply regardless of ecological surroundings. So the bush–village contrast operates as a more general opposition between 'out there' and 'over here', between nature and culture. Masks emerge from 'there', whatever the exact nature of 'there' may be: the bush versus village dichotomy is 'good to think'.[50] Dichotomies are never so simple in practice, as John Picton showed among the Nigerian Ebira, since the village and the bush are often mediated by a middle category such as 'field' or 'farm',[51] the cultivated part of the wilderness; for the masks such mediation is not needed, however, since they bridge the conceptual divide themselves.

Coming out of the bush the masks create their own ritual space. Usually the village has pre-set spots where the masks perform, on the edge of the village for instance, but wilderness is hard to contain and in many cases, masks run through the streets of the village accompanied by a lot of noise, thus liminalising the whole village. The fact that masks stray out of their pre-set stage enhances their show of raw bush power. For the Pende of DRC, Zoë S. Strother remarks: 'Masks are matchless in their ability to transform the most banal of public spaces into an oneiric world outside of time, where the normal rules no longer apply.'[52]

Spirits form the second major association, and are usually just that: spirits. Sidney Kasfir remarked of the West African mask that it is not 'a simple catalogue of the supernatural world. More often it consists of middle- and lower-level spirits in the hierarchy of belief, or spirits of deceased ancestors.'[53] This kind of spiritual middle management is conceived in many forms but, often as spirits of the bush, underscores the wilderness referent. Eli Bentor

49 Such as among the Beng (Gottlieb 1982) or the Ebira (Picton 1989), among many others.
50 For the wilderness as a cognitive category see Jackson 1982 and Schildkrout 1989. An example: the Baule 'use the poles of bush and village as principles to organise the world': Vogel 1997a: 42.
51 Picton 1989: 86.
52 Strother 2008: 19.
53 Kasfir 1988a: 6.

remarks: 'I found that in most Igbo mask genres, masks represent ambiguous spirits of no precise nature.'[54] The associated spirits can be threatening, cajoling, or comforting, and are often mentioned only in connection with the masks as an association that first comes to mind.[55] Between cultures, this link with spirits is general but variable: sometimes spirits, unnamed and unspecified, seem to cling to the mask top, as we saw among the Dan of Côte d'Ivoire.[56]

Usually the association is less direct, but it does bring into focus the fundamentally human nature of these spirits.[57] As William Siegmann pointed out, spirits are deemed to have much in common with people 'such as emotions and desires, and often want to participate in the world as tangible beings'.[58] Already in 1964 Hans Himmelheber noted for the Dan in Liberia that only by entering the world of the human beings can the spirits satisfy their cravings for companionship, solicitude, food, drink, music, physical beauty, and personal adornment.[59]

Ambiguity is part and parcel of indigenous religions, but in the case of mask rituals acquires an additional dimension. Whatever masks may be considered to represent, they can never be identical to the thing they portray – the very point of René Magritte's famous painting. Effectively a mask is an apparition with a human being playacting inside, so any association with the otherworld must remain highly flexible. For the Baule masks Alain-Michel Boyer calls it *présentifier*: masks 'presentify' the otherworld,[60] implying that the otherworld is not so much represented as it is made present in the mind, so presentified; people think of these otherworld associations, but usually only afterwards when they reflect on the performance; or are asked about its 'meaning' by a researcher.

The third association is with ancestors, a highly relevant and significant type of spirit in Africa. However, considering the iconic position of ancestors in many indigenous African religions, masks are less connected with ancestors than one might expect. In rare cases a specific ancestor or someone recently deceased belongs to the performing mask, but then the

54 Bentor 1994a: 332. See also Colleyn 2011 on this issue.
55 Bouttiaux 2009.
56 Fischer 1978: 18.
57 From a non-fideist standpoint their very existence would depend on humans as a projected reality, but such an observation does not respect the man–spirit relationship as it is experienced, nor does it do justice to the lived world of masquerades.
58 Siegmann 1980: 11.
59 Himmelheber 1964, cited in Siegmann 1980: 11.
60 A.-M. Boyer 2008.

attribution tends to be made after the performance.[61] Throughout, the link between masks and ancestors is little elaborated on and remains vague; rather, masks and their rituals are routinely referred to as 'things of the ancestors', an indistinct but general notion that imbues the rituals with the authority of the otherworld but does not explain much about the masks themselves. And while there are many indigenous religions that are dominated by ancestors but have no masks, there are also many African indigenous religions, usually also without masking, where ancestors play no part whatsoever.

Victor Turner relates how he wrestled with the ancestor connection in his research of the Ndembu of Zambia.[62] On the one hand, the terms are almost identical: shade or ancestor = *mukishi*; one mask = *ikishi*, and masks plural = *makishi*; yet there was little consensus among his informants on what exactly the relationship was between the shades and the masks, and Turner received quite contradictory answers. The interpretations ranged wide: 'the *ikishi* is a shade that died and from a specific tree at his initiation site took up the form of the mask costume'; 'a shade that wants to dance in an *ikishi* costume will sway inside the body of the dancer, who then gives it a different name, to be renamed at the shrine later'; and finally '*makishi* come from the ground, and after the dance return to the ground, so they die again'. In the end, Turner called it 'a problem that perplexes and divides Ndembu quite as much as it does the anthropologist'.

Ancestors as such are more ambivalent than they are usually credited for, since they are quick to punish for transgressions – especially for lack of attention – and some masks reflect this ambivalence. For instance, the Annang in southern Nigeria distinguish between good and bad ancestors, since for them the transition from disembodied spirit to ancestor was a perilous journey: some were definitely more successful at it than others, and those who had failed were considered notoriously malicious. The Annang *èkpó* masks that represented 'good' ancestors were rendered much more beautiful.[63] Anyway, spirit, death, and bush are close neighbours: a notion from West Cameroon holds that at death the human spirit enters the bush and unites with a bush spirit, and that they return together in the form of a mask.[64]

61 For instance among the Igbo (Njoku 2020: 187), and also to some extent among the Yoruba (Noret 2013).
62 Turner 1969: 241–243.
63 Akpan 1994: 53, Pratten 2007: 30. Also the spelling Anang is used in the literature. The term *ekpo*, in its many variations, can refer to masks, associations or ethnic groups.
64 Michael Rowlands, personal communication.

The fourth association is more mundane. Surprisingly often, people are represented in masks; usually personages in the typical village scene – such as the beautiful girl (also danced by a man), the old man, or the diviner. As Michèle Coquet remarks: 'The human figure is in fact one of the great obsessions of African iconography',[65] and that holds for masquerades as well. These persons are not specific individuals, but stereotypical categories that feature in public mask performances.[66] Chapter 9 concentrates on this theatrical aspect.

What are seldom presentified are the deities, the denizens of the upper echelons of the otherworld. Masks in Africa are usually not gods or deities. Occasionally, leaf masks like those among the Bobo get close to the divine,[67] and some association with the sun and the moon may be mentioned, as in the Congo region,[68] but these are exceptions to the rule. If the masks presentify anything other than themselves, their referents occupy a conceptual layer between heaven and earth, such as the bush and its spirits – meaning that the relation between man and mask is not vertical but horizontal. Masks stem from the edges of human existence, where the village morphs into the bush. As be-things from the margin of the lived world, they bridge the gap between the human world and the bushy otherworld; this otherworld-at-the-side is not just a neighbour, it is quite different and powerful, a kind of horizontal transcendence.

The main issue with masks is not what they look like, but what they do: the clue is in the performance. Pierre Bourdieu characterised the human being as a *pense-bête*,[69] a thinking animal, but in the mask performance he becomes a *danse-bête*, a dancing animal, a be-thing in captivating movement.[70] The mask does its utmost not to look like a human being, but its dance places it inside the human frontier again, especially in Africa, where dance is the ultimate art form. It is by dancing that the mask links the two worlds: the human and the spiritual. And even more, by dancing the mask becomes alive; as the Yoruba say, 'Dance brings vitality to the body', while

---

65 Coquet 1995: 33.
66 Like the hero: see Nwabueze 1989.
67 Le Moal 1980: 245.
68 Grand-Dufay 2016: 100.
69 Bourdieu 1990: 11.
70 Not all ritual movement is dance; Till Förster describes a Senufo ritual that consists mainly of men walking closely behind each other in absolute darkness (Förster 2019: 111–113).

the Ejagham praise the vitality of a mask: 'He turns round, round, round, to show he has power in dancing.'[71]

Essentially, the basic script of a mask performance is quite straightforward: the mask comes on stage, dances – alone or with others – and leaves the stage again. Since with the mask the otherworld appears, it is the coming on stage itself that forms the high point of the ritual. In the vignette in the Introduction we saw the Dan mask appear after elaborate preparations with careful staging; after that it did dance – and in that case also spoke and sang – but it carried the day by appearing. Masks do not dance alone, but all their attendants, musicians, and interpreters just add to the apparition. We will see mask liturgies with many other elements, but they all start with the 'Great Entry'; after this initial shock of the ultimate other, anything the mask does renders the inherently strange apparition more familiar.

Masks and power

What these four associations of masks share is power, one of our key notions. 'Masks and mask performances are also indices of the Urhobo notion of power', Diakparomre remarks of these Nigerian masks.[72] In many African worldviews one finds a notion of otherworldly power as a defining characteristic of deities, spirits, or ancestors, but also existing in a less circumscribed form as a non-personified power.[73] The classic *mana* concept from Oceania comes close,[74] and one finds this broad notion in many forms, ranging from occult power to any kind of power that cannot be seen. In Côte d'Ivoire the concept of *aze* or *ase* is used, which also has occult associations ranging into witchcraft,[75] a notion of the incommensurable that is recognisable all the way to Yorubaland.[76] The concept of *nyama* in Mande languages is more ethically neutral, a kind of force often compared to electricity.[77] Shared power is another aspect of *nyama*,[78] or 'exceptional energy unleashed by action'.[79]

---

71 R. Thompson 1974: 9.
72 Diakparomre 2010: 475.
73 Ellis and Ter Haar 2004.
74 Van Baal and Van Beek 1985.
75 Ekoué and Rosenthal 2015; we use the word occult here as a synonym of 'religious' (Ter Haar and Ellis 2009).
76 Abiodun 1994.
77 McNaughton 2008.
78 Colleyn, cited in Gagliardi 2010: 94.
79 Gagliardi 2010: 92.

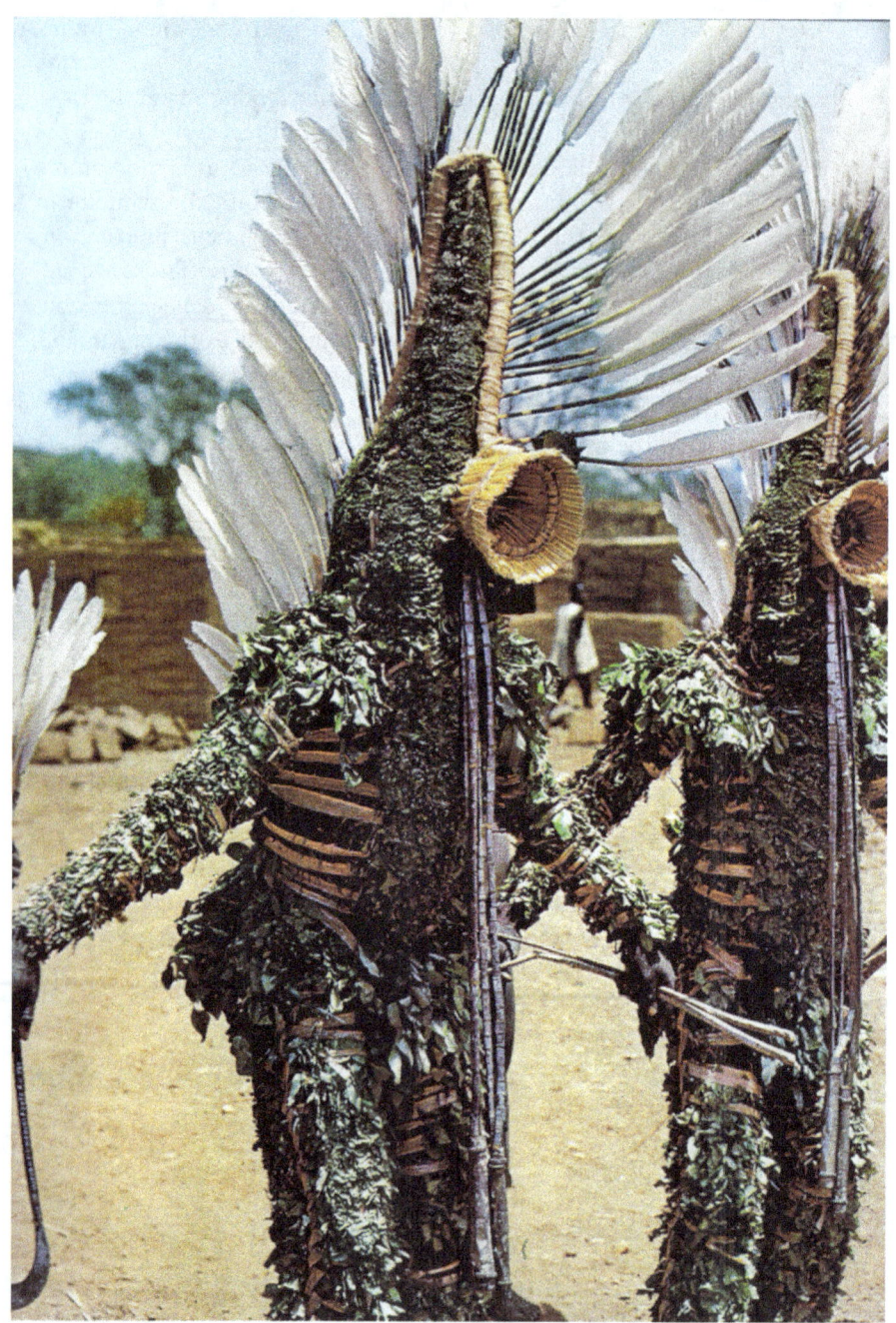

Figure 2.3. Leaf masks of the Bobo. Burkina Faso, 2005. Photo: Christopher Roy.

The Senufo term is *nyambe*, 'potential dangerous energy or force inhering to certain animals'.[80] Similar notions are *tsav* in Tiv[81] and *panga* in Dogon; many Dogon villages have borrowed also the Bamana word *nyama*. Power in this form is an attribute of the otherworld, of the uncanny and the bush, needed but dangerous and with its own agency, an essential aspect of the unseen. This is very much an attributed power, constructed in discourse and belief, and attributed by people to objects: a 'theology of power'. Human power, the social reality, is considered impossible without the religious kind.

All power is ambivalent, a notion well illustrated by the Pende from the DRC. All carvings gravitate to the chief, masks as well as statues – which are exclusively for him – and in their accumulation increase the chief's power over his people. The many sculpted heads (both Pende statues and masks are predominantly portraits of people) are supposed to gaze at the chief in order to watch and stand guard over him, but also to protect the chiefdom from the chief, restraining him from abuse of power. So the carvings are in a delicate balance with the political might of the chief. At the end of his life, all these power objects should not be inherited and must be destroyed completely, since power accumulated over one generation is more than enough.[82]

Now, if masks are power be-things, how do they accrue that power and how do they manifest it? Masquerades acquire power by bridging two worlds: the human one of daily life, and the otherworldly one. 'Heaven and earth' are close in Africa, and daily existence is tightly interwoven with the otherworld, shot through with an immediate familiarity. Masks are powerful because they come from the otherworld, a distinction that is not so much hierarchical as spatial, less 'up there' than 'over there'. As Mary Douglas has shown,[83] crossing boundaries between worlds generates power, and this is what masks routinely do. A prime attribution of power is through what Richard Fardon calls 'therioanthropy', the blending of animal and human features, a crucial aspect of many masks.[84] All over the three zones this mixture is found, and in Zone 1 it dominates. Usually these tops are dubbed animal masks, and often it is quite clear which animal is hinted at: bush buffalo, various types of antelope, water bird, monkey, hare, hyena, crocodile, chameleon, and even leopard. They can be portrayed very

---

80 Gagliardi 2010: 95.
81 Abuku 2008: 21.
82 Strother 1995.
83 Douglas 1966, 1973.
84 Fardon and Stelzig 2005; Schildkrout 1989.

elegantly as in the Bamana *ciwara* headpieces, or with an unerring eye for detail and proportion like the Guro tops; or they can be carved just in large bold lines with decorations that have little to do with the animal itself, like the Mumuye tops. Often the headpiece itself fuses the human and the animal, such as an animal beak on a human skull, like the Chamba headpiece,[85] which crosses a whole series of borders. These animal referents have an inherent ambiguity, and one sometimes has to guess which animal served as inspiration. Among the Jola peoples, Peter Weil noticed costumes looking like snail shells, with horns on top of an impressive headpiece, all made of fibre.[86] The headpiece of the Fali mask, in North Cameroon, shows a trap to catch wild animals as part of the array on the head: the human side is never far away either.[87] So crossing boundaries is the proper calling of a mask, and when different borders are crossed, the bush–human divide is among them. It is the wild animals that are represented, because the domestic ones are considered stupid and powerless.

The core of the masks' sense making is in their moving performance: they enter the village, dance between people, and move back to the bush again. Masks dance, and as Robert Thompson made abundantly clear, a major component of African art is movement: 'Africa introduces a different art history, a history of dance art, defined in the blending of movement and sculpture, textiles, and other forms, bringing into being their own inherent goodness and vitality.'[88] Masks cross the border between culture and nature, and as 'be-things in-between' cover the epistemic distance between different worlds, the one lived in and the one lived from, while the be-things that emanate from the bush need humans to bring them to life.

Fardon calls this the 'fusion of worlds',[89] meaning the fusion of the animal world and the human one; but one must realise that both worlds have been virtualised before being fused. During his initiation, a young man transforms himself into a mask – not into the animal as such but into the idea of the beast, a generalised view of animal-ness, so bush and village meet halfway to create a mask. One ready icon, for instance, is formed by the horns on human heads,[90] a sure sign of fusion-into-power. What appears

---

85 Fardon 1990, 2007.
86 Weil 1971: 280; similar costumes are found among the Balante of Guinea Bissau: Fagg 1980: 30; see also Mark 1987.
87 Gauthier 1988: 244.
88 R. Thompson 1974: xii.
89 Fardon 2007.
90 R. Thompson 1974: 133.

in a mask is not part human and part animal, but an imagined combination, an apparition that Descola calls a 'chimera'.[91] It combines parts and pieces of various animals with human elements in such a way that the illusion is created of a living organism that can act and perceive on its own; in Alfred Gell's terms, a piece of art with its own agency.[92]

Also visually, the mask as top–plus–costume is by no means identical to the animal, nor does it strive for a lifelike rendition of the beast; when African artists aimed at doing so, the piece would come out quite differently; in 1972 Fraser and Cole remarked: 'To the best of our knowledge the African artist never attempts *mimesis*, the exact imitation of life forms [...]'.[93] Of the Jukun and Chamba masks, Fardon remarks that they are 'the materialised form of a set of associations rather than the representation of some entity other than itself'.[94] Indeed, masks are first masks and then presentify something else. One Jukun mask exhibits this virtuality to a high degree: the headpiece has a *trompe l'oeil* characteristic, a cow from one angle and a bird from another.[95] Thus, in masking, two imagined worlds fuse. Masks are icons of the animals, not their double; they evoke the idea of the beasts but are never identical to them.[96] Since the presentified bush equals power when it merges with the human world, the result is a short, intense display of force – that is, the appearance of the mask. The more mixing, the more power, as the following example from the Senufo shows (Figure 2.4a and b). The *wambele* costume is cotton fabric woven in narrow strips and painted with geometrical motifs, while all variants of its wooden headpiece feature parts of different animals, an example of materialised power.[97]

The mask scenario is part of a wider ritual complex in which the power of the mask stems from the sense giving during the performance. Pierre Bourdieu points out that any ritual power is grounded in the positions of those who perform, view, or comment on it. The power of the mask is the power of the ritual, which means it derives from, and in turn constructs, the power of those that perform the ritual. Analysing ritual speech acts, he

91   Descola 2021: 305. Recently Philip Descola published this major volume on the way cultures make figurative images, highlighting the interaction between nature, fantasy, and setting.
92   Gell 1999, see Descola 2021: 639.
93   Fraser and Cole 1972: 306.
94   Fardon 2007: 125.
95   Fardon 2007. For the Mambila, the Northern neighbours of the Jukun, similar problems of interpretation hold, see Zeitlyn 1994a, 1994b, 2020.
96   This holds not just for African masks, but for masks the world over. Descola 2021.
97   Veirman 2001: 235.

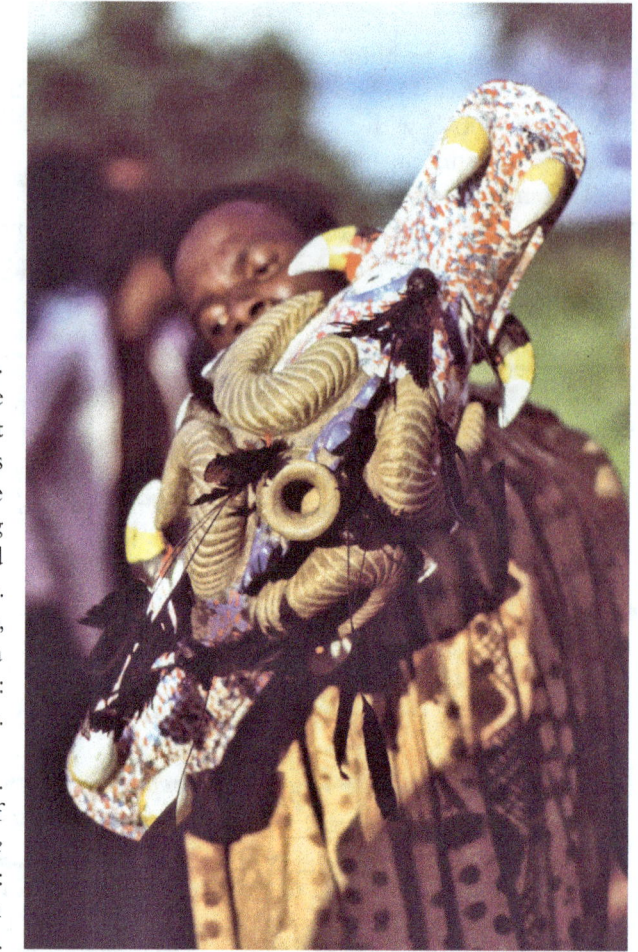

Figure 2.4a (right).
After the burial the
wambele dancer, just
visible, takes off his
headpiece, seen here
from above featuring
two horned
composite animals.
Near Korhogo,
Senufo, Burkina
Faso, 1979. Photo:
Till Förster.

Figure 2.4b (below).
Side view of
another *wambele*
headpiece. Photo:
Metropolitan
Museum, New York.

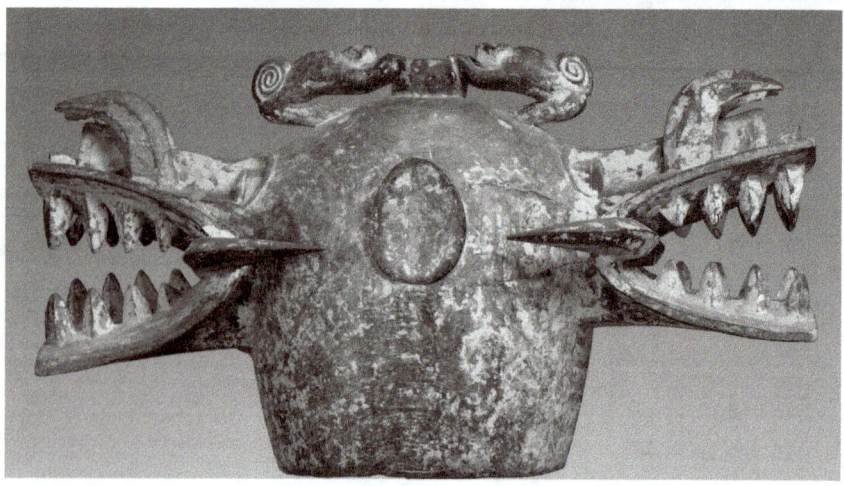

states: 'For ritual to function and operate it must first and for all present itself and be perceived as legitimate, with stereotyped symbols serving precisely to show that the agent does not act in his own name and on his own authority, but in his capacity as a delegate.'[98] 'Delegate' here implies that the performer derives his right to take part in ritual from a social body outside the ritual itself. In masking, this delegation of power is crucial, since one must earn the right to perform and be known to have earned it, an authorisation that is constantly repeated and actualised during the performance of the ritual itself. The whole setting of the dance, the drums, and the admiring viewers, as well as the men on the side who adhort the mask to do its utmost, all conspire to a field of authority, relying on the shared knowledge of the initiation the dancers have undergone, and the hardships they have endured to finally arrive at their actual performance. This authority is experienced more than perceived: 'rituals have another sort of power that resides in their ability to incubate symbols deeply into bone, belly and breast, which is to say in their capacity to establish webs of connectedness.'[99] The power of the mask ritual is in both its performative and symbolic conventions, and the pathway that has earned the dancers the right to participate in this performance.

Thus the ultimate source of power is in the eyes of the beholder, and the same theatre that induces power also frees the mask from standardised interpretations. Whatever its visual details, the mask in its theatrical setting is both an invitation to sense giving and power attribution, and a framework for free signification. As Richard Schechner put it, 'Once an action is framed as "theatre" spectators read messages into whatever they witness'.[100]

Tradition, prototype, and invention

Thus far we discussed masks in very general terms, loose associations, and an impersonal notion of power, defining masks as be-things that are not reducible to the representation of something else. In this we followed the Africans themselves, who indeed rarely explain their masquerades, as many scholars have noted. For the Limba of Sierra Leone, William Hart wrote: 'As to the meaning of the whole performance, my Limba informants had nothing to say. It was marvellous, that was as far as they would go.'[101] Hart

---

98 Bourdieu 1992: 115.
99 Grimes 2014: 303.
100 Schechner 2003: 154.
101 Hart 1988: 64, 67.

was clearly flummoxed by this lack of explanation, which even extended to the word for the masquerade itself: *gbendekolo*. Nobody knew what it meant – and nobody cared. This holds, in fact, for many African rituals, and other anthropologists have reported similar experiences. Audrey Richards remarked in the case of the female circumcision rituals of the Bemba: 'It is obvious that a complete interpretation [...] is unlikely to be given [...] even by ritual experts.'[102] For the participants, the main challenge in these infrequent and complicated rituals is not to understand what they mean, but to perform them correctly, since they participate in them only rarely. The more colourful and complex the rites are, and the more people experience the ritual in body and action, in dancing and admiring,[103] the less they will be inclined to explain them: it is the performance that counts, not the interpretation. And owing to the absence of religious authority, one cannot expect the mask rituals to possess a definite, consciously expressed meaning; anyway, these are religions of orthopraxis rather than of orthodoxy,[104] where beliefs are 'rarely formulated [...] as they do not need to be'.[105] Consequently, little explanation of what these strange performances 'mean' is available for the participants, the audience, or the odd anthropologist or art historian.

It seems paradoxical: people invest great energy and effort in actions they are hard put to explain – at least they cannot explain why these rites take this form. Individuals may incidentally raise these questions and construct meaning while performing rites, viewing them, or musing on them. Boys who are initiated are not taught what the initiation masks mean; instead they are taught how to become a mask, the crowning moment being when they really dance as a mask themselves. So their primary meaning will be: 'I am a man now!' Any further meaning they must construct themselves, if they are interested in sense seeking at all.

Jonathan Z. Smith characterised ritual as 'paying attention',[106] and this is what mask rituals do *in extremis*: they pay attention.[107] What exactly they pay attention to is another matter. It is important to realise that this has

---

102 A. Richards 1982: 113.

103 See also Michaels 2006. R. Marett's adage from 1909 comes to mind: 'Primitive religion is not thought out, but danced out' (Van Baal and Van Beek 1985: 68). Although voiced at the time as a critique of evolutionism, the notion fits well both in the new cognitive approach and its insights into ritual; see Vàsquez 2011.

104 Kapferer 2013; Whitehouse 2004.

105 Bell 1997: 191.

106 J.Z. Smith 1987: 25.

107 Not just mask rituals, but also African Christianity aims at spectacular performances, often on screen; Meyer 2015.

two solid reasons. First, in any religion, including script-based religions, explaining the form and content of a ritual is surprisingly difficult, an observation that has led Frits Staal to the notion of the empty ritual, of rules without meaning – at least any meaning that can be coherently explained by the participants.[108] This is what we see with masks: informants tend to be at a loss when asked for explanation. A specific form of non-explanation surfaced when S.F. Nadel asked his Nigerian Nupe informants what their mask meant to them. In the first instance they referred to it as a spirit, one of the basic associations mentioned above. And then the author notes:

> There is another, esoteric explanation [...] rarely offered in so many words. It was given to me by the Master of the [secret society], when he said that the [mask] was not a spirit but a 'strong secret', that is a knowledge or skill of a mystical and powerful kind.[109]

The informant explaining this to Nadel bore the title 'Master of the Monster'.[110] The point is that any analysis should leave the mask rituals intact to be experienced; they are to be understood not through decoding, but by being part of the performance.[111] The proper way to understand a mask is to dance it, the second best way is to enjoy the perfomance.

This reticence towards explanation regards specific ritual forms. For major ritual complexes as such, general goals tend to be clearer in people's minds – for example, initiation rituals are there to make men out of boys and responsible women out of girls, and funerals should transform deceased kinsmen into ancestors; crops must grow, justice should be served, and order restored. Rites of passage especially tend to be straightforward in this regard. And since many mask rituals belong to this category, this at least provides a generalised sociological meaning; but emic explanation usually stops there.

The fact that ritual is so hard to explain highlights the so-called imagistic mode of religiosity. In his theory about the two modes of religiosity, Harvey Whitehouse depicts the doctrinal mode as one of frequent rituals with an authoritative exegetic structure behind them;[112] the eucharist mentioned in Chapter 1 is one instance, a rite often repeated and even more often explained in sermons, part of an official doctrine that is purposefully taught

---

108 Staal 1975, 1989. See also Van Beek 2007.
109 Nadel 1954: 191.
110 Nadel 1942: 142.
111 This resembles the notion of *ekdoche*, the non-judgmental approach advocated by classical phenomenology of religion; Van Baal and Van Beek 1985.
112 Whitehouse 2004.

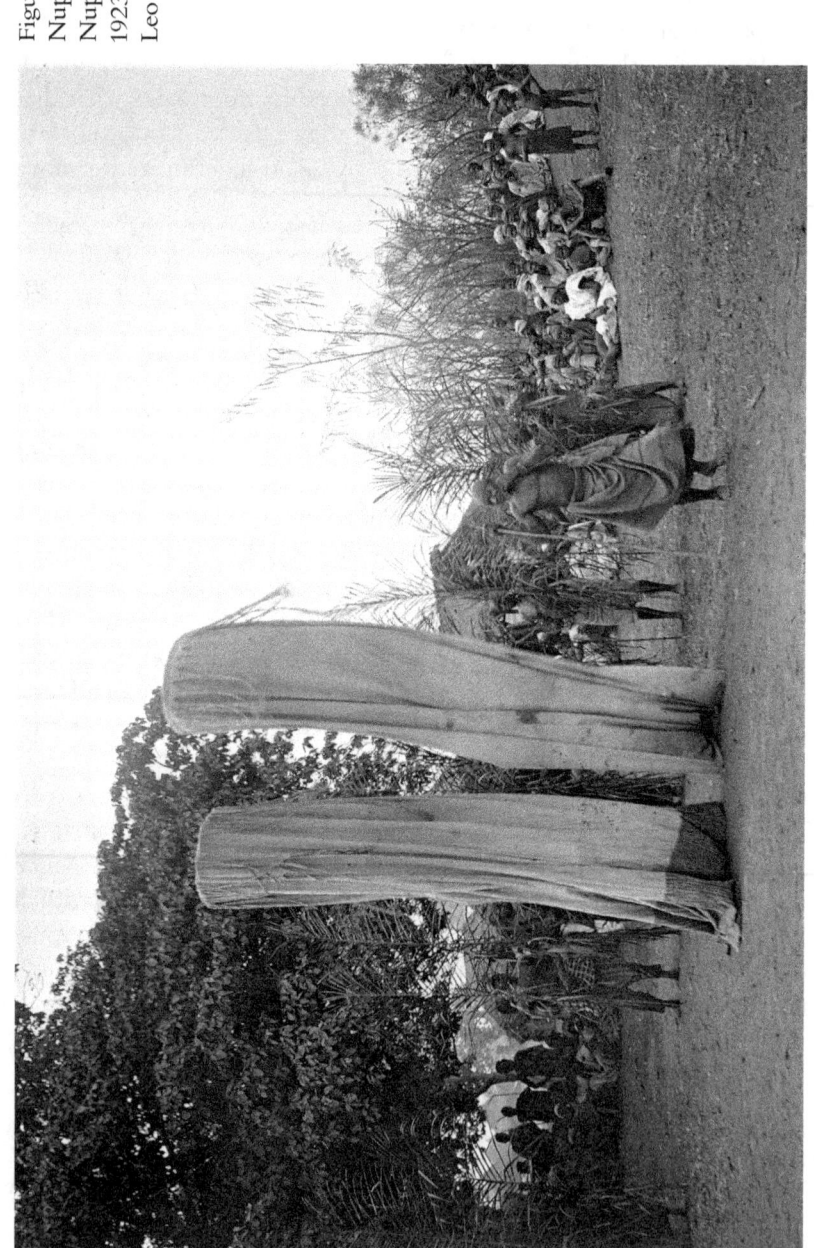

Figure 2.5.
Nupe masks.
Nupe, Nigeria,
1923. Photo:
Leo Frobenius.

by professionals. The imagistic mode, on the other hand, centres around infrequent rituals that are often large and colourful, in which there is not only no authority but also no standing interpretation: they must be participated in and performed correctly. Spectacular as mask rituals usually are, their challenge is in the performance, and thus their meaning is the embodied action itself, with post-hoc reflection taking second place.

Often participants solve this quandary by stating that they perform these rituals because it is 'tradition', or 'a thing of the ancestors', which for them suffices as both explanation and motivation. Such rituals are deemed to have remained the same since the dawn of history, handed over from generation to generation roughly in their present form. This is, in fact, the way these religions present themselves, as unchanged since the ancestors, faithful to the ways and mores of the olden times. Actually, it is neither an explanation for the rite nor a measure of its age, but a reference to authority, an *argumentum ad auctoritatem*. By appealing to tradition, the whole weight of the authority of the past and of the power of the foregone generations is brought to bear on today's practices, defining the present form as beyond debate. Invoking tradition is a means to give legitimacy to one's actions – be they beliefs, rituals, taboos, or stories – endowing them with the 'powers that were'.

In actual practice rituals change continuously: new elements filter in, either through chance, choice, or external developments, and with incidental inventions or adaptations these are incorporated into the liturgy without much ado. Tradition is not the same as history. For instance, in a Kapsiki ritual against crop disease, one of the clan representatives was ill and had to be replaced by his friend, who happened to be from another clan. The officiating smith told the anthropologist that henceforth the clan of that friend would send a delegate, since it was now, according to the officiator, 'traditional'.[113] 'Lego ritual', Paul Post calls this phenomenon:[114] new blocks can be added to the ritual edifice and old ones discarded – not a very African metaphor, but one that is clear enough.

In this way all newness is blurred by reference to the ancestral past, and what is called 'tradition' may well be of recent origin, hence the notions of 'invention of tradition' or 'reinvention of tradition' that have gained wide exceptance in Africanist circles; in the dynamics of masking these are crucial as well.[115] 'Tradition' is the result of a specific dynamic of change, slow, gradual, and somewhat fitting into the existing corpus. Yet that invention

113 Van Beek and Olsen 2015.
114 Post 2007.
115 Hobsbawm and Ranger 1983.

is neither sudden nor haphazard; in Strother's terms: 'Invention of tradition presupposes traditions of invention',[116] for even if tradition does flow, it is not completely fluid, and change follows rules. Also this flexibility does not mean that tradition has no content at all. As Roy Wagner put it: 'The widely cited idea of the "invention of tradition" should not blind theorists to the fact that such traditions, as cultural continuities, have existed in many places and times, to one degree or another.'[117] Tradition means a dynamic of gradual adaptation, but also of content.

So we see rituals drift through time, change piecemeal, and adapt to the contingencies of history and to new circumstances – and in the case of masks also definitely to impulses from human creativity.[118] Some continuity, however, is guaranteed both by the fact that the changes are usually small and by the discourse on tradition itself: this has been done since ancestral times and, yes, it is the same ritual. Even if the sum effect of all incremental changes is considerable, the perception is that the link with the past is unbroken and intact.[119] The concept of 'prototype', as developed by Alfred Gell, addresses this:[120] the culturally constructed, imagined model of what an object should look like – such as a mask. Much of the drift is variation on this prototype, which may slowly change over time while serving as an interpretation of the present in terms of the past.[121] Masking traditions are quite open and show creative pathways for invention, but must stay recognisable.[122]

The prototype has an owner, either a village, a secret society, a family, or even an individual, for there is always a story behind a particular mask. Legitimacy is essential: the right to dance a particular mask must be recognised, which implies that masquerades can be sold or even stolen. This ownership may include also rights to prayers, to praise songs and exhortations, to shouting in the ritual language, and even sometimes to specific music tunes and drum rhythms, as well as to insight into the history of a particular mask.[123] The prototype is an all-inclusive bundle of these features, so a prototypical

---

116 Strother 1998.

117 Wagner 1981: 144.

118 Hallam and Ingold 2007.

119 P. Boyer 1990; see for a more general theory P. Boyer 2001. For an example see Homann 2020.

120 Gell 1999.

121 Nooter and Roberts 1996. See Hersak 2012 for a local application of the concept.

122 Geary 1996, 2008.

123 Chapter 7 contains a case in which historical knowledge won a court case about ownership of a masking tradition (Willis 2018: 145).

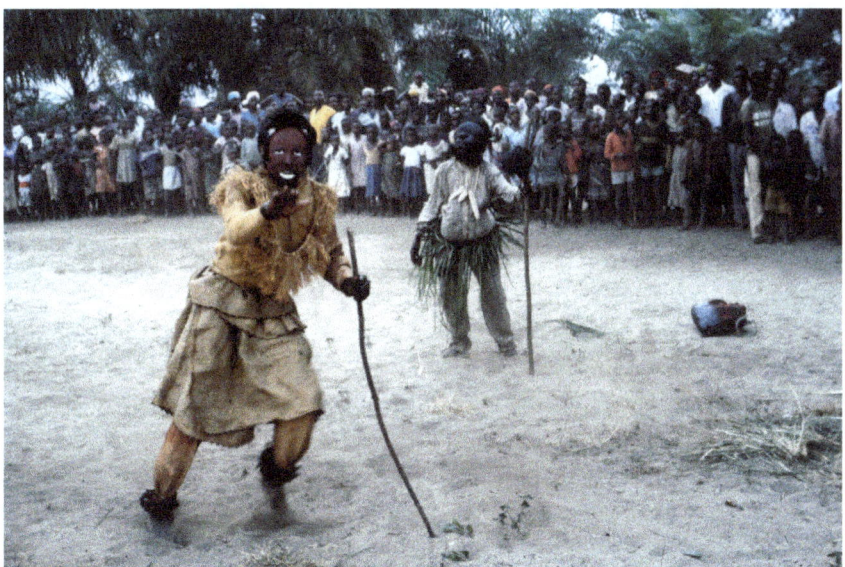

Figure 2.6. Gambetshi Kivule performs the mask *gindongo (gi)tshi*, with the clown, *tundu*, watching. Nyoka-Munene, Pende, DRC, 1989. Photo: Z.S. Strother.

definition of a mask should read: mask = costume + headpiece + paraphernalia + music + dance routine + legitimacy + knowledge.

The prototype allows for creativity, but within the bounds set by the culture, since not all societies appreciate individual creativity in the same way. New masks can mean either the revival of old forms that have disappeared, or new variations on the prototype. What masks do offer is a domain for creative expression that is safe and appreciated, shielded as it is by the gentle blanket of public secrecy that precludes any direct confrontation with the expected norm. This creativity can result from life's experiences, allowing for an outlet of frustrations that are part of life; Zoë S. Strother furnishes the following example, in effect the story behind Figure 2.6.[124]

It must have been in 1970 that the young Gambetshi climbed a mango tree to gather some fresh fruits, when immediately from below an older woman called him, asking him to give her the mango he had picked. Of course he had to comply, but every time he got a mango, someone older requested the fruit. Exasperated, Gametshi made a song about this trial from the older generation and developed a dance to go with the song. He improvised a burlap costume and at

---

124 Strother 1995.

first used a pierced calabash to cover his face. But when people responded well to his performance – he was a gifted dancer – he obtained a proper costume and consulted a real sculptor for a nicely carved top. He insisted on a headpiece with a new face and a costume without fibres, one in which his strident dance came out well. The mask-plus-dance was a great success and other dancers copied it, for this issue with the older generation struck home with many youngsters. The new mask thus caught on, and in doing so it developed: a fuller-skirted costume, a more classic wooden face-top, and a shift from the complaints about the elders to a veiled critique of the failing of DRC state.

Invention is welcome in Pende culture, where carving is a specialised profession.[125] The carved tops of Dogon masks follow simpler lines, and most dancers carve their own headpiece. In 1988, the first author witnessed a young man carve a new headpiece. It was not for a funeral but for a tourist performance, and the carver felt free to include a new animal: a sheep. Already he had thought out what the dance should be, since he had seen something like that when working in Côte d'Ivoire – a country full of masking. So he carved this top and danced for the tourists, and even for a film team working in the village at that time. At the end of the film shoot the director bought the 'sheep mask' and that was the end of that type, for this innovation did not take hold. Neither the creator nor his colleagues produced such a piece ever again, and the animal masks in Tireli remained focused on wild animals, not on domestic ones: there are limits to the invention of new masks.

Forms can also be reinvented. In the 2008 masquerade in Tireli one older dancer wanted to distinguish himself from his peers with a rare mask; he chose the mask of the Samo, a group at the southern border of the Dogon, using a headpiece that had fallen out of fashion.[126] This spectacular mask was recognised by the older men, who then lauded the dancer for his safeguarding of the past.

Conclusion

In this chapter we have sketched the main features of masks and masquerades, their relation with power in its many forms, and their internal dynamics. In the next chapters we move into the dynamics between masquerades and the arenas, the second tier of testing, but the first test of our model starts here: How do the ethnic groups in question comply with our masking profile? For the Cameroonian Dìì peoples, with whom we started, history

---

125 For many African cultures the same holds. See for instance Messenger 1979.
126 For the Samo or Saman see Holder 1998, 2001 and 2002.

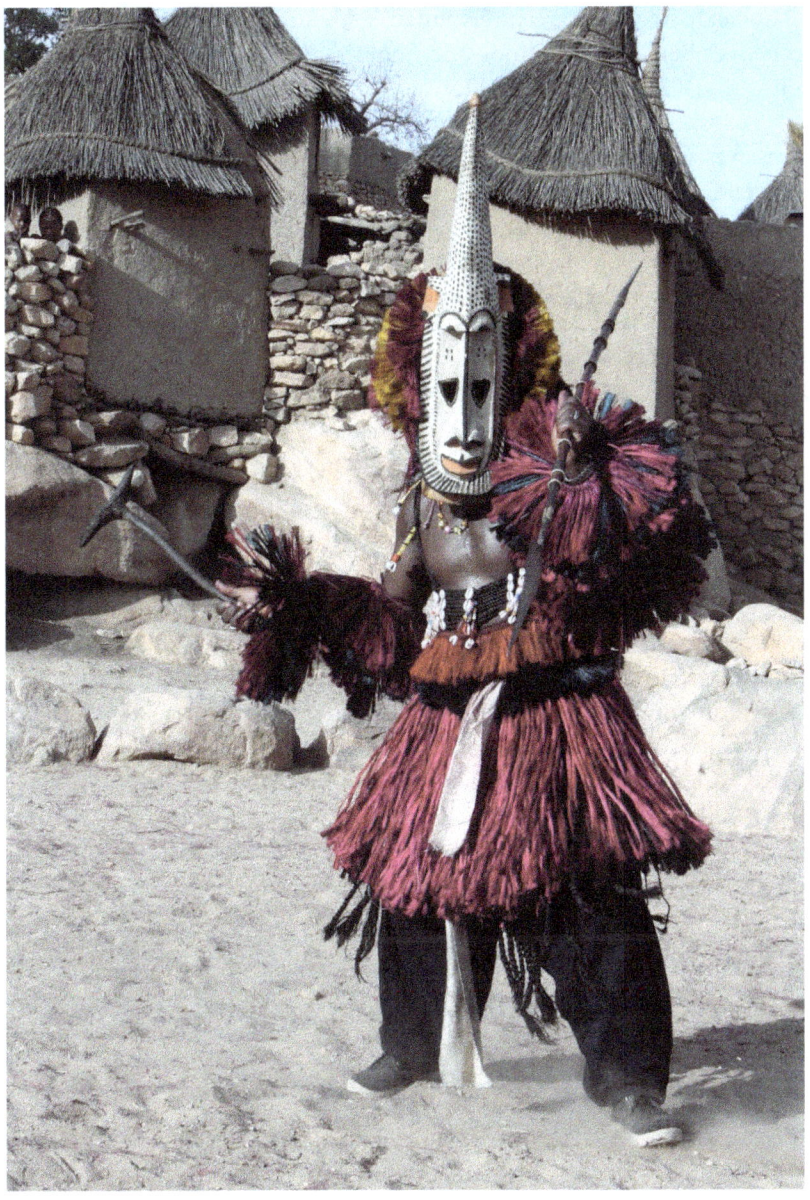

Figure 2.7. Mask *èmna samo*, representing the Samo neighbours of the Dogon. Tireli, Dogon, Mali, 2008. Photo Walter van Beek.

and societal structure are intertwined with similar groups in the Upper Benue area between Cameroon and Nigeria, and in the Alantika mountains, such as the Chamba, Komo, Dowayo,[127] and Duupa. Like them, the Dìì conform well with the Type C profile, for these societies had to defend themselves against the marauding Fulbe – and other groups – in during the nineteenth century. In this cultural area most groups are patrilineal and have rituals with masks, but some do not, a difference based on the structure of the patrilineages, and to some extent on the presence of shorthorn cattle, important because of their ecological adaptation and thus endowed with local symbolism.[128] Among them the Chamba, former raiders in this area, form a heterogeneous society that is hard to classify, but they do have double descent, and they definitely mask. They have one high-profile type of mask that is active during the initiation of boys.[129]

The Pende of Zone 3 form a typical Type D community, based on the 'House' with varying levels of political centralisation, and indeed with masks, used in boys' initiation.[130] The same holds for the Limba in Zone 1, deep in the interior of Sierra Leone. The Chewa share characteristics of Type D, but are situated in a dryer environment with a mixed economy, forming the largest group in Malawi. Matrilineal, and with a considerable degree of political centralisation, they do fit the profile to some extent, but the main mechanism for masking is less the structure of the village than it is the Nyau system of secret societies, which has shown considerable resistance to change.[131] This is a feature they share with other masking cases on the eastern side of the 'cattle corridor'.

[127] Barley 1983.
[128] Taurine cattle, not the zebu. See Seignobos and Thys 1998.
[129] In fact, the Chamba form one of the better described cases in West Africa: see Fardon 1990, 2006, 2007; Fardon and Stelzig 2005; Stelzig 2009.
[130] The work of Zoë S. Strother has been foundational for us: see Strother 2008, 1998, 1995.
[131] Boucher et al. 2012; Kubik 1993.

3

Masks and Masculinity: Initiation

'When you durst do it, then you were a man'
(Lady Macbeth to her husband. Shakespeare *Macbeth* 1.7 49)

'Manhood is only important if you care.'
(Gilmore 1990: 217)

Chewing the mask

*The rains have passed and the harvest is ripening in the fields. A group of young boys,
aged ten to fifteen years, sit down on the ground somewhere in a wooded spot around
a Bobo village in the west of Burkina Faso.[1] The youngsters are not alone, for older
boys with scowling faces and a threatening demeanour surround them, instructing the
smaller ones on what they should do. The older boys form the age-set just senior to
the youngsters, who in fact are in the process of forming the new set. What the young
boys are doing is highly significant: they cut branches from a tree species considered
sacred throughout the region, and put together a mask costume made solely out of
those leaves: the* sahasahala *(the quick one). The boys are excited, as they have finally
come out in the open, here in the bush where everything is going to happen. This is
the year when they should start their long initiatory trajectory, and they welcome it. In
order to arrive here, they had to ask for the rituals themselves in a propitiation to the
elders that forms part of the ceremony. No less than three times they had to submit
a formal, ritual demand for initiation, through the intermediary services of the smith.
Reluctantly, consent was finally granted after gifts of beer and chicken, and yesterday
night the initiation had begun. In the pitch-dark they had been taken from their homes
and placed inside a dark room, naked, cold, and frightened, surrounded by – judging
from the sounds that came from the outside – a battle raging between people and
beings uttering high-pitched cries. Food was offered to them, but it was food suited*

---

[1]   This vignette is based on the meticulous research of Guy Le Moal, 1980 and 2008.

for an orphan's funeral. Their only contact with the outside was through a few smiths who came into their hut – nobody else; it had been a long, hungry, and scary night.

This morning they had awakened with the loud, shrill cries of a mask posted right at their door. Each of the boys had to exit through the leafy legs of the mask and run a gauntlet of stinging blows by other masks, while a smith took them by the hand, leading them as fast as possible out of the village into the woods. The oldest boy came out first, and he had to show his courage and determination by receiving the whipping without crying, even without flinching. Arriving at their bush destination, the boys were told that this was 'the place of death'. Leaf masks received them at this place, and when all the children had arrived, panting and bleeding, one mask posted itself before the frightened youngsters. 'What is this?' their monitor asked, and the boys answered: 'Death.' That was what they had been instructed to do, and the monitor made all the boys say it. Then the mask slowly took off its headcovering, the foliage that formed a high crest resting on his shoulders, and showed himself to be a man, just a man. And he was not a stranger either; they all knew him well – one of the respected men of their village, a kinsman in fact. This was the essential revelation: someone was inside the mask, someone they knew well. They all had to call out his name – his normal, proper name – using the correct kinship term; he was one of them.

And that is where they are now for their next phase: they must become more or less like him, so they have to make a mask of their own, with the right kind of leaves from the correct trees.[2] Their teachers, both the older age-set and their accompanying smiths, make them do something else as well, which they had not expected. Of course, they had more or less known that men were inside the masks, but they were not allowed really to see that – and certainly not talk about it – and now they cannot escape that knowledge: the masks are 'us'. The symbolic way to achieve this unity between them and the mask is revealing: each boy takes a mouthful of leaves, the core of the mask, and slowly chews on it, letting the juice run into his mouth, down his throat, and into his stomach. He masticates the mask, digesting its essence. The smiths make all the boys spit some of the juice into a small hole in the ground; the mask is thus given back to the earth from where it stemmed.

The boys' ordeal is not over yet, as the remaining masks whip them again, while the smith explains that the secrets they have just learned should be kept hidden from non-initiates and should not be spoken about. After the flagellation they are asked what they have just learned and seen, and now the boys should be on the alert: 'Seen what? Heard what?' When the mask shows its fingers and asks the initiates to count them, suddenly none of the children can count to five. They learned their lesson, so they keep silent and feign ignorance. In later rituals they will carry a small stick in their mouths

---

2   Often these trees are considered to have special properties, medicinal or symbolic, and this may be part of the instructions.

to remind them of the silence that should reign over masks. Back home the boys are received with honour, given white clothes and an old, well-used hoe, and they participate for the first time in a sacrifice by the ritual elder, feasting afterwards with their relatives.[3]

For the Bobo novices, this first rite marks just the beginning of a long initiation trajectory, which has as its characteristic elements the separation from mothers (even becoming orphans), the notion of death, physical tests, and fright, all of it leading to a revelation that carries little information. Later the same boys will be subjected to new phases in their initiation sequence, for Bobo initiation is one of the most elaborate on the continent, a major ritual complex spanning some fifteen years, and masks are essential during the whole sequence. Initiation is a core business for masks. Male initiation as such has always been central in ritual studies,[4] and the tripartite structure of these rituals – separation, marginal phase, reintegration – is well established.[5] These elaborate rituals carry a high symbolic load,[6] and form a crucial factor in gender definition, which for initiation means the construction of masculinity.[7]

When masks figure in initiation, children have often prefigured these appearances themselves in a playful form, as boys' masquerades. Long before adulthood arrives, such mimetic dances can form a trajectory into the 'real thing' or simply be an emulation of the adult form, but they also appear independently of adult ceremonies: masks seem to be waiting to be reinvented, and African boys continue to reinvent them; as do girls.[8] Masking is, after all, a fascinating game: 'We should not forget how joyful and playful they are for those involved',[9] Simon Ottenberg and David Binkley stress, highlighting the many instances where boys play with masks well before their initiation. Of course, all children in the world put masks over their faces, but this is not the same as a masquerade inside a culture. Significantly, all African cases of child masking stem from known masking cultures within the Crescent, so for a child's play to develop into an accepted juvenile expression, there must be an adult tradition.

---

3   Le Moal 2003: 72.
4   See Grimes 2000.
5   Van Gennep 1960.
6   Ronald Grimes 2000, 2014; Catherine Bell 1997; Rappaport 1999; Gilmore 1990; Geertz 1980.
7   See Paige and Paige 1981: 37 ff and Moor 2009.
8   Cameron and Jordán 2006; Yoshida 2006. See for the adult form Jordán 2000, 2014.
9   Ottenberg and Binkley 2006: 8.

The ease with which children mask themselves shows how deeply engrained masking can be in these cultures and how much of a central cultural focus it is. Developing their own masks, the boys prepare for an adult life of masculine performances and in fact take part of their education into their own hands: 'The child does much of the work of self-education, using older persons as a role model.'[10] When the children's masking reflects older forms, such as among the Dogon[11] and the Senegalese Wuli,[12] their masquerade reflects the arenas within the society in a playful way. In urban settings, children tend to create new masquerades, with a mix of adult forms and media-inspired drama, developing divergent styles.[13] They thus serve as mediators between their parents and the modern world, even sometimes as political antennae for the community, attesting to the role of masks in identity construction.[14]

Separation from the mother

In all initiations the first phase is separation, implying that the youngsters are 'stolen' – forced, abducted, or however one may call it – from the home they grew up in with their mothers, and brought to the initiation place in a show of force. In Bobo initiation the masks performed this task, heightening the strangeness of the abduction and adding to the shock of losing the home; but this is not standard. Among the Liberian Dan, the boys are snatched from their beds and brought to the circumcision camp, without the masks; the masks will present themselves later.[15] Usually it is the kinsmen who abduct the boys, either their older brothers or other male kinsmen. Usually it is their paternal kin who do the 'stealing', even in matrilineal societies, for this abduction highlights the kinship bond of the father. The father usually leaves this task to his kinsmen, for it is his 'family', however conceived in matrilineal societies, that brings 'their progeny' into the initiation. Or in

---

10 Ottenberg and Binkley 2006: 23. Binkley (2006) notes examples of this process, and Maples (2018) descibes it in Freetown, Sierra Leone.
11 Van Beek 2006.
12 Weil 2005.
13 Such as among the Igbo, Mende, Yoruba, and in Guinea-Bissau and Ouagadougou; see respectively Okeke 2006; Hlavácová 2006; Nichols 2006; Cannizo 2006; Baird-Hinckley 2006.
14 Argenti 2001, 2014.
15 The data on the Dan are from the long-term and extensive research of Himmelheber 1960, 1979; Fischer 1978; Fischer and Himmelheber 1984. The description of the performance is based upon Reed 2001, 2003.

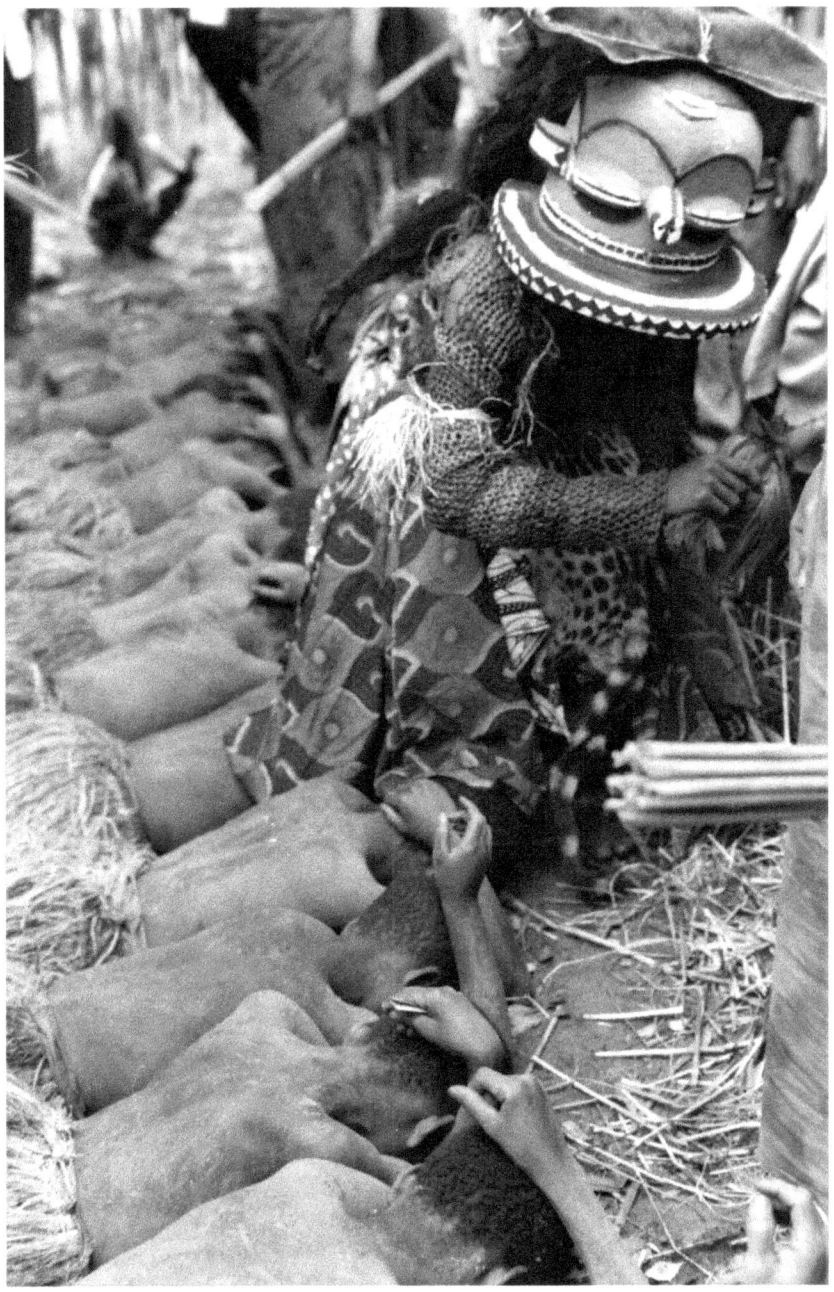

Figure 3.1. *Kipoko* mask supervising Kibetelo ritual during Chief Kende's boys' initiation into the *mukanda*. Ndjindji, Pende, DRC, 1987. Photo: Z.S. Strother.

a patrilineal society it might be the mother's brother who performs the initiation, even in a different village, as in the Jola of Senegal.[16]

In principle, the abduction should be a surprise, and this also applies in societies without masks. For the Wagenia of DRC, André Droogers reports that the first batch of initiands was abducted from a football match that the elders had organised for the occasion, as the latter recalled with considerable mirth.[17] The surprise concerns only the exact moment of abduction, since the boys have undergone extensive preparations in their dress, in lessons and admonitions.[18] If there is no circumcision, as among the Kapsiki of northern Cameroon, the abduction scenario may still hold: lifted from their beds by the male kinsmen in the depths of night, the boys are huddled into the bush for a two-week period of initiation. At any rate, the novitiates are 'thrown abruptly into a state of becoming'.[19]

What Van Gennep has named rites of passage, Pierre Bourdieu calls *rites d'institution*, a term that focuses on the insertion of a person into a new but already existing group.[20] These rites are meant to create a difference between people, between neophytes and the initiated, between men and women, between young and old, and the point for the boys is that they enter a world of new differences, no longer the familial distinctions of hearth and home, but the daunting differences of adulthood. In our terms: the boys transit from a home into an arena. All initiations stress this transition, but masks highlight it with two additional 'unfamiliarities', the bush and the secret, and thus add an exclamation mark to a common transition.

This world of new differences shows in many symbols. Frederick Lamp suggests that the form of the *bondo* mask of the Temne is based upon the butterfly's chrysalis, an icon of metamorphosis and of life springing from death, a rare but powerful illustration of rebirth.[21] Masks exaggerate the transition, and intensify the rituals around them. The gentle and safe sphere of the home is ruptured, and the world has turned against them, a world that is inherently strange through the masks. And yet they themselves have asked for it, sometimes even insisted on being initiated; this is one ordeal they have opted for. They must be aware of some of the trials that await

16 Mark 1992: 147, note 33.
17 Droogers 1974: 71.
18 Not all initiations start abruptly. Among the Bukusu of Kenya, who have no masks, the transition to the circumcision grounds is very gradual, De Wolf 2006: 99.
19 Janssen 2007: 218.
20 Bourdieu 1992: 117–127.
21 Bentor 1994a, note 10. For a general view of symbolism, see Sperber 1974.

them; nevertheless, from a combination of social pressure and desire to be among the adult men, they have embarked on this perilous journey. The major drivers for this guided choice were their father and family, and the presence of their friends, all in all hard to refuse – or a rare motivation: they want to know the initiation secrets.[22]

It matters how old the boys are at initiation. The Bobo children are quite young, in the range of ten to fourteen years old, while initiands elsewhere are often between fifteen and twenty. Masking initiations tend to recruit younger boys, while non-masking initiations see older neophytes appear in the bush, which correlates with the fear and fright that the mask liturgies rely upon for their effectiveness. But age depends also to a large extent on the frequency of initiation. For instance, the Jola of Senegal space their *bukut* initiation over fifteen to twenty years, making for a levy of initiates that range from tender boys to young adults. When these older initiands enter the sacred forest for the *bukut*, they show off their maturity in a spectacular dance, brandishing their cutlasses and guns as fierce warriors: they already embody the new differences.[23] When the initiation leads to formalised age-sets, as occurs in East Africa,[24] the boys may be older still, with a wider age range between them, and for them initiations are repeated later in their lives. However, in these latter cultures there are no masks, which gives initiation a different slant.

Initiation should be daunting for a boy, as Figure 3.2 illustrates,[25] but this holds for his immediate family too. For the mother of an initiand the abduction of her son is highly ambivalent: she hears her small boy disappear into the night, out of her range and control, venturing into dangerous territory, and she realises that, although this is part of his coming of age, the days of easy intimacy with her child are over. If anything, it is the involvement of masks that highlights the fact that her boy is now completely out of her reach. Also the risks are real, and she has certainly heard of boys not returning from the bush; their mothers never receive any message about the death of their son and never see them again. Such a serious concern is fuelled by the tales of the men, such as when the Ndembu speak about a monster that is going to eat their son. On the other hand, the mother is proud that she has raised

---

22 For reasons given by the initiands to enter initiation, see Droogers 1974: 65–67; P. Richards 2022.
23 Mark 1992: 44. See also Mark, De Jong and Chupin 2014.
24 Bernardi and Kerzer 2009.
25 The mask is called *kalelwa*, the boy is a *kandjandi*. See Verswijver et al. 1995: 14, and Crowley 1972: 27.

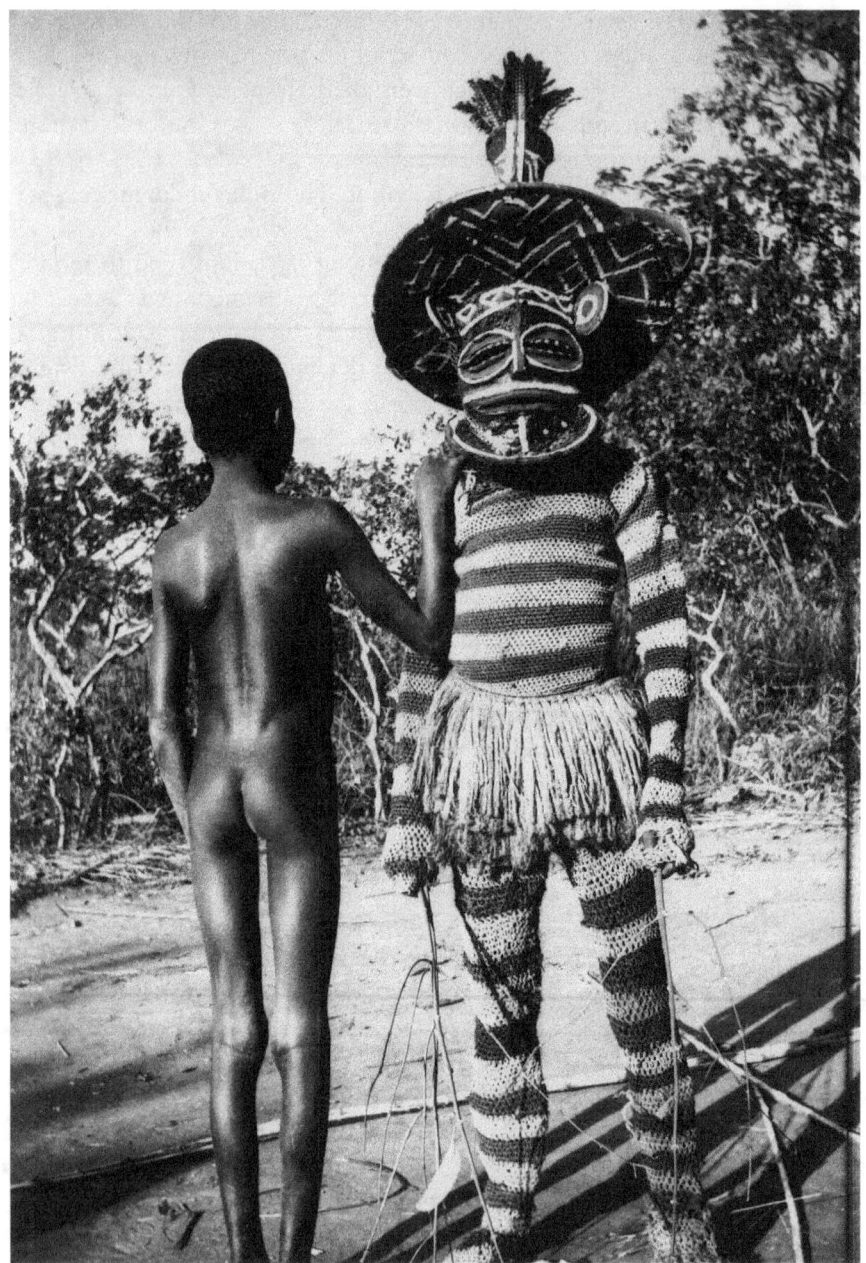

Figure 3.2. A young initiand facing his initiation mask. Chokwe, Angola, 1949.
Photo: E.P. Marchal.

her son this far, and raised him well enough to face this trial unflinchingly. If he passes all tests, the credit will be for a large part hers – more so than his father's – so she will shine at his homecoming. But that is way off in the future.

Liminal revelation

The first stop after separation is 'outside', in the non-village – meaning somewhere in the bush, the initiation camp. During the preparations for the initiation, this camp is rebuilt, always on the same spot, since the village has its own sacred layout and the initiation site is part of this. The Bobo arrangement is very specific and demands considerable preparation, but simpler measures abound elsewhere: a fence, a spot in a sacred grove, a lean-to. Mountains are not abundant in the Mask Crescent, but for mountain peoples, like the Fali of North Cameroon, a cavern may serve as masking retreat.[26] The Dan set-up, described below, is a hut made of straw mats, a simple replica of a normal habitation. Initiation camps have a specific layout and often are spatially structured – for instance, oriented to the cardinal directions; to specific features in the landscape, such as pools; to fissures in rocks or large trees that often function as sacred sites, such as among the Yakö of southeastern Nigeria.[27] And just as often it is history that dictates the site of initiation; Bobo villages and altars are laid out along the pathway that the original settlers used to arrive at the spot and found the village.[28]

Though in daily life such spaces may be quite unassuming, open to anyone, or even cultivated, during the rituals only the initiated or the neophytes are allowed to enter them. Gauthier mentions that at the sacred spot of the Fali village, officiators had to look closely to find it and dig out the needed ritual implement.[29] Often villages have their own special area of bush set apart for initiation, like the so-called 'sacred forest', a rather small patch of forest left after the rest of the land has been cleared for cultivation, but the term 'forest' may stretch it thin. The Wagenia insisted on calling their initiation place

26 Gauthier 1988: 227.
27 Among the Yakö, the initiands follow a historical pathway to greet special trees and stones: Forde 1964.
28 Le Moal 2003.
29 Gauthier 1988: 226.

'forest', even if there was not a tree in sight.[30] The term 'forest' may refer to a former forest, but more generally just conveys the idea of the wilderness.[31]

In a small clearing inside this 'forest', huts are arranged like a mini-village: the initiation camp. Around these huts, which must be repaired for each initiation period and are quite makeshift anyway, are located specific ritual spots for sacrifices, tests, encounters, or dancing places – any of the specific rites that make up the total complex of the initiation. The whole camp is surprisingly close to the village, just a short walk away; while it should be out of sight, it may be within earshot. Most masks require musical accompaniment, which can be heard in the village. But this is not a problem; it adds to the mystery, provided they stay out of sight. Special houses where the masks are stored may be deeper in the woods, as in Mende initiations, or in fenced-off places like the Dan camps.

The closeness to the village adds to its liminality. Bush itself is not liminal; bush is bush, and nor are the spirits of the bush liminal; they are simply spirits of the bush. It is when they come near the village that they become in-between, and then they appear as masks. The boys are in liminal territory since they are at the interface between village and bush, near both but really inside neither. If camps are very close to the village, and actually well in sight, like the Wagenia one, reed mats will shield the initiands from the prying eyes of their mothers, and that is sufficient; sounds may carry through the veil of invisibility. Liminal spaces are not out of communication; they are in controlled communication with the outside. And the men should be in control – or the masks. After all, the ritual eminence of the initiation camp can only really be felt when people are checked at its perimeter: a visitor to the Bobo camp must show that he is circumcised, while the non-initiated are forbidden even to approach the site.

This liminal space is where the new differences are brought to bear on the boys, for a camp is completely male, devoid of any women and children, a mini-society, where the next generation of adults is fully in the hands of men – and in the case of circumcision that is quite literally the case. Masks serve as a link to the 'deeper bush', the roots of power in this male-only world. Together, men and masks are responsible for the birth of a new generation of men, an all-male parturition with its proper birth pangs. In the camp the boys are undressed, stripped of anything that reminds them of their childhood, and must often be naked, a mark of the foetus.

---

[30] Droogers 1974: 269.
[31] The sacredness of these groves is not based on a rich ecosystem but simply on ritual use: Sheridan and Nyamweru 2008.

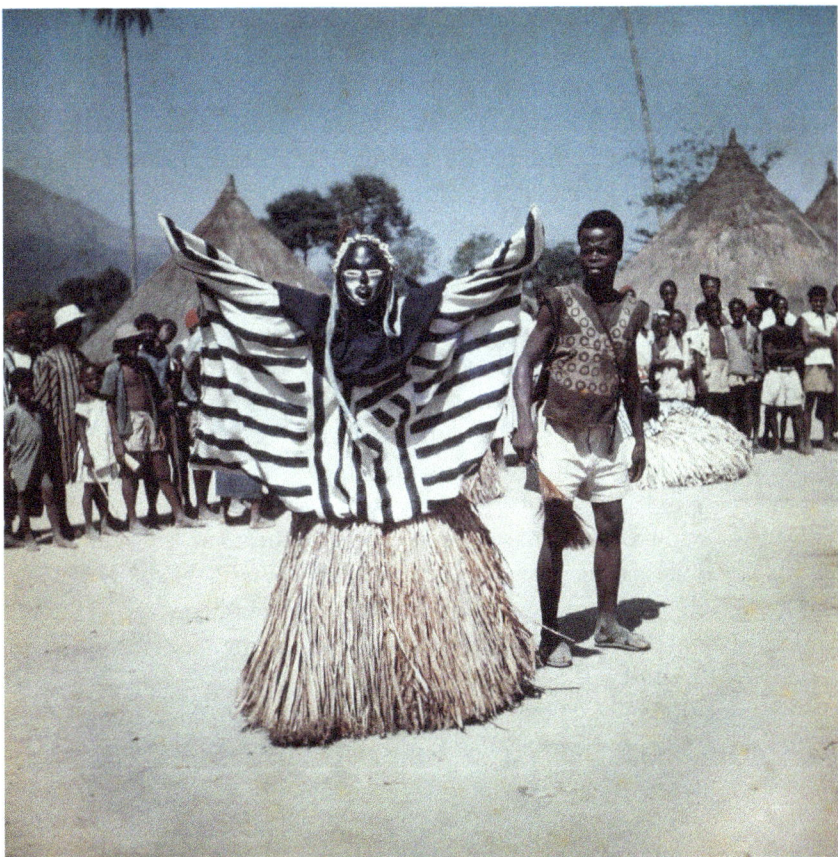

Figure 3.3. The mask *nyon nea* in full apparition, the mother mask that has ritually devoured the boys and given birth to them again. Dan, Côte d'Ivoire, c. 1950. Photo: Michel Huet.

Sometimes they are painted by their abductors, often with white kaolin in nicely contrasting white patterns, or they smear themselves: they become identical, and devoid of familial ties; blank slates on which new definitions can be inscribed. Thus, for the moment, any gender arena as such is defined as non-existent, women have ceased to exist, and all power is fully male: a virtualised masculine world.

Not yet human, the boys are ready for the first major element of their initiation, the revelation of the material nature of the mask: the 'monster', 'scary thing out there', or 'bush spirit' is, after all, quite human. Not only do the Bobo boys see how a leaf mask takes off its headgear in front of them, the same even happens a few years later during their second tier of initiation: at that time the candidates witness a mask made of fibres take off its top. Evidently, this second revelation cannot hold too much of a surprise: the initiates are older now and are already allowed to know that masks are human. But it underscores the fact that this showing of the masker's face is critical, a core rite found throughout the Mask Crescent.

This basic revelation can take various forms. With the Salampasu initiates of DRC, this was a straightforward act: 'Near the beginning of the initiation period [...] the maskers took off their masks and revealed themselves to the boys.'[32] Among some of the Pende peoples of DRC, this rite takes a more poignant form. At the beginning of the initiation camp several masks gather and one of them, the *ngolo*,[33] clothed in fibres overlaid with long shiny green leaves, approaches the initiands and sits down. The chief then exhorts the boys: 'Don't be afraid, don't be distracted; concentrate.' The boys know what to do but hardly dare to; their fathers have explained to them that they have to launch themselves at *ngolo* and rip off its headpiece. Armed with switches, the other masks close in on them threatening to whip them, and finally some daring boys dart out and throw themselves at *ngolo*. The first are unable to dislodge the headpiece, but their fathers keep the other masks at bay and help the boys tear off the top of *ngolo*. The boys show themselves to be strong enough to 'steal' the secret.[34]

The revelation of the mask's humanity is enveloped in a shroud of silence, in two ways: first, contrary to its other appearances, the mask removes its headgear without any music; and second, no one speaks about it afterwards. Such a revelation-in-silence is crucial in most initiations with masks, and forms an essential difference from initiations where no masks are involved. Masks highlight the secret as core of the initiation, and the initiands are now on the 'inside' of that secret; they have become initiates to the mystery, the ones who do not speak.

The next phase is for the initiands to become masks themselves. Among the Fali the boys are shown the mask deep inside the initiation cave, and each one must put on the costume and dance in it. This dance actually forms another test, for they have to dance in the heavy costume until they are exhausted, while being flogged on the back.[35] But more often this familiarisation with the mask is done in two steps: making them, and performing in them. After the revelation, the Bobo neophytes start making

32 Cameron 1988: 38.
33 Meaning 'strength'.
34 Strother 2008: 14, 15; Strother and Kakema 2020: 258.
35 Gauthier 1988: 239–240.

their own masks, which takes up most of their time in the bush in both their initiations: they make leaf masks during the first, and at the second initiation they make the quite intricate fibre masks. More than any other type, fibre masks are suited to a prolonged initiation since they demand cultivation, extraction, drying, dyeing, plaiting, braiding, and finally making the fibres into a costume; making such a mask is an ideal task for a 'bush school'. Making mask costumes is a core symbolic act; with their own hands they transform the raw bush into an otherworldly presence. Finally, as the logical end to the initiation, the initiates dance as a mask themselves, though during this bush phase their performance is limited to the camp.

Wooden headpieces add another dimension, that of craft and art. Carving is difficult and not for everyone. Some wooden headpieces are easier than others, and youngsters may have a go at it – many of the Dogon initiands make their own headpieces – or ask someone else to make one, but many mask tops demand a skill that belongs to the realm of artisans and craftsmen. These can be smiths or specialised carvers, and their services are indispensable in the initiation.[36] In the Guro and Dan initiations – two neighbouring groups famous for their intricate carving – these artisans come into the camp during the bush period and show how a headpiece is carved. Even if the production of such pieces is beyond the reach of the initiands themselves, they must become familiar both with the technique and, more basically, with the fact that these carvings are also the products of human hands.

In some mask-driven initiations this liminal revelation comprises almost all the mask does. Among the Chamba peoples of northern Cameroon and eastern Nigeria,[37] the mask wears its headpiece – a round, ridged skull with circular ears, a huge flat protruding beak, and two curved horns at the back – on top of a fibre costume. About the only thing this imposing mask really does is to take off its large wooden head in the presence of the boys. Fardon notes: 'Grown men insist that as children they had no notion that there was a man inside the mask.'[38] Knowing how much of a public secret masks usually are in Africa, this is surprising, but then Chamba neophytes are very young, and Fardon's respondents were much older. Also, this statement fits in well with the general norm of non-disclosure that surrounds masks, while mask dances are not frequent in Chamba culture.

Ronald Grimes recounts how some informants of an Amerindian group, the Hopi, related their severe disappointment when the *kachina*,

36 See D'Azevedo 1979.
37 Fardon 2007.
38 Fardon 2007: 98.

masks they had been taught were gods, turned out to be human, even family; some children never quite recovered from that shock. He calls this 'initiatory disenchantment', the rupture of an illusion. Other informants from the same group, however, 'in place of their naiveté [...] developed an adult spirituality founded upon one of the most widespread and fundamental religious paradoxes. Sacred people, like sacred objects, are both ordinary and sacred.'[39]

In African initiations, this revelation of the 'sacred ordinary' has been reported occasionally as a surprise, but not as a disappointment, since in the great majority of cases it was something they already knew, more or less. Another important difference is that African masks are not considered gods. Nevertheless, the paradox does remain. The boys have made these masks themselves, cultivated the hibiscus or raffia, extracted the fibres, coloured them, and plaited them into the costumes. They obtained the cowry shells and other decorations at the market and sewed them onto the costume. Sometimes they also carved the headpieces, painted them, and put in the bit for their teeth after fitting it for their jaws. Therefore, the mask becomes theirs in all possible ways; yet it is also a mask, something from 'out there'. Paolo Israel mentions a similar dilemma about the Makonde boys: from sticks and cloth they had to make a tent-like contraption and then perform with it, in a pretence that it was a lion or an elephant, and he wondered how they could possibly believe it.[40]

The answer, as often, is that they do not believe, and yet they do. Familiarity with sacred things does not breed contempt, but generates an additional layer to the power objects, with secrecy adding specialness to the familiar. Despite the deep familiarity, when the performance takes place, it is more than just a costume or a tent. Masks are an inherent paradox of make-believe.[41] When performing the ritual, any cognitive ambivalence is overruled by the experience of the moment. Dancing as a mask is exhilarating while still retaining an otherworldly side; it is not a question of belief but one of experience and existential involvement. Whatever one believes, dancing is dancing, with its own logic and with an admiring public that effaces any doubt: whoever performs as a mask is a mask, for however fleeting a moment.

---

39   Grimes 2014: 136–137.
40   Israel 2014: 233.
41   Picton 1992.

Mask and circumcision

Worldwide, one element stands out in boys' initiation: circumcision. If any act characterises a boy's coming of age, it is the painful procedure on his penis, and the same holds for Africa, both within and beyond the Crescent. Though not all ethnic groups circumcise, and circumcision may well occur much earlier in a boy's life than initiation, the link between initiation and the penis modification is strong.[42] All cultures include sexuality in their definition of masculinity: becoming a man implies moving into sexuality. Already in 1908, Arnold van Gennep pointed out that initiation does not lead to sexual activity as such, but from a *monde asexué* to a *monde sexué*, from a sexless world into one in which sex and intercourse are normal issues; a boy's sexuality and his procreative potential are now on the social agenda, approved and expected in due time.[43] Somewhere in the rituals of manhood, his genitals come into full sight.

Masking and circumcision seem to occur independently of each other; circumcision is found throughout the continent, and within the masking societies of the Crescent one finds initiations with and without circumcision. However, the combination of the two is significant, and to glean the impact of circumcision on mask rituals we give two examples, Dan mask rituals and the Ndembu *mukanda*; the two show masks in different roles.

The initiation of Dan boys[44] implies circumcision as well as masks, and is a village affair. A wealthy man who wants his son initiated takes the initiative in the whole endeavour, and engages some other elders to guide the procedures, including a smith for the cutting and a specialist in protective magic. The required masks are procured from those who own them. The father needs four types of masks: the first two, the initiation masks proper, both presentify the great bush spirit Nana; the third is called a 'falcon' but has a human face; and the fourth represents a monkey; the latter two play a subsidiary role in the initiation. The man consults neighbouring villages and the ritual authorities of the power associations, who will later pay a visit to the camp to check whether all is performed correctly. His initiative starts a collective initiation, since both boys and girls are initiated at the same time but in different locations; regarding the girls, women singers roam the village to entice mothers to hand over their daughters.

---

42 Anthropology knows a long-standing debate on circumcision in initiation. Paige and Paige (1981) give an overview, plus their own theory, which concentrates on fraternal interest groups. For our masking theory this debate is only marginally relevant, because of the near ubiquity of circumcision on the continent.
43 Van Gennep 1960, French original from 1908.
44 The description comes from Fischer and Himmelheber 1984.

During the night before the first day, all children are snatched from their beds and, accompanied by dancing and drumming, are led in the direction of the sacred grove where the campsites have been laid out. The girls have their own camp not too far from that of the boys.[45] At sunrise, the actual operation for the boys starts immediately; when finished, a gunshot tells the mothers waiting at the edge of the area that it is done. From a hut made of mats, the voice of the spirit Nana is heard, a high-pitched chirping sound that is translated by an assistant. The mask, called *mandorple*, moves over to the village and – with a similar transformed voice – asks the women of the village to provide food for the boys, speaking in the language of a neighbouring group. In fact, this is the initiation language that the boys must learn; hence, an interpreter is needed for the women, who may never show that they understand the initiation language. Often mask and women jest with each other, in a skirmish of linguistic expertise that is very much part of Dan culture.

The next day sees the girls excised, and both enter their weeks of healing. Their time in camp is filled by instructions, first how to properly greet the camp leaders, the other adults, and the masks, whenever present. With each new item the boys must learn the relevant songs; learning the accompanying dances will come later when they are healed. They sleep in their camp in a hut made of plaited mats and perform the menial tasks required in a small settlement, such as fetching water. The girls have their sleeping huts inside the village, but never with their parents.[46]

The wounds require attention, as the men fear infections. Boys who die during the initiation – an event not unheard of – will haunt the village forever; besides, the small bunch of youngsters are all close kin. The first week is filled with wound care, with songs and with the first lessons in plaiting; the boys must make a whip to clear their way through the high grass and to chase off spiders attracted by blood. Ten days after the cutting, the boys start to dance, learning the moves of new dances to the tune of drums and a flute.

Two weeks after the operation most of the wounds have healed, and teaching starts in earnest for another two weeks. As is common in initiations, the first lesson is the mask taking off its headpiece for a short time. Henceforth, the boys must sing for every request, especially to the mask, who hardly ever stops talking in its chirrupy voice, considered to resemble

---

45 Information on the details of girls' initiation is scarce.
46 Usually boys and girls are initiated in alternating years, but in the year of the study the initiations were performed simultaneously.

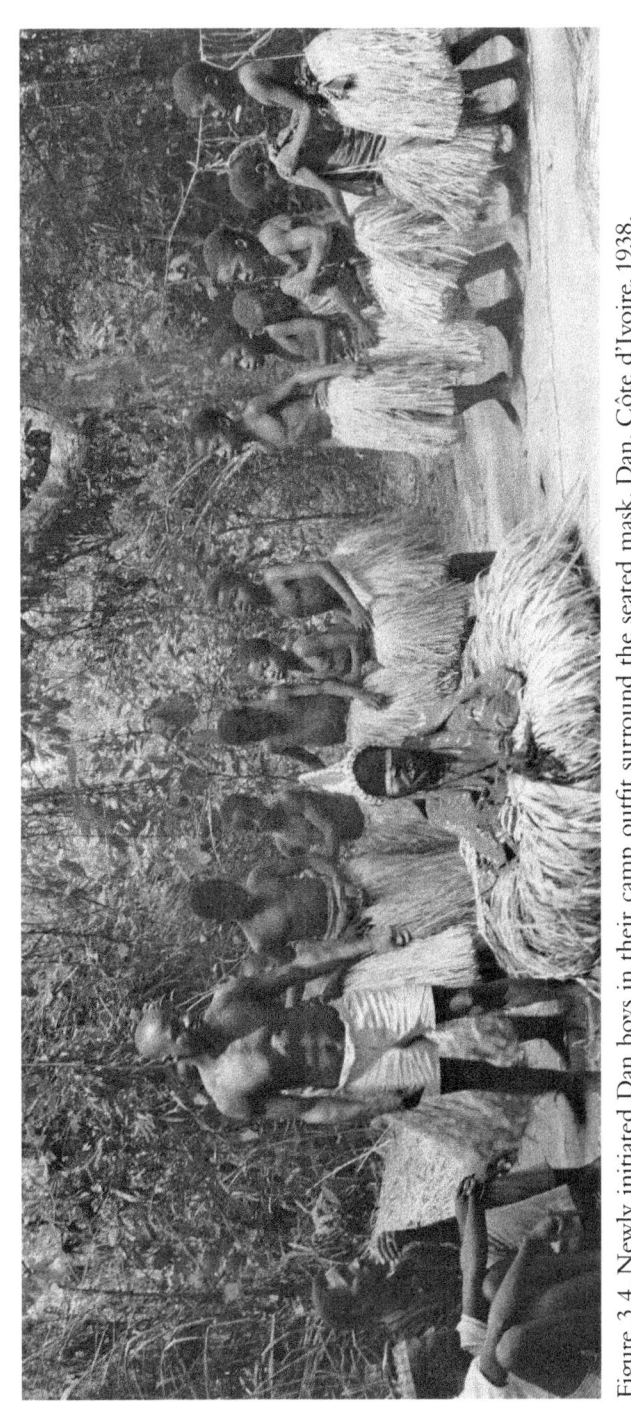

Figure 3.4. Newly initiated Dan boys in their camp outfit surround the seated mask. Dan, Côte d'Ivoire, 1938. Photo: Hans Himmelheber.

a bird of prey; they also learn to imitate other animal sounds. Following their dreams, carvers make the headpieces of several masks inside the camp, with the boys watching. The real revelation for the Dan boys is that they have never seen headpieces being carved; this is always done out of sight. Plaiting is important in this culture, and the boys are taught at length how to procure the fibres from the raffia palm to plait mats and roof covers, crafts the Dan are quite renowned for. Most of these techniques they know already, but they must now grow proficient and 'own' their products, which are used to help widows in the village, a kind of assistance that is imprinted upon them during this liminal period. They also make their own skirts that form the basis of the mask costume; the upper part of this costume is usually a blue-white blanket or cloth, but the boys make only the skirts, which they wear for most of the remaining time, the last twenty of the total forty days, as seen in Figure 3.4.

The actual instructions come from the camp leaders and adult visitors who teach them the initiation language. The boys learn how to make traps and hunt for mice in the bush, but mainly they are taught dancing, chanting, and making music. Each of the songs they learn, over fifteen different ones, has its proper dance routine and usually requires specific musical accompaniment, with improvised instruments that the boys learn to make and play. The performances they practise hinge on these two prime African arts: dancing and speaking. In order to speak well, one must use proverbs, tales, and riddles,[47] in the great African tradition of verbal performances. This is taught quite explicitly; the boys must make a long line, hung with small symbols plaited from grass: a clothesline of proverbs and sayings. The symbols on the pegs serve as mnemonic devices for the proverbs, and the novices must remember them well, along with their explanations and specific occurrences, plus the company in which they can use them. Gradually, the boys grow into the performances, also into their role as as masks. They have seen the inside of the mask and witnessed headpieces being cut, and now they watch how a miniature mask is made, which will serve as a permanent link with the real mask during their adult lives.[48]

The final days are filled with a farewell from the bush. The *mandorple* mask protests the boys' return to the village, since it does not want to say farewell to its sons. The boys are tested on whether they know all the songs;

---

47 Riddles are important in African speech performances; see Harries 1970; Blake 2010: 59.
48 Miniature masks are found dispersed over the Mask Crescent. For instance, the Lega use them on a great variety of occasions. Generally, they serve as a sign of the owner and may even be tied to a fence to indicate ownership; Biebuyck 1973: 167.

and since they perform well, the mask eventually gives in, provided a final witch-cleansing is performed – for it does not want to see its children ill. The final day arrives forty days after the first cuttings. All masks come into the camp, hug each other, and say farewell to their children. The boys are now dressed in blue and white cotton, while a younger brother carries their skirts for them. The girls come out at the same time, so from two sides the village is replenished with new adults, with people who are now complete, who know how to behave, how to work, and especially how to speak, sing, and dance. The new initiates visit all the homes of the players in this whole process, in a village-wide festival of great rejoicing.

This case is based upon a rare day-by-day account of what happens in an initiation camp,[49] and while it illustrates many aspects of initiation, it highlights the initiation masks as constant companions to the boys, more than as frightening presences. The next case, which is quite renowned,[50] describes a different role for masks.

Among the Ndembu of Zambia the circumcision itself is central, its dangers, its symbolism, and the joint experience for the boys, and Victor Turner analyses at length the social dynamics that lead to the establishment of a *mukanda* ritual.[51] When the Ndembu initiands encounter the masks on their way to the circumcision camp, these *makishi*, referred to as 'monsters' or 'devils',[52] should frighten the boys enough to transform them into an obedient flock, but for the rest of the *mukanda* the masks are not overly present. The ritual itself is characterised by an intense focus on the genitals. A host of symbols refer to the penis in its circumcised form, especially the glans in full view, ideally dry, hard, and 'white', with medicines aimed at attaining a strong erection. Any uncircumcised boy is equated with a menstruating woman; the actual operation is performed with the boy sitting spread-eagled, 'like a woman', and the making of the main medicine (*nfunda*) features a ritual of symbolic, more or less homosexual intercourse. This *nfunda* medicine consists, among other items, of the ashes of foreskins of former initiates, tying the new neophytes to all the penises of the past. When the novice tastes this, as he must, 'he is given back his body'; and the 'place of dying' is where circumcision is performed. A series of food taboos aims at attaining an erection good for a series of copulations, and the taboos are explained to the initiates in these terms during their seclusion. Visitors

49 Himmelheber 1979.
50 Through the descriptions of Victor Turner.
51 The description is based upon V. Turner 1967: 189–250.
52 E. Turner 2012: 183; V. Turner 1967: 188.

must show their circumcised penis as proof of being initiated, before being allowed into the camp. During their seclusion, the novices move through the camp hopping, which is likened to the movement of the penis in the vagina.

The *makishi* masks get relatively little attention during the bush period. At the end of the seclusion masks suddenly appear in the boys' camp, whipping them once, after which the boys' fathers will shield their sons from further castigation. It is then that the boys see that the mask has a penis, a circumcised penis with a dry glans. The masks themselves have a stylised human-like headpiece, worn almost horizontally, with designs in red, black, and white, the classic colour triangle of the Ndembu. They wear a mongoose skin on their back and sport a beard made from sable antelope, holding a switch of eland tail; the bush is everywhere. Black is a major colour among masks, a clear association with death that contrasts with the white and red symbolism surrounding the boys. The masks have a stage identity – meaning, they have names, such as *katotoji*, the fierce one; *mvweng'i*, the grandfather; *mudimbula*, the one with the pipe; *chikumbu*, the bald one; and *chizaluki*, the mad one.[53] In the village, the masks approach the singing women and dance with them, handing them salt for the new food. The women have already been brewing quantities of beer from the moment the *makishi* appeared. After the homecoming festivities, elders take the masks to the village shrines and call upon the name of an ancestor. Thus, each mask is equated with a particular ancestor, one within living memory, and people realise that it was this ancestor whose shadow was moving in the mask – a curious *post-hoc* interpretation.

Circumcision rescripts the role of masks, since the boys need time to heal, so there are weeks to be filled, with teaching, exercise, performances, and ordeals. Teaching is not a prime task for masks, so they tend to appear only at the start and towards the end, as the Ndembu *mukanda* shows; in Chamba, circumcision in the presence of the masks is even more marginal; the masks come in, as it were, as an afterthought.[54] If the masks are present for the whole period, like the Dan masks, they grow familiar and serve as intermediaries for the village, supporting the boys in their ordeal. In Zone 3 the combination of circumcision and masking is common, as it is among the Pende of DRC. When the Belgian colonial government forbade

---

[53] The latter three may have been borrowed from the Luvale, who have more masks than the Ndembu; masks easily cross ethnic boundaries and the *mukanda* complex as such is widespread. Also their stylistisc relationship with the Lunda is well-known: Pritchett 2001.

[54] Fardon 2006.

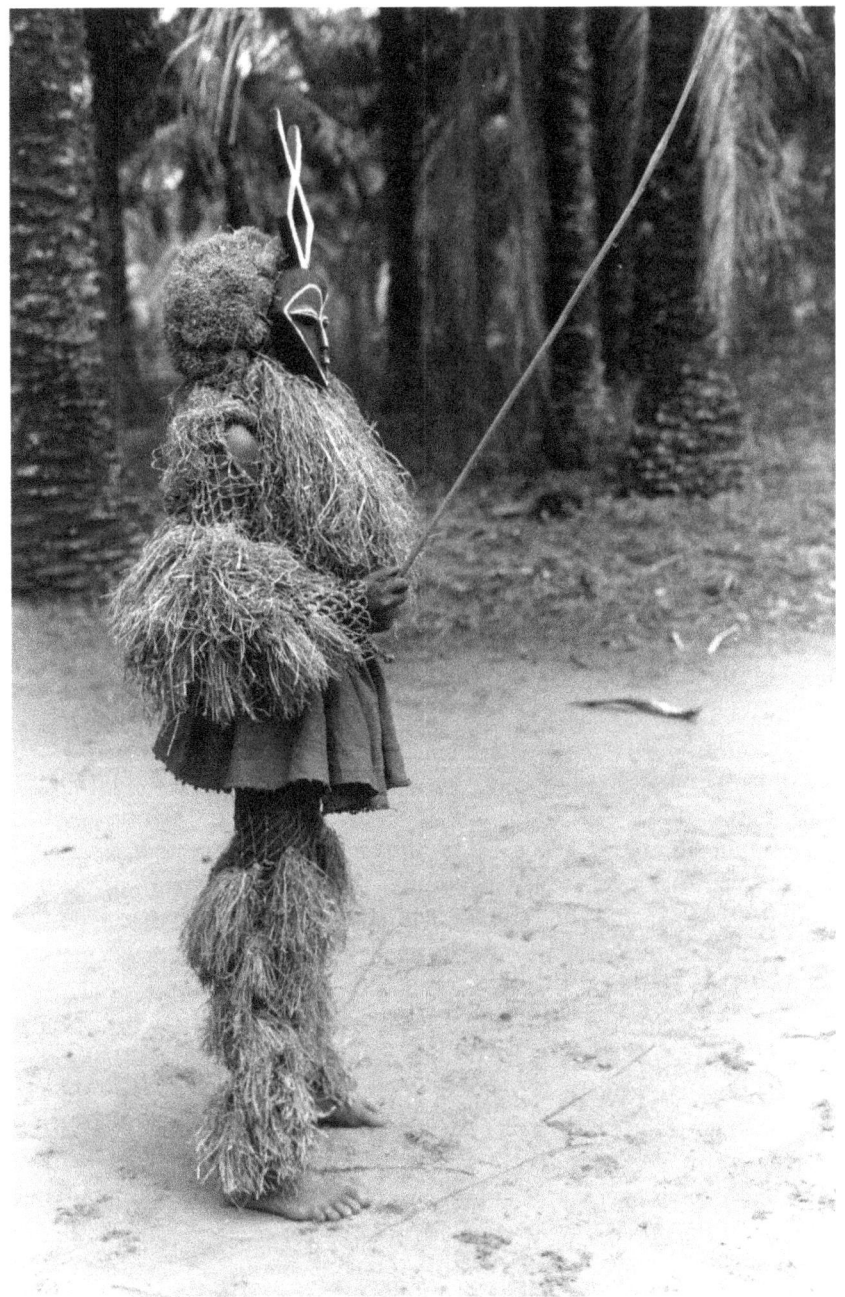

Figure 3.5. Chief Kisonji carved the mask *thangi* for a camp in 1987. Pende, DRC, 1987. Photo: Z.S. Strother.

circumcision in the camps and transferred the operation to birthing centres, some of the Pende henceforth deemed the initiation void; consequently, the Kwilu Pende stopped the *mukanda* in the 1930s and the central Pende in the 1950s. However, the eastern Pende considered the initiation too valuable to give it up, and they defined the unmasking, called the 'touching of the mask' – which had always preceded the circumcision – as the central ritual, and thus retained the *mukanda* as such,[55] shifting its focus back to the masks.

Ordeals are omnipresent in initiation; both with and without masks, the road to masculinity is a pathway of pain. Whipping is the most common, but African initiations use a whole gamut of corporal punishments. The small Bobo novices ran the gauntlet of whipping by masks, and during the entire fifteen years that their trajectory to adulthood will last, whippings will be the order of the day. Blood is to be drawn and pain should be evident; the same holds for the Dan and Ndembu initiands. Boys' initiations are more a pathway of pain than the initiations of girls, for enduring pain is considered the first step on the road to becoming a man. 'In initiation we all suffer', a Kenyan Gisu elder told Jean la Fontaine;[56] the way into adulthood is not easy, not even for those who initiate the boys. Mende boys receive small wounds on their backs, to be explained as the teeth of the monster that gobbled them up – read the mask. The pathway of pain should leave its traces.

Surviving hardship is what counts. In the Fang ethnic group of Gabon the initiands had to collect provisions for the entire ritual period and to fell a specific tree from which emblems – such as a hunter, panther, python, wild pig, or other animal – were to be carved. The core event, as usual in mask-driven initiations, was the appearance of the mask: wearing a horned headpiece, surrounded by acolytes, and evoking the spirits of the dead, it frightened the youngsters at the start of their ordeal.[57] The candidates were then required to prove their courage by plunging into a long tunnel lined with nettles, dung, ants, and other terrifying obstacles. They were forced to eat repulsive food and undergo numerous hardships. The full initiation period could last as long as a year.

Throughout initiation, pain is first and foremost seen as a test of perseverance, courage, and 'being a man'. Sometimes it is simply a question of endurance, as when the young Fali initiate is put on his hands and knees, and the mask puts stones on his back; he must stay put under all

55 Strother and Kakema 2020: 261.
56 La Fontaine 1985: 194. The Gisu have no masks but do circumcise at initiation.
57 Lagamma 2007: 24.

circumstances.[58] But also the way in which he endures may be important, and his family may watch to see whether their boy flinches or cries, and honour is bestowed upon him if he suffers with dignity – a sign of adulthood. But this suffering also serves other purposes. Pain is inflicted by adults, in principle by the elders who oversee the initiation, though usually by proxy: they let younger adults perform this handiwork. Undergoing the harassment is thus also a sign of submission to authority, of respect for the adult initiates, and in the end a signal that the boys agree to fit into the village hierarchy.

The masks themselves may whip the boys, like among the Bobo, but more often the young men who themselves have just been initiated castigate their juniors, and these whippings are often more severe than when inflicted by the older generation. Eventually, the Bobo whipping masks take off their headgear and ask forgiveness from the youngsters, explaining that this had to be done[59] and that there should be no hard feelings in the village. So the test of pain is also a test of forgiveness, of being able to let personal animosity go, to realise that to live closely together as a village one must forgive and forget. Forgiving one's torturers shows not just a model of adulthood, but also shows that they have internalised the powers that seemed to overwhelm them and have incorporated, in the most literal sense, the forces of the bush.[60]

Pain is not the only test, however. The Bobo youngsters had to provide rote answers to standard questions. They were tested on one essential element in initiation, keeping secrets, and the first test is muteness: the boys are taught to be silent, to say nothing, to pretend ignorance. Other tests are more physical, such as jumping a rivulet, running a course, or pulling oneself up by the arms.[61] The idea is that anyone can do this – and if not, he will be helped. The boy's pride may suffer, but he should pass anyway. Most tests in girls' initiations are of the same ilk: 'We do not let them fail', a Bemba woman told Audrey Richards during the *chisungu*,[62] their girls' initiation.

Ordeals during initiation are found the world over, ranging from terrifying and daunting, to just painful, to symbolic and gentle. Most initiation theories focus on the idea of the adult generation putting up barriers for the next

58 Gauthier 1988: 240.
59 Le Moal 2008.
60 Bloch 1992.
61 Like among the Kapsiki of Cameroon: Van Beek 2012.
62 A. Richards 1982; La Fontaine 1985: 174.

one,[63] and in our scheme this is the local field of masculine power asserting its internal structure and hierarchy: the novices learn that by becoming a man, they are in the first place fundamentally different from a woman – the gender arena – and they are in the second place part of a male power arena, but at the bottom rank. The ordeals both symbolise and reify those differences in power: ordeals imply order. With masks, another power source enters the equation, that of the bush, and throughout the Crescent the neophytes learn that it is the men who have access to these powers, not the females. So initiation with masks imbues a power field with the tensions of a gender arena.

Symbols of gender: Death and food

During the liminal period the gender arena shines through symbolically in some surprising ways. Initiation is routinely described in terms of death; the initiands are often qualified as being dead or foetuses. Turner remarks: 'Liminality is frequently likened to death, to being in the womb, to invisibility, to darkness, to bisexuality, to the wilderness, and to an eclipse of the sun or moon.'[64] The Bobo simply call the place of initiation 'death', and the boys are 'officially eaten'. Neophytes are naked on the ground as newborns and are treated as corpses; they must lie or crouch in a foetal position; and they are reborn through the mask-who-is-death – whipped as if they have no senses. A corpse is a no-longer-being to whom one still has to say a farewell, while the foetus is a not-yet-being waiting for a transition in order to be welcomed. This is being betwixt-and-between.[65] In the pathway leading up to the revelation, the young Fali neophytes are threatened with instant death: 'Go away. If you stay, your head will be cut off.' Each youngster is accompanied by a male kinsman who guides him through the process and makes him stay on this pathway to masculinity.[66]

Another symbol of 'not-yet-manhood' depicts the initiands as 'women'. The Ndembu initiands are called 'wives', even 'first wives', and are entreated to 'marry' – in fact, they must marry *nyakayowa*, the mask representing Ancient Woman, at the very moment when they see it has a circumcised penis.[67] A logical consequence of the preceding stages would be that the final rites in the liminal phase enact birth, but that is too much a woman's prerogative to

63 Paige and Paige 1981.
64 V. Turner 1991: 95, cited in Bowie 2009: 155.
65 Janssen 2007: 224–225.
66 Gauthier 1988: 236.
67 E. Turner 2012: 179.

be used as a male symbol; birth is the very stronghold of women. In girls' initiation, birthing symbols dominate; or, as among the Eagham of Cross River, Nigeria, a mask appears after she has finished her seclusion, which happens after birthing her first child, and is ready for marriage.[68]

One prime symbolic act of becoming human is acquiring language: the neophytes – the word itself is revealing – must learn to speak correctly and to sing songs they have often heard, which are taught anew. A special initiation language, if present, adds to the symbolism of being renewed as an adult: new life, new language, topic of the next chapter. Thus, the symbolic 'return from death' is not so much birth, but language: learning to speak like an adult, someone who knows the new differences – and who knows to keep silent. So the gender arena is verbalised: the old existence is symbolically defined as belonging to the female realm, the new human must learn a masculine language. The all-male society teaches the neophyte an exclusively male language, and as part of a newly created group of brothers without women, the young adult reenters the village. The liminal period abounds with denials of the role of the women, symbolically stressing that the only world that counts is the masculine one.

One other issue is food, which is also a polyvalent symbol. Eating is a sure sign of being not-dead, so food is associated with life, and abundant food with wealth and power. A pervading African image of the rich man is the 'eat-all', and the powerful are said to have 'a great belly', like the symbol of powerful ingestion: the elephant.[69] Many initiations feature an eating spree during the liminal phase, especially in initiations without masks. For instance, after their seclusion, Kapsiki boys in Cameroon are considered to have grown in bodily stature. When they re-enter the village, their mothers pretend not to recognise this tall and handsome stranger with such a beautiful, fat body; this is a lot to ask from two weeks of overfeeding, but the mothers play their part.[70] After their long stay in the circumcision camp, the Wagenia boys of DRC hoped that they would have grown nicely fat, and when the anthropologist showed that most of them them had actually lost weight – life in the camp is not that easy – they were disappointed.[71]

It is in the initiation of the Masa and Tupuri, living in the Chari and Logone floodplains in northern Cameroon, that this notion of gaining weight, even growing fat, is dominant. In fact it is more drinking than eating, and it is called

68 Röschenthaler 1998: 40.
69 Fabian 1983.
70 Van Beek 2012.
71 Droogers 1974.

the *cure de lait*. The youngsters – they are considerably older than the Bobo, Dan, or Ndembu novices – gorge themselves with milk during months of seclusion, consuming thousands upon thousands of calories per day in cow's milk, and these cattle raisers do indeed succeed in becoming quite fat during their initiation.[72] This massive intake of calories transforms lanky boys into semi-obese men, and one could forgive a mother for not recognising her son after this indulgence. But in these cultures there is never a mask to be seen – not with all these cows – though they have neighbours who do have masks. In non-mask initiations the symbolism of fatness is more pronounced than in rituals with masks, and in girls' initiations it is almost ubiquitous.

Even if food is a symbol, the people at the initiation site must be fed. The point is that the camp remains dependent on women for food, since the African reality is that the women oversee food, masks or no masks. How to solve this quandary? When sacrifice is involved in the mask rituals, as in the Cross River Region of Nigeria, it is the men who do the cooking – for instance, of the sacrificial goat, roosters, and plantains.[73] But sacrifices are prepared by men anyway and can never supply a steady stream of meals, for the bulk of the food is not sacrificial at all, nor is it always meat. Food is the realm of the women, so the real world of the home intrudes into the virtual one of the initiation camp, and the gender arena shows itself in the daily meal.

If neophytes reside in camps, food is a perennial challenge. Novices may fetch water, light fires, wash, and plait, but they do not cook, and neither do the adult men around them – let alone the masks. We saw the Dan solve this catering problem in a humorous way: the initiation mask constantly begged the women to give food for their own children, underscoring the fact that the one who cooks holds the reins on food. During their initiation, the Wagenia initiands were also fed by their home mothers, and a constant tension reigned over food; in their case the adult males stole from the food, another sign of a broken maternal link.[74] The Ndembu women cooked their sons' food on a special fire, the *mukanda* (initiation) fire, following specific instructions: balls of mush without any salt, the latter being considered harmful for the healing of wounds. Yet, when speaking about masks, men insisted to the women that 'monsters had eaten their sons', and they had a 'knowing laugh' about the women's gullibility.[75] Of course, women knew exactly for whom they

---

72 De Garine and Harrison 1988.
73 Ivor Miller, personal communication.
74 Droogers 1974.
75 V. Turner 1967: 201, 224, 231.

cooked, and one could seriously ask who was fooling whom and which was the more gullible gender.

The women do know the difference between symbol and reality, and are aware that the boy they are feeding is alive; but they must speak as if he is really dead. Beryl Bellman described the linguistic codes the women use to express their hidden knowledge; they will never say anything directly to that effect, lest they be punished severely by the *Zo*, the chief of the masks, but they revel in oblique hints and metaphorical speech, even using riddles, parables, proverbs, and dilemma tales – a very African form of verbal art. Theirs is an 'active non-knowing'.[76]

So each boys' initiation is based upon a paradox: separated from the village, the boys bid a ritual farewell to home-and-mother, while they are still connected to them by the umbilical cord of food. The mind may be in the bush, but the stomach is still at home. Thus, as a symbol of the gender arena, the counter-symbol to male initiation is the domestic fire with its classic three hearth stones, and the fundamental opposition is between the wilds and the domestic fire. With each meal the boys eat, the gender arena is present in the camp, so food provides the initiation ritual with a symbolic opposition that is crystal clear. The women cook cultivated food over home fires in a particular cultural domestication of the bush, while the myth depicts the boys as being eaten by a monster:[77] the human child is transformed into uncooked flesh devoured by a non-human be-thing – representing the destruction of culture. The case of the Masa boys is illustrative: they grow fat not on cooked food but on milk, quantities of milk – a food of the bush, not of the fire. How fundamental this contrast is can be seen in one image that would be impossible in African thinking in the Crescent: nothing is as ridiculous as the idea of a mask that cooks.

Communitas and age

Victor Turner coined the term 'communitas' for a crucial aspect of the liminal phase: the notion of unity, equality, and bonding.[78] It hints not just at being together but at being similar, even the same, despite initial differences, despite the structural cleavages between groups. Communitas runs against the structural constraints of society, a short moment where all are equal,

---

76 Bellman 1984. See also Taussig 1999: 7.
77 V. Turner 1967: 239.
78 V. Turner 1969.

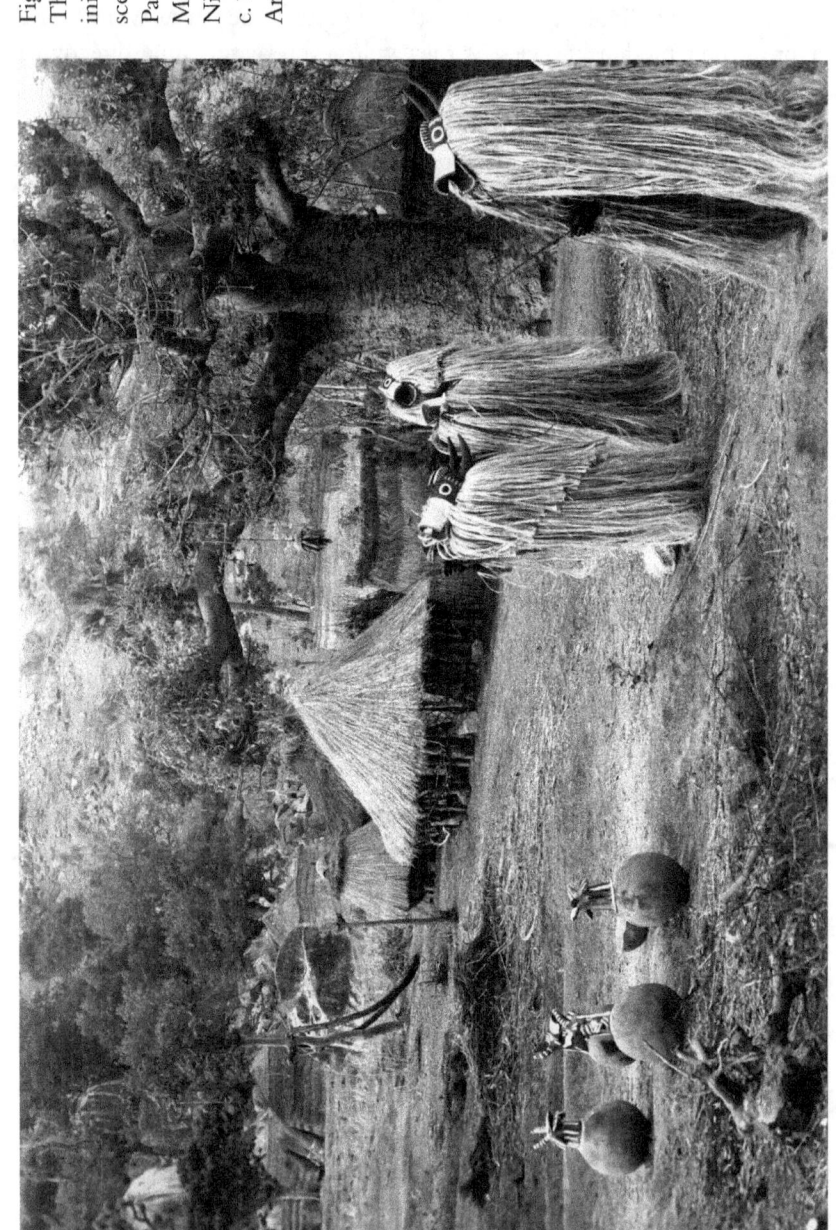

Figure 3.6. The Mumuye initiation scene. Pantisawa, Mumuye, Nigeria, c. 1970. Photo: Arnold Rubin

despite all the evidence to the contrary, and occurs in a fleeting moment, experienced in what his wife Edith Turner called events of 'collective joy'.[79] The boys start out naked, are gradually clothed in identical garments, and reappear in the village as age-mates, a collective unity.

Communitas is the positive expression of the disappearance of the old differences, of wiping the slate clean before bringing on the new differences, in Bourdieu's terms, and is what the boys generate under duress, bombarded with symbols indicating that 'things are not normal'. Circumcision changes not just the foreskin but also the experience of one's own body, highlighting one's vulnerability and the connection between status and suffering. That experience is the same for all, older and younger novices, and as a proud remembrance for the older age-sets forms a commonality that effectively erases all previous differences. Masks add to that experience by striking terror in the young hearts, and by severing preexisting bonds, but they also comfort through new bonds and offer a venue to become something very different oneself; Figure 3.6 well illustrates that mix between strangeness and familiarity.[80] In the bush the boys rely only on their comrades-in-distress, and the bonds generated during that time will last – in short, a communitas of duress.[81]

The clearest expression of communitas in the Turnerian sense is in the homecoming of the boys, their reintegration into the village. However painful or peaceful, however exhilarating or tedious, the liminal period ultimately ends with going back to the home village. This may be a simple resumption of daily activities, just going back to normal, or it may be very elaborate and constitute the very apogee of the whole initiation complex.

In the case of circumcision, the transition from bush back to the village is more acute and homecoming is more pronounced. Edith Turner provides a splendid 'emicised' description of the final part of the initiation of Sakeru, a Ndembu boy:

> They all lined up. Each guardian chose a boy who was not his own and lifted the child on his shoulder. Each one was a chief now. 'The return!

---

79 E. Turner 2012.
80 As an art historian, Rubin was traveling through the Benue River area in order to record art in context; for an analysis of that journey see Rubin 1985, and more generally in Gagliardi 2011. The masks consist of a fiber cape, headpiece, and not much else; the boys are naked underneath, and when viewed from the left their bodies are in full sight.
81 Through emotional information processing; see Finkenauer 1998: 285, and also Kelly 2002.

The return!' They ran full tilt down through the forest in the open, into the public world that the boys had not seen for three months. 'Yey, yey, yey!' shrieked the women in joy, ululating their tongues. The boys were carried around the centre thorn bush in a streak of black and white spots, each boy clacking a pair of sticks behind his head. The mothers ran around in an outer circle looking for their sons. 'There's his guardian, I see his guardian. But he's carrying someone else! Where is my son? He must be dead. Yey, yey! They've killed him. Eh! Why, where is he, Sakeru?'

'War leader now, Mama!' called down Sakeru from his height.[82]

Her husband called it a 'scene of complete uninhibited jubilation',[83] the clearest example of festive communitas, of collective joy. Ndembu boys are initiated at a young age; but also homecoming forms an absolute social highlight when older neophytes return from circumcision.

Masks are often absent in this final phase, which makes sense since their work is finished. Even among the Senufo peoples from Burkina Faso, who use masks for almost all ritual purposes, the final festivities are without masks.[84] At the end of their initiation cycle, which has lasted almost seven years, the 'new adults' come together again in the *ngoro* festival to celebrate the end of their long period of hardship. Each initiated young Senufo man chooses an unmarried girl to accompany him in the dance and on his tour of the surrounding villages. Musicians play xylophones, various drums, and flutes; it is party time. The scene is dominated by a special figure, *syonfolo*, 'Master of the horse'. The dancer carries a wooden horse (*syon*) between his legs, attached to his shoulders by two chords. His costume consists of a net, strips of leather, and pericarps, which swirl around his body when he dances, with a whip to chase the dancing girls. He looks like a mask but is not a mask, and indeed there are no masks present.[85] In homecoming the newly initiated are redefined: masks have become men.

However, one must contextualise Turner's idea of communitas, for it seems rather one-dimensional, merely aimed at non-difference. In practice communitas in initiation has more faces, and each society seems to have its own kind of difference that is effaced during the rituals. The matrilineal Ndembu villages are fluid, a Type D community with built-in tensions and dilemmas, and fundamental equity is stressed as an antidote of individual

---

82 E. Turner 2012: 179, 180.
83 V. Turner 1967: 255, quoted in E. Turner 2012: 180.
84 See Gagliardi 2015 for an overview of the breadth of Senufo art.
85 Förster 1988: 76; see also Förster 1993.

strivings towards excellence. In other cases the liminal times of initiation introduce new differences. The Kuba initiation[86] in DRC, also Zone 3, starts with making distinctions within the group of boys, when the elders select certain boys as leaders and others as followers. Such a stratification is deliberate, since the leaders aim to raise not equals but leaders and followers who will fit into the highly hierarchical system of Kuba villages; the assigned leaders have a much easier initiation period than those destined to become commoners. The new differences that the initiands learn also include the ways they must relate to the other males in the village: they prepare for the local power arena. In other initiations, the new levy of boys must choose their own 'chief and counselors', functions that will remain in place.[87] So during liminal times not even communitas escapes the cultural definition of which distinctions are relevant in real life.

Masquerades as such generate their own hierarchies as well. For example, the Igbo are characterised by equality in social relations, with little concentration of power, yet their masks stress internal difference: 'Critical to nearly all Igbo masking is a hierarchy of participation and knowledge among males, paralleled by a hierarchy of mask types.'[88] Also, initiation produces a definite hierarchy among villages based on first arrival on the spot, especially in Type C societies.

Our theoretical model posits that masking societies have other political cleavages than just the lineage system, and a prime one is age. Through its rhythm over the years initiation defines age as a societal factor, which produces both equality and difference. The joint experience of the initiands makes them members of a new group, crosscutting the usual lineage and territorial arrangements, which can morph into an actual organisation based on age, a pervasive form of masculine organisation in Africa. The bush transforms the boys into partners; in African kinship idiom, they have acquired 'brothers' – a wider definition of brotherhood that also entails obligations; they are expected to help their initiation mates, whose sisters they are not permitted to marry, since that would be incestual.

Age grading as a principle exists throughout Africa, but the degree of organisation of these grades varies across the continent, from a loose aggregate of age-mates, to echelons of mutual help groups, to the grid of society itself.[89] In principle, masks are not needed for this process of age group formation. Whatever the importance and structure of the

---

86 Binkley 1987, 2010.
87 As among the Kapsiki of North Cameroon: Van Beek 2012.
88 Cole and Aniakor 1984: 110.
89 The age-set analysis is based on Bernardi and Kerzer 2009.

age organisation, initiation always plays a major part in its genesis, with discernible but varying elements of communitas. The most articulated age systems are found in East Africa, where societies such as the Oromo in the African Horn or the Maasai of Kenya are to a large extent structured along age lines. Each transition to a new age position involves initiation, fixed in rites of passage; however, masks figure in none of these rituals; they are all cattle-keeping societies with high bride wealth.

Also in the Mask Crescent, relative age is important, but age systems are of a different nature. Whereas in East Africa the age groups form primarily warrior groups, in West Africa age leads more to organisation of labour. In the Crescent one sees age groups as companion systems, loose cooperative groups that will continue to support each other throughout their lives. One major task is performing bride service for each other's marital commitments, which fits in with the low bride wealth that we noted. Girls' initiation does not lead to age organisation, and women tend to associate more with their husband's age group than with one of their own. Also, in the Crescent initiation is not a prerequisite for an organisation based on age; Dogon villages know an elaborate system of age groups called *kadaga*, which are determined by birth order and a quotum system on the number of births in the village, without initiation. This is certainly a masking society, but initiation into masks is part of the funeral proceedings independent of the formation of age groups (see Chapter 5).

Though the age factor generates groups of equals, it also brings in a difference between the successive age groups; relative age underwrites an ascending scale of power, and the existence of these groups regulate the tension between old and young. When a society is organised by secret societies, the topic of the next chapter, initiation-*cum*-masks leads to a strict structuring of society where age is translated into increased power through ascending initiation grades, an aspect we mentioned in Type C. The masking profile stressed age as an integral part of the power arena curtailing lineage interests. The interplay between descent and age is a major way in which the male power field morphs into a proper arena. When the masks help to forge a new age group on the anvil of shared experiences, they balance the authority of age with that of the lineage, and when the mask rituals during initiation highlight the collectivity of initiated men versus the new age group of neophytes, they in fact reproduce the social dilemmas that inform the niche for these very masks.

Masks and masculinities

So far, we have defined both genders primarily in opposition to each other, but they also vary within themselves.[90] Gender is a social construct, so multiple versions of male identity can exist between cultures, and even within in a single culture.[91] One major aspect of masculinity is that it has to be established and maintained: there is an 'imperative to prove masculinity',[92] and manhood must be tested and demonstrated: masculinity is not a given but an achievement.[93] Novices have to show courage, assertiveness, and even aggression, proving first that they can thrive far from home beyond their mothers' care, and second that they can maintain themselves as denizens of the male world that awaits them. One can fail in one's manhood, and cultures have their own models for failed masculinity, such as the 'rubbish man' or the *schlemiel* of Jewish culture.[94] Real masculinity aims not just at being 'a good man' but at 'being good at being a man'.[95]

Furthermore, masculinity must be achieved in stages, in a process that takes time, even a lifetime. A dominant model mentioned in most studies on African masculinity makes this clear: a 'real man' marries several wives; fathers a row of children, with sons who defer to him, and daughters who accede when he gives them in marriage; is a brave warrior but also wealthy and a good provider; speaks wisely in the company of men, where he is respected; possibly holds a position of power; and has a good relationship with the otherworld – the spiritual side is never far away in Africa. In short, a real man is a 'big man' – an ancestor in the making. This model of manhood can be found in many African societies, but the priorities vary between cultures. It is within reach only for the happy few, since it requires lifelong success on all fronts.

For women, motherhood is the hegemonic model, combined with the faithful wife, the harmonious co-wife, and the astute cultivator. This successful femininity is more within grasp than successful masculinity; of course, nature may deny a women progeny, but that is bad luck, not any fault of her own; the insistence on the other aspects varies with culture. Generally, a woman 'is'; a man must become, or 'nature turns a girl in to a

---

90 For Western masculinity studies: Edwards 2006; Howson 2006; and Lusty and Murphet 2014. For Africa: E. Thompson 1997; Jónsson 2006; C. Cole et al. 2007; and the historical overview of Miescher and Lindsay 2003.
91 Jónsson 2006: 28; c.f. Hodgson 2003.
92 Shefer et al. 2007: 3.
93 Gilmore 1990: 36, 38.
94 Ibid.: 100.
95 Ibid.: 30.

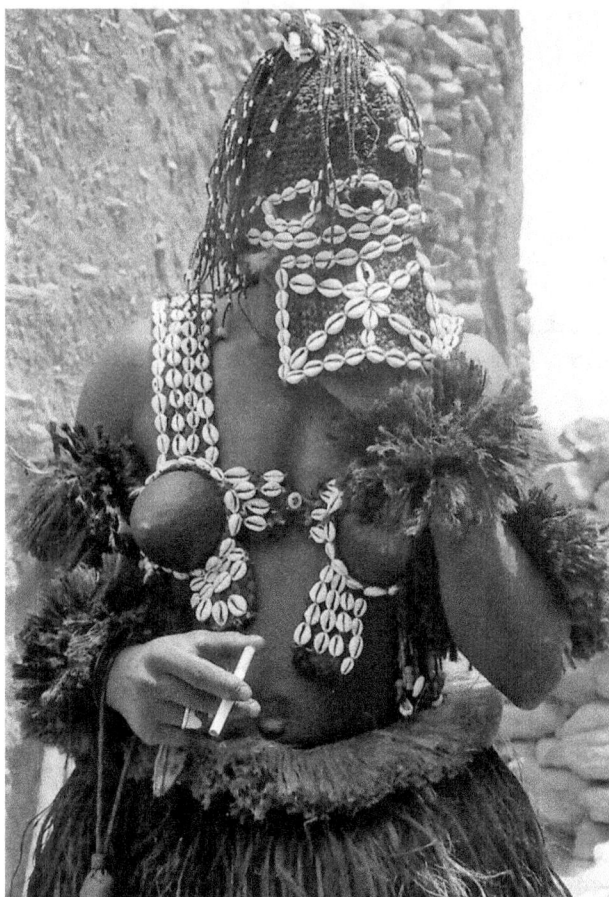

Figure 3.7. Despite its overt femininity, this *tingetange* mask combines two types of masculinity, by taking a smoke after its performance and by being a mask. Amani, Dogon, Mali, 1989. Photo: Walter van Beek.

woman, but a boy needs ritual work to become a man'.[96] So the initiation ritual may serve as a lens for the various pathways into manhood.[97]

Initiation accomplishes four things. First, the youngster is set on a long pathway into manhood that will have other signposts along the road, such as marriage, children, and social responsibilities: initiation opens the gate to the road towards masculinity. Second, all people around the initiate know that he has set this course and are committed now to assist him on this road. In a comparison between Gisu and Bukusu initiations in Kenya, Jan de Wolf notes that the roles and attitudes of the boy's family toward him

96   Shefer et al. 2007: 7.
97   Sparks and Post 2015.

change when he has performed the rites.[98] A boy who has just come back home from the circumcision camp sees that his place at the hearth has shifted, for he is on the way out, eventually. Some initiations leave visible marks, such as cicatrices on the head, which show to everybody not just that the boy is initiated but also into what group. The most important change, however, the circumcision, remains quite hidden; people know about it and may surmise it as a covert mark,[99] which he can never undo. So initiation transforms kinship. Third, the boy has acquired age-mates, brothers beyond his lineage. However, the fourth and crucial change is sexuality and marriage. In principle, all boys' initiations take place before their first marriage. This relation is even stronger for girls – for whom the first marriage often equals their initiation – but the order is there with boys as well: first initiation, then marriage. A boy's male identity hinges primarily on his place in the gender arena; his position in the power arena comes later.

But initiation has many faces, and the habitus of these rituals makes a difference in the construction of masculinity. Overviewing initiation rituals with and without masks, four models of masculinity emerge: the *warrior*, the *father*, the *virile/fertile male*, and the *wild/powerful male*. Dramatising male gender roles, initiation as an all-male endeavour does not simply create a man out of a boy, but also helps to 'create a male culture in which *a man is made among men*'.[100] Masks colour especially the latter two of these models.

In societies with segmentary patrilineage systems – which have no masks – the first association with male adulthood is war: the boys are initiated to be warriors. During their liminal period they dress as warriors, carry spears and bows-and-arrows, roam the village perimeter, and exhort gifts from visitors. In East African cultures this is almost standard; their intricate age organisations form the backbone of society, grouping the initiated men into broad age-based clusters called age-sets. Each set has its own roles in society and collectively goes through a series of phases in male life, such as warrior, husband, father, and elder, with rituals to demarcate each transition. Characteristically, the warrior age-set is not allowed to marry before another set has replaced them as warriors; the relation between initiation and sexuality is complex but always present.[101] The warrior model of masculinity appears also in other parts of Africa, for the image of the fierce fighter is a compelling one. Mask-driven initiations usually do not stress warriorship: masks are not warriors, nor do they produce warriors.

98 De Wolf 2006: 103. Both are Kenyan peoples, so without masks.
99 Van Gennep 1960: 72; Stewart and Strathern 2014: 32.
100 Janssen 2007: 222; emphasis in the original.
101 As among the Samburu of northern Kenya: Gilmore 1990, ch. 7.

Our second model of masculinity relates to social fatherhood. Ronald Grimes remarked that 'many initiations in small-scale societies do not produce men and women, much less generic adults, but rather potential fathers and mothers'.[102] The Kapsiki of northern Cameroon – who do not mask – initiate their boys parallel with the girls at the time of the latter's marriage ceremony. For the Kapsiki girls their wedding equals their initiation, with a singing contest for all young brides in a specific cavern at its apogee: a public spectacle that forms a highlight for the village. The boy-initiands swarm around the admiring crowds, in support of their sisters and fiancées among the singing girls.[103] It is not the separation of the sexes that is stressed here, but the supreme importance of marriage, and the initiatory symbols stipulate male adulthood in terms of marriage: the boys become potential husbands.

In matrilineal cultures, it is rather difficult to give substance to paternity, and ritual helps. The ritual is *around* the boy, but not just *about* the boy; organising the ritual is high politics in the village, and having one's son among the initiates is a public sign of fatherhood.[104] But even more poignantly, circumcision can serve as a statement of fatherhood against the boy's more structural links to his mother's family.[105] The clearest example is from the Ndembu, where during the procedure the father stands behind his son with an axe in hand, to strike out against the circumciser if he harms his son. He is the parent on the spot, not his wife's brother. Turner has analysed the initiation proceedings as a tug-of-war between the sexes and between the fathers versus the maternal uncles, stressing the 'masculine aggression against mothers in a matrilineal society',[106] in short, as a gender arena.

In patrilineal societies with masking, fatherhood is much less an issue, and circumcision tends to be a separate ritual that occurs well before initiation. In these cultures a father has another important ritual at his disposal to claim his paternity: sacrifice. Home sacrifices unite the family around a sacrificial victim, in a communal meal presided over by the father, a ritual not found in

---

102 Grimes 2000: 109.

103 Van Beek 2012, 2015.

104 Paige and Paige 1981 posit that when the father allows the elders to cut his son's penis, he submits himself to the authority of the elders. Yet the father's role in shielding his son points more toward his fatherhood than to his submission, while in a matrilineal society these elders have little authority anyway. Paige and Paige cite examples only from outside the Mask Crescent, as does La Fontaine 1985.

105 In the Muslim world very young boys of just over three years old are circumcised; here the claim to ritual paternity by the boy's father is dominant, coupled with a recognition for his wife, who has gifted him with a boy: it is now a family with a son (Crapanzano 1981; see Bell 1997: 56–58).

106 V. Turner 1967: 193.

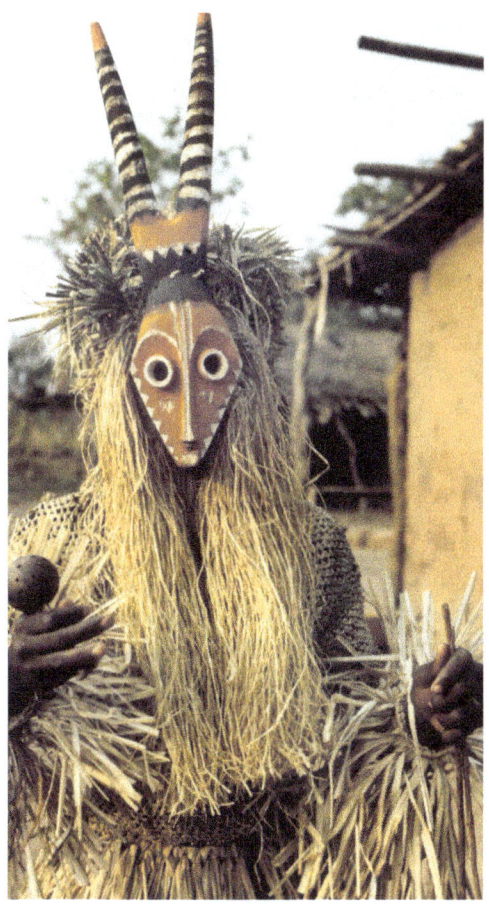

Figure 3.8. *Thengu ya lukumbi*,
commissioned from artist Ngoma
Kandaku Mbuya for the *mukanda*
of Chief Mukunzu. Ndjindji,
Pende, DRC, August 1987.
Photo: Z.S. Strother.

matrilineal societies. With this ritual killing and by presiding over such a meal,
the man proclaims his fatherhood over the family; Nancy Jay's classic analysis
of sacrifice shows how this link between sacrifice and paternity works.[107]

The third model focuses on sexuality as such: the virile and fertile man.
In some initiations, virility is referred to in veiled terms, but often, especially
in Zone 3, genitals form a central symbol in the mask-related initiations and
play a large role in songs and sayings. Among some Pende peoples of DRC,
for instance, Zoë S. Strother observed how the very young initiands were
vexed by the fact that they had to sing about their mother's genitals, obliged
to insert her name in lines that referred explicitly to anatomical details. At the

---

[107] Jay 1992.

beginning of the camp their embarrassment was tangible, but at the end even the youngest sang the bawdy songs with great gusto.[108] In these initiations the penis is a crucial – and often surprisingly direct – symbol. Actual sexuality is not yet on the agenda, and this first stage on the pathway to masculinity is purely verbal: the novices are now 'men' because they can speak or sing about sex. Thus, sexuality transforms into a state of mind generated by an indeed rather bawdy discourse. The link with the matrilineal descent is evident, since the ritual overstates the role of the male in procreation, as a counterweight to the weak social position of the men.

The fourth model relies on the power that derives from the bush. 'Real power' stems from beyond the village perimeter, and can be harnessed exclusively by men provided they become partly bush themselves, as masks: masculinity as a gatekeeper to the otherworld. Initiation is a way of becoming not just an adult, but one with the option of becoming a mask himself, an option closed to women.[109] It is by repeatedly crossing the line between village and wilderness that men become contained wilderness, completely 'masculine'.

This is the antagonistic definition of masculinity: powerful men of the wilds in opposition to domestic women. Masks render male initiation a major achievement that is out of the women's reach, transforming boys into men in a way that girls can never be made into women. So masking tends to define masculinity in direct opposition to femininity, through a ritual supremacy of the male over the female that symbolically denies the evident biological complementarity.[110] This models puts the gender arena right onto the stage: masks as wild, powerful be-things seemingly subjugating women, only to be contained by the men.[111] Masks do not domesticate the boys as much as empower them, heightening the gender gap, just as they harness the difference between initiate and novice.

In the end all models aim to turn the individual proclivities of the boys into socially acceptable goals for adult men, for ultimately masculinity is defined in terms of the well-being of society, which should take priority over purely individual ends. Models of masculinity are thoroughly social, and initiation feeds into this. Or, as David Gilmore puts it: 'Manhood ideologies always include a criterion of selfless generosity, even to the point of sacrifice. Real men are those who give more than they take; they serve others.

---

108 Zoë S. Strother, personal communication.
109 See also Cornwall 2003.
110 Chapter 5 will elaborate on this topic.
111 See for instance Kasfir 1988c.

Real men nurture their society.'[112] What masks add is a direct link to the otherworld, so the use of masking in initiation offers the males an exclusive power base in ritual competence and religious primacy, ultimately defined as beneficial to the community at large. In doing so, masks overstate the male contribution to society by grounding masculinity beyond human society.

Conclusion

Power and gender arenas formed the core of this chapter, for if masquerades address these arenas anywhere, it is in male initiation. In this chapter we saw a range of societies pass by, both with and without masks, and the masking societies fit in well with our profile. In the northern part of Zone 1, Type C societies dominate, and the Bobo and Bwa defensive villages clearly show the characteristics mentioned. Suffering from the depredations of Fulbe raids for much of their history in a countryside with few natural defences, their exuberant masking traditions are well described. In the southwestern part of Zone 1 this holds also for the coastal societies of Wuli and Jola, with their large rice-cultivating villages, which are self-sufficient and highly endogamic, shielded by water and forest. In this zone Type D is relevant to the Dan. Their independent villages, in which hunting is important, are linked by complex systems of gift giving and power associations,[113] and they are inveterate maskers; their headpieces are renowned.

In Zone 2, Type C is also well represented in the Fali and Igbo.[114] They had, or still have, mask rituals. The Mandara Mountains on the border with Cameroon and Nigeria, where the Kapsiki live, show Type A societies with segmentary systems limited to the village, and with high bride prices. Indeed, they have no rituals featuring masks. Zone 3 is dominated by Type D, the frontier village, which characterises Ndembu, Salampasu, Chokwe, Kwele, and Fang, who all masked, at least in the past.

112 Gilmore 1990: 229, 230.
113 Fischer 1978: 76.
114 To some degree this also holds for the Bobo: Saul 1991.

4

Secrecy and Power

'Secrecy is one of man's great achievements'

(Simmel 1950: 320,
cited in Finkenauer 1998: 50)

Writing on the mask

During the 1989 mask ritual in the Dogon village of Amani, Mali, some youngsters in their enthusiasm had painted their name on the kanaga *(antelope) headpieces of their masks (Figure 4.1); the horizontal bar offers a fair writing surface. Of course, they wanted to show off both as dancers and as 'literati'; however, for the elders of the village this was a problem: now everybody who could read would know – and would be obliged to recognise – who was dancing that mask. And since literacy was not that scarce any longer, this was a bridge too far. Consequently, the elders decided that henceforth no names were allowed on any mask headpiece; and this injunction has been followed closely in subsequent dances, also in other villages. During the large 2008 mask ritual in the neighbouring village of Tireli, where schooling is now standard, nobody painted his name on a headpiece.*[1]

This small clash between modernity and tradition highlights the central secret of masking. By the simple act of writing, the *kanaga* entered the world of school and daily life, and with the written name of the proprietor it became less of a mask and more of a personal billboard.[2] Since the main taboo still held that women and girls were not supposed to know that a man was dancing as such a mask, and surely not who the dancer was, the elders of Amani were completely justified in their prohibition: the 'public secret' had to be kept intact. Their well-reasoned rejection of this novelty showed how much they were intent on patrolling the borders of this ritual

---

1   See Van Beek 2018. Polly Richards records a similar incident (Richards 2022).
2   The first author bought the headpiece from its owner just after the mask festival.

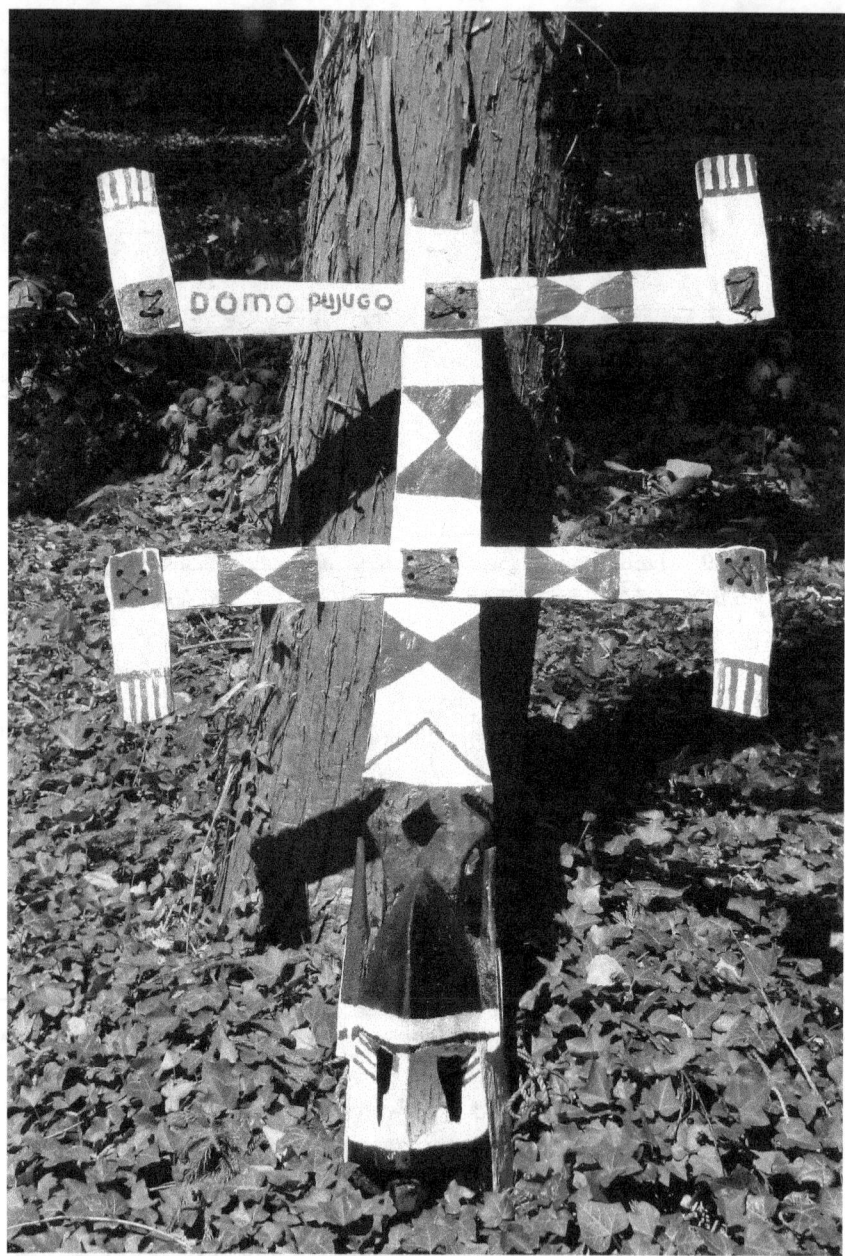

Figure 4.1. The headpiece of the *kanaga* mask. Amani, Dogon, Mali, 1989. Photo: Walter van Beek.

world. Masks do change with every new *dama* (mask ritual: see Chapter 5), a dynamic they are very much aware of, yet this new development threatened the very essence of masking.

Dimensions of secrecy

At the heart of masking lies the secret. In large stretches of the Mask Crescent, secrecy finds its organisational form in secret societies – which in the Dogon case happen to be absent.[3] What could be more 'African' than a secret society? Masks loom large in the old exotic images: strange apparitions roaming the deep jungle, scaring outsiders while engaging in unspeakable rites in the depths of night. The combination of secrecy and masks reinforces all the stereotypes about the 'Dark Continent', encapsulating the mystery of wildness and the threat of the ultimate other.[4] As is often the case with stereotypes, the reality on the ground is less exotic and more understandable – but also more interesting. Three questions will guide us. First: what are the dynamics of secrecy in mask performances and in secret societies – thus, what does the notion of secrecy entail in practice? Second: what is the role of masquerades in the initiation into these kinds of societies? After all, these secret societies are often also called 'initiation societies', and with good reason, since initiation is their *raison d'être* – not just the initiation of boys into manhood but also of adult men into higher grades in the society in question. As mentioned in Chapter 1, such organisations are also dubbed 'power associations', with equally good reason. Third, the continuous background question: how do these rituals nestle inside the societies of the zones?

It will come as no surprise that inside information on secret societies is relatively scarce. Access is difficult, as the border control of these groups is strong and essential to their existence. Also publication of research is restrained, because once inside a group the participating researcher must agree with the restrictions on sharing information with outsiders.[5] Finally, these societies have withdrawn at the coming of the world religions, and are disappearing in a modernising Africa. So the information is restricted. Still, given these barriers, the secrets of Africa have always taunted researchers;

---

3   The Dogon have no secret society. *Awa*, which in some of the literature is sometimes referred to as a masking society, is simply the word for mask in the initiation language Sigi so.
4   Coombes 1994.
5   Setlhabi 2014.

and though not abundant, from the 1980s onward reliable and rich sources of information on secret societies appeared.[6]

The psychologist Catrin Finkenauer[7] devised a convenient matrix to classify secrets, using two axes: specific versus broad content, and high versus low social accessibility. Specific secrets consist of incidents, details, once-in-a-lifetime happenings that are kept hidden – such as driving away after hitting someone with a car. Broad secrets concern a more general picture of one's life – for instance, homosexuality in a culture that does not accept it, or broad historical facts that a government wants to cover up, such as a historical genocide. Accessibility regards the notion of sharing: who else knows, who may know, and who may share with others? The lowest accessibility is evidently the individual's secret that nobody else is even aware of: the secret of the murderer or the embezzler. Highly accessible are the public secrets that everybody knows but nobody speaks of – or the secret that just one person does not know, all others participating in a charade. For example a surprise party, or a problem all one's colleagues know about while together keeping the boss in ignorance. The crucial point is that both axes are independent of each other, a finding that is essential for the analysis of secrecy. Filling in a grid with examples results in Table 2.[8]

Table 2. Dimensions of secrecy.

	Specific content	Broad content
High accessibility	Shared specific secrets	Member of forbidden groups
	Family secrets	Secret societies
	Industrial secrets	Initiation secrets
	Professional secrets	Gender secrets
		Government secrets
Low accessibility	Traumatic experiences	Hidden sexual preference
	Causing accidents	A double life
	Criminal acts	Anonymous donor
	Magic tricks	Anonymous author/ artist

6   Jones 2014.
7   Finkenauer 1998; see also Wismeijer and Bots 2009: 29.
8   After Wismeijer and Bots 2009.

Today in the north, transparency is the norm and secrets have a negative connotation. Individual secrets may well lead to hard questions: Should I tell the other? Can my relationship stand it? Can the other be trusted to keep the secret?[9] Whether it leads to soul wrestling or is considered a cherished possession, most people clearly have some sort of secret, at least in Western society where people know relatively little about each other. Secrets are an integral part of social life, and Finkenauer remarks: 'imagine a world without secrets. The result would be devastating.'[10] Compared with an African village, Western society makes it easy to hide aspects of one's life and personality from most of one's fellows – sometimes even from a spouse.[11] Privacy should not be considered secrecy; privacy concerns information that the other has no business knowing but that in principle everyone shares. A secret is something that is relevant to the other but that the other is denied access to, or is even unaware of.[12]

For masking, the most interesting axis is the second one: accessibility or sharing, how the secrets are communicated. Clearly, the secrets of masks are in the top right cell of the table, the public secrets, and here the relevant question is, who has the keys to disclosure – meaning, who has both access to information and the right to speak about it? Sharing a secret involves selection, for the essence is that some categories of people are denied access, while those in the know are aware of their prerogative. In the words of Michael Taussig, 'secrecy is orchestrated disclosure'.[13]

The landmark study on African secrecy is that of Beryl Bellman[14] on the *poro*, the male secret societies of the Kpelle in Liberia. During lengthy fieldwork he embedded himself in several secret societies, which sounds more difficult than it in fact was. Of all African initiation society systems, the *poro* and *sande* are the most famous, the male and female power associations that for a large part define social life in these regions; and their secrecy complex has accrued its own qualities. The patrilineal Kpelle villages are rather small, between one and two thousand inhabitants, but they contain an astonishingly large number of power associations. Bellman reports twelve

---

9   Wismeijer and Bots 2009: 126. This negative valuation needs some revision; see Finkenauer 1998, Barrett 2007, and Frijns 2004.
10   Finkenauer 1998: 282. The authors thank Catrin Finkenauer for her comments.
11   Caughlin and Vangelisti 2009.
12   For this distinction between secrecy and privacy, see Finkenauer 1998: 25 and Warren and Lasslet 1977.
13   Taussig 1999.
14   Bellman 1984.

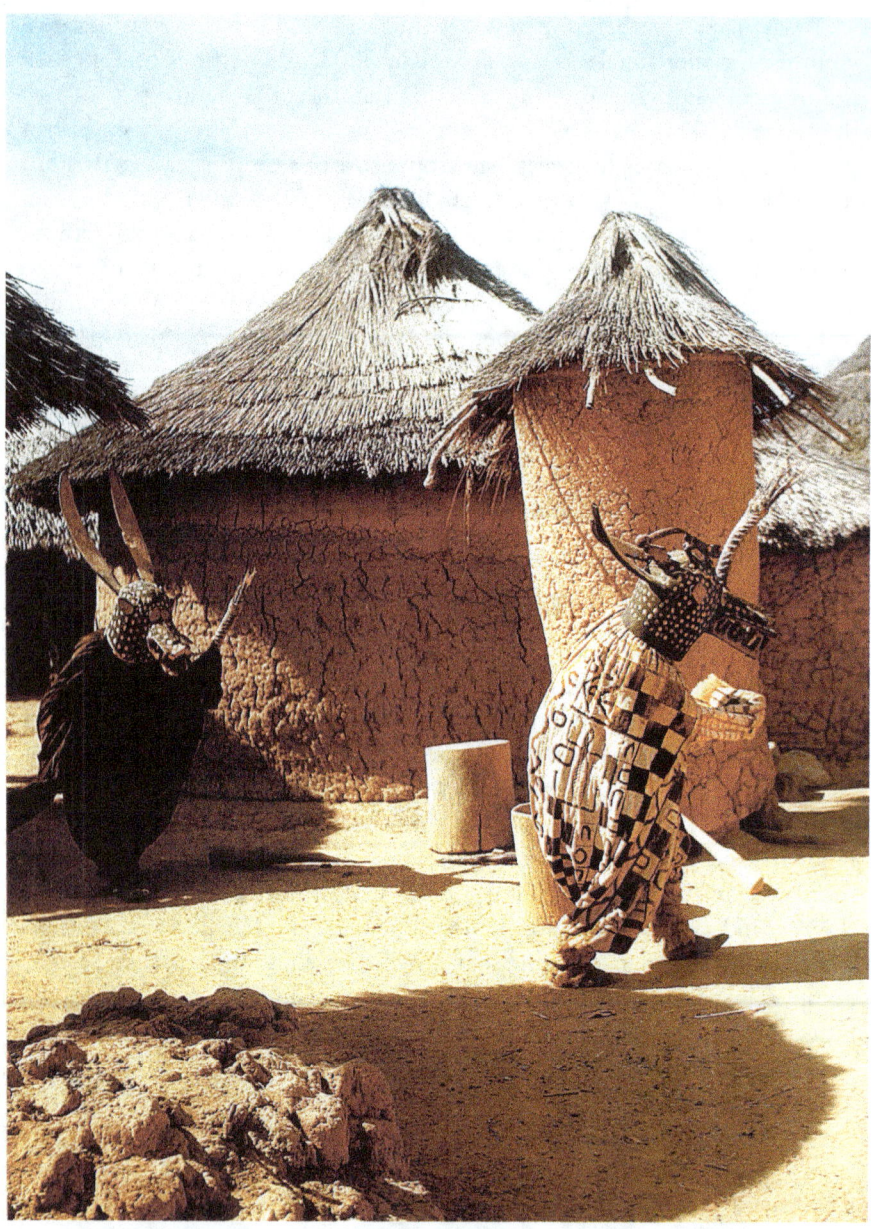

Figure 4.2. Arrival at a funeral of the *ponyugo* masks representing the *poro* association. Tyongofolokaba near Ginématyali, Senufo, Côte d'Ivoire, c. 1950. Photo: Michel Huet.

in a village of 1,500 people,[15] which means that 400 adult men must staff a dozen secret societies. One man can be a member of several, and these *Zo*, the individual associations that comprise the *poro* structure, are a crucial feature in the village and intervillage organisation. Some of them are male, *poro*, and some are female, *sande*. These names, *poro* and *sande*, are found in a broad swathe of territory from Sierra Leone and Liberia to Côte d'Ivoire and even beyond, in various forms.[16] Over that huge area the dynamics of secrecy are quite similar, as is their relation with the masks – sometimes called 'devils'[17] in Liberian English, or more generally 'bush-things'. Beyond the *poro–sande* system, other associations are also active.

For men *poro* membership is optional, but it is expected that a man joins the *poro* in his own village, with his patrilineal kinsmen. Kpelle associations are graded: all young men enter as members in one, another association comprises the leaders of the village. Initiations are rare, occurring every twelve to eighteen years, during which the various *poro* associations assist each other.

The female counterpart of these *poro* societies is the *sande*, the women's organisation, which is taboo for men. The *sande* have their own bush school, where all young girls must go and remain for a year, undergoing scarification and formerly clitoridectomy. The men used to stay for years in the bush for the *poro* and the women for the *sande*, but that has been reduced to one year. As with the *poro*, a special chapter of *sande* comprises the female leaders of the town, recruited along the lines of matriliny, with its own initiation and agency: they oversee a fenced area in the middle of the village where the women's hut is located. No man will ever venture there. When the *sande* initiation is in session, these women rule the village, assisted by a mask that is furnished by another, male society, the *mina*. Our next chapter looks at this *sande* organisation, for such female organisations are scarce in Africa. In addition to the *poro* and *sande* societies, five other types of secret organisation fill in the niches of socio-religious life, an impressive array of secret societies for such a small-scale society. Masks figure in many of them at selected spots and for specific functions. Political and ritual life in these communities is shot through with these power associations – and so with notions of secrecy – all in all, an immense occupation with things secret.

The Kpelle have no word for secrecy; they simply call it *ifa mo*, 'do not speak', and Bellman analyses their notion of secrecy as a language game, as a series of strategies of speaking about things that one should not speak about,

---

15 Ibid.
16 See for an overview M.J. Adams 1980.
17 Bellman 1980.

of hinting at the unmentionable. All things pertaining to the *poro* are out of bounds for women, just as anything relating to the women's association is forbidden for men. The secrets separate the genders quite effectively: secrets make differences between people.[18]

All secrecy discourses have rules of expression, verbal codes, and voice inflections that go with them. In the Bamana language it is called 'question speak';[19] other languages have their own term for hidden speech, but throughout the discourse on concealment is essential. Eli Bentor notes: 'As an Arochukwu friend told me: "If I am going to dance the Ekpe [mask], I will tell my wife that I am going to the nearby town, but she will know".'[20] This is what Finkenauer calls the 'reciprocity of secrecy';[21] one partner does not tell, and the other does not ask – in fact, a shared element in such a marriage.

So not speaking is crucial in the language game of secrecy, in the form of silence or evasive speech, hiding the fact of being informed; the need for silence was the first message for the Bobo initiates. Non-communication is difficult between people, so not speaking is a form of controlled communication. All initiands learn to keep their mouth shut, for even as an insider they are not allowed to hand over this 'information' to anyone else; the distinction between 'knowing' and 'right to disclosure' is drummed in from the start. Novices find themselves on the lowest rung of the ladder of secrecy and learn that only the ones 'higher up' can decide who may know and who may not. Thus, performing secrecy involves distinction between the various echelons of disclosure, and generates social differentiation and status through ascending ranks.[22] So, inevitably, wherever secret societies operate, there is an initiation inducing youngsters toward silence, and for an example we turn to the Minyanka in Mali.

Initiation societies and the empty secret

The sacred forest, a stand of trees quite distinct in the savannah landscape, marks the western horizon of the Minyanka village in southern Mali, housing a single hut and granary between the trees. On a flat earth altar right in front of the hut a white chicken lies sprawled on its back; the initiation is under way.[23]

---

18 Which is the original meaning of the term 'secret': that which is separated.
19 Hoffman 2017: 112.
20 Bentor 1994a: 331.
21 Finkenauer 1998: 287.
22 See Simmel 1950: 315, Förster 2019: 100.
23 For this case, see Jespers 2011, 2013, and Colleyn 2002b and 2002e. For a comparison with Bamana Komo or Kòma, see Zobel 1996.

At the side of the hut a rack of headpieces of masks lines the wall, plus a few other ritual paraphernalia, including a mask costume. A Komo functionary, called 'messenger of the alliance', presents the chicken each boy brought along to the elders – 'This is the chicken of so-and-so' – who hand it over to the chief of the Komo, *komotigi*, who in his turn passes it to the chief of the knife. The latter slits its throat and lets the blood drip on the masks lined up on the low rack along the wall, invoking loudly:

> Nanakoro, old hyena,
> who calls the children of the village,
> who works like this day and night.
> Here is the chicken *perikolo* [initiation] of […].
> His parents came over to give us this chicken.
> If they came to betray the Komo,
> Please kill them, Nanakoro,
> Here is your child.[24]

The master of the knife throws the dying chicken on the ground and all watch to see how it died, on its back or on its belly, after the usual flapping and running around. It ends on its back. Good – and the men cry out '*anibari*' (you and your words), a variant on a common greeting, but mandatory during this Komo ritual. The messenger picks up the dead chicken, shows it to all people, and the master of the knife disembowels the chicken over the masks.

'Look at it', the *komotigi* commands the boy, who has to notice that the intestines have disappeared. From the hut comes a strange noise like the roar of a lion. The youngster has heard this many times before from afar, but now it is terrifying, up close and ominous. The noise is made by a friction drum that belongs to specific masks, but this he will learn only later.

> 'What do you see?'
> 'The intestines are not there any longer.'
> 'Very good. If you go tell the village what you have seen in the Komo,
> your own intestines will go into the Komo hut as well.'
> 'I will not do so', the novice is expected to answer.

The circle of initiated men in the courtyard teach the boy some passwords he should utter when he meets the mask, and then warn him, in chorus: 'May the Komo kill you if you betray him.' A last roar of the lion's voice signals to the youngster to take his leave. After him another boy takes his

---

24 Jespers 2013: 45.

place, for the same ritual, until all boys of that initiation group have had their chicken sacrificed and it has been impressed upon them that if they spill the word, they will spill their own intestines.[25]

After this first phase, the neophytes are ready to witness the mask performance at the annual ritual of the *Komo sanyèlèma*, right after the joint initiation. In the open space inside the grove, the mask tops are lined up: both types belonging to the Komo. In plain sight the headpieces of the *warakunw*, heads of beasts, lie on the ground, some packed with bristles, others without them. This is the first time the novices see them, and they are expected to greet them in a loud and clear voice with the proper formula: '*ju ta siya.*' The initiated men, seated around the masks, respond, '*ju guba*' (move your foundation/bottom), and the novices sit down, now among the initiated.

These *warakunw* headcoverings are intimidating; to the European eye they look hideous: each is a large black horizontal mask covered with stumps like warts with bundles of porcupine bristles. Everywhere the piece is coated with a thick crust of blackened blood, the result of untold sacrifices. The dome-shaped mid-part of the headpiece is set with animal skulls and with bone fragments of people who have died a bad death.[26] They presentify no specific animal, and form the epitome of the fierce wilderness – sometimes named 'hyena'.

There are two variants of *warakunw*: one without the bristles – the mothers; and one with them – the daughters; both are indeed female. Each headpiece gets its share of sacrificial blood. Still other headpieces, of the *jaraw* (lion) genre, lie in a thicket of dense bush near the grove, hidden from sight. They too are shown to the novices, and they also receive sacrifices – specific ones: a young, mature rooster and ram, all white.

Up till now all action has taken place inside the hut or the grove, but at nightfall the scene moves to the village. When the kitchen fires have died in the compounds, sounds are heard from the outside: the voices of lions. Women and uninitiated boys hide in their huts when the masked figures with the *jaraw* tops come running from the forest, circle the village, and emit a vocal roar. Most noise comes from the friction drums, but only the initiates can see that. They are fast, these masks, fleet of foot, circling the village at full speed. For the frightened women and children in the village it seems as if the roars of the lion are coming from every direction; they are

25 Ibid.: 47.
26 Despite the horror that these normally elicit: see Jespers 2011.

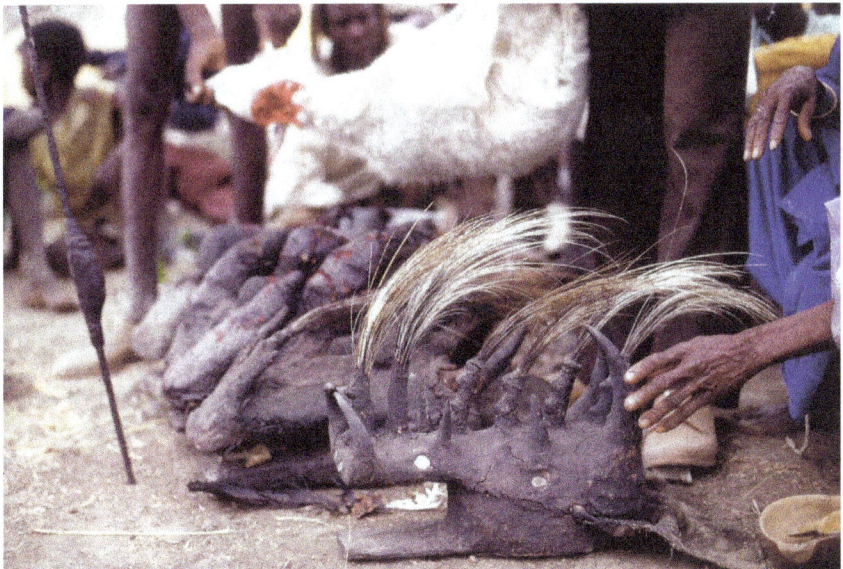

Figure 4.3. *Warankunw* masks during sacrifice in the Komo power association. Bougouro, Mali 1980. Photo: Philippe Jespers.

surrounded by the voice of the wilderness. Especially witches and sorcerers should beware, for they cannot stand this auditory onslaught. A few elders may exclaim, 'God is growling' or 'The lion has made the voice of the master heard; the child of Komo has nothing to add'.[27]

Then the *waranw* masks, the 'beasts', enter the village. Their costume is striking: a huge cloak covered in the feathers of vultures or other birds, such as guinea fowl, if there are not enough vulture feathers around, with the headpiece right on top of their head. Their tops covered with coagulated blood, these masks dance barefooted under the heavens, moving with ease and grace in their huge cloaks; without face coverings they have a good view of their surroundings; there are only initiates around. And the masks speak. In its mouth each mask has a mirliton[28] so they require an interpreter, an attendant who is also a conversation partner.

In his analysis Philippe Jespers focuses on the inversions in the *waranw*'s appearance: the cloak-costume represents a vulture but has feet on the earth; the very earthy headpiece, on the other hand, looks up to the sky

---

27 Jespers 2011: 208

28 A common instrument in masks: a reed stalk closed off with some membranes that move with the mask's breath and distort the sound of its voice.

and conveys the message of the stars to the people. From time to time the mask even lifts the headpiece straight up toward the stars. Capturing the 'light' that comes from above, the mask communicates with his interpreter, predicting the future to the initiates and as such acts as a diviner. His helper is considered blind: 'The beast's head takes the light of a star and thrusts it upon a person. The star's light falls upon them and the words come.'[29]

Compared with the initiations in the previous chapter, this first entrance of the boys into a secret society is surprisingly gentle; the pathway of pain is practically absent, with few reports of whippings. The common elements are, as ever, familiarisation with the mask and imprinting the need for secrecy and silence. Differences, however, abound in this context. The boys are initiated one by one, swearing a specific oath to an organisation of adult men, not to last year's initiates: the boys are entering a structured society with a cult centre. Power objects form the core of the association, also absent in village-based initiations, and here the mask tops themselves are among these objects. Often these objects are assemblages, which through their fusion add power to the object; in their construction, the makers 'favor materials that to their knowledge hail from diverse and sometimes distant sources'.[30] Showing them in ceremonies, or rather pointedly not showing them, highlights the power of the association. One major function of these objects is as repositories of blood sacrifices, which in other masks is not common. Finally, the separation of the genders is extreme, the non-initiates participate only as terrified listeners when the masks come out, and the main presence of the masks is via sound.[31]

The Minyanka, the group whose Komo rituals Philippe Jespers studied in southern Mali, speak a Voltaic language, but their Komo association is part of the Mande cultural complex, which comprises a much wider area. As part of a roster of similar societies, Komo associations are important,[32] dominated by blacksmiths, an endogamous group of specialists in Mande societies.[33] Especially among the Bamana peoples, the central group of the cultural complex, at least seven of these secret societies are found[34] with varying social importance. A man can be a member of more than one,

29 Jespers 2011: 210.
30 Gagliardi 2010: 141–142, 179.
31 Exceptions occur: Susan Gagliardi notes that the highly educated daughter of a leader danced in Komo ceremonies; Gagliardi 2010: 207.
32 Aden 2003; Dieterlen 1988.
33 As elsewhere in Africa, McNaughton 1988, 2002, 2008.
34 Zahan 1960; Dieterlen 1988.

and each of the associations comprises several cult centres, strewn out over the various villages. Thus, one can choose a Komo oneself, though village membership determines to some extent which one is chosen. But at the same time participation in the Koré, Ciwara, or any other association, is an open option. So these are associations of choice that initiate upon entrance after a trial period, and all of them feature masks.

Often a few women are initiated into these exclusively male societies, to cook for them and to assist them during sacrifices. This is quite usual in Africa. Such women are called, for instance, the 'sisters of the masks', and the taboo does not hold for them. They may not, however, dance with the masks themselves; they are still women, and their familiarity with the masks stems from a special initiation or from the circumstances of their birth. For instance, among the Dogon these *yasigine* are women born during a *sigi* ritual, which takes place every sixty years.

Some of the associations resemble age grades, belonging to a certain phase in one's life. The Ndomo or Ntomo association, for instance, was formerly for boys before circumcision.[35] In principle, all boys from one village were expected to aspire to membership of the Ntomo chapter of their village. It demanded an initiation – all secret societies do – and involved different masks. Age structuring was intense in Bamana society. After circumcision, the Bamana *ton*, or age-set, united all circumcised males to serve in public duties for the ward or village and in agricultural assistance, but the *ton* mainly functioned in entertainment by means of theatre and dance, the latter featuring its own masks.[36]

After the revelation of the mask in one's first secret association, what is the function of the mask in subsequent initiations? How often can a mask be 'revealed'? After the coming of sexual age, Bamana boys can choose to enter the Koré association. Initiation into this association follows the usual pattern: seclusion, some suffering, a variety of instructions, and symbolic tests. Verbal dexterity is central: they must memorise chants, recitations, riddles, special greetings and hunting magic, and practice ritualised forms of expression between initiates, such as speaking in sentences of a fixed number of words (twelve, fourteen, etc.). After one week they find their spiritual double in the water, paint their musical instruments, acquire a new soul, and purify themselves in fire. Toward the end they perform sacrifices, wrestle with each other, and at the very end of their initiation they are

35 For Ndomo and Koré, see Zahan 1960, and Colleyn 2002d. The same held for the Nupe: Nadel 1942.
36 Imperato 1980.

introduced to the mask tops, which they wash and paint again, a quite intimate way of dealing with these power objects.[37] On the very last day they perform libations over the headpieces, just before returning to the village as new Koré initiates.

In these later initiations masks have a different function, for the initiates do not form the target audience of the masks, they just prepare themselves for the mask and rejuvenate the object. The point is that mask performances in secret society initiations are not directed at the novices, but at the non-initiated people in the village. The more secret these societies are – and the more secret societies there are – the more they show themselves in public mask performances. For the Koré this is during a rain dance at the end of the dry season and at funerals in mock battles with torches to liven up the burial proceedings. The new initiates are simply the new youngsters of the troupe, the rookies who will gradually learn to dance and perform, but for the moment must just view them from the coulisses of the theatre. Mask performances of secret societies are much more public than the discourse on secrecy would suggest. Or, as Gagliardi puts it for the Senufo: 'Power associations always have an audience in mind.'[38] About the *sigma* mask in northwestern Ghana, Césare Poppi wrote: 'The existence of the "secret" must be proclaimed widely and loudly on as many occasions as possible.'[39] As billboards of the secret, masks are the public face of the initiation society: secrets must be kept, but the fact of their existence must be advertised.[40]

Even if the mask in question has neither male nor female character-istics – as exemplified by Figure 4.4 – any show of a secret society is fully gendered, and wherever masks perform, the gender arena is on stage. The power association serves as a major player in both arenas, that of gender and that of power, with the advertised secret serving as a vehicle for men to gain power over women, while in its internal discourse the process of hiding is translated into male supremacy.

The secret equals silence, and any search for cognitive content, called 'encyclopaedic content',[41] is unproductive, as it is simply the wrong quest. As early as 1971, Ervin Goffman wrote: 'As countless folk tales and initiation rites show, often the real secret behind the mystery is that there is no

---

37 Colleyn 2002a: 98, 99.
38 Gagliardi 2010: 168.
39 Poppi 2013: 187.
40 In Europe there are 'open days' to visit the buildings of secret societies such as the Freemasons, when no rituals are performed.
41 Jansen 1995.

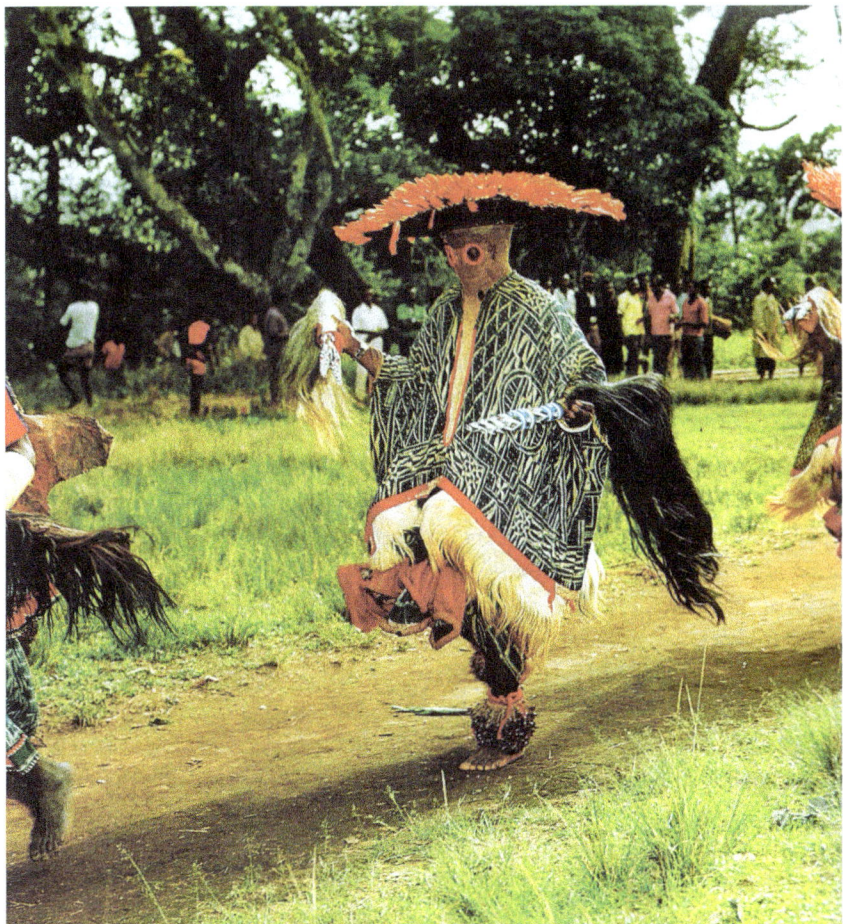

Figure 4.4. Secrecy must be advertised: the *kurosi* secret society on show with the *tso* dance. Bamenda, Cameroon, c. 1960. Photo: Michel Huet.

mystery; the real problem is to prevent the audience from learning this too.'[42] In African initiation the audience does know, but keeps its silence.[43] In the Crescent the masks embody this empty secret by enveloping it in an experience hard to put into words anyway. 'Secrets were revealed in terms so proverbial and enigmatic that I realized it would be virtually impossible to tell them, even if I wanted to', as Mary Nooter recounted her initiatory

---

42   Goffman 1971: 76.
43   Even if the audience is out of sight, this still holds: Gagliardi 2018a.

experience.[44] Till Förster explains: '"Knowing *poro*" means to have acquired the tacit knowledge that only orthopraxy conveys.'[45] Initiation entails an existential experience, not increase in knowledge.

The point is that initiatiory secrets are cognitively empty, since the basic revelation is in fact public knowledge. What the boys learn is which symbolic objects are used, the sayings and proverbs of their culture, while practising skills they have already mastered; in fact, they learn what they already knew, only better. Plus, they learn the unfathomable. Some of the texts they must memorise are hardly understandable, yet are never explained, as for Pende initiates: 'The boys learned to sing the song as they concentrated on their dance steps. Nonetheless, on examination, it turned out that the words were as opaque to them as they were to the authors of this essay. Nor did anyone attempt to explain the song to the initiates.'[46] Indeed, what is drummed into the initiands is not a body of cognitive information, but how to keep the border of secrecy intact: they learn that their 'tongue is their own worst enemy'.[47] The language game aims to keep outsiders from knowing that, after all, there is no 'real secret'.

This game of hiding leads into a world of codes. On the *ékpè* initiation in Nigeria's Cross River Region, Joseph Akpan notes: 'The main secrets are the series of code words and dance steps that a member learns when he goes through initiation.'[48] Coding and recoding are the name of the secrecy game: signs of recognition, passwords, signals, riddles, proper exchanges of greetings – all the linguistic tools to define themselves as members of the secret society, as the ones who 'know'. Hand signals and written signs may be part of the instruction. In the *ékpè* initiation society in the Nigerian Cross River Region, this has evolved into the *nbìsìdì* signs, which encode a host of items of daily culture in their own society.[49] Messages in these signs hint at hidden things, but they carry little actual content and never provide new information. Initiation codes are not Enigma machines; rather, they call up the secret society in the eyes of the initiated, messaging: 'Another one like you is here', someone from the same power configuration and the same gender. Codes define the contestants in the arenas.

---

44 Nooter 1993: 57.
45 Förster 2019: 107.
46 Strother and Kakema 2020: 269.
47 Colleyn 2002c: 188.
48 Akpan 1994: 49.
49 Miller and Ojong 2012: 273.

There is another conceptual issue with the notion of the secret. We have been using notions of both the secret and of sacred objects – like the sacred forest – say, the hidden and the holy, but these two concepts only seem different, while in fact they are very close. The secret–public polarity, which is foundational for this chapter, runs parallel to that of sacred–profane, which has developed in the study of the world's written religions, and is still a major issue in religious studies. The secret and the sacred are both defined in terms of separation and interdiction; for instance, Émile Durkheim defined the sacred as *séparé et interdit*,[50] separated and prohibited, and any definition of the secret would entail similar terms, while both are protected by taboos. The philosopher Sissela Bok comments:

> The sacred and the secret have been linked from earliest time [...]. Both are defined as being set apart and seen as needing protection. And the sense of violation that intrusion into certain secrets arouses is also evoked by intrusions of the sacred.[51]

So, what the Africans define as 'off-limits to the non-initiated' and thus 'secret', northern researchers tend to label 'sacred'.[52] Ferdinand de Jong remarks that his French-speaking Jola informants in Senegal had trouble distinguishing 'secret' from 'sacred',[53] and for good reason: in French (and in English) the two are quite similar, but Jola language has a single term to cover both: *nyau-nyau*, forbidden. The same holds for other languages: the Dogon call their main masquerade, the apogee of their ritual life, simply *dama*, forbidden.

In quite a few cultures researchers make a distinction between sacred masks and entertainment masks.[54] What is at stake is that some mask rituals are only for initiated insiders, while others are open to everyone, so the issue is relative accessibility, exactly the factor of secrecy. In this book we prefer to use another concept instead of the sacred: power, a notion that is central in indigenous religions and shows in its masquerades; Chapter 1 noted the two notions of power, interhuman and a more mystic force, and the latter is meant. For Africans, differences in accessibility represent gradations of

---

50 Van Baal and Van Beek 1985: 106, Molendijk 2010: 64.
51 Cited in De Jong 2007a: 9.
52 Middleton 1987.
53 De Jong 2007a: 8.
54 The actual term used for the 'sacred masks' seems to be 'masks of the forest': Bouttiaux 2013b; A-M. Boyer 2008.

power: some masks are more powerful than others: a power expressed by audience exclusivity, and by being consistently gendered.

A curious example of this exclusivity is the reticence that Susan Vogel reports among her Baule informants: most of their art was not to be looked at, but should be kept hidden from outsiders – which in their case was just about anyone. That held for their famous 'spirit spouse' statues, but also for a specific category of masks: 'Among the Baule, the secret's very existence must be hidden. More private than secret.'[55] The fact that there is no initiation in Baule villages is significant in this respect, as are the vivid memories of informants when they happened to stumble upon such an object.[56] On the other hand, the category of entertainment masks is well delineated: they are not 'masks of darkness', but 'masks to look at'.[57] In the emic valuation of both categories of masks, the three notions 'secret', 'sacred', and 'power', merge.

The sound of secrecy

Masquerades are loud events, shows of power and masculine noise; in Figure 4.5, just out of sight, custodians blow a bull horn, while the crowd makes rhythms with sticks.[58] The power of masks resides mostly in their soundscape, which comprises three kinds of noise: the actual sounds made by the masks themselves; the musical accompaniment of the performances; and the way they are addressed by the initiates – the mask languages.

First, masks often make animal noises; they grunt, roar, whistle, squeak, snarl, bark, growl, or bellow, imitating whatever animal they are inspired by.[59] For a dancer, non-speech comes easily since most carved headpieces are held by the teeth on an inside bit, so sound without articulation is the only option – which is essentially what animals produce. But it is seldom very loud, unless they respond as a troupe to the ritual elders. Masks sometimes carry their own instruments. As a means of preparing for their first masquerade, Dogon youngsters visit the village men's houses at night, beating small slit drums they have carved themselves: 'Toc toc tac, toc toc

---

55 Vogel 1997b; Gottlieb 1988: 123.
56 Ibid.: 125.
57 Ibid.: 136.
58 Miller's explanation: 'The *etangala* mask performance during the New Yam Festival 2016 to greet the Obol Lopon (Town Head) and his wife on the palace patio.' Ivor Miller, personal communication.
59 See for the Mumuye Bovin 2011.

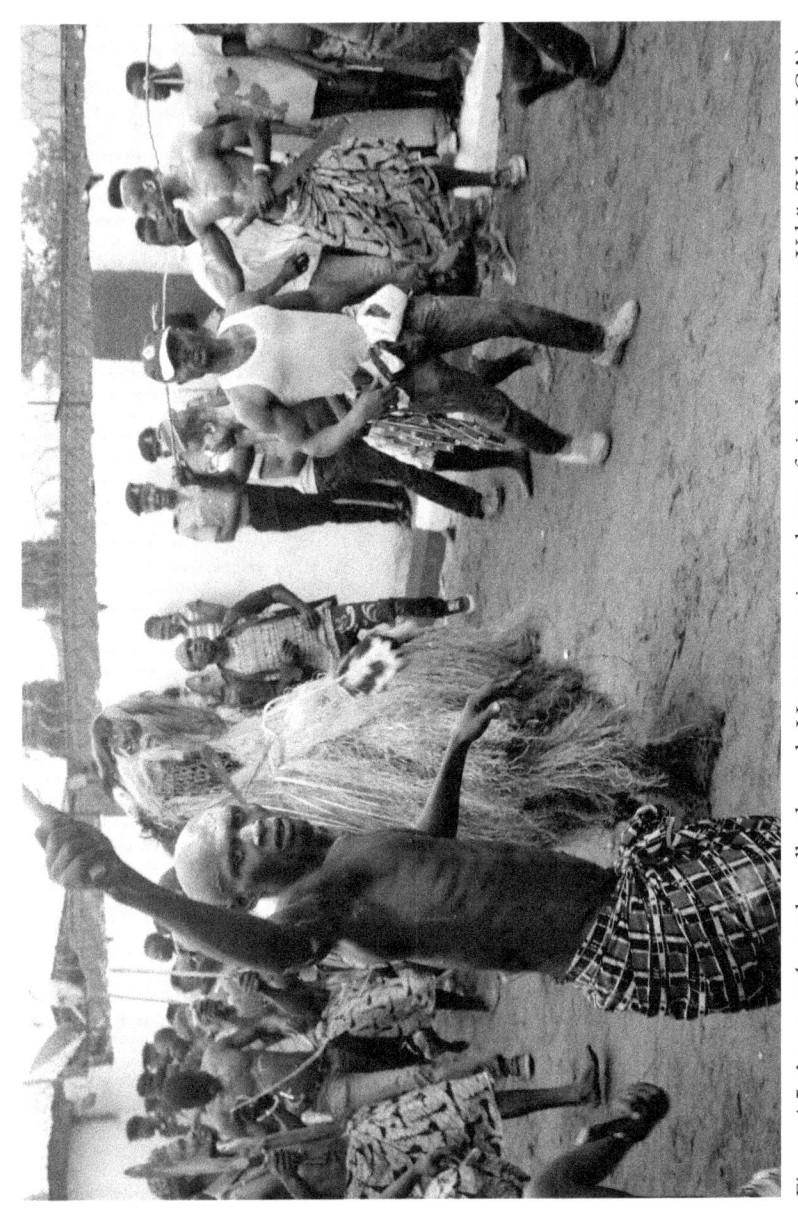

Figure 4.5. An *etangala* mask walks through Ugep town in a show of ritual testosterone. Yakö (Yakurr LGA), Cross River Region, Nigeria, 2016. Photo: Ivor Miller.

tac, toc toc tac', they advertise to the village that the mask festival is coming. They are in just long trousers, and will later dress up as proper masks, but then without their own musical devices.

But some masks are just sound and do not even exist in any material form: these 'auditory masks' consist only of noise to create the illusion of a 'presence'.[60] Such auditory masks are generated by a variety of means, always at night. For instance, a set of sheep horns are blown on one side of the town, with a group of men singing in unison; then they suddenly fall silent, and at the other side of the village another group makes the same noise, their sounds alternating. For the women hiding in the village, it sounds like the 'devil' is flying from one end to the other, as the weird sound produced is hard to interpret. Other masks announce themselves using stick drums, scrapers, flutes, horns, or bull roarers, interspersed with human voices, shrieks, and shouts by initiates, men slapping their arms against their torsos – all carefully orchestrated to create an illusionary presence. Throughout the world, bullroarers serve the same purpose with their deep roar, either single or in several places at the same time. Such a simple slice of wood, whirled at the end of a string, has a penetrating effect in the quiet of the night: the whispers of the wild, the voice of the ancestors, the mark of the mask. At Dogon funerals a bullroarer is whirled at a moment when no other masks figure; that sound is their collective presence, the great mask.

The women and children who have been ordered to remain in their huts form the awestruck audience for this acoustic violence. The mask 'is there', the mask 'walks', 'masks are everywhere' – and everyone can hear it![61] At least, that is the impression the men hope to create, and in the stillness of the night such a sudden din coming from all sides is impressive enough. One may shut one's eyes, but never one's ears. Susan Gagliardi, who as a woman researcher experienced the masks from the female side, describes these effects and remarks: 'The prohibition against women seeing certain power association performances does not exclude them from the event because they can legitimately hear and otherwise experience it.'[62] Evidently, it is less clear to children where the racket comes from; a belief in the nightly bogeyman comes easily to them. Some Kpelle boys stated that before entering the bush camp they did not know that masks were men in disguise, let alone that some masks consisted only of noise.

60 Lamp 2013: 86. See also Lamp 2011, and Jespers 1995.
61 Lifschitz 1988.
62 Gagliardi 2010: 151.

Second, a large part of the soundscape is created by the musical instruments, for masks 'expect' to be received with high acoustics, and their
public appearances are noisy feasts. Bells, horns, and scrapers accompany
the masks, as do the inevitable drums; percussion has a special relation
with rites of passage.[63] The boisterous performances contrast sharply with
the silence that reigns during the camps, the initiations, and the sacrifices,
as well as with the silence that the boys are taught over and over. Michael
Rowlands analyses loudness as a ritual expression of power. Sound penetrates
all barriers, and thus forms a major instrument conveying power differences, since the right to make loud noises tends to be one-sided. Like the
auditory masks, performances provide a sonic bath for the audience, which
is expected to listen in silence, for it is the powerful 'other' that has the
right to loud noise. Writing about masks during a death commemoration,
Rowlands remarks: 'The intention is to create a sonic envelope that includes
the powerful sound elements of animal and non-animal elements in the
bush and will exclude people of the compound of the deceased […]'.[64]
The musicians and the shouting men broadcast the power of the mask to
all within hearing distance: loud noise separates participants into powerful
producers and subordinate listeners.

The third element of the soundscape is the sound that is thrown toward
the masks, the way people address them. Only the initiated are allowed
to address the masks, the prerogative of specific ritual elders, initiators, or
village speakers. And when they speak to masks, it is seldom in common
conversation but in loud exhortations, in strong warnings, and in shouts of
praise – all part of the acoustic din that surrounds these silent be-things. But,
more important, they use a special language for the occasion: an initiation or
a mask language. This can be the language of a neighbouring group, genres
of pig Latin, or a separate secret initiation language.[65] The Bobo neophytes
were taught a special initiation language during their stay in the bush and
were regularly tested for their fluency. This language itself is not very hard to
learn but does need practice; it is a derivate language of Southern Bobo in
which common words acquire a new meaning or consonants are switched
within words, a common strategy for 'secret' languages. The Dogon of Mali
know two kinds of language: their common language and a mask language,

---

63 Needham 1967.
64 Rowlands 2007: 200.
65 Pig Latin is the generic name for play languages made by switching and reduplicating
consonants and syllables: Blake 2010: 227.

Sigi so.[66] The mask myth relates how this secret language was given to them by bush spirits, the *jinu*, in order to converse with the masks, which must be addressed in bush language. Sigi so is a restricted derivate language, showing a 20 per cent overlap in vocabulary with Dogon, and should be spoken by all males, and – officially – by no females. After each loud peroration, the masks in unison shout their high-pitched cries as a response: Sigi so is a signal language, part and parcel of the soundscape of secrecy.

This kind of initiation language is not restricted to masking societies,[67] but the idea of a secret language fits in well with the general fascination with secrecy in these cultures and with the purported male supremacy. The women of the village are considered ignorant and unable to comprehend what is said. If the mask language is a neighbouring one with a patrilocal marital residence – which is often the case – at least some wives stem from such neighbouring groups. These in-marrying women are more proficient than the men in the dialects or languages of the neighbours, and such an initiation language is easy for them. Also, pig Latin languages are not hard to decipher. Just as with the masks, the women's professed ignorance is part of the carefully constructed edifice of male dominance.

Ethics, society, and secrecy

To a large extent secrecy is a language game, and it is an engaging one. Constructing secrets, keeping them in a closed group, distinguishing oneself from others through the veiled disclosure of their existence – all this is great fun[68] and begins at an early stage in life.[69] As Oscar Wilde put it in *The Picture of Dorian Gray*: 'The commonest thing is delightful if only one hides it',[70] an enjoyment that becomes alluring when tied to a secret organisation. In Zambia, Kenji Yoshida noted how young Chewa boys were fascinated by the secrets of the Nyau, the power association, and in their own boys' masquerade constructed their own 'secrets' – meaning riddles and codes as variations on the adult ones.[71] This rendered the passage into adult society easy later in life. Both the child's and the adult's play with secrecy is seductive

---

66 Leiris 1948.
67 The Sara in southern Chad have an initiation language and no masking tradition: Jaulin 1971.
68 Luhrman 1989.
69 Ottenberg 1982.
70 Cited in Wegner et al. 1994: 8.
71 Yoshida 2006: 223–225.

since it creates distinction between the knowing and the ignoramus, offering a fascinating form of symbolic capital.

That attraction is only increased when the media write about secret societies, such as the Nyau. A southern African tabloid reported in a piece entitled 'Going behind the Nyau masquerade',[72] that 'bizarre and unspeakable things' happened during the initiation rituals. The term 'unspeakable' is right on the spot, though in a more literal sense than the journalist meant: people indeed cannot speak about it; as to 'bizar', the most 'bizar' things tend to be for public show. Such a report does help in heightening the attraction and power of the secret society, and highlights the notion that some people 'own' rituals that others lack. Secrets are property, as Simmel's classic work stresses, and as such a way of elevating oneself:

> The strongly emphasised exclusion of all outsiders makes for a correspondingly strong feeling of possession. For many individuals, property does not fully gain its significance with mere ownership, but only with the consciousness that others must do without it.[73]

Hiding induces scarcity, so secrecy adds value to ownership, expressed as power, and the orchestration of disclosure is read as 'implying that secrets are too powerful to make public'.[74] The secret is an 'adorning possession' made more powerful because its exact nature remains vague.[75] Or in the words of Mary Nooter: 'The substance of secrets is less important than the social delineation resulting from their acquisition, ownership and controlled revelation.'[76] 'Controlled' is the operative word, for the excluded others should know that they have no access to that 'property'; as Fredrik Barth put it: 'The value of information is inversely proportional to how many share it'[77] – at least, the number who can avow that they share it.

If secrets are an asset to be cherished and an argument for power among groups,[78] they can be sold or bought as part of an economic transaction, a kind of property that in the hands of secret societies can become economic capital. Secrets can be monetised, and in fact they are continuously converted

---

72 See https://www.sundaymail.co.zw/stranger-than-fiction-going-behind-the-nyau-masquerade, consulted 15 January 2021.
73 Simmel 1950: 332.
74 Luhrman 1989: 139.
75 Newell 2013: 141.
76 Nooter 1993: 60.
77 Barth 1973: 217.
78 Simmel 1950.

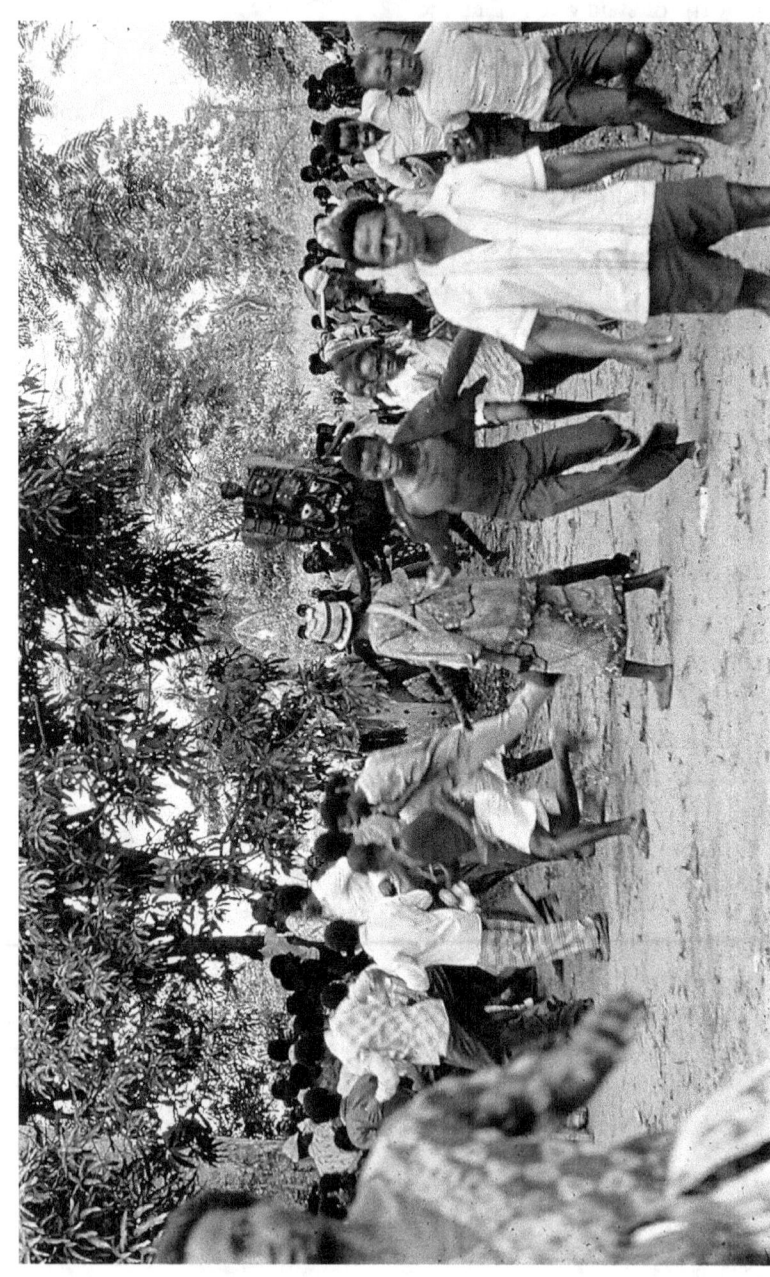

Figure 4.6. The power of secrecy: when the *epa ekpo* mask comes into view, the uninitiated flee but the initiated man in the middle does not react; there are no women present. Annang Ibibio, Cross River Region, Nigeria, 1976. Photo: Jill Salmons.

into cash: advancement through the ranks of the society is expensive, both in fees and feasts, and people must pay their way up the ladder. But also between communities this can be the case. The nineteenth century in Ekpo, Cross River Nigeria, saw a strong growth in secret societies; central lodges branched out over various ethnic groups and 'turned a handsome profit in selling the rights to secret lore necessary to set up certain of the secret societies'.[79] This seems contradictory since secrets are empty, but what is commoditised are the authority and the right to disclosure that are essential in the whole secrecy complex. Ute Röschenthaler, who traced the network of *ékpè* purchases throughout the Cross River Region, noted how the relay of the secrecy complex gave rise not only to a meshwork of monetary transactions, but also to guardianship over the correct implementation of these *ékpè* branches.[80] The model of a chain of franchise holders easily comes to mind. One corollary of this structure is a certain conservatism in these associations and performances: they are bought and licensed in this way and would lose the authority of the source if too many changes were made. Franchises do not lead to innovation.

In its inherent authority the 'secret produces an enormous enlargement of life',[81] always hinting at an invisible presence just around the corner; the fact that there is nothing there makes no difference. It may be an illusion, but one that rests upon authority. For this reason, the auditory masks offer such a clear example of the 'mask illusion': present in sound but always out of sight, perennially invisible yet an acoustic imposition, they embody the constructed nature of the secret, highlighting the fact that at the heart of the initiation is an empty secret, a cognitive vacuum, and even an acoustic presence is not strictly required. One Jola mask is completely mythical; people speak about it, but it never appears, is never even heard, and all authors agree that it does not really 'exist'. Of course, that mask is considered the most powerful of all, too powerful to really come on stage.[82] Perhaps one could call this the ultimate mask, the one that nobody sees or hears and nobody wears or dances, a mask constructed by words only, a real secret. In any case, what does it mean to 'exist', in masks or in secrets?

Since secrecy can exist well without proper content, the dynamics of secrecy and thus of producing 'secrets' will not stop at initiation, for secrecy

---

79 Miller and Ojong 2012: 279.
80 Röschenthaler 2004, 2011. For the history of a single masquerade in this tradition, see Nicklin and Salmons 1988.
81 Simmel 1950: 330.
82 Langeveld 2003; more on this mask in Chapter 6.

creates immaterial capital that can grow by adding more 'secrets'. This alluring play on secrecy knows no end, and newly constructed secrets serve as tools in attaining ever higher initiation ranks. Consequently, secret societies always have internal grades: initiates are expected to move toward higher levels of secrecy – meaning, to breach other linguistic and behavioural fences. There is no end to secrecy, since it is not a state but a process, not about content but about distinction. Thus, *poro* societies have various echelons within them, each shrouded in its own secrets and with its own linguistic border protection.

There is one difference: these higher grades are sub-associations of equals, colleagues in fact, so they no longer have public secrets at their disposal that could be 'revealed'. They can, however, express occult progress in other ways. One is the genre of mask that is used in ceremonies, such as masks abounding in the symbolism of royalty and power. Thus, the *kalengula* mask of the Leopard society among the Bakwa Luntu comes on stage in an enormous headdress of feathers with a carved top in the shape of a ram, another symbol of kingship, while the costume sports a leopard skin, the ubiquitous royal sign throughout much of Africa.[83] Secrets are ranked, and so are masks.

Another way to show advancement in ranks is by very small tops. The *bwami* association of the Lega in DRC highlights its ladder of esoteric progression: members of the most advanced level in the second-highest grade are permitted to have miniature masks – maskelettes, as the author calls them.[84] In public dances these are proudly shown, in the hands, on the body, against the head; they are usually inherited from family members or other high-graders. Showing off such a maskelette in the public dance indicates another level of intimacy with the mask, one of holding the keys to masking.

But masks are less efficient in producing secrecy here, so these higher grades need different ways to distinguish themselves from similar groups or lower grades. How to construct ever more 'secrets'? The answer lies, as often, in coding. Fredrik Barth found among the Bakhtaman in Irian Jaya that further grades reversed the earlier teachings: what in an earlier grade was right was now left; what was bad was now good.[85] New 'content' means code switching. In a way, this is a recipe for endless initiations: the codes will be reversed at the next sub-stage of secrecy, and that is exactly what happens. If some content does enter, it is of a personalised kind. In Africa such sub-grades often specialise in various types of medicines (involving both herbal/somatic and magical means), and most of this knowledge is of the magical kind

---

83 Petridis 2005: 55, 58. The same holds for their Luluwa neighbours: Petridis 2005a.
84 Kingdon 1995: 301.
85 Barth 1987.

and highly individualised. At his initiation the aspirant member is tested on whether he knows what medicine belongs to whom. Bellman recounts how he was probed for such a higher grade. Among a range of 'medicines' he had to pick the 'head medicine'; he pointed at several, and each time one of the men present told him that was his medicine – so finally he chose the right one, and thus he passed.[86] This kind of 'knowledge' finds its foundation in the recoding of reality rather than in actual knowledge, reflecting a similar process in masquerades.

Since secrecy produces power, medicine as an African power source is often mentioned in association with masks. Hans Koloss points at this as the way the Cameroonian Oku define their masks, as be-things with medicines,[87] and one mask among the Nigerian Ebira dances with a large bundle of medicine on its forehead; this pig mask is one of few in that tradition with a headcover, and thus may be seen by women.[88] The term medicine covers all magical means of whatever source and kind, that are deemed powerful: medicine is materialised power. The same holds for the sacrifices performed on headpieces: the sacrificial blood enhances the power of the object, with visual remains that should stay. Even if their content is virtual, the power of secrets is real.

Secrecy is seductive and has a complicated relation with ethics.[89] On the inside of the secrecy game, ethics reign. What the boys learn in the camp is propriety: to show respect for the elders, for the masks, and for their instructors, but also for women, for their mothers and sisters, and for authorities and foreigners. They must be polite, submissive, helpful, diligent, and they must work hard. In short, the norms and values of the society at large are hammered into them, and they learn that the secret societies should help people in need and be supportive of governments and of village secular authorities.[90] In a very direct way, ethics inherent in the organisation are tied to the taboos on disclosure, so the two, social ethics and disclosure ethics, are inextricably mixed: whoever discloses without authority is defined as antisocial,[91] and also in this way secrecy reinforces the ethical side of masculinity.

On the outside, however, this ethical side is not evident. As the Nigerian Afikpo say: 'Masks show that the secrets are everywhere',[92] but secrets also

---

86 Bellman 1984: 51.
87 Koloss 2012.
88 Picton 2009: 307.
89 Schulz 2000.
90 Akpan 1994: 53.
91 See Ugwu 2017.
92 Ottenberg 1982: 176.

create distrust. Secrecy is a game with high stakes, which when well played produces a tight-knit village society, connected in a large network with other similar villages. The warp of secular authority and the woof of power associations can produce a social fabric of authority that would otherwise be much more fragile. But as scholars point out, this authority is hegemonic, cannot be contradicted, and may well be oppressive.[93] David Pratten[94] convincingly shows how, in both colonial and anti-colonial fiction, the mysteries of the so-called man-leopard murders in Sierra Leone and Nigeria used a compelling imagery of secrecy, with pernicious rumours linking crimes to secret societies and their masks. For the excluded, the secret is unpredictable, uncontrollable, and thus an easy target for conspiracy theories. Once things go wrong, the association harbouring it becomes an easy scapegoat: secrecy takes a toll on trust.

Consequently the high internal moral stance of secret societies stands in sharp contrast with their reputation in the outside world – and within Africa, where they are often feared, distrusted, and blacklisted, viewed with apprehension and scorn. In Europe they have been persecuted, and governments in Africa have also reacted to them. For instance, the *poro* system in Guinea has been outlawed and its initiations have been forbidden – and yet according to *poro* lore the whole system stemmed from Guinea. Thus, in this country the system went underground, and Guineans come to Liberia and Sierra Leone for their initiation.[95]

The standard accusation against *poro*-like societies is murder: killing people to make medicines. In indigenous medicine sacrifices form a common element of medication, and tales of human sacrifice come easily. However, ethnography has shown that stories of homicide and cannibalism are very efficient means of 'othering', by defining the other group as sub-human, and that the actual incidence of these atrocities is much lower than the tales would lead one to believe. This does not mean it cannot happen – for instance *muti* (medicine) murders are known in South Africa and elsewhere – but in fact there is no evidence tying this evil to secret societies, just rumour and the fear of the secret. The intense communication within these societies renders such atrocities implausible, and any blatant transgression of their ethical stance is likely to be an individual aberration. The Mande *jeli* (bards) explicitly state that anyone who commands the secrets must be thoroughly ethical. The master of

---

93   Miller 2011; oppressive even up to the point where secret societies were involved in the slave trade: see Pratten 2007: 52.
94   Pratten 2007.
95   Bellman 1980.

the word must be credible, which depends not just on delivering a believable story but also on moral rectitude. Only a righteous man carries authority in the words he utters and certainly in the secrets he conceals, masks included.[96]

As we look at how actual masquerades play into both arenas, rituals associated with secret societies show how the two are linked: gender and power merge as connected arenas. The masks separate both genders as effectively as their initiation societies do; we see a certain symmetry in the male and female societies, but the latter are rare. It is essential that secrets produce power, both between the genders and between echelons of male initiations, so in both arenas. Masks and power associations are joined at the hip, and if anything guarantees the survival of masquerades it is the secret society. Like the border between the genders, the border of the secret is carefully patrolled, and masks seem to be its most effective guardians.

Conclusion

Secret societies are linked closely to Type C communities, and the cases discussed in this chapter fall well within our masking parameters. Manding, Bamana, and Minyanka are core groups in the larger Mande cultural area and share much history between them. All are based on rain-fed horticulture in a dry savannah environment; the people live in an open terrain with few defensive options, part of a long history involving slavery. Type C communities with defensive villages are thus well represented, each in its own way, harbouring powerful secret societies, most of which have masks as a focus point of cultural attention. The *poro–sande* complex, like that of the Kpelle, finds its base in the Type D forest frontier villages to the south of Zone 1; we will come back on the *sande* in Chapter 6. Zone 3 is the natural habitat for Type D with its proclivity for secret societies, a trend recognisable in the societies of Pende, Lega, and Luntu.

---

96 Jansen 2018a, Jansen and Roth 2000.

5

Death and its Masks

'The acceptance of death is the highest point on the way of initiation'

(Hampaté Bâ, in Fölmi 2015: 256)

Singing at the mask

Silently gazing at the compound entrance, a dozen men sit in one corner of the courtyard, one of them with a drum. They are tired, as they have just finished over two hours of singing in front of the house of Balugo Say, whose funeral this is. Together they have sung the twelve mask songs, each to its own melody and drum rhythm, each repeated six times. None of the singers was allowed to move, stand up, or talk during the performance, which went on for hours; but now they are finished. Content after a job well done, they wait for the last phase of the complicated liturgy of the Dogon funeral, for with their singing they have set the stage for the appearance of the mask, to round off the farewell to the deceased. Silently and almost surreptitiously, an ajagai mask walks into the compound, led by an elder. The headpiece of this all-fibre mask consists of a plaited hood with eyes on all sides,[1] its costume a thick flurry of red fibres over black trousers. The two climb the forked ladder onto the roof of Balugo's house. Down in the yard, all watch the mask and its attendant dance alongside all the corners of the roof; nobody utters a word as this mask operates in absolute silence. After dancing, the mask climbs down, enters the house, and takes a few personal belongings from the chest of the deceased. As quietly as it performed, the mask emerges from the house, looks around seemingly without noticing anyone, and then runs to a nearby cavern where it throws Balugo's belongings into a deep crevasse. As a red shadow it disappears between the rocks and houses of the village and never comes back to the house. One by one the singers slowly take to their feet, speak in hushed voices, and go home. Balugo has left now — he has really, truly left; and the long wait for the second funeral is on, to take place in the next years.[2]

---

1 The name refers to a stinging insect.
2 This did not materialise owing to political insecurities in Mali. The funeral was in 2008, and the second funeral is still not in sight.

In Africa funerals are core rituals. 'Your funeral is the most beautiful day of your life', is an expression often heard about African funerals. Marc Bloch once remarked: 'In South-east Asia one can write a monograph on birth, in Africa on death'[3] – and that is precisely the case. Funeral dances and celebrations magnify the deceased's former greatness, since in these dances all deceased are pictured larger than life, being ritually 'over-conceived', glorified in their final and finest hour, an apotheose of ultimate identity. The community stresses their great achievements, emphasising the great loss for those who remain behind and their deep inability to cope with a future without the deceased, but express this in a great and captivating show. Africans confront death with a vigorous assertion of life and thus turn from grief and sorrow to 'a realisation of life in its most intense quality'.[4] Such an exuberant performance of the deceased's life is what underlies most spectacular African death rituals, in order to face death properly and to propel the kinsman without regrets onto the voyage without return.[5]

The reason for the importance of death rites is fundamental: Africa is a continent of relations, of links and networks between human beings – through kinship, friendship, membership of associations, and territorial and commercial relations, but relations first and foremost. One's social persona in Africa depends primarily on other persons, and the definition of self or identity depends on one's position in that meshwork of relationships. Elaborate birth rituals are rare on the continent, since a baby has no links yet to anyone other than its mother. During its lifetime the newborn slowly accrues relations, and thus gradually acquires an identity; they are not born someone, but they become someone. The death of an old African man or woman, on the other hand, involves the loss of a nodal point in the fabric of society, and these knotted relations must be disentangled and severed, so their social identities are acted out in large funeral performances.

Most funerals on the continent do not feature masks; but within the three zones, if masks are present, they usually appear somewhere in the farewell liturgy. Many reports on masking state that masks dance at funerals,[6] but what exactly their performance entails is often not very clear. In modern times funerals have changed much owing to Islamisation and Christianisation, and the role of masks in funerals has decreased. Nevertheless, when masks do appear,

---

3   Marc Bloch, personal communication.
4   Wilson 1939: 24, cited in Metcalfe and Huntington 1991: 57.
5   See Van Beek et al. 2022.
6   As among the Yoruba, Chewa, Limba, Bobo, Jola, Ekperi, Kuba, Kurumba, Hemba, Bobo, Baule and Guro. For an overview, see Bouttiaux 2009b: 207–227. A more detailed description on the Mossi is found in Roy 1979: 80–87.

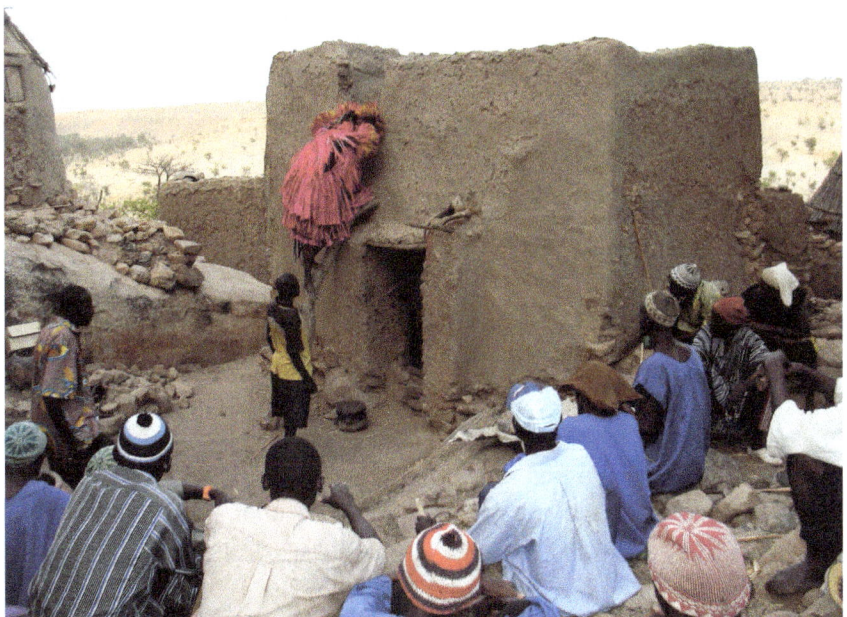

Figure 5.1. The *ajagai* climbs on the roof of the deceased's house with the elders, who have just sung the farewell songs, watching. Tireli, Dogon, Mali, 2008. Photo: Walter van Beek.

they have a significant role inside a much wider ritual repertoire, and we will gauge how the social arenas shine through in defining the deceased's identity.

Funerals are large and complex rituals, so it helps to distinguish phases in the ritual proceedings. As for terminology, burial is the handling and inhumation of the bodily remains, and the first funeral is the collective farewell that the community bids the deceased. Both can be done at the same time, as in Western societies where the burial is the apogee of the funeral. But in Africa these often are separated. After this first farewell comes an intermediate period of mourning and adjustment, the liminal period. Then, sometimes after years, this in-between period is concluded by commemorative rituals, a ritual complex called the second funeral. So the structure of African funerals, first-*cum*-second, is three-fold:

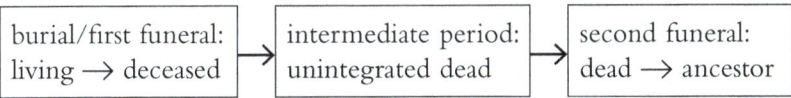

Figure 5.2. The basic structure of funerals in Africa.

This is a similar triad to that of initiation: separation, liminal period, and reintegration, only over a longer time scale. Whereas the first funeral marks the transition from living kinsman to dead person, the second funeral embodies the change from deceased to ancestor, and thus elaborate second funerals are the hallmark of societies where being an ancestor comprises the final identity.[7]

Burial and the farewells

One major aspect of the whole complex of funeral rites is that they 'establish social continuity despite the mortality of human beings',[8] and it is this continuity that dominates social analysis. But the fragility of life is basic, and one should never lose sight of the emotional aspect of rituals, and certainly not of death rites. First and foremost there is grieving, since these rituals are essentially about loss, about a forced farewell from a loved one, and they give form to this final separation. Such deep emotions are universal in humankind, but various cultures have found diverging ways of handling them, using rituals as tools for psychological coping. Although our analysis focuses on collective effects on the community, these emotions should not be lost from sight.

The rituals of the first funeral effectuate three kinds of farewell:[9] from the living person, from the corpse, and from the social persona. The first stage can be called 'cultural mourning'. The living must realise that someone they knew and loved is has transited from life to death and will change further very quickly, the blunt reality of biological death. From beloved kinsman to stinking corpse is a matter of days, especially in the tropics; this short window of transition implies that the community must redefine the deceased very rapidly from a person into a thing. Mourning provides the cultural means to do so, highlighting the deceased's identity, especially his belonging to a particular family.

Lamentations, mainly by the women, commence immediately after death and last until the burial. The inner circle of kin must communicate the death while they mourn, for their private loss must quickly become public, embedded as the private identity is inside larger social circles. The act of dying is as silent as can be, but the crying, wailing, and shouting

---

7   The classic study is Hertz 1907.
8   La Fontaine 1985: 115.
9   Following Metcalfe and Huntington 1991.

that ensue give vent to emotions and spread news of the death by sound. At some stage, musicians come in, such as the West African griots[10] or smiths,[11] for mourning requires dancing and dancing demands music, so the noise level rises.[12] Death has its definite soundscape, an event for loud, explosive bangs. Sound mobilises the larger social environment and draws the larger community into the loss – musicians first, then the more removed kin, lineage elders, and representatives of age groups. Among the Dogon, the youngsters of the family climb up onto the roof of the deceased's hut and fire blanks with their flintlock guns. In these cliffside villages the sound of the explosions – they charge their muskets as heavily as they can – ricochets against the high cliff and rolls over the whole village. Incidental shots may indicate a hunter, but a continued volley of gunfire is unmistakable: death has arrived.

This first stage exudes only grief and a deep sense of loss. The mourners laud the great person the deceased was, the 'house post that has crumbled', and lament their profound loss, defining themselves as orphans, a common theme in African mourning: 'Where can we go? We are all alone now.' With the loss of this person, all identities are changed. Cultural mourning starts with 'de-conceiving' the living person into a dead one,[13] and thus redefines the kinsman as a corpse. By public grieving, the family also evens out the emotional impact of their loss: while expressing acute pain over the bereaved, they assuage their own emotions by increasing those of other participants, thus homogenising grief. This cultural form is intended as a support and a help, but may not be sufficient for people who feel the bereavement acutely. Jean-Paul Colleyn noted a girl who grieved for her dead mother and had to be induced to dance, for that was 'the way we do it'. Her heart was not in it, but she reluctantly started to pace out her grief on the floor to the rhythm of the music; it seemed to help.[14] The first author witnessed how his Dogon informant, Meninyu, led the other elders in the funeral of his close friend, Yengulu, and then had to step aside for a moment and grieve in silence. After wiping his tears, he joined the others, resumed dancing, and from there could take the lead in the rituals again. Masks are not involved with the individual persona of the departed, so this first farewell does not

10 Jansen 1995.
11 Van Beek 2015.
12 Metcalfe and Huntington 1991: 38.
13 Barley 1995: 117.
14 Colleyn 1987.

feature them. Masks neither wail nor mourn; they are be-things that arouse emotions but are not supposed to have them.

The next stage is the farewell from the corpse itself, the burial, and most of the corpses in Africa are inhumed, a farewell in which the logistics dominate: time is short, and the corpse can be around for a few days only. In the vignette, Balugo's corpse was not in sight. A few hours after his demise his body had been wrapped in a white cotton blanket, placed on a bier, and covered with its personal death blanket. Warned by the gunshots that Balugo's sons had fired from his roof, young kinsmen arrived from the ward; two of them took the bier on their heads, and with other barefooted and barebreasted youngsters in tow, they made the deceased 'ride as a cavalier' to his grave. The Dogon do not have to dig a grave; the caverns right above their heads high up in the cliffside serve as the last abodes for the dead, so burial can be very quick. It was in one of those caves that the carriers removed a heap of bones from his predecessors, placed Balugo's body, and covered it with the old bones of his ancestors.

Not all burials are that quick. In the Kuba funeral the body is kept above earth as long as possible, for their leave-taking liturgy is based upon a present corpse, and people must prepare. So they bury after three days, which is about as long as Africans can postpone burials without cooling technology, just long enough for the whole social network of the deceased to come to the funeral, witness the deceased in person, and participate in the farewell dance.[15] Not only the family must de-conceive the deceased, so does the wider circle of relatives and relations, which takes time.

But identity is not just a series of nesting circles, up to the larger social identity, it can also itself be an arena. The first issue in any burial is who the corpse belongs to. In Western societies, where burial and funeral coincide, the family makes all decisions regarding the funeral, meaning the widow or widower and the children; the undertaker does not deal with the family at large, nor with the deceased's close friends or colleagues, though church affiliation may determine who runs the funeral-*cum*-burial ceremonies. National laws set the limits for the corpse's disposal, but strife over inheritance is almost a cliché in the West.[16] In African societies the ownership of the corpse is more complicated, and can become an overt arena. A famous court case in 1986 in Kenya had to decide between the rights of the widow and those of

---

15 As among the Kapsiki of North Cameroon, Van Beek 2015.
16 The state is present in all burials through the so-called 'necropolitics', Ferrandiz and Robben 2015, but less in Africa than in other continents.

the deceased's lineage.[17] After the death of her Luo husband, who had been a prominent lawyer, his widow from the Kikuyu – a group with different burial customs – wanted to bury him at their Nairobi farm where they had lived all their married life. However, his younger brother – on behalf of the patriclan to which the deceased belonged – wanted to bury him in Luo grounds, following Luo ethnic customs. Who had the legal right to bury the remains of the deceased? The District Court decided in favour of the widow, but this verdict was later reversed by the Court of Appeal. The legal arguments in both courts assessed the relative weight of the colonial-derived official law in its confrontation with customary law – in this case the Luo one. Both types of law are recognised in Kenya, as they are in most of Africa, so in judicial terms this was a typical case of dual law conflict. Ultimately, the deceased lawyer found his resting place in Luo territory – where he had never been before.

This was outside the Crescent, where the identity arena pitted the widow – so the nuclear family – against the patrilineage. Inside the Crescent the lineage is less strong, and in general the ward, age group or secret society tend to handle the corpse and organise the funeral; in Balugo's case his sons cleaned his body and then handed it over to the young men of the ward, so to the age group. Also a specialist group such as the blacksmiths, a group with a special status often as a caste-like organisation, may have major role in the funeral proceedings,[18] as part of the larger community.

The third stage of farewell focuses on the social persona and highlights the separation of the individual from the community, and it is here that the masks operate. The example comes from the Senufo living at both sides of the border between Burkina Faso and Côte d'Ivoire, a group where masks are present in many rituals, and certainly during this first funeral.

Burial by masks

An old man has died, a respected member of the *poro* of his village,[19] and his family prepares itself for the many things that must be done. Women

---

17 See https://hitchhikersguidetolaw.wordpress.com/2015/06/15/death-and-burial-in-the-african-context-a-case-study-on-kenyan-customs-and-kenyan-customary-law/, consulted 29 May 2020.

18 For the Fali, inside the Crescent, see Gauthier 1969, and the Kapsiki just beyond it, Van Beek 2015.

19 The description is based on a funeral among the Fodonon, a subgroup of the Senufo.

immediately start to mourn for their beloved one, and his son sends a messenger to inform the *poro* lodge. While the news of death quickly spreads through the village, the *poro* members gather in the lodge to make their masks ready for the ritual. At the house the family mourns all night, while a son gathers the honour signs the deceased has accrued in his life and places them at the door for everyone to see. Among these signs is a staff for the best cultivator, a much-prized distinction. In the following days, guests start arriving, kinsmen and neighbours who present large gifts to the family. Kinsmen usually arrive with food, as many people must be hosted; friends and *poro* relations hand over cloth and baskets for the burial. Senufo society is matrilineal and patrilocal, so lineage members tend to live far apart, and these arrivals will go on for a considerable time. Death means collecting obligations, and in the villages further away people consider what they will have to contribute to the funeral, which can take on the form of dance teams, a *kpoye* (xylophone) or a harp-lute.[20]

When they are sure that everybody knows of their loss, the women start a long cycle of mourning songs, called the 'cord of weeping', extolling the virtues of the dead. Just before noon they hear drumming from the sacred forest, and they stop. Quickly all uninitiated persons hide behind huts and doors, out of the way, because the *poro* of their kinsman is coming, and these loud drums are the sound of secrecy. The first masks to appear are red-brown apparitions with large tufts of fiery-red fibres on their heads and arms, whirling around, dancing, jumping, and running – very agile. These *nafiri*[21] will serve as guardians of the ensuing dances, as the masters of ceremonies, a whole troupe of them. Strange bush-creatures they may be, but first they greet the deceased, for he was one of them. With a crack of their whip they order the drums to be silent, and then they start their ritual greeting. Backing and stooping under the low doorway, they circle the body three times and then walk over it, ever backward, also three times, then leave the house, again walking backward. Once outside they immediately engage in a fierce dance, lashing out at each other with long fibre whips; after all, the deceased has suffered for his younger fellow *poro* members, so now some suffering from their side is his rightful due. The men of the family and the neighbours close in on their performance, but the women keep their distance. After a tour of

---

20   Glaze 1981: 160

21   *Nafiri* is a special mask found only among *jeli* of Manding origin and in the region of Dikodougou among the Fodonon, while absent in most parts of Senufoland. We thank Till Förster for this information.

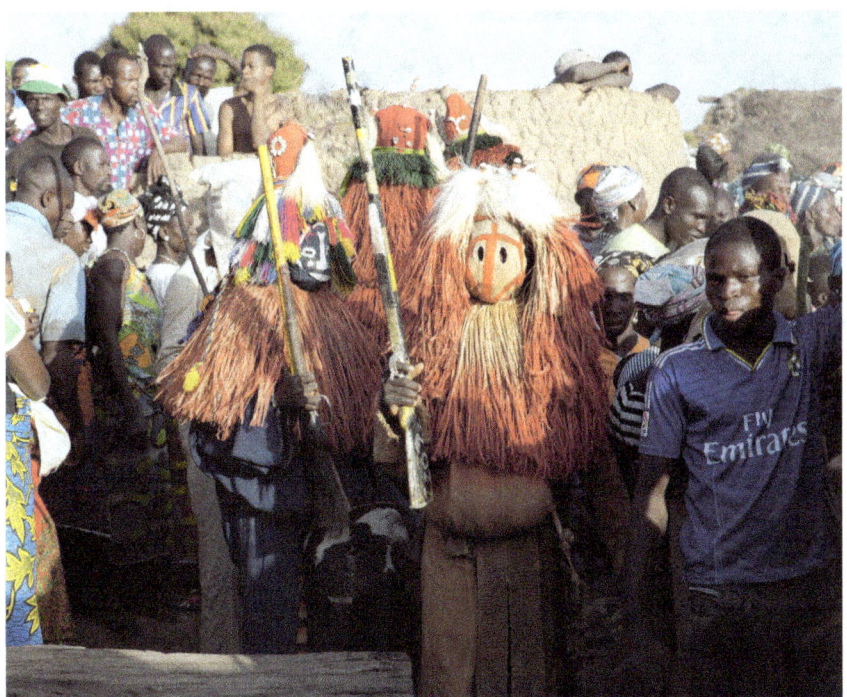

Figure 5.3. The *yalajo* masks, here carrying toy rifles, are highly social masks who like to be in the thick of things. Senufo, Côte d'Ivoire, 2016. Photo: Till Förster.

the village, in which they collect cowry shells for the *poro*, the *nafiri* masks head back to the huts in the sacred forest.

In the afternoon, a different sound pervades the courtyard, the strange buzzing of mirlitons, voice disguisers: the *yalajo* masks are coming, the funny ones. The family is the first to greet them and to receive blessings when the masks call upon the ancestors for good health. These masks look clownish and do act the part, but jesting is more than mere amusement.

In fact, it is less the face that is considered funny than the language. *Yala* is the onomatopoetic part of the name and means 'to babble'. The masks speak to everybody they encounter at the ritual site, ask 'funny' questions that only initiates of *poro* will understand and answer correctly. The masks thus know who is entitled to watch the following rites and who is not. Till Förster relates how some young townspeople arrived on their motorcycles, and the masks immediately focused on them, since they were clearly not *poro* members. A

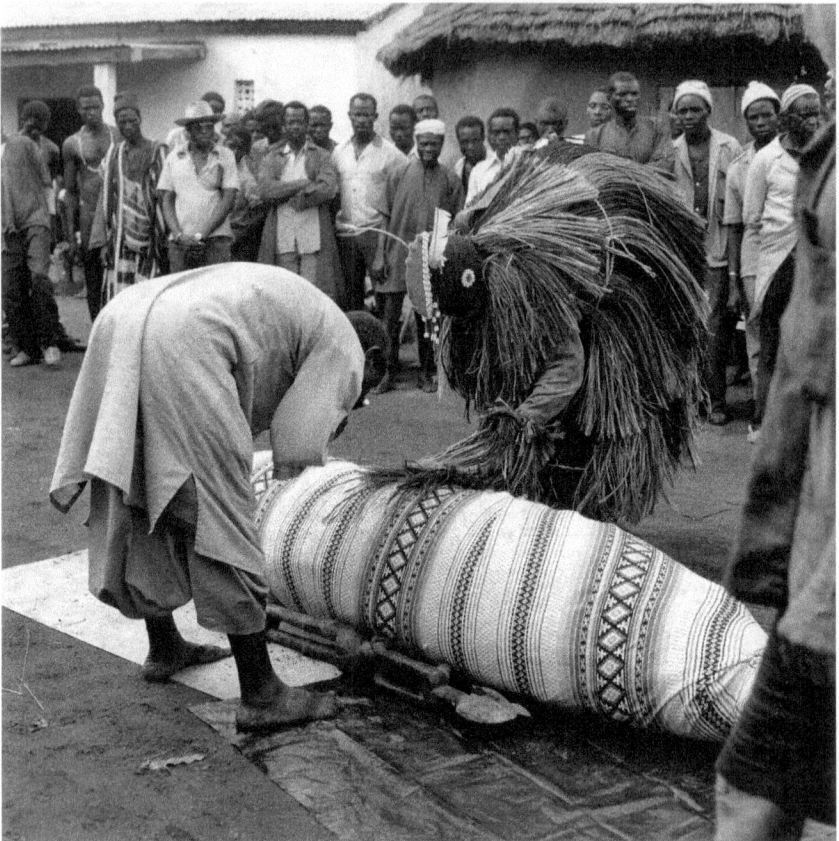

Figure 5.4. A ropemaker mask, assisted by a ritual elder, prepares a corpse for burial, while an exclusively male audience watches the proceedings. Tyelihaka, Côte d'Ivoire, 1986. Photo: Till Förster.

yalajo mask offered them a cowry shell and a little plastic doll without arms,[22] and with his disguised voice posed some seemingly absurd questions, which were in fact passwords for members of the *poro*. The young bikers failed the test, were severely chastised with the whips and had to pay up.

While the family and the rest of the village begin dressing for the funeral proceedings, the hunters' association appears, clothed in the special costumes one sees throughout West Africa: earth-coloured vests covered with amulets and medicine holders. Though important throughout West Africa, they are not

---

22 Or some other insignificant little object, a rusty nave of a bicycle, or an old school book: Förster 1988: 47.

masks. Storytelling is their forte, and the night will be filled with it. During the night bards arrive, another specialist group, who with their one-stringed harp-lutes regale the audience with well-known recitations and songs between individual mask performances.

The burial itself follows soon afterwards, either the next day or some days later in the case of a large event, and during the burial the family gradually cedes the stage in favour of the *poro*. After elaborate preparations, a large group of *poro* initiates of the various initiation classes comes from the sacred grove to the village with an ensemble of musicians and two specific masks called *gbon*.[23] The latter form the centre of the performance and wear crimson and cream-coloured fibre costumes, holding a walking stick in each hand. Their large helmet top sports long antelope horns and an open snout with teeth, ears, and large eyes; so the bush has fully arrived.[24] On their way to the compound they drop to their knees as a gesture of respect for the dead man; rising again, they lean on their walking sticks and shake and tremble as if they are old people. In the meantime, diggers have prepared the grave, an underground burial chamber, and three *poro* elders butcher a goat at the graveside. All matrilineal kinsmen present, plus friends and age-mates, partake of the meat.

The family moves in again for the next social highpoint, a ceremony of cloth-giving. All the relations of the deceased present their gift of cloth to his oldest son, as a sign of appreciation and an opening for future relations with the family – including marriages. A stack of these cloths are chosen as burial cloths; and when the *poro* elders sew the body into the cloths, another mask, the ropemaker mask, watches the proceedings.[25] This is the ritual highpoint of the farewell. Sewn inside the cloths, the deceased is no longer a corpse but something suited for burial, a further step in his deconception and signal for a series of mask performances at several places in the village.

The ropemaker masks start a whirling dance as a symbolic farewell to the deceased. The wrapped-up corpse is laid on the dancing floor in front of his house, and one mask, crouching, dances over it, from the feet to the head, swishing its heavy raffia skirts. It does this three times, in remembrance of the three grades of *poro* that the deceased has mastered, the three

23   Again, these masks are specific to the Fodonon.
24   See Figures 2.4a and 2.4b for examples.
25   The ropemakers and their mask are of Manding origin, belonging to artisanal groups that gradually moved into Senufoland till around the 1920s. Celibélé – the location of the photo in Figure 5.4 – stems from the Manding term *jeli*. We thank Till Förster for both picture and information.

times he has been reborn. Calling out his initiation name,[26] the mask in its deformed voice urges him to rise and speak. When no reaction follows, the mask acquiesces and the elders sing: 'We will follow you. He has returned to the country of the ancestors [...].'[27]

After some other mask dances, the corpse is carried to the meeting place of the elders, with its massive, thick-roofed men's house. There, musicians with tall, slender drums call in antelope masks in splendid woven costumes topped with long horns, followed by a pair of *yalajo*. The ropemaker mask runs in, kneels at the side of the corpse, and utters piercing cries, while an elder sings the praise of the deceased, ringing an iron bell to call the spirits. At this place in the village no women are present; uninitiated men and children also give the dancing place a wide berth, for this is strictly *poro* business.

Finally, the *poro* members take up the corpse and carry it to the sacred forest, a route that is thought to be led by the lingering spirit of the deceased, for during this last journey the corpse must point out its successor.[28] Pairs of *nafiri* from all participating *poro* groups take turns at whipping and running around the corpse. Finally, a few initiates carry the corpse at some speed to the graveyard, and to the accompaniment of drums carefully place it in the horizontal chamber.[29] The *poro* elders fill the entrance and close the grave.

In our short overview we have had to skip quite a few mask types, especially the ones present during the nightly vigils before and after the burial; however, few cultures have a mask farewell that can match this Senufo funeral.

The funeral as initiation

The intensity of the mask involvement with the corpse among the Senufo is rather exceptional, but the main arenas are clear. It is not the direct kin group that owns the body but the secret societies, and the ritual stage is dominated by the masks. Identity is always gendered, but in this – undoubtably male – first funeral, masculinity is highlighted and the role of the women downplayed, with almost no input from wives, sisters, or mothers. During the liminal time of burial, the field of gender is no longer an arena, for

26 The honorary name for initiates who completed their six-year initiation cycle.
27 Glaze 1981: 190.
28 If the latter is present. If not, the carriers will search without finding a way, a sign that the dead will follow the living back from the grave. A deceased person unable to point out his successor may become a wandering being causing misfortune to his descendants. Information from Till Förster.
29 Glaze 1981: 192.

the masks dominate completely. Also the power arena is redefined: in this Senufo burial the power association exerts its dominance over any lineage connection, which in this matrilineal society means that the association treads into the power voids of the matrilineal system. Such a secret society serves as a kind of second family, not by descent but by choice and with members of one gender only – in fact, a super-family of brothers and fathers whose powers are strengthened by initiation, oaths, and secrecy. So the burial and the funeral both testify, loudly and clearly, the males as overlords, as creators and re-creators, over any claims of the matriline.

The ritual form of this symbolic hegemony harks back to initiation: secret societies equal initiation, and what the masks effectuate in a funeral is a second initiation. When the Senufo mask acknowledges, greets, and honours the deceased, it highlights their public stature and makes the farewell less personal, since they become less a kinsman and more a mask-person. The mask passing over the body is an inverted symbol, as is the backward walking of the *nafiri*; ritual inversions in funerals highlight liminality, just as in initiation. What is hinted at is an inverted initiation: the mask sits on the corpse, out of sight of women, and takes off its head cover. This occurs not just in Senufo rituals; in the Baule funeral, the mask called *akplowa ngoie* approaches the corpse lying on the ground and greets the dead person, dancing around the bier. Carefully the mask lays some fresh leaves on the corpse, shakes up some of the branches of the bier, and chasing away some flies, takes off its top; a chorus accompanies his actions, with shouts of 'Go back to the bush'.[30]

This similarity of first funeral and initiation testifies to a basic symbolic logic: the deceased is initiated by the masks for a second time and thus sent to his next level of existence. At death, therefore, the core of the initiation is replayed, but with a twist: the mask sits down on the deceased, who is lying on the ground; the latter is honoured, not cajoled or tested. Such a symbolic inversion resonates with the situational inversion between initiation and burial. During their initiatory pathway to adulthood the boys learned that masks were – at a certain level – just men, and that they themselves could become masks. Initiating the deceased elder for a second time signals that he is no longer an adult who can wear a mask, but is now a mask who can no longer be an adult. He is a thing of the bush, of the ancestors.

30   Vogel 1997a.

The Mundang of northern Cameroon take this initiation logic one step further in their funeral, as Alfred Adler points out.[31] The corpse is buried very rapidly, and then divination must indicate when the farewell rituals will take place, after a few days or a week later. In the early morning the drums call the *muyu*, 'female masks', belonging to the deceased's clan and completely covered in black fibres. With whips and intimidating falsetto voices, these apparitions clear the area before the house of the deceased. Meanwhile the clansmen gather leaves of the shrubs that furnish the mask fibres,[32] and they use these as a screen to cover the second genre of masks, the *mundere*, the 'male masks', at their dramatic entry. The *mundere* are clothed in fibres similar to those of the *muyu*, but sport impressive head crests, plus a waterfall of long fibre 'hair' around their heads; when dancing, they twist these into a circle of swinging hair.

Arriving at the house, the drummers start the rhythm of the initiation dances, and while women and uncircumcised boys keep their distance, the men start the song called 'crossing of the water', metaphorically describing the initiation journey. The men keep singing and dancing as 'new initiates' along the village roads, 'with the gestures, the atmosphere and the state of collective excitement they experienced in the bush at the time of their initiation'.[33]

This second initiation intensifies when the son who will inherit from his father – the Mundang are patrilineal – enters the dancing circle. Behind him two men, dressed only in cache-sexes with their backs painted with ochre and white dots, clamp a large knife between their teeth, the 'crocodiles'. They throw themselves on the heir and pull down his trousers, and while assistants hold him firm, each of the crocodiles brushes the heir's penis three times with the huge knife, throws it down, and tosses some sand on the 'wound'. In this way the circumcision is repeated, not by the masks but by what one could call 'anti-masks': naked, painted, visible beings from the water, armed with real knives. Now the heir is fully liberated from the 'crazy spirit' deemed to reside in the prepuce, and a satchel with protective medicine is tied around his neck, wrapped in the same leaves of the mask costume. So here it is the heir who is initiated twice.

In the Aro funeral, just west of the Cross River area in Nigeria, such an inversion between initiation and death is played out in spectacular theatrics.[34] Up to the time of the ritual, the fact of death is all but denied; people pretend

---

31 Adler 1994: 96. For the influence on their ethnic positioning, see Schilder 1994.
32 *Piliostigma reticulatum* (in Mundang *pwere*) Adler 1994: 95.
33 'les gestes, l'atmosphère et l'état d'excitation collective qu'ils ont connus en brousse au moment de l'initiation' (Adler 1994: 96). Translation by the first author.
34 Based upon Bentor 1994a.

that the person is just ill, ailing a bit. After elaborate preparations the mask ritual is held, in which two rows of initiated men from the *ékpè* lodge move to the house of the deceased. Seven times the procession is held, for each of the seven initiation grades, and each time a specific mask dances between the rows of initiates. The fifth mask portrays an old and sick man, staggering with a cane. Throughout the ritual people keep pretending that the dead is still alive, but when the old man-mask enters, people whisper that this old man is very ill and is going to die. When the mask leaves the house again, the drum rhythm picks up and the mask starts dancing at full tilt. Tension reigns in the audience: 'He is cured. The dead man is alive!' – an excitement tinged with fear. Who cured whom is left conveniently unclear, for it may mean that the dead person healed the sick mask. When the last, seventh, procession with a majestic mask has entered the house, the deceased is finally dead, for they have 'taken *ékpè* back', an expression referring to the funeral.

Here the masks do not engage in a second initiation but in undoing the first one, in a day-long inversion of the initiation stages of the *ékpè* society. 'Death rituals are symbolic representations of the ambiguous liminal state of the deceased', state Metcalfe and Huntington,[35] as this case illustrates well. All in all, the various 'deathways' with masks all refer to initiation, either adding a second one or undoing the first, underscoring this very ambiguity: death is the final coming of age.

In short, the relation between initiation and death is a structural inversion. In initiation, boys die symbolically to attain an adult identity; the loss is symbolic and temporary, while the societal gain is real and permanent. In death the reverse is true: the loss is painfully real, any further existence of the deceased is symbolic, and the societal loss is permanent. So the two transitions are fundamental opposites of each other: the first is about gain, the second is about ultimate loss. Initiation and the first funeral form a ritual pair that symbolically mirror each other.[36]

The individual and society at funerals

In death all deceased are 'over-conceived', but it does make a difference who dies. When chiefs or kings die, all hands are on deck, and all masks will show up. Chapter 7 investigates the intricate relation of kingship and masks, but in many instances the rites of enthronement of a new chief or king closely resemble both initiation and funeral. The ruler-to-be is

---

35 Metcalfe and Huntington 1991: 111.
36 In masking societies, funerals for women are different from those for men.

endowed with special powers in a ceremony in which some of his social persona is taken from him; he must die as a person in order to become chief. Symbolically the incumbent dies, and as a new persona receives the attributes of kingship that will completely dominate his own personality, so he is revived as an embodied ruler whose powers are integrated with his physical body.[37] Masks are the cherry on the cake in these ceremonies, acting as public celebrations of a newly formed powerful identity.

Yet, when the king really dies, the masks must put in a strong appearance in what is in fact a larger version of the standard funeral procedure. For instance, masks form the highlight of the Limba funeral proceedings, forty days after the burial,[38] in a huge public feast for the whole community. In Chapter 7 the Kuba of DRC form a major example in respect to kingly power, but a brief prelude on their burial is apt here, since it shows how masks handle differences in social status.[39] At village level this highly hierarchical society is shot through with titles, honorific epithets, that initiated men acquire during their life and that form the essence of their social life. A similar hierarchy pervades the various masks, each of which occupies its own echelon in rituals. Thus, burial of a non-titled man calls for a lower-ranking mask, but when a man with an important title dies, the top of the mask pyramid is called out.

The mask's role is to initiate the actual burial on the third day of death. The two previous days a lower-ranked mask came out to prepare the premises, and the burial day sees the deceased in an open coffin under a shed. The mask in question dresses in the initiation camp, deep in the forest behind nine raffia screens of secrecy, adorning itself as a visiting chief with the appropriate signs of rank – among which are plumes of specific birds. A young initiate runs to the village shouting 'Broom, broom', for the women should sweep the village clean and cover all refuse; the mask is coming and will certainly fine them if they do not clean up. Then, with trumpets sounding and guns being fired – a reminder of the battle fought in order to capture the mask from a neighbouring group – and surrounded by musicians playing the instruments of initiation, the mask walks through the nine raffia curtains and arrives in the village.

A significant intermezzo follows: in song, the women bar the be-thing's entrance into the village, and the mask must negotiate for right of entry, through its accompanying elders. That done, with a ceremonial gift for the

---

37 Warnier 2007.
38 Hart 1988: 62. See also Hart 1987, 2019, and Ottenberg 1988.
39 This description stems from Binkley 1987.

women, the mask proceeds to parade through the village, preceded by a rattle like the homecoming of the initiated boys, but also like the installation of a new chief; the iconography is similar. The mask's pathway ends at the shed with the deceased, and all women flee to their huts; the power within the village is now in the hands of the mask. The men shield the coffin from view with raffia mats for the actual farewell. Slowly the mask walks toward the coffin, taps it three times on the side with some fresh plant leaves, and starts a lengthy oration to the corpse.

> You were taken away. This mask is your mask of honour, a never-ending power and an endless life. The mask dances with power and strength. Let those who are still alive grow older. They are your elders of the village [...] Go in peace to the world of the dead men. As we are honouring your death, give us the physical strength to dance.[40]

This – much longer – verbal address to the dead man's spirit reflects the general attitude of fear and distrust of the intentions of the recently deceased man, who may become jealous and vindictive if he is not properly honoured; David Binkley stresses the ambivalent relationship with the dead. When finished speaking, the mask remains inside the shed and the other men bury the body. On their return the women start emerging from their hiding places, and the funeral dance begins with the masks, both the higher and the lower ones, at the centre. The masks themselves remain taboo for the women who risk becoming infertile or ill by touching them, or even just touching their footprints, so they must keep some distance.

The address places the mask in a peculiar position: it acts on behalf of the community toward the deceased, in order to send him away to the land of the dead, but the intimate link of the mask with that realm is never mentioned in the text. So the initiation symbols effectuate a double transition: the dead man is now initiated again into his new reference group, the dead, while the mask, as a be-thing of the bush, is transformed into a human, a new chief speaking on behalf of the living. The mask's little altercation with the women fits into this: as the new 'chief' it must win over support from the basic source of power in the village, the women; at the same time, as a mask, it is a threat to their fertility.

The plea to the new spirit to be kind and gentle exemplifies a very widespread discourse toward the recently dead, irrespective of masks, titles, or secret societies; what is special here is the mask offering the discourse.

---

40 Ibid.: 90. For the aspect of power in Kuba masks, see Binckley 2021.

Binkley does not mention a voice disguiser, so the speech must be audible and understandable. Although the deceased is present at this ritual, the mask commands the dancing scene, accentuating in speech that the deceased's identity was well defined by his titles and thus belonged to the ranking system. This pyramid of titles culminates in the chief, which in this ritual is the mask itself, so in essence this mask represents the male power organisation, just like the secret societies of the Senufo.

The power field is very much present at this Kuba funeral, but in such a way that the arena aspect is downplayed: there is little contestation or indeterminacy; the mask represents the political structure of the society, reinforces its hierarchy, and reestablishes its dominant relation with the women, consonant with the general support that masks deliver to the Kuba kingship, as we shall see in Chapter 7. In these first funerals with masks the major arenas of gender and power lose their indeterminacy, acceding to the temporal hegemony of the mask organisation, and the issue of identity becomes the main field in the ritual performances. Thus, at the end of his life an initiated man takes his leave of the nested identities of his living career, to find his ultimate destiny in a new, collective – and nameless! – one, between the masks and the ancestors. In essence this carries the deconception of the deceased one step further, and the masks are instrumental in doing so.

Masks also deindividualise the funeral by siphoning off attention from the corpse. By 'stealing the show', they effectuate a shift from the notion of loss to the experience of otherness. It is a double shift: from familiarity to strangeness, but also from loss to acceptance, since as be-things they dance. Dancing is emotion, an expression of sorrow that develops inevitably into an enjoyable experience. At a Western funeral, mourners convene for 'condolences with tea and cake', and the atmosphere tends to turn light and joyful with all these old acquaintances one has not seen for a long time; the Dutch with their Calvinist heritage tend to feel a little guilty. With dances at African funerals, this is much clearer and also culturally vindicated, for in the exuberance of the masquerades mourners intensify the ritual explosion of life that is so characteristic of African funerals. Masks are a crucial addendum to these festivities, officially in honour of the deceased but actually for the benefit of the living. When masks are present, the corpse not only becomes someone else, but also may be forgotten.

At the funeral of Balugo Saye described in the vignette, at the height of the funeral dance a sizeable delegation of masks from Ireli, a neighbouring village, came in to give a splendid performance. Afterwards, their ritual speaker explained – in mask language – that they had come to honour Balugo, since his son Apomi, an important man in Tireli, was not only a great friend of someone from Ireli but also employed him in the NGO he presided over. So the Ireli masks showed up – and showed off. Not to be outdone, the ritual speaker of Tireli – also in a show of fluency in Sigi so – thanked the people from Ireli profusely, stating that the village would be in their debt forever. During the long and loud orations, the name of Balugo was never mentioned. So the masks depersonalise the funeral, their anonymous presence of primal power overshadowing any qualities of the deceased. With masks and their performance, life is regaining its vigour again: masks do not mourn, but rather de-mourn.

Masks and the second funeral

As shown in the funeral scheme, the intermediate period until the second funeral helps the bereaved to adjust to their changed position in life. Sons and daughters and especially widows and widowers get time to mourn and redefine themselves as a new social persona, one without the deceased. The deceased has now entered an intermediate existence: out of life but not yet part of the realm of the dead, someone to whom farewell was said but who is not yet reintegrated as an ancestor. The length of this period varies from several months to many years, and daily life is not too different from normal, save for those very close relatives whose status has changed most and who mourn longer. Rituals are few in this period, but taboos abound. Widows and widowers especially have their own after-death rhythm and may be subject to specific rules; for instance, they may not approach altars or sacred spots for at least a year.

Masks are never visitors during this intermediate period, and their absence is revealing: this is the time to adjust social roles, and the village must resettle within itself without interference from an ambivalent otherworld. Nevertheless, there is a waiting for the second funeral, which takes place years later. Mourning tapers off and the new identity gradually establishes itself, when children learn to live without their departed parent, and widows and widowers establish new relations. Estates must be settled in debates that take time, sometimes years. Since masking societies tend to be not the wealthiest ones, large inheritances are rare. The Senufo case is illustrative, since there is hardly any inheritance at all. Their matrilineal system precludes sons inheriting from fathers anyway; also between a mother's brother and a sister's son there is almost no flow of goods. Their norm is that a person's goods should be exhausted at his death, used for the funeral feast, and distributed as much as possible.[41] Actually, inheritance between close kinsmen is frowned upon, an arrangement that fits in with matriliny, where the lineages are rather weak and do not command strategic goods. A title system like the Kuba one also helps here, since the expensive titles result from personal investment and cannot be inherited: matrilineal death shrouds have no pockets.

After the intermediate period, the second funeral shows a variety of rituals. This can be a ritual to finish off the tomb,[42] but in several cultures the end of mourning comes with large, spectacular rituals, and here masks appear on the scene again. In the literature they sometimes are called 'commemoration feasts', while in fact they signal the end of the mourning period and are part of the whole funeral complex. Our example comes from the Dogon of Mali.

Masks dominate the second funeral among the Dogon of Mali.[43] The mask feast, called *dama*, lasts a month, and we highlight one major moment that illustrates the masks' contribution to this final farewell. The time is May 2008, the setting is the Teri Ku ward of Tireli, a village at the foot of the Bandiagara cliff. The high points in the *dama* liturgy are five days in which the masks enter the village from the bush in large numbers, each day from another cardinal direction. The description focuses on the third and largest arrival, one of the last days of this ritual-packed month.

The *dama* is nearing its end. The initiates have made their costumes and headpieces, the leaders have repaired the drums, each ward has reroofed its men's house, and a host of other ritual preparations have been made. The initiates have walked through the sleeping village tapping their slit drums and have carried their first outfits, black ones. Four days ago they came into the village for the first time as the 'red masks', with red fibre costumes, and from that day until the end of the *dama*, women are forbidden to leave the village. The bush is now taboo for them; the word *dama* in fact means 'forbidden'. This means that the men now have to fetch water themselves, as the wells are outside the perimeter of the village proper. Seeing men go out and fetch water is highly unusual, a strange sight, and the men are quite self-conscious about it.

This day is the most valued of all *dama* days, called *manugo sugo* (the descent from the dunes). In the morning the masks, with a plaited hood as

---

41 Glaze 1981; Förster 1988.
42 As in Kapsiki funerals; Van Beek 2015.
43 The Dogon data stem from the first author. For descriptions of the mask rituals see Van Beek 1991a, 2006, 2012, 2018, 2022, P. Richards 2005, 2022.

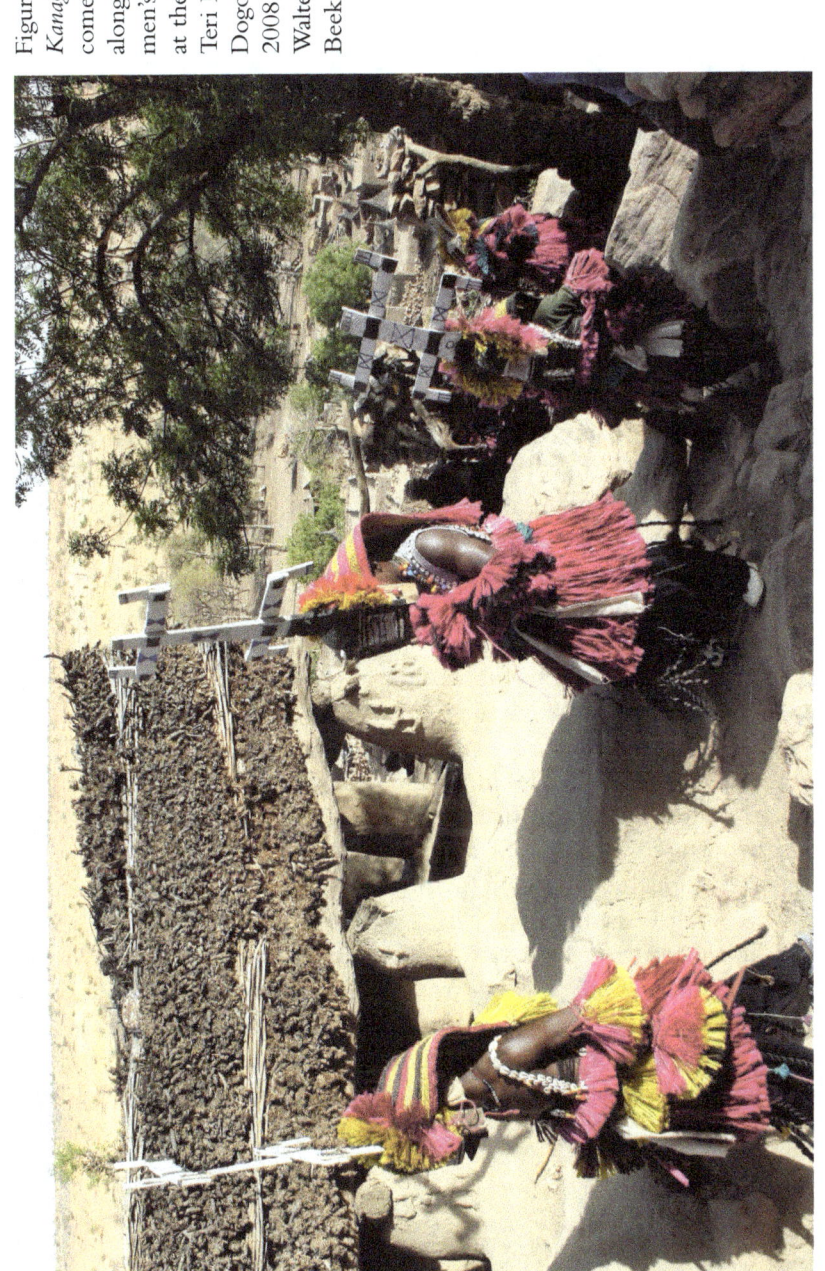

Figure 5.5. *Kanaga* masks come on stage alongside the men's house at the *dama* of Teri Ku. Tireli, Dogon, Mali, 2008. Photo: Walter van Beek.

headcovering, come one by one down to the rim of the village, carrying a carved headpiece in a sack. Of course women are nowhere in sight. At a small hangar used to store grasses, the masks unwrap their headpieces and put them on top of the thatched roof, and head for the dunes without any headcovering, led by some old men. During the afternoon, the whole village gathers gradually near the dancing place, and the *yasigine*, the sisters of the masks who are not bound by taboos on masks, set up their beer near the scree rim. Around 4 pm the main event gets underway: led by the elders, a long winding file of 'naked masks' emerge from the bush, put on their headpieces, and start to dance.

This is the first time that all the masks of Teri Ku show up in one dance, and the essence of this day is that they arrive as one large troupe; the entire bush comes. The opening is spectacular: the *èmna tiû*, the tree masks, lead the way with their five-metre-high headpieces, and with eight of them it is indeed a small walking thicket of trees – a dancing forest, in fact.[44] Sitting atop a house near the grounds, the waterbird masks tie on their two-metre long stilts and come in next.[45] They must perform early in the programme, as fatigue would make their dance dangerous. But by far the largest group are the *kanaga* masks, presentifying antelopes, making up about one-third of all the sixty-odd masks. They performed their own dance four days earlier and made a great impression, and now they dominate the general dance, prancing and sweeping their 'horns' through the dust. The old men are everywhere, beating the earth with their sticks while shouting exhortations at full force in the mask language.

Rabbits are a popular mask with the younger dancers; three of them enter the dancing ground, looking anxiously at the audience. Suddenly their fears materialise in the form of the mask of a hunter, who points its spear at them, and the three little masks crouch together in a corner, a little hunting scene much appreciated by the audience.

The rabbits have hardly left when a gazelle mask bursts onto the scene, its long horns pointing backward, running fast to the rapid beat of the drums. It is usually alone; this is a mask that demands a good runner, and with its limited vision that is no mean feat. Other masks follow, depending on the composition of this ward's troupe – in this case, a healer's mask. Silently walking with its headpiece crowned with four human figures, the mask does not really dance but slowly perambulates among the audience.

---

[44] Sometimes called *maison à étages* (two-storey house). In the cliffside villages the referent is the tree spirit called *jinu*. See Figure 11.2.
[45] See Figure 9.4.

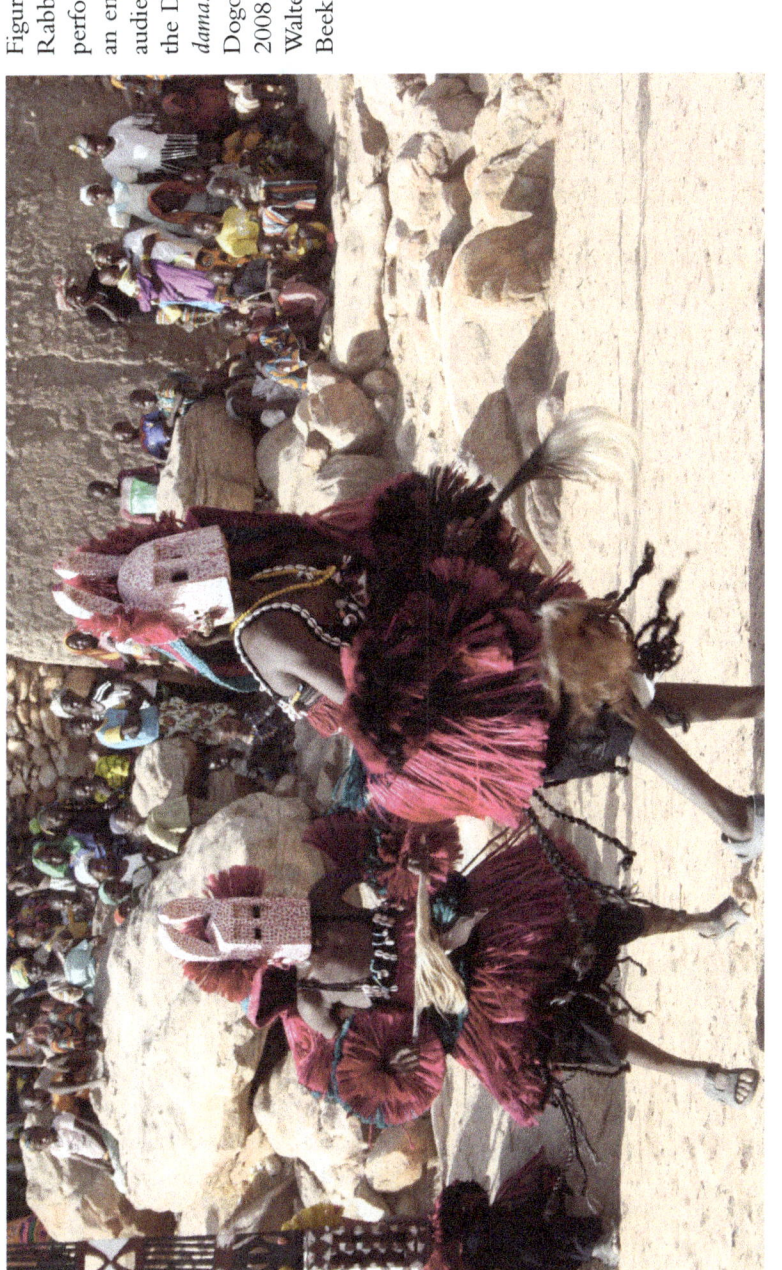

Figure 5.6. Rabbit masks perform for an enchanted audience at the Dogon *dama*. Tireli, Dogon, Mali, 2008. Photo: Walter van Beek.

From time to time it halts, kneels, takes some medicine from its pouch, and hands it to an onlooker, who is then expected to thank the mask and hand over some money. This is a doctor making rounds – a role for an older dancer who is less forceful and vigorous but with good judgement and some theatrical skills.

The other masks perform one by one or come on stage in small groups according to genre: the bull, three other antelopes, two hyenas, a monkey, the marabout, the Samo, the shaman, the Fulbe, a white man, and one pupil mask; additionally, a *sadimbe* arrives on the scene, representing the woman who, according to the myth, found the first masks. After their appearance from the bush in a troupe, most masks continue their dance solo or in small groups, while the other masks sit down on the stones that line the dancing place; effectively, the masks dance for both the regular audience and their own colleagues.

For about two hours the masks dance constantly and then end the masquerade in a final show in which again all participate. The long line of masks dances one round and then each mask runs into the village; the last ones are the rabbits, who leave the dancing ground empty in the falling dark. As a final farewell to this great day, the four *yasigine*, the 'sisters of the masks', slowly circle the grounds holding their calabash spoons in one hand, while with their other hand they symbolically wipe out their own tracks as well as those of the masks with long fly whisks, lifting the taboo from the dancing ground.

Celebrating life

Dogon masks show their provenance from the bush with utmost clarity: they come into the village from the bush; they presentify animals or people from the bush; they do not speak but utter high-pitched cries or animal sounds; and they respond only to the Sigi so language of the *jinu*, the spirits of trees and thus of the bush; plaiting a mask shirt is called the work of the *yènèu* – another type of small bush spirit. Thus, the masks presentify the bush coming into the village, and with these entries they are in fact recharging the village, since after a long series of losses it has been gradually depleted by the accumulated deaths. Such a collective loss must be replenished, and it is the masquerade that does just that – with the therianthropic masks embodying the power of the virtualised bush: they fuse the worlds.

Arriving from the bush on this day, the masks are 'naked', without headpieces, and so when out in the dunes they are undifferentiated bush entities, almost indistinguishable as masks; by donning their tops they emerge as distinct individual be-things. Characteristically, at their entrance they have to be guided by the drums and the elders, for when the invisible materialises it has to learn how to dance, so the elders lead them by showing the essential moves. When the bush-things approach humanity, they must humanise themselves as be-things, meeting the bush–village opposition halfway;[46] the worlds of men and of the bush can fuse only if they meet each other on the hemmed-off dancing ground that is the essential middle ground between bush and village.

The *dama* is both a second funeral and an initiation.[47] The specific moment of the boys' initiation was a few weeks ago, when they donned black costumes with plaited hoods at the top of the cliff and descended into the village; but their initiation is mostly just their participation in the *dama*. By practising their dancing routines, making their masks, getting accustomed to wearing them, and then performing before the whole village, the boys are initiated. For the Dogon that is sufficient initiation; circumcision occurs at a much younger age.

The relationship with the dead does not show in the public dances; for that aspect one must follow the masks outside the strict dancing grounds. Early the next day, before coming out to dance again, the masks will visit the houses of the deceased and dance on their roofs, as the sign of final farewell. During the *dama* there are some other ritual farewells to the dead, but they do not feature masks. All in all, the main contribution of the masks to the second funeral lies less in their relation with the deceased than in the inversion of death, in bringing about new life from death – in short, in fertility and regeneration. The contribution of the masks lies in their arrival and their dancing, which suffices to transform the dead into ancestors; just as the boys are initiated mainly through their participation in the *dama*, the dead become ancestors through the feast itself.

What remains is the gender arena; also in second funerals. The exhortations by the Dogon elders highlight the gender gap: 'This is not for children. If you see a woman, beat her. Greetings, good heads, who came running. All the women are afraid; beat them.'[48] The women watch from a respectful distance as an indispensable part of the audience (Figure 6.2).

---

46   A notion of Michael Rowlands.
47   This combination is not rare; see the Chewa Nyau initiation (Yoshida 2006: 226).
48   Van Beek 1991b: 159.

The total complex of the *dama* is much more than a farewell for the dead and an initiation for youngsters; it also represents a ritual *coup de force* by the men: a male appropriation of female fertility. As Bloch and Parry remarked about funeral rituals in general, they regenerate the community.[49] The Dogon *dama* marks the end of a long intermediate period, and even if ancestors are not overly central in Dogon religion, the dead, at least those with living progeny, do become ancestors. It is after the *dama* that they can be reborn, meaning that their names can now be reused for children born after the masquerade; after the *dama,* the village expects a boost in both children and crops.

Though closely associated with death, the masks do bring in new life, and at this second funeral the men perform a ritual play of procreative self-sufficiency – that is, the masked men claim to control the sources not just of power but also of fertility, and thus of life, which fits in well with the initiation side of the *dama*. By moving freely over the death–fertility axis, masks revitalise society, not by extolling the deceased but by presentifying a creative force that is external to society. The bush comes in and replenishes the village with power and energy, with life and fertility, but this peremptory male grasp on reproduction is a male-only fertility, a *contradictio in terminis*.

This male fertility is based on the logic of liminality, the symbolic inversion that characterises so many rituals. In daily life as well in other rituals, the men are fully aware of the fact that the future of the village is in the hands of their wives, sisters, and daughters, and during other rites they fully and abundantly express that sense of dependency. But that is expressed without any mask present. In effect the whole negation of female fertility during the liminal mask times actually emphasises, in a quite dialectical way, the fundamental importance of the women in society. As a slippery grip on the source of life, this ritual appropriation of fertility is ultimately doomed to be short-lived, a splendid chimera of male power during a fleeting time-out-of-time of liminal glory, set against the solid-groundedness of the women. By addressing the gender arena in this fashion, masks attest to their own ephemerality.

The Dogon *dama* is held at long intervals, but such commemoration rituals can be part of a regular ritual calendar. John Picton describes the masquerades among the Ebira of Central Nigeria in which the dead are deemed to revisit the village of the living, which they do at the very moment the old year becomes the new one, the new moon of late November–early

---

49 Bloch and Parry 1999.

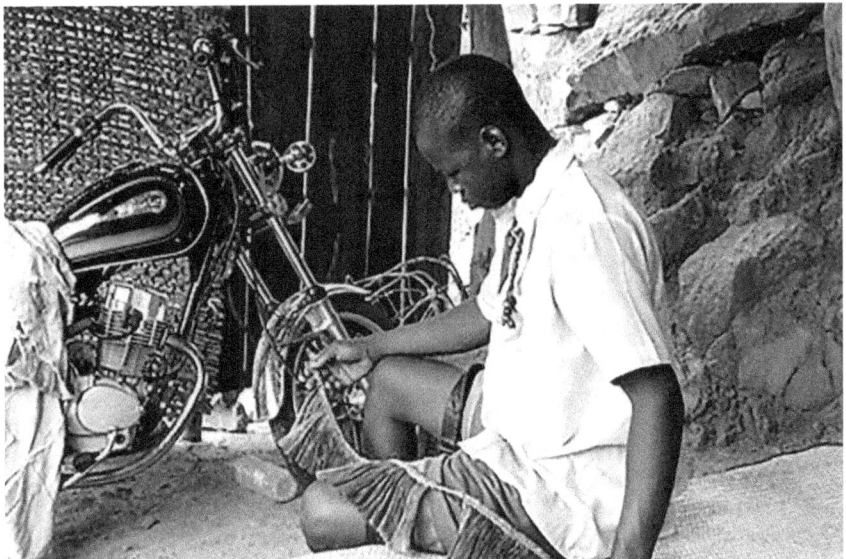

Figure 5.7. Domiyon, a young initiate just back from the capital, inspects the fibres of his dance mask for the *dama* of Teri Ku. Tireli, Dogon, Mali, 2008. Photo: Walter van Beek.

December.[50] These *ekuechi* festivals close a series of year rites, on a night where the masks of the night come to chase the night's evils, meaning witchcraft, considered both a woman's evil and a source of their energy and strength. The night starts with the '*eku* of the stamping feet', at the rhythm of two split drums intoning the melody of the sentence, for the main performance of these masks is verbal. They are masks that pronounce oracles and hand out directions for healing, but mainly they sing, which is unusual. For each season they must come up with new songs, singing at houses and in the square, paying special attention to houses where sons have died. Their performance is judged by their verbal excellence, not their dancing and certainly not their attire: often they wear only a face cover when women can see them; their verbal role suffices to define them as masks. But they are much more than just bards, for their masking role allots them oracular insights.

Some time after this ritual a deceased Ebira elder was expected to revisit his descendants as *ekuoba*, the stretching *eku*. Here the costume was highly significant: the dancer was wrapped in a long and wide tube of cloth

50 See for Ebira masking Picton 1988a and b, 1999, 1990, 1992, 1997, and 2009.

pinned together over his head with some relics of the corpse sewn into a cloth on top – there was no head discernible. Without face or limbs, such a mask resembled a buried corpse, but also this mask demanded oratory skills, and knowledge of poetics and invocatory recitations. This genre of mask has been on the wane among the Ebira since the 1960s, in favour of a mask type in which the performer is freer to choose headpiece and costume. What has remained are the ways in which both the gender arena and identity dynamics join hands in the funeral rites.

Second funerals also address the other arenas, and for some modern aspects of second funerals, we turn to Cameroon. In the more urbanised parts of its western provinces, these festivals of the second funeral are often called commemorative celebrations. The Cameroonian Grassfields form a good example, where in pidgin they are called 'cry die'[51] and where these festivities are not on the wane; on the contrary, they are getting ever larger. This series of celebrations starts with food exchanges and eating, a feast that extends well into the night, even in the sense of a proper vigil. It is late at night when the women must be suddenly shut inside the compound because the first mask shows up. On the rhythm of drums, accentuated by loud horn blasts, mask and attendants dance around the grave, situated near the compound, leaving after ten minutes for the bush.

This is just the opening, and during the following day a plethora of performances celebrate the deceased and the ancestors, with dances, songs, gift exchanges, food, drink, and mask dances. The masks appear as part of dancing groups representing other neighbourhoods, or are sponsored by local families, by the remaining secret societies, and even by the churches. In hybrid performances, masked groups mingle with teams that dance in uniform, a mixture that is not seen as problematic since they all share in a huge joyous celebration. These commemorations have become more popular with modernisation and the loss of traditional authority, plus the rise of Christianity. The increased wealth of the area means that individual families, not just the traditional elite but also the new wealthy, can spend more on their own ancestors; thus, ironically, one sees a 'proliferation of ancestors' in modern times.[52] Meanwhile, there is a characteristic uncertainty about these very ancestors, about their relation with the deceased and with the masks in question. Opinions range from the dead being called back by the celebrations either to take their share or just to see the celebrations, to the

---

51 Jindra 2011: 112.
52 Ibid.: 123.

celebration as a gift to the ancestors. Dancing always pleases ancestors; that is certain for everybody, so the contribution of the masks is clear: 'The masks take away the ancestors',[53] who are best kept at arm's length; modernisation has not changed that.

In this Cameroonian case, wealth and status increasingly define the arenas of power and identity, with the proliferation of second funerals following the rise of wealth in the region. The mixing of masks and modernity shows not only that mask rituals are very adaptable, but also that they fit well into certain strands of African Christianity. After all, 'ancestor' is a term with many meanings. Big spending at funerals has been noted in many instances,[54] and funerary expenses can weigh heavily on descendants. Comparing the relative neglect of the elderly in southern Ghana with the lavish burials after they die, Van der Geest speaks of 'funerals for the living', since the costs of the farewell weigh heavily on the offspring.[55] Such expensive feasts do generate social capital in Africa, but it is highly questionable whether these benefits weigh up to the costs. It is not masks that induce such mega-spending – southern Ghana has no masks – these feasts are costly in other ways. Actually, when mask groups are sponsored to embellish a funeral proceeding in Cameroon, they are not the largest item on the budget; on the whole masks are relatively cost-efficient, and also in modernising situations, masquerades point more to identity than to wealth.

Death rituals are about existential confrontation with the termination of life. Masks provide a special angle on mortality, highlighting the continued vitality of the community in contrast with the irreversibility of personal death, a paradox all societies must come to terms with. As 'metaphors in action',[56] masks are used to represent change, to effect change, and to block change. Since they 'embody a paradox, they can express other paradoxes of human life'.[57] Humans are born to depart again; the point is not to struggle against the fact of death but to render one's life into a work of art. As the old Roman saying goes, *dum vivimus, vivamus*: now that we have chosen to live, let us really live. Thus, the underlying over-assertion of male power in the mask dance, its insistence on new energy, wisdom, and life – even on exclusive male fertility – is a pathway of cultural coping, a way to live with what is unique in humankind, its sense of its own mortality. And it is through the masks' strong association

53 Ibid.: 124.
54 Van der Geest 2000; Jindra and Noret 2011; Noret 2013.
55 Van der Geest 2000.
56 Tonkin 1976: 242.
57 Tonkin 1988: 246.

with death that their performance highlights a timeless farewell over the short span of living time. Whatever may happen after death, life is right now and right here – and what a life it is! The final consolation is that as long as the masks dance, and surely for as long as one's sons, nephews, and grandsons keep dancing, new generations will emerge.

So in death the arenas of gender, power, and identity accrue special dimensions. What the masks do during the first funeral is highlight the religious status of the men through their second initiation: the powers of the bush claim the dead males as people of the bush, highlighting the bush powers that distinguished them from women during their lives. Initiated men, these liturgies assert, are of a different kind than women, commanding forces that are essential for the well-being of the community, but out of reach to the opposite gender. The second funeral pushes this line of thought even further: the future of society is in the hands of men, and of men only. Significantly, in modern death celebrations this aspect has faded away, ceding the stage to an identity arena that is defined increasingly in terms of wealth and religious affiliation.

Conclusion

The Senufo and the Dogon peoples, both of Zone 1, are representatives of Type C communities, with a long history of defending themselves against slave raiding. Senufo society follows our masking profile down to the last detail: it is matrilineal, with women who are proud to feed their families without either bride wealth or inheritance; and it shows one of the most intensive masking traditions on the continent, coupled with a high appreciation of aesthetics. The patrilineal Dogon used their cliffside villages as a defence during the slave raiding days of the Macina realm. Cultivating sorghum and pennicetum, their main production is in the hands of men, but bride wealth is low and the position of women is strong. With the *pax colonialis* they dared to move out into the plains, and, characteristically, their new villages never developed a local masking tradition: masquerades remained a thing of the cliffside. They have no secret societies, but do have an age organisation; masking is an affair of the whole village, directed by the seven oldest men.

In Zone 2 some major examples stem from the Nigerian Middle Belt, which shows a large diversity in masking profiles between groups with similar agricultural practices.[58] This chapter mentions the Ebira, living at the juncture of the Niger and Benue rivers, who cultivate maize, sorghum,

---

58 Ballard 1971.

peanuts, and yams in sizeable villages. Formerly they preferred the high places in their hilly area as a defence against marauders hunting for slaves, leaning towards Type C. Patrilineal and patrilocal, they have neither secret societies nor a pervading age organisation, but do distinguish between first and late coming lineages, like Type B, and their segmented lineages are not tied to land. Hierarchical organisation came rather late to the Ebira.[59] The gender arena, though, is clearly marked, and their mask rituals follow gender lines closely, with cloth masks dominating – geographically they are close to the Yoruba area. But even if the communities show mixed type features, the arenas are definitely there.

Another group in this region in close interaction with the Yoruba are the Nupe, mentioned in Chapter 2. In open countryside bereft of defendable sites, just north of the Niger river at the confluence with the Kaduna, they live in large villages or towns.[60] Land is not in short supply and the rivers offer stretches of arable land, the basis of diversified food production. Agriculture is primarily a male occupation, while women are engaged in the marketing of produce and control tree-based crops, such a shea nuts. Social organisation is based on the 'house', and patriclans are limited to the quite self-contained village unit, in which also an age system operates. These age grades are modelled after the hierarchical political system – especially in the capital – and extend only to adulthood: young men have three grades of six years each, extending into young adulthood, while girls have one grade ending at marriage. The age associations' main functions are educational and recreative.

These Nupe villages are part of a complex kingdom with an intricate political organisation, extending to craft guilds. Historically waves of political centralisation washed over Nupe country, from the south (Yoruba), from the north (Fulbe), and from internal war lords. Theirs is a slaving polity, both externally and internally, and they were instrumental in the supply of the Atlantic trade: at the time of Nadel's research 'half a century of wars and raids had denuded the country of people who could with no great difficulty be made slaves'.[61]

Overall they fit our profile only marginally: the gender arena is not overly pronounced, and power configurations are clear. However, they have neither cattle nor other inheritable wealth, their bride price is evened out by a high dowry, and they do have an intricate title system, also for women, while

---

59 Sani 1993, Segun 2018.
60 This description is based upon the classic work of S.F. Nadel 1937, 1942, and 1954.
61 Nadel 1942: 104.

historically slavery was a crucial factor. But then, their main mask is highly peculiar, just a cylindrical tent carried around on a pole. It functioned in the initiation of boys and combated 'witchcraft'; but with ongoing Islamisation, both these functions dwindled. Its form stands out from all other masking types, but does fit into their early Islamisation, while it also reminds us of the centrality of cloth among the Yoruba.

The following two peoples of the Middle Belt will be mentioned in Chapter 7. The Tiv have a clear-cut segmentary patrilineal system, Type A, and indeed have no masks, and as such this large group adds to the cultural diversity of the region. At the eastern limit of the Belt, the Jukun, descendants of the Kororofa realm of old, retain a centralised and hierarchical chieftainship, but have splintered into many small groups.[62] Under the threat of the Fulbe and Chamba raiders, they developed Type C communities, with masking for initiation and youth groups.

---

62 Meek 1931, Rubin 1974, 1982, Wele 1993.

6

Women: Pivot of the Masks

'The hen fully well knows when dawn is coming,
yet she lets the cock make it known to the world.'

(Akan proverb, Rattray 1952: 136)

The first mask

Before they became known among people, a group of dye, *spiritual beings living in the bush, left the savannah and moved south to the forested area. On their sojourn in what is now Ivory Coast, or so the story goes among the Guro, they met women who were collecting water.*

'Please give us water; we are thirsty.'

The women deliberated among themselves, discussing this normal request from these strange beings. In the end they refused:

'We have barely enough for ourselves; we will not give you any.'

Disappointed and thirsty, the dye *moved on and encountered men who were drinking palm wine.*

'Please give us to drink; we are thirsty.'

Immediately the men cut down a number of palm trees and served them drinks. As they were satisfied, the grateful spirits taught the men how to sing and drum, how to make the costumes of the mask, and how to dance as dye *masks. They explained: 'When we asked the women for a drink, they did not give it, but you, the men, served us drinks. That is why women are forbidden to see us dance. Now we are for you, the men.'*

In a dream a sculptor received instructions how to carve the headpiece, and thus the mask was complete − for the men, not for the women.[1]

This Guro myth is typical, for throughout the Mask Crescent stories explaining the appearance of masks are remarkably similar. Origin myths among the Bobo, Senufo, Dogon, Dan, Baule, Guro[2] and many other ethnic groups, relate

---

1   Fischer 2008: 133.
2   Himmelheber 1960: 11–12; Evanoff 1985: 56; Aubry et al. 1988: 133; Langeveld 2003: 129–130.

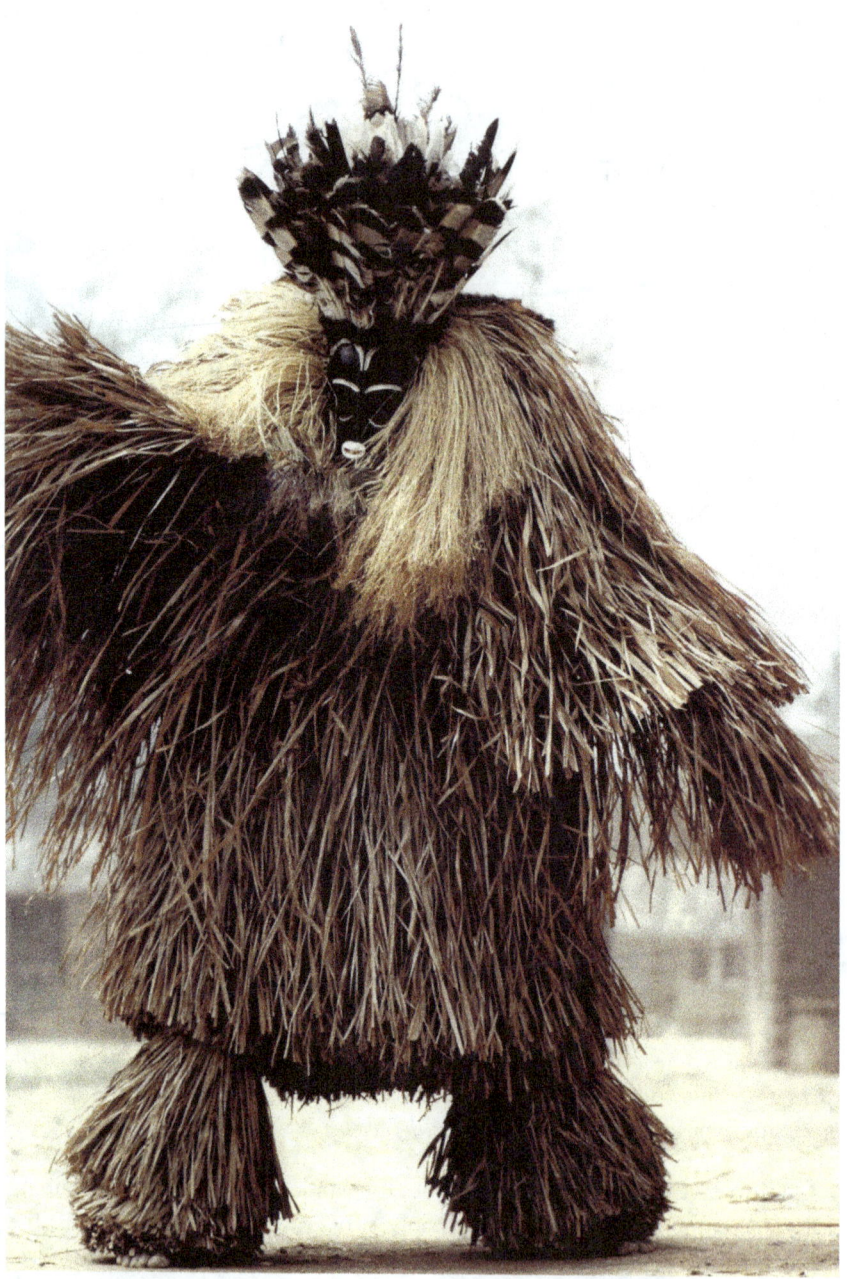

Figure 6.1. The *dye* mask the women refused to host. Guro, Côte d'Ivoire, 2008.
Photo: Eberhard Fischer.

parallel stories. Almost to a fault it is a woman or a child who first encounters the mask somewhere in the bush, and brings it into the village, and then the men appropriate control over these 'bush-beings', excluding the women and children. In fact, two parties are crucial in these tales: women and the bush – two elements that usually are separated, for the bush is male territory. In some cases the bush as such is enough to generate the masks. The initiates of the Dìì in Cameroon learn that a man saw a hedgehog in the bush that rolled up in defence and used the skin of its back to cover its head. Impressed, the man brought it back from the bush to frighten the women.[3]

A third theme is the secret, the dividing line between the genders, especially when secret societies are operative. For instance the Senufo tell how the coming of the masks also meant the arrival of secret societies.

> In the beginning, *poro* was with the women […] When the men finished preparing the meals of pounded yam, the women came out of the sacred forest of *poro* to take the food. But the men were forbidden to see the secret things of *poro*. If the women came out dressed in *poro*, the men had to hide, leaving the dishes of food outside the house. The men were too tired and thin. They had to hide while the women ate. Then […] the creator god said, 'No, I cannot leave *poro* with the women – they are too wicked and sinful.' So he seized the *poro* and gave it to the men.[4]

Poro here simultaneously stands for the society, the mask, and the secret; they are indistinguishable, and this whole complex has been relegated from the women to the men, who took better care of these powers. For the Gola of Western Liberia, Warren D'Azevedo stresses the primacy of the *sande*, the women's organisation: 'In the beginning, it is said, there was Sande. Women were the custodians of all ritual and the spiritual powers necessary for defining sacred tradition in the interest of the ancestors.'[5] The founding myth relegates the origin of Gola society to the power – and secrets – of women. Later a war produced the power of man, so the *poro*, and the ritual calendar was to alternate between four years of male and three years of female dominance, each with its own 'secrets', an arrangement in which the gender arena resonates through 'all interpersonal relationships by its rigorous codification of male and female roles'.[6]

3 Muller 2001: 62.
4 Glaze 1981: 91–92.
5 D'Azevedo 1973: 127.
6 Ibid. 133.

Also without any mythical ascendance women may serve as the prime link to the masks. A Jola version attributes the arrival of death to the attraction of masks:[7]

> A woman came into the bush and saw the spirits dance as masks. She was intrigued and wanted to dance herself. She was told: 'If you want that, you have to die eventually.' She agreed and danced. When she returned to the village, Death followed her. In the village she died, and people started the funeral proceedings. Fascinated, Death followed the funeral feast with its mask dances and was enthralled. 'When I came here, I intended not to stay in the village, only until that woman died. But now that I have seen your beautiful feast, I will remain in the village to participate in more of these.' And thus Death stayed among the people, after coming in with the mask.

The mythical variations address details in internal social relations; the overall constant is that in the myths the men have a secondary relationship with the mask and are basically dependent on the women, or children, to be where they are now.[8] In one instance a legendary queen is reported to have invented them,[9] but the standard provenance is that they come from the bush, with the women bringing them into the village. So at the basis of the mask is a discourse on gender, one that ranges from antagonism to complementarity.

Gender domains

At first sight, the ritual masculine power of masks certainly seems antagonistic to the women. Quite a few commentators define women as victims of men's dominance, unable to resist male aggression, and see their fear of masks as a sign of submission. The many references to women being chased away before a mask serve to reinforce this masculine view.

However, there is a female flipside to this battle of the sexes, as Sidney Kasfir and Henry Pernet have pointed out.[10] On closer inspection, the power of masks is strangely dependent on both the daily work of women and their

---

7   Langeveld 2003.

8   Myth and ritual in Africa are usually not very close. See De Heusch 1994 for Central African examples.

9   Among the Kuba, the wife of the culture hero Shyaam is said to have invented two mask types: Vansina 1978: 58, 60.

10   Kasfir 1998a, Pernet 1992. The whole issue of *African Arts* edited by Kasfir gives ample evidence of the crucial importance of women in masking; see also Weil 1998, Cameron 1988 and Röschenthaler 1998.

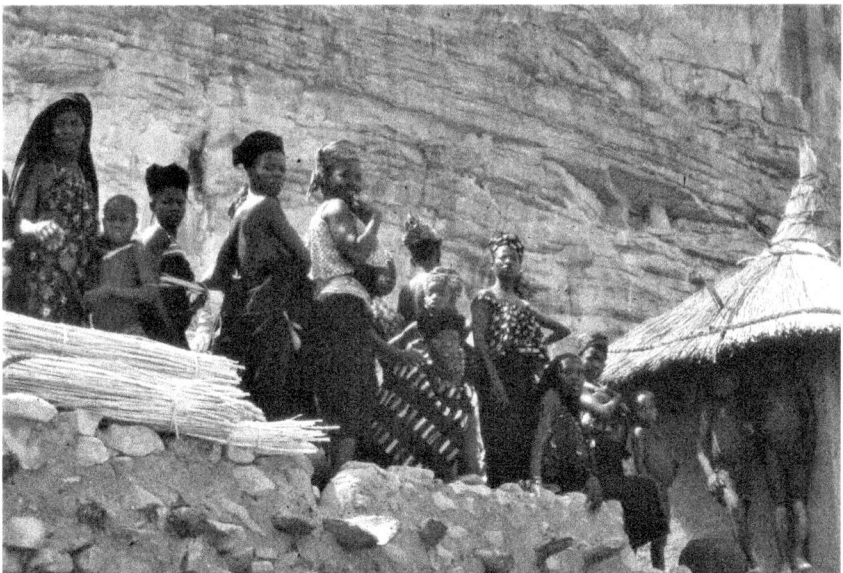

Figure 6.2. Young women watch the masks from a respectful distance high on the slope. Amani, Dogon, Mali, 2002. Photo: Walter van Beek.

fertility, but more precisely on their cooperation in keeping the charade intact. Time and again it is stressed by informants that women are supposed not to know the 'secret' of the masks, whereas it is crystal clear that they are perfectly aware of it, even of some of the details. Women play the part, and to understand why, we must view masks from the women's side. Their complicity in the mask phenomenon appears to offer women a definite benefit in their relationship with the men, a benefit they may express in private. Ottenberg relates of an Afikpo woman who gave the dancer, her husband, a gift some time after the ritual: 'I saw you do a fine thing once'[11] – the discourse must remain oblique.

Yet even if women know the main things about masks, that does not mean that they are comfortable in their presence; they are not so at all, because they have not been initiated into them, have not struggled with them, so have no right of familiarity. As David Binkley reports on the Kete of DRC: 'A Kete woman told me she would be terrified of the masquerade figures, even if she knew that her husband or son was dancing

11   Ottenberg 1982: 180.

that mask.'[12] The actual masks need not even be present; even the dance routines of the mask are taboo for women. A Dogon funeral is the stage for many dances, often with men and women dancing together. At a recent funeral, both boys and girls started out together in the evening, dancing in line, but when it was completely dark, the drums switched to the intro rhythm of the masks, and immediately all girls left the circle; they kept watching, but never entered the dance although there was no mask in sight; they needed no warning.[13]

The female exclusion of the masks tends to be balanced by a female realm that is out of bounds to men, since despite the spiritual powers that materialised in the masks and their performances, women do retain their own sources of strength that are in no way subservient to the masculine ones. Purported male supremacy is balanced by a counter-discourse on female power. Or, as Boyer states: 'The mask […] may constitute the most efficient means for the men to battle against a female preponderance that is always ready to affirm itself.'[14] This aspect, together with the fact that in some cultures women have their own take on the masks, either having the men dance for them, or even dancing with the masks themselves,[15] precludes any easy assessment of female submission in mask rituals.

A crucial factor is the strong social position of African women in the local ecology, solidified in their households and underwritten by a pronatal attitude shared by both genders. In her critique of mainstream social anthropology, the Nigerian scholar Ifi Amadiume uses the term 'matri-centric units', and especially in polygynous households this holds well.[16] Of course, such a 'female preponderance' is only a problem when men define it as such. In African village life – the basic scene of mask rituals – men and women each have their own domain, spheres of activity that they control, inaccessible to members of the other sex. Certain activities,

---

12 Binkley 1987: 93.
13 The dance took place in Amani, 7 May 2022. The authors thank Ibrahima Poudiougou, Amadou Guindo, and Issa Sagara for their rapport on this event. John Picton relates how among the Ebira women were curious about what exactly he was. Suddenly a man shouted: 'Eku is coming out', and immediately all women left (Picton 1988b: 187).
14 A-M. Boyer 2008: 56. 'Le masque […] constitue peut-être le moyen le plus efficace employé par les hommes pour lutter contre une prépondérance feminine toujours prête à s'affirmer.' Translation by the first author.
15 A splendid example is Peter Weil's account of the various masks worn in the past by women's organisations among the Mandinka (Weil 1998).
16 Amadiume 1997: 18.

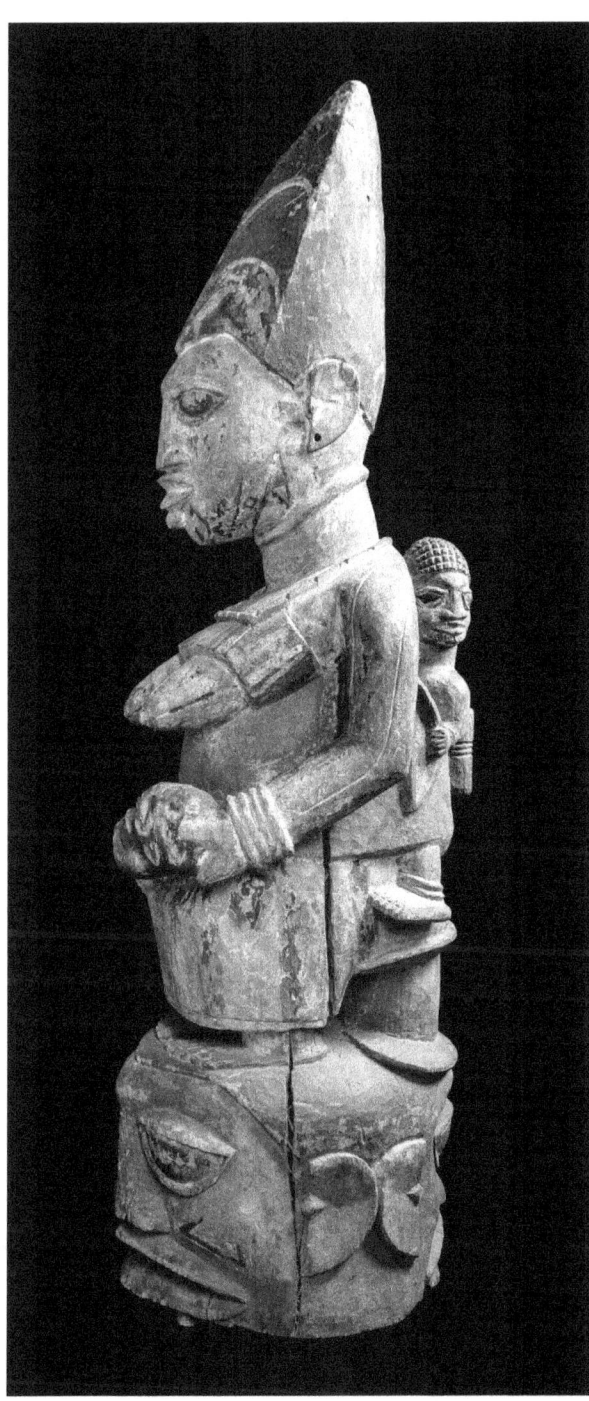

Figure 6.3.
Motherhood as
a mask. An *epa*
headpiece. Yoruba,
Ekiti province,
Nigeria. Photo:
Afrikacentrum,
Cadier en Keer.

such as food cultivation, carrying foodstuffs, and preparing meals at home, are seen as typically female – that is, as belonging to the female domain. Other activities, such as the manufacture of iron tools, warfare, and the production and marketing of cash crops, are considered as belonging to the male domain; work is gendered in the Crescent – and beyond. One seminal study of gender relations in West Africa, entitled 'Female and Male in West Africa' – note the order of the genders – has as its main theme 'Male and female spheres: separate and connected'.[17]

Members of the two domains do not cross the borders that separate them. Even living physically very close to each other, which African men and women do, they have clearly demarcated spaces within the compound and often have their own economic activities. A woman has her own hut, her own granary, her own *trésor*, as it is called in French, and of course she is the first port of call for her children; in short the matricentric unit mentioned above.[18] Kinship terms often distinguish brothers of the same mother from brothers of the same father, a distinction that permeates the life of a polygynous family and forms a recurring theme in myths and folk stories.[19] In Ghana for instance, the separateness of spouses,[20] the cooperation and conflict between the sexes,[21] and the role of polygyny and divorce,[22] all are based on this very African definition of a marriage as a working arrangement with domain demarcation and gender complementarity.[23]

As said, in the Crescent women do most of the cultivation. Also in societies where men do take pride in cultivation, like the Senufo, the women dominate agriculture and are equally proud of doing so; the contribution of the men, which is substantial, is viewed by the women with some disdain, since the continuity of the family and the village is seen as in women's hands.[24] In this culture, women act also as diviners, another crucial intermediary position between humans and the supernatural world. The Dan award a prize for the best hostess of the village, in the form of a highly decorated serving spoon for rice.[25] And throughout,

---

17 Oppong 1983: 70.
18 Amadiume 1997.
19 Van Beek 2015, 2020.
20 Abu 1983.
21 Vercruijsse 1983.
22 Hagan 1983: 192–203. See also Vellenga 1983.
23 Goody 1973b.
24 Glaze 1981: 74.
25 Himmelheber 1979.

the households are run by women taking care of children, food, and their husbands; they rule the domestic sphere.

In 1972 the anthropologist Sherry Ortner published an article that has become the subject of prolonged debates under the title 'Is female to male as nature to culture?'[26] Her topic was why in all cultures men are dominant and the position of women is one of cultural inferiority. Of course, the ways of male domination vary widely between cultures, as do the actual positions of women, but there is indeed no society in the world where the tables are completely turned, and only few where the playing field between the genders is wholly level. So the question is very apt.

Looking at cultural valuations of the genders Ortner posits a generalised association of men with culture and women with nature. It is not so much the biology of the sexes that generates this universality as the way cultures construct the life spheres for men and women upon the basis of these biological differences. Women, who give birth to babies and must suckle them, are routinely assigned the duties of the domestic sphere, the tasks of cooking, caring, and cleaning, leaving the cultural side of politics, religion, and the maintenance of order, and thus the making of society, to the men. Domestic families in themselves do not make a society; in fact, they have conflicting aims and goals, so the male tasks are crucial for the larger whole and thus gain a higher cultural valuation. Since women are part and parcel of this culture, they share this hierarchy of values and consent to their – officially – lower position.[27]

This article, many times reprinted, has inspired a large debate on the universality of gender inequality within the interaction between biology and culture. Ortner's observation of a pervasive gender imbalance is clearly visible in Africa, and evidently the issue is of importance for the gender aspect in mask rituals. But how does this male–female dichotomy relate to the opposition village–bush that is crucial in masking? Our mask definition contrasts the village (culture) with bush (nature), and associates the village with woman and bush with man; Ortner's dichotomy seems different. The question is what we mean by 'nature'. In the equation nature = female, nature means the biology of the female body, the bio-mechanics of reproduction and lactation – and is hence an individualised nature. The bush, on the other hand, is very much an environmental, generalised nature, relevant to the whole of society. So the bush is gendered and male

26 Ortner 1974.
27 See McCormack and Strathern 1980.

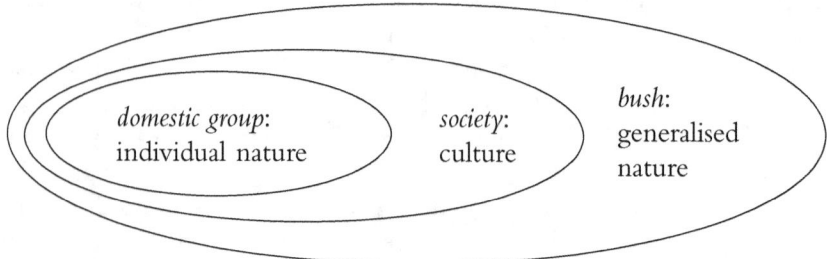

Figure 6.4. Man and woman between nature and culture.

because it coincides with basic male activity, that of making a society through the regulated input of the external nature. Figure 1 shows this in diagrammatic form.

So the two different oppositions of nature and culture come together on the domestic–society–bush axis.[28] From our angle, the male gendering of the bush in mask rituals reinforces the masculine structures of society in its confrontation with the domestic unit, the domain of the woman embodying individual nature. We are speaking about generalisations here, and it is well to heed Henrietta Moore's warning that such schemes are not always found on the ground: 'The feminine and the masculine in cultural analysis are frequently only tangentially related to what actual women and men do or believe.'[29] One factor ignored in many debates is the simple fact that men are physically stronger than women. Audrey Richards quotes a Bemba woman who remarked drily: 'In the end, we cannot beat them up, but they can [beat us up].'[30] That, too, is biology.

If in return for this domestic power, the women must relinquish official positions that represent the community to the outside, how large is this price? Since men usually fulfil the public representative roles while women work in their homes, in the eyes of the outsider the latter seem to be dominated. However, the judgement on this gender imbalance hinges on the question of which of these two domains, the public and the private, is the more important one. Different continents provide different answers

---

[28] Gendering – even sexualising – a society's relationship with aspects of its environment, is not uncommon; one evident example is smelting iron, which is consistently and creatively gendered (Rowlands and Warnier 1996).

[29] Moore 1994: 163.

[30] A. Richards 1982: 125.

in this regard; in effect, the public–private dichotomy is a Western one, where the interior of the house is invisible from the outside. In African villages, life is much more in the open – perhaps not always in full sight, but within earshot in any case. The reason Bamenda men give for their public dominance is also revealing: 'Yes, a woman is like God. And like God she cannot speak. She must sit silently.'[31]

Kaberry relates an Ibo case where the men tried to impose a rule that the women did not like, even trying to have them pay fines. The women got together and organised a walk-out. Together they left the village, leaving all children behind, except the suckling babies. So the men had to care for crying children, carry water, bring in firewood, and do the women's work – meaning, they had to try their hand at cooking as well. 'They endured this for a day and a half, then went to the women and begged them to return. They gave them a goat and apologised formally and informally. The women returned!'[32] What makes this case ironic is that the ruling of the men was about the right of the women to have lovers on the side; the men had decided that their spouses had to renounce these lovers and pay a goat to their husbands in compensation. And this was what provoked the female walk-out![33]

A crucial factor is that these African cultures are fiercely pronatalist: fertility is a prime value, children are welcome and needed, and motherhood is highly honoured. This aspect and the food production-*cum*-cooking together form the firm foundation of the women's domain, their power base. Matrilineages in Grassfields' cultures[34] are called the 'buttock of the house', because 'all people come from there'.[35] Throughout, fertility means motherhood, having a child and feeding it, so procreation and cooking are closely entwined. When we mentioned cooking in initiation, the implication was that the bond of motherhood was not really severed, neither for the boy who must eat, nor definitively for his mother who cooks – even though officially she must think he has 'been eaten'. 'The functions of a woman as mother and giver of food tend to be so [...] fused in African thought that it is difficult to separate them in analysis.'[36] And she

---

31 Kaberry 2005: 152.
32 Ibid.: 147.
33 Within the Crescent this is not unusual; for the free arrangements of Balante women, see Temudo 2019.
34 The Grassfields house both patrilineal and matrilineal groups.
35 Kaberry 2005: 17.
36 Ibid.: 151.

cooks for the whole household, including visitors; hospitality is a prime expression of her being master of the house. 'The pride which a woman takes in dispensing hospitality [...] to her husband's guests is one of those intangibles most difficult to document.'[37]

Masks follow the domain distinctions between the genders, and accentuate them. In cultures where masquerades belong exclusively to the men's domain (which is in fact almost everywhere), women will make no attempt to participate in them, even if they could. In the rare reverse case where masquerades extend into the women's domain, the men will never cross the border into the female domain. What the women produce is what the men also value greatly, and the fact that men must rely on masking to bolster their own position is indicative of where the real power lies. Masking is an effective tool in border demarcation, for the more strongly the men define their domain as off-limits for women, the more the female realm is shielded from the men.

So at the centre of the gender arena stands the female domain, based on the creative powers of fertility. But fertility is fragile. In general in the Crescent, while the women know they are looking at costumed men, they are still looking at powerful be-things inimical to their own fertility. The dancing young men may be theirs, but the powers are not, and the women are aware that they cannot command these powers directly without incurring harm; the only way to handle them is through their men. By performing their part of the secret, the women suspend their disbelief, for there surely must be something in these be-things, and whatever women think and say among themselves, they must perform according to this suspended disbelief. Something of the otherworld is present, and acting against it would incur a serious risk, and an unnecessary one at that.

An example: at a small well in a Dogon village, Yasaa, the wife of the first author's host asked him to remove a bundle of red fibres – part of the mask costume – lying alongside the path to the water: 'Walter, we cannot get to the well; please remove that mask for us.' He picked up the fibres, she got her water, and he replaced the 'mask' after she had left. Some man had put it there to reserve this well for his cattle. What would she have done without him? His female co-researcher told him she had removed it once for her, but was told not to touch it with her hands: take two sticks and put it aside. If neither of them had been present, Yasaa would probably

---

37 Ibid.: 97.

have done it herself in the same way, remove the fibres with two sticks and discard the sticks afterwards – not touching the stuff, for it is still a mask.

The mask threat to fertility is pervasive. Certain Baule masks must wear cotton girdles to catch their sweat when dancing, for whenever their 'mask sweat' reaches their genitals, the masker will become infertile himself.[38] While seemingly playing second fiddle, the women are very much aware of their back-seat driving. The Ashanti proverb used as an epigraph for this chapter captures this eloquently: the hen seems to accept that announcing dawn belongs to the cock's domain. She lets the cock do it, even if she seems subservient to him, but it guarantees that he will not interfere with her business, which is laying eggs; after all, that is what being a chicken is about. If not, you are eaten.

Celebrating femininity

As far as masks are concerned, women are either the target audience or the target non-audience; the difference is actually moot. When the rituals are taboo for women, this fact is always stressed to mark the special quality of the occasion: not for women! Most masks may be taboo to touch, but not to look at. When a Baule dancer performs the *kpan* mask, moving with slow and stately paces, the mask may itself manifest the strong position of women in their culture; but what would that mean for the dancer himself without admiring female eyes? As a mask dancer told Susan Vogel: 'If the women aren't among us when we dance, it has no sweetness.'[39] Christopher Roy reports how the spectacular serpent mask was adopted from one Bwa village into another, since it would attract more girls to the local performances.[40]

As Paolo Israel indicates, this may well be one of the motivational engines of masking,[41] since dancing without a female audience is rather pointless everywhere. However, it puts the performer in a quandary, since for this audience he is supposed to be unknown. As Jedrej put it: 'Representing the invisible in a visible form, his visible self has become invisible';[42] or in the words of Simon Ottenberg, the dancer has a double absence: he is not onstage, but not in the audience either.[43] With his face hidden behind a

---

38 The *kwam kple* mask; A-M. Boyer 2008: 52.
39 Vogel 1997a: 180.
40 Roy 2003. See for a general overview Roy 2007.
41 Israel 2014.
42 Jedrej 1980: 226.
43 Jedrej 1980; Ottenberg 1982.

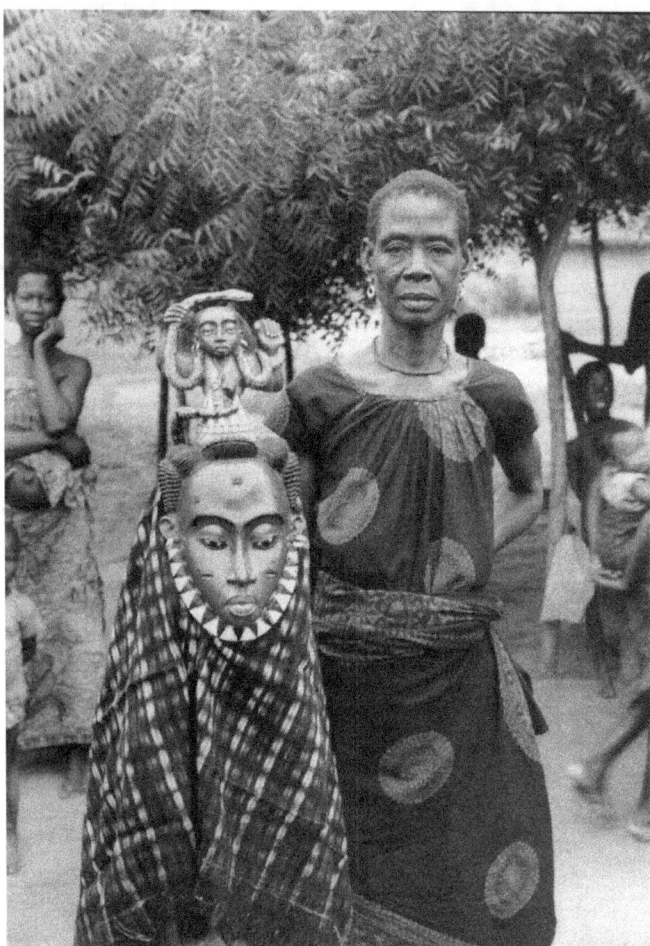

Figure 6.5. A Baule woman and her portrait headpiece. Baule, Côte d'Ivoire, 1972. Photo: Susan Mullin Vogel.

wooden top and his body covered with cloth or fibres, not much of the dancer is visible. And yet he hopes that the female audience not only appreciates his performance, but also will recognise who he is, otherwise much of his effort will have been in vain. In trying to shine, the dancer must be content with anonymous excellence, counting on the secret not to hold. So at the very heart of the mask performance is a gender charade: collectively the men perform a dance based upon a masculine secret, pretending that the women are not party to that secret; but at the same time, the individual dancers calculate that this pretence is part of the play and that the women do know, and indeed recognise individual dancers – while remaining silent about it. To the men at least. And that is exactly what happens. Thus, masquerading dramatises the separation of gender roles as well as their mutual dependence.[44]

But the involvement of women goes further than simply being present. As mentioned in Chapter 2, quite a few masking cultures have tops depicting women and girls, usually in alluring forms, and generally they tend to honour womanhood through masks – the other side of the gender coin. The Ibibio have the pretty girl,[45] the Dogon the young girl, the Senufo their beautiful woman[46] – all of which are danced by men but portray women. The Baule in Côte d'Ivoire provide another example of this masking category, a culture that is clearly in love with its own masks. Baule women have a multilevel relation with masks. For a *blo* masquerade, a man commissions a so-called portrait mask (*ndoma*, double) to represent his wife; he will then don the head cover and a woman's outfit, including fake breasts, while she proudly escorts him, enjoying the way the masker celebrates female beauty and womanhood.[47]

The bond between a woman and her 'double' is close and lifelong; it becomes part of her identity. The dance itself, though performed by a male dancer, is considered a woman's dance, gracious in style with women participating alongside it. When the woman in question becomes too old or too weak to come out, she asks her daughter to take her place. Also, when the husband becomes too old to dance, he has his son perform as mask.

This *blo* dance, in which a woman dances next to a male dancer wearing her *ndoma*, is an uncommon phenomenon in Africa, where men and women do not usually dance together, and certainly not with masks. But there are also other ways in which women use mask performances actively in support of their own positions in life, enhancing and glorifying the female domain. One is in children's masquerades, such as in the Luvale groups of Zambia. Boys and girls together organise play initiations, modelled on the *mukanda* mentioned in Chapter 3, in which women participate, though some basic taboos still hold. The real initiation will come later, but this one is not just for fun; it is for the mothers. 'Women claim that a major purpose of the masquerade figures is to play with the initiates' mothers, to honor them and to make them happy.'[48]

44 Picton 1989: 74.
45 Borgatti 2003.
46 Glaze 1975.
47 See Vogel 1997a: 137 for details about this piece.
48 Cameron and Jordán 2006: 239–240.

In the following example the women are not in opposition to the male masks but, fully aware of their procreative powers, they enlist the support of the masks in the festive celebration of their own motherhood. No mask genre typifies this dynamic better than the Yoruba *gelede* in southwestern Nigeria. It is fitting that the first UNESCO recognition of a masquerade was for these Yoruba dances,[49] since more than any other mask performance these are the ones that celebrate womanhood.

Toward midnight on the day of the festival, the entire community meets in the marketplace with mats, chairs, lights, drink, and food, as they know the night will be long. The drummers take their seats and everyone is ready, when suddenly to the sustained rhythm of the drums a mask appears, dressed completely in white and moving slowly in a stooping manner, suggesting that 'she' is very old. Elders of the *gelede* society rise and pay their respect to her, while a choir sings praise songs: 'Mother, Mother, child who brings peace to the world, repair the world for us. *Iyanla*, child who brings peace to the world.'[50] After circling the area a few times, the mask leaves the market place and another mask takes its place, with songs to honour the mothers, the gods, and the elders of the society. Though impressive enough in their own right, these masks form just a prelude to the arrival of the high point of the evening: *oro efe*.

Two assistants enter the marketplace and kneel with special medicines that will protect *oro efe* during the performance, followed by the head of the *gelede* cult and her assistant, all clad in white as a sign of respect for deities and the 'Great Mother'. The two strike a special gong, assuring *oro efe* that all is safe. A flute player commands the crowd to be silent. Then, finally, with all attention focused on the entrance, the mask *oro efe* appears, moving slowly with its elegant white costume, ankle bells rattling, a horsetail whisk in each hand. This is the 'bird of the night' mask, 'Great Mother', *oro efe*, the most powerful of *efe* and *gelede* forms.

The mask moves slowly, majestically, manifesting the pride, patience, and endurance that are characteristic of womanhood,[51] and sports an elaborately carved headdress with a white face topped by a multicoloured superstructure that displays snakes and woodpeckers. This is a singing mask, and its praise

---

49 Since 2008, the *gelede* dance has been acknowledged by UNESCO as an intangible cultural heritage. This paragraph has also benefited from the special issue on *egungun* in *African Arts*. 1978. Vol. 11, 3.

50 Drewal and Drewal 1983: 24. The work of the Drewals is foundational in Yoruba studies; see also Drewal 1974a and b.

51 Prince 1961: 798.

songs comment on events in the community since its previous appearance, comments given in humour or satire, but always with an undertone of deep concern. The mask offers prayers for the well-being of the community but also hurls curses at those who have offended society: they will die by fire or by insanity. *Oro efe* directs its songs and comments to spiritual forces – and above all to the mothers – first solo and then joined by the chorus and the public for the refrains, always to the strict rhythm of the drums. This spectacle lasts throughout the night. At dawn, *oro efe* quietly leaves the arena.

The *gelede* festival is a large one, containing a host of mask dances, and it has evoked commentaries by the dancers themselves: '*Gelede* is the secret of women. We, men, are merely their slaves. We dance to appease our mothers.'[52] Dancing *gelede* affects the quality of life in the community and may avert drought and other calamities. As one dancer observed, 'It is necessary [to dance]. It is in order to get good crops.'[53] Fertility in Africa has many faces. Never is this more evident that when a *gelede* dancer wears the most female of all mask attributes: a belly-mask. Figure 6.6 shows two of these masks, portraying not just women but pregnant ones. Here, the female secret is out in the open, for some to reminisce over, for many to aspire to, and for all to admire. The glory of women is the power of fertility, a power source men can only longingly try to emulate symbolically.[54]

By dancing *gelede*, the masks bring *asè* into this world, a power affirming life and providing security, and the *efe gelede* festival is full of this *asè*, full of its positive side:

> Although *efe* contains humorous anecdotes and satire, they are only a superficial aspect. *Efe* songs possess vital power (*asè*), which is activated in the pronouncing of the words of all *efe* songs regardless of their subject matter.[55]

Witchcraft is the negative side of the same *asè* coin, and so the masks speak out against this misuse of the force. The praise songs, speeches, dances, headpieces, and rituals all possess *asè*, which is also deemed to stave off drought and other disasters, while public prayers are especially directed at women who want to have children.

Yoruba women are honoured in the *gelede* cults, but steer the proceedings as well. Prior to the festival the women meet with senior men in the

---

52 Beier 1958: 5.
53 Drewal and Drewal 1975: 38.
54 Lawal 1996.
55 Drewal and Drewal 1983: 38.

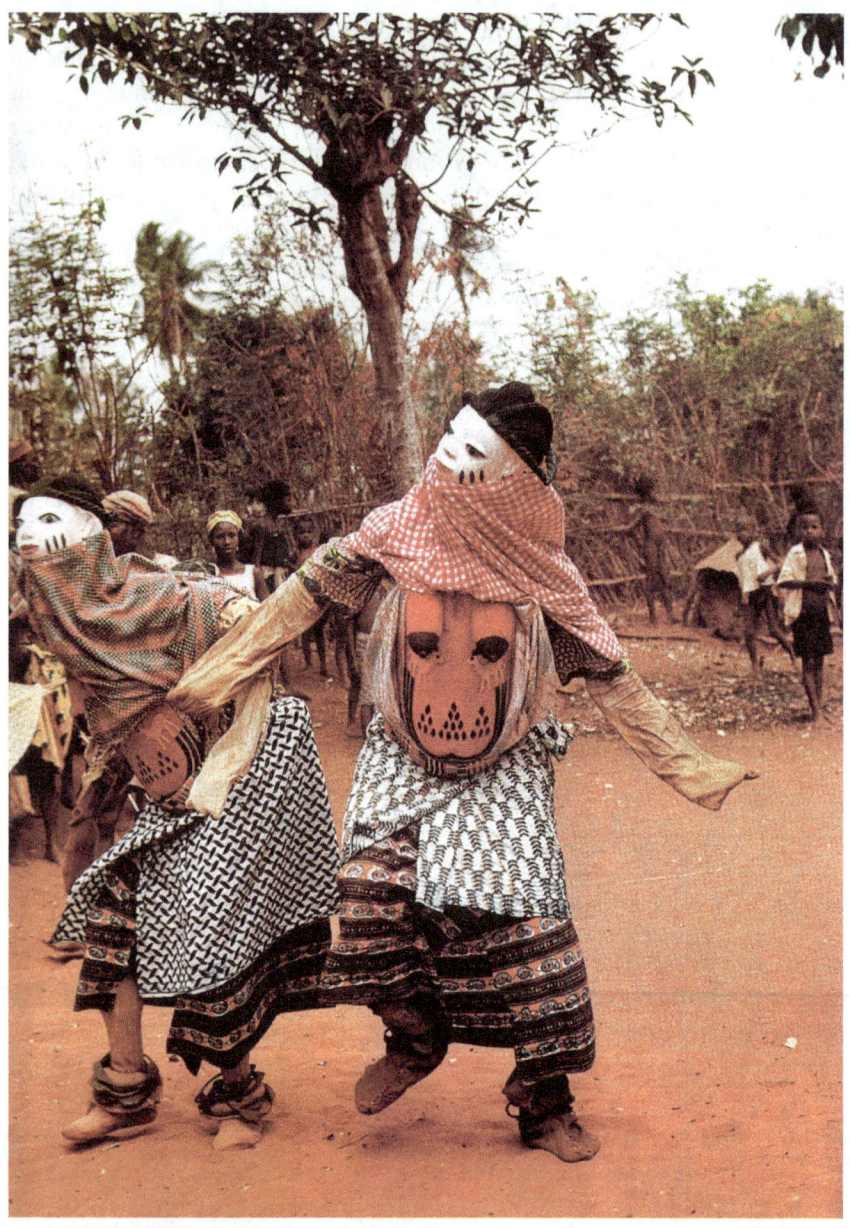

Figure 6.6. Adorned with beauty, breasts, and a prominent belly, two *gelede* masks, representing female twins, provide a burlesque interlude during a major festival. Cové region, Benin, c. 1950–1960. Photo: Michel Huet.

organisation of the festival to evaluate the past year. Together they decide on the events that need to be commented upon, the praise songs, the wording of the speeches, and how the new headpieces would have to look. So, behind the scenes Yoruba women affirm their powerful position in society through the manipulation of the *gelede* festival, controlling the masquerades without anybody noticing it, and thus strengthening their hold on social, moral, and political matters in the society.[56]

All masquerades are also products of history. As John Willis has shown, the *gelede* masks probably developed out of the older *egungun* – also urban, see the next chapter – shifting from an attempt to control women into the idea of celebration of motherhood. Later the female role in masking became much wider, when the mother figure was complemented by that of the wife, a model that fitted palace women.[57] In some cases women may well be authorised to organise a masquerade, for example, a daughter who fulfilled her father's final wishes by organising a mask performance in his remembrance.[58] Yet women do have to respect some boundaries. The historian Nwando Achebe tells of an exceptional Igbo woman who, under colonial rule, had a remarkable career, even extending into masking.[59] She was exiled, forced into prostitution, and then became a multilingual merchant and ally of the British coloniser. Back in her area of origin she became a crucial aide to the British and acquired several colonial positions, climbing from headman to warrant chief, and by the mid-1920s she had become king in her paternal Nsukka division. In 1939 she decided that as a 'man' she would organise a masquerade, by creating a mask with its accompanying spirit. That was a bridge too far: the Igbo elders, already rebelling against her running the daily operations of the state, seized and confiscated her masquerade and sued her. In court, the British colonials, never loathe to change sides, backed the elders and she lost her privileges.

The relationship of women with masks is complex, and one curious possibility is realised among the Jola and Mandinka peoples of Senegal and The Gambia,[60] the option of the mythical mask mentioned in Chapter 4, one in which the female version surpasses the male one. Masks may be good to dance; they are also good to think. The mask in this case is the *kankurang*

56 Gore 2007.
57 Willis 2018: 132–133.
58 See Willis 2018: 145–150.
59 Achebe 2003; see also Willis 2018: 154.
60 See https://ich.unesco.org/en/RL/kankurang-manding-initiatory-rite-00143, consulted 1 September 2018.

mask, an all-fibre mask made from the bark of special trees (Figure 10.1). With its deep ochre colours it is an impressive apparition in boys' initiation camps in the sacred forest – out of bounds to women, of course, a taboo underscored by the slashing knives that the mask may wield.

A persistent secret tradition holds that a female variant of the *kankurang* also exists. Deep in the sacred forest, a female *kankurang* is thought to consist of just fire, a being enveloped in flames, much more powerful than the male version – so powerful that it never leaves the forest. The mask may not be seen at all, in fact, except at a certain time during the excision of girls, where it ensures the proper healing of the wounds.[61] On just one night, when the excised girls lie on the ground, forbidden to fall asleep and strictly prohibited from looking at the mask – their heads are covered with a shawl – this female *kankurang* is reported to protect the novices against evil forces. Only the Manding women mention this mask, which is thought to be controlled by blacksmith women. Kirsten Langeveld treats these two masks, the male and the female, as complementary, which fits well into the generalised gender discourse on masks. But in the end the female version may never actually have been present; it may just have been spoken about.[62]

From their side, the Jola men also have such a mythical mask, called *ifan bondi*. It may appear as a *kankurang* mask but cannot be summoned; it emerges of its own accord, is invulnerable, can multiply itself, notifies others of its presence by a certain sound (a rooster's crow), and has a special smell. This mask never comes into any village and, of course, is considered the most powerful of all. Its myth tells of a brother and sister. The brother danced *kankurang*, and his sister disguised herself as a man to know the secrets of the mask. Her brother noted the smell of woman inside the sacred forest and received the order from the elders to seek her out and kill her, having been promised that he would then remain *kankurang* forever. He found his sister, beheaded her, and united her magical powers with his to become *ifan bondi*.[63] Masks, therefore, do not need to exist in actual reality but can also be merely the subject of discourse. In any case the mask rituals constitute a meta-discourse, a symbolic way to 'speak about the other gender'. The last myth is telling: men and women have their own sources of power; and joined together after an almost incestuous murder, they become an invincible and eternal being. But still invisible!

---

61 Langeveld 2003: 126–127.
62 This resonates with the way women's associations used masks among the Mandinka (Weil 1998).
63 Langeveld 2003: 125, 132.

Women dancing with masks

The next step up the ladder of female involvement in masks is found in girls' initiation. These rites centre on marriage and motherhood, with symbolism around blood, fire, and cooking, all linked to the girls' bodies. Often residing in a seclusion hut, the girls are expected to eat, dance, and sing, and especially to grow fat, while relearning all the domestic tasks that they already know so well. Submission to authority, speaking properly, and honouring their prospective husband – these qualities are taught during the period by older women. Masks may figure in the rituals; girls of the Bemba, Chewa, and neighbouring Nyanya,[64] all in Zone 3, witness a mask performing at the end of their initiation, danced by a man.

In Zone 1, among the Senegalese Manding, the *sengko* mask, a bark and bamboo contraption, was central in girls' initiation.[65] It started with the girls' sleeping out on the village square at full moon, where during the following day they learned the songs of the mask, especially their responses to them. During the second night the *sengko* came from the bush with its assistants and 'inspected' the girls to determine whether there were any witches among them. Fearful of the mask, the girls tried to get up, but their caretakers, kinswomen, forced them down again. Content that there were no witches, the mask started to sing its song and carefully listened to their sung responses, threatening the little girls if they made mistakes. Most of the night was spent in dancing. First the mask danced by itself, while the girls' mothers presented gifts to its assistants; then the initiated women danced with the *sengko* in a highly sexualised show; the women presented the mask with their headscarves, which were tied to its top-knot. No one could leave the square, for only 'witches' would shrink from the spectacle; so for the whole seven hours of the mask's performance, the audience had to stay.

The final afternoon saw the girls, in shining, red-coloured outfits, gather in the square again for the last rite: the 'run'. The group of girls had to run a gauntlet from the side of the square to a special tree, while halfway across the square the mask and its assistants tried to block their way. Armed with whips they lashed at the girls, who were helped and shielded by their female guards; the latter took most of the blows. Eventually all girls arrived at the tree, the first girl receiving a special title. At the foot of the tree the mask assistants showed the girls a few secret/sacred objects, including a jar with sour milk. All the girls had to taste the milk and heard that they should

64 A. Richards 1982: 179, 180.
65 This description is based upon Weil 1987. See also Weil 1971.

never reveal these secrets to the uninitiated; no explanation was given. The initiated girls took the first girl on their shoulders into the waiting crowd, where she was honoured in a great dance. That evening the girls dressed in fine clothes and headed back to the square, and resumed the dance with the mask, which lasted until dawn. This time the mask did not fade back into the night, but the women and girls picked up pebbles, as instructed by the woman leading the initiation, and threw them at the retreating mask: 'Go away! We don't want you! Go back to the bush!' and the ritual was over.[66]

We are not overly informed on girls' initiations,[67] and certainly not on those featuring masks, but this important case shows some systematic differences with the boys' encounter with masks. The mask as a threatening apparition, the whipping as a test, the instructions on how to respond properly, and the dancing and drumming, this much is similar. Also, at the end of the seclusion both come out and with some drama are shown to the village, a moment referred to as 'revelation'.[68] But it is not the inside of the mask that is revealed, but the new outside of the bride. Here the village square sets the stage, and the leader of the proceedings is a woman. The main test is not so much what the girls perform, as determining their status as potential 'witches' – presumed witchcraft is a perennial focus of mask actions in general, a topic of Chapter 8. Also, the mask dances mainly with women. The main additional symbols pertain not to death but to food, in the form of eggs and fire,[69] and the symbols are not of rebirth but of procreation. All in all this is an intriguing ritual reversal, showing the flexibility of masking in its core function as an agent of maturation.

It is the Mende women who take the mask logic to its final step: they themselves dance with the masks. The context is that of secret societies, that hothouse of masking. The large area in West Africa where *poro* associations are found, the whole coastal area of Zone 1, also harbours *sande* associations, which are exclusively for women.[70] In most groups that have *sande* organisations, the masks are just for men in their *poro*; but in Sierra Leone, the *sande* members in Mende society wear masks as well, which is almost

---

66 Weil 1998: 98. The woman-centeredness of this initiation is underscored by one of its central symbols, the elephant. Peter Weil analyses its as being self-sufficient and matriarchal, whereas the marginal males are only needed for insemination. Other associations with the elephant are knowledge and understanding, initiation and abundance.

67 Brown 1963.

68 Imeh 2012.

69 The article is called 'Fighting fire with fire' (Weil 1987); fire refers to bush fires, the mask itself, and domestic fires for cooking.

70 M.J. Adams 1983, 1980. See for their public power MacCormack 1975, 1979.

unique in Africa. The masks are a nice example of the fusion of worlds that we saw earlier; the costumes are made of black-dyed palm fibre, typical bush material, but their helmet-shaped headpieces show human faces with finely carved hairdresses and ringed necks. The dancer's feet are hidden in stockings or shoes. The maskers embody not only the *sande* association but also have their own spirit, *ngafa*. Secret societies almost automatically involve initiation; and, indeed, *sande*'s main responsibility is the initiation of girls into the association, a precondition for marriage in Mende.

On the first day of their initiation period, the girls are collected from their homes and escorted into the camp by older women and *sowei* masks. *Sowei* is the title for women with the highest rank in *sande*. While it is also used for the masked dancers, it refers fundamentally to the 'Great Mother'. The name *sowei* stands for ideal human beauty; and the headpiece especially, slightly different in every mask, is the idealised image of female bodily perfection and power.[71] In the camp the girls are received by a wild rush of masks and women together, in a dramatic display of female power, masked and non-masked. Immediately upon their arrival in the bush camp the girls are excised.

The role of the *sowei* during the initiation period is all-important. They act on behalf of the entire *sande* association, take care of the girls during the excision and the period of recuperation, and stay in touch with the villagers. The *ndoli sowei* (the *sowei* who dances) is the masked *sande* representative, its tutorial spirit, and appears in the village after the completion of each stage of the initiation period. Two or three days later, while the initiates remain in the camp to heal their wounds, one *ndoli sowei* mask leaves the camp, ritually dressed and accompanied by other women. Its personal attendants announce the mask's arrival on the scene by calling out the mask's name in full voice, in a chant that resembles wailing. The attendant carries a straw mat, which she may drape over the mask's lap when it sits down, or use as a screen if the mask wishes to rearrange its costume. This mask does not so much dance as walk slowly and silently, since it is waiting for the recuperation of the girls. It is still a time of danger, too early for celebration. The mothers of the initiates know nothing yet about the condition of their daughters, and they too are anxiously waiting. In the meantime, the women who arrived in *ndoli sowei*'s company run through the village, shouting, rampaging, and creating havoc, which nobody can object to. After some time, the mask and the women return to their camp.

71 Blier 1986.

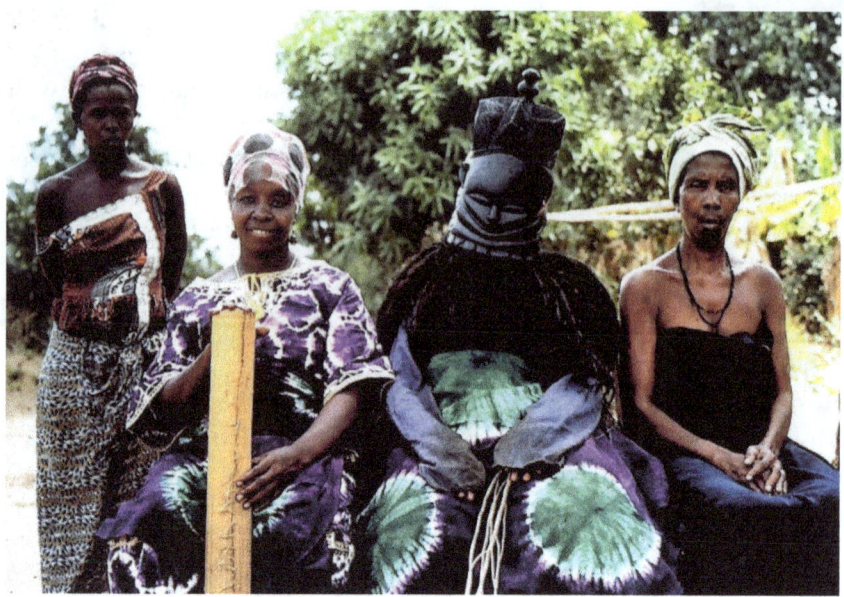

Figure 6.7. *Ndoli sowei* with accompanying *sande* initiates. Bandajuma Kovegbuami, Kenema district, Mende, Sierra Leone. Photo: Ruth Phillips.

About two weeks after the excisions, the *ndoli sowei* mask appears in the village again, this time to announce that the initiates will return home the next day. Of course, the girls' mothers are relieved that their daughters have recuperated well, so now is the time for rejoicing, singing, and dancing. Several *ndoli sowei* masks, all in their black raffia costumes but with varying headpieces, join in the celebrations, which will last all night.

The next day witnesses a long line of women appear in the village, walking solemnly in a row, accompanied by the *sowei*. The newly initiated girls, women now, are easily recognisable: their upper bodies are covered with white clay; they wear head ties and special strings of beads diagonally across their chests, as a mark of their newly conferred status as marriageable adult women, fertile women ready for procreation – but also members of *sande* now. The line of *sowei* and initiates dances at certain spots in the village, joined by *sande* officials. The scene of homecoming is joyful, though not as exuberant as with the boys' re-entry from the bush; there is a quiet, slow-burning sense of joy in the village. From now on the girls will stay with their parents during the daytime but return to the camp for the night, and they will remain dressed as initiates.

The final release of the girls from the initiation camp takes place some two months later. After bathing ritually in the river, at last away from the watchful eye of the mask, the new members of *sande* are welcomed back into the village. There they are congratulated and receive gifts, with a general village dance for the newly initiated members of the community, the girls themselves behaving in a graceful and disciplined manner. At the end of the festivities, the *ndoli sowei* hand the girls back to their parents. The initiation is over.[72]

Every *sande* mask receives its own name when the spirit that inhabits the mask reveals its identity to the mask's owner in a dream; these names are proudly displayed and fully known. A man never makes his association with a particular mask known, but a Mende woman considers the mask as her personal possession, and does not object to being photographed with it, even holding the headpiece in her hands. When viewing the mask itself, as in Figure 6.7, the contrast with the male masks is clear. The headpiece does not express alienness, but beauty. When a male mask represents beauty, it represents the ideal of the other sex, of female excellence in the eyes of men. The *sowei* masks do not hint at anything outside themselves; they are just themselves. They rarely dance; they just walk around, dignified and with poise, and they sit on chairs. Male masks walk, dance, swirl, and run, but they do not sit, unless watching other masks; for the Mende *poro* masks, of which there are a lot, the same holds. Women's masks behave like the dignified women they are; they talk and sing, and when they must rearrange their dress, they are simply shielded by a mat. The dress of the female *sowei* mask bears little reminiscences to the bush, and sometimes it is difficult to see in the old photographs who is the mask and who are its attendants.

Thus, women who dance with masks perform their own persona, not in order to be something else but to be the best they can be. The absence of a public secret is striking. These are masks that cherish and honour domesticity, fully at home inside the village, rooted inside the house. A picture like Figure 1.4 is quite revealing in this respect: the woman sits proudly with her mask in her lap, while her husband and son stand next to her in deference.

The Mende women's *sowei* takes masks as far as women can go with them. The ultimate version, in which women would have masks but not men, does not exist in Africa. In the end, also for the Mende, the involvement of women with masks is a corollary of the male occupation with them – not the other way around; the male masks are the original, while the female versions

72 R. Phillips 1995: 97 ff, Bledsoe 1984.

are a reflection. This does not mean that women's issues are secondary to understanding the African mask phenomenon, for that is not the case, not by any means. For African masking, as we have stated from the onset, the arena between the genders is fundamental. Also, in men-only masks the women are always present as the idea of femininity opposite to the mask. In women's masks this inherent and implicit antagonism against the other sex is simply not there; they operate fully within their own gender and within their own domestic domain, secure in its demarcation and not intent on dominance over the public domain. In women's masks masculinity is simply not in the picture: women suffice in themselves.

In their role as domain demarcators the male masks delineate, highlight, and empower the male part of the gender arena, defining it as out of bounds for women; as such, they create a male corner in which men are deemed self-sufficient in all relevant matters, including fertility and procreation. The sources of life they preempt, however, are virtual and stem from an association with death, an inherent paradox that is at the heart of masquerades. The women's domain, on the other hand, is not virtual but real, and not through death but through birth; the women's masks simply accentuate that solid basis. 'Because women make a secret of birth, we make a secret of death', as one Chewa informant formulated it.[73] This opposition between 'power from death' and 'power from the body' harbours an underlying competition: which is the ultimate source of power. Whenever the battle is actually waged, as we shall see below, the outcome is clear, and it is not the men who come out on top.

The mask of the woman is her body

Dusk falls over a small Baule town near Yamoussoukro in Côte d'Ivoire. From several houses, women emerge and head toward the far end of the main street. The women, mostly elderly, are clad in single white cloths that barely hide their naked bodies. Gathering around their leader, they anxiously await the signal to start *adyanun*, their ritual dance through the town. The occasion for the ritual is serious: in several villages in the area, women have died from mysterious diseases. Divination has indicated that the cause must be attributed to witchcraft.

The chief had already taken measures to combat the problem. Two months earlier, he had called the *poro* to come in with their masks, and that is what they did. The *bo nun amuin* masks, imaginary animals (with horns and a

73 Yoshida 2006: 234.

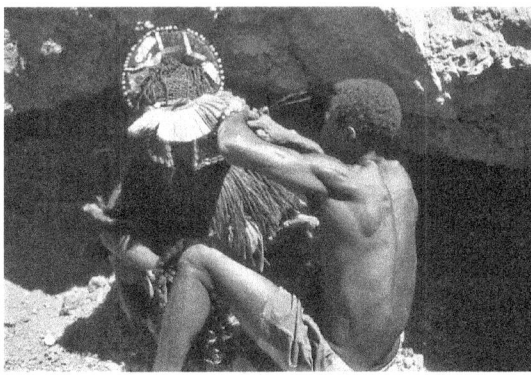

Figure 6.8. When a male mask is damaged during the dance, it must be repaired out of the sight of women. Tireli, Dogon, Mali, 1980. Photo: Walter van Beek.

large boxy muzzle showing rows of teeth), danced in the village, venting their aggression on the unknown transgressors. The frightening outfit of these spirits 'of the bush' made quite an impression, and the women and non-initiated had to hide in their houses.

It is two months later now, and last week another woman died from the same symptoms, so the mask dance did not halt the disaster, and sterner measures were called for. Thus, the chief called on the women to invoke their spirits, the *amuin bla*, more powerful than those of the men. And here they are, the women of the town, joined by women of surrounding towns and villages, conscious of the evil that threatens their homes. Unlike the men two months ago the women do not wear masks; their outfit is the ultimate contrast, a simple transparent piece of cloth, which in fact means that they are considered naked. The mood is one of anger and aggression against these evil forces of witchcraft.

Suddenly the women's leader strikes up the ritual song of *adyanun*, signalling the beginning of the dance. She sings at the top of her voice, ending each verse with a shrill whooping cry that is repeated by all the women present, three times over. The group of women starts moving forward, almost running shoulder to shoulder, while clapping their hands and singing. They run through the town, from one end to the other, side-tracking between the houses. The sound of their voices is frightening and can be heard throughout the town. No men are in sight and no children: they hide in their houses. They believe that seeing naked women dance their *adyanun* may kill them. 'Powers of women are supreme', the Baule say.[74]

---

74 Vogel 1997a: 172.

'Naked' women, in whatever manner, not only form the absolute visual opposite of masks, they also trump the power of the bush, and the Baule are by no means unique in this respect.[75] The main issue is the power inherent in womanhood itself, for women do not derive their power from some external spiritual source as the masks do, but from their 'womanness', their fertility and, basically, their sexual organs.[76] Their power is vested in the creative power that enables them to bear children. These Baule women do not need masks to activate their spiritual forces; they simply dance, angry and shouting, with their body parts in full view. No male power can ever beat that. The women's power is not 'of the bush' but comes from the force of their own biological nature. And anything that derives from their body is powerful, as the next example shows.

The occasion is a feast in the western Cameroon city of Foumban, during the yearly commemoration of the investiture of the sultan. While Njoya III and his dignitaries install themselves at the entrance to his palace – a magnificent building on the UNESCO World Heritage List – they are waiting for three spider masks to form part of the festivities. Suddenly the masks are there, fierce and dangerous. With a seemingly uncontrolled anger they charge at all bystanders, flailing about with their clubs, and scattering the people in all directions. With ropes tied to their arms, youngsters try to contain them, but the masks are too strong. In the entourage of the sultan a few elders point wooden sticks set with copper wire at them – another attempt at control. But the three masks calm down only before a rather different type of control: a young woman with a child on her back waves a scarf at them. Immediately the masks are subdued, for here they encounter a superior force: the scarf is drenched in the woman's breast milk.[77]

The mask of the woman is her body. Time and again the tales about masks dwell on the forces of women's bodily fluids, from breast milk to vaginal fluids and menstrual blood – especially menstrual blood.[78] The whole masking complex, in all the three zones, hinges upon this fundamental opposition of male versus female power, symbolically typified in the contrast mask versus menstrual blood.

---

[75] Other examples are given in Kasfir 1998a, Cameron 1988, and Röschenthaler 1993.
[76] Makinde 2004.
[77] We thank Michael Rowlands for this case.
[78] For instance Carlson 2019.

> Menstruation is a profound mystery, the noxious flow of a substance
> so potent that contamination can diminish the fertility of the land,
> confound male virility, and interfere with the successful pursuit of
> goals in war, hunting, litigation […] Yet it is this substance that is the
> vital force of life, that ceases to flow when a child begins to form in
> the womb […] its monopoly by women constitutes a potential threat
> to the principles of social order […].[79]

Menstrual blood is the icon of female force, and womanhood is defined
in terms of menstruation. D'Azevedo's quote, collated from his male Gola
informants, underwrites Alma Gottlieb's insistence that the worldwide
phenomenon of menstrual taboos cannot be explained by simple pollution.[80]
In fact its symbolic connection with fertility can go in different directions:
the menarche of a young girl may be culturally feted,[81] or hidden from
outsiders; menses may signal a conception missed as an unfulfilled procreation and a fertile body not living up to its purpose, yet on the other hand
menstrual blood may be considered the very substance from which a child
is born, with conception involving the stopping of the flow through the
semen of the man.[82] And the concept of menstruation may have different
connotations than the blood itself.[83]

In the spring of 1985, the following story circulated in Monrovia, the
capital of war-torn Liberia, as reported by Warren D'Azevedo.[84] Two
well-to-do Monrovian women made frequent trips to the north to visit
friends, but they were always bothered by soldiers of the Kran group along
the road and endlessly searched until they paid them money. So they decided
to put an end to this harassment. The next time they were stopped, they
were forced, as usual, to open the trunk of their car. 'There is nothing of
interest', the women told the Kran militia, 'see for yourselves.' When a
soldier opened a bag, he and his colleagues shrank back in horror, covering
their faces as if burned. The women drove on and repeated the scene at
every checkpoint with the same success. They were never bothered by
any militia again. The bag in the trunk contained menstrual napkins, used
ones, in full view.

---

79 D'Azevedo 1994: 354.
80 Gottlieb 1988; Buckley and Gottlieb 1988.
81 Gottlieb 1988: 66.
82 A. Richards 1982.
83 Lamp 1985, 1988.
84 D'Azevedo 1994: 346–347.

When D'Azevedo brought up this story with his male Gola informants, they were shocked. For two reasons: first, that he spoke about such matters at all, for this was 'woman's business' – a man could only hint at this, through allusion and innuendo, and never speak openly, so the ethnographer had made a serious breach of etiquette. But the second shock was the idea that these women might be Gola, their own women. After some deliberation the men decided that such could never be the case: their women were too well-behaved – the *sande* association had taken care of that. In fact, the idea that these women might have been 'their own' was unbearable, so they explained to the ethnographer:

> Those Kran soldiers deserved to learn a lesson. Their guns and big talk were useless to them. They were helpless. Women are strong. You must not push them too far. They will do anything when they are vexed. No, it could not be Gola women who did that. They are too well-trained and would be ashamed.[85]

Wishful thinking, we think, on the part of these Gola men. Women all over the Mask Crescent will turn the tables of power when men transgress the borders of their masculine domain or misuse the power allotted them, as defined by the women. 'An intimate rebuke' is what Laura Grillo calls this in her major overview of FGP, female genital power,[86] a power quite evident to those shell-shocked policemen. These raps on the male knuckles can be institutionalised, like the *titi ikoli* practice of Bakweri women. When they believed it necessary, they wrapped their bodies in green leaves, leaving their sexual parts exposed, and sang songs that were embarrassing to the collectivity of men.[87]

The realitive effectiveness of FGP measures can be gauged from the Dogon *puro*, a punitive march, which either men or women may engage in. The male variant aims to berate the women in the village collectively for some infraction, at least in the eyes of the men. In 1989 in Tireli it started in the early morning with whooping mask cries, when sloppily dressed masks started to gather in the men's house. Each man was easily recognisable in these 'naked' masks, so all women had to remain inside their huts. The ire of the men was kindled because the women had been cutting the wrong trees for firewood; men liked to suck the fruit of this tree, but the women

---

85   D'Azevedo 1994: 347.
86   Grillo 2018.
87   Ifeka 2009. The custom had hardly changed in 2002 compared with accounts in the much earlier fieldwork of Shirley Ardiner in the 1950s. See Ardiner 1975.

needed its branches as firewood. The 'masks' tore the offensive branches from the stacks of firewood, and brought them to the men's house, which generated hot debates and flaming speeches about the wayward women. Meanwhile, the women remained in their huts, silently amused and not overly impressed, it seemed.[88] The male dominance at the men's house was further diminished by the presence of some older *yasigine*, sisters of the mask, who as initiated women were totally undaunted by this male display of righteous wrath. The verdict was severe: all women had to pay a fine so this would be a lesson they would never forget. However, none of the men even bothered to inform the women; all husbands paid the fines on behalf of their wives, and by noontime life in the village resumed its normal rhythm.

The female *puro* has a different impact. In 2008 word reached Tireli that in Banani a women's *puro* was on the way. The next morning the first author went over there, to witness a strange sight. One large compound at the edge of the village had been completely obliterated, its wall dismantled, the house broken down, and the granaries destroyed. Two women were searching amidst the rubble, dishevelled and sad, trying to find their belongings. What had happened was the following: their husband had a long history of abusing women in the village, a reputation that grew worse over time. Protests were raised against his transgressions, and complaints were lodged at the departmental chief's office, who sent over a gendarme to warn the man and to settle matters – which meant mainly to keep the women calm. It was too little and too late, since the women of Banani had decided to end these abuses once and for all by organising a *puro*.

All the women of the village came to the culprit compound and took off their clothes, meaning their blue cotton wrap-skirts. With naked genitals they walked toward the compound, the menstruating and pregnant women in front of the group: menstrual blood and fertility went hand in hand. The gendarme saw them coming and immediately fled. Methodically the women began taking down the whole compound, stone by stone, with the women of the house standing idly at the side. Nobody could do anything against this display of female power. The abusive owner was nowhere in sight; he had fled at the first sign, out of the village, out of Dogon country, and out of Mali. He was never seen again. His two wives eventually got

---

[88] The story is from the first author, who had a female colleague on the spot, reporting the reaction of the women.

hold of their personal belongings, moved out, and married elsewhere. The compound was never rebuilt.[89]

Among the Dogon, menstruating women are expected to stay in a special compound out of sight, but here they led the troupe. In general, the monthly blood signals both potential fertility and its dangerous fragility, representing a deeply rooted female power that at the same time generates a society and forms a threat to its male half.[90] The fact that in rural Africa women do not menstruate very often, through pregnancy, breast feeding and hunger, may even add to its symbolic poignancy.[91] Menstruation is the iconic 'woman's business', and completely out of bounds to men. Audrey Richards notes that the Bemba girls during their *chisungu* initiation are taught never to show even a single drop of menstrual blood to their husbands,[92] since viewing menstrual blood is something no man can stand. This is as cross-culturally valid as it gets in Africa, only inside the Crescent this part of the female symbolic repertoire is squared against the power of the mask.

One corollary is the special position of post-menopausal women in the Mask Crescent. At the heart of the Senufo *poro* is a female spirit, *malёёo* ('ancient woman', meaning post-menopausal), that is the main spiritual power guiding each *poro* society. Women, as we saw, have their own society, yet participation in *poro* activities is not fully restricted to men: young women may join *poro* dances in public. But when these girls marry, they are excluded from all *poro* activities; only after they reach menopause can they resume them and even opt to be initiated into *poro's* secret affairs.[93] Among the Dan peoples one of the most powerful masks was *bu gle,* which in the olden days would bless the men before they left for war and accompany them into battle. On its return the mask was welcomed by old women, and the mask was given to a post-menopausal woman for safekeeping. She would also take care of the medicines and other magical objects that protected the masker during his performance.

Grillo points out that these older women are much more than just 'cross-over men' whose 'drying up' has shifted their feminine identity into an almost masculine one. In a host of examples she shows how these 'Mothers', as they are called, 'are post-menopausal women, who having surpassed the defining

---

89 Van Beek and Banga 1992.
90 Weil 1998: 29.
91 Buckley and Gottlieb 1988: 45.
92 Glaze 1981: 88.
93 Glaze 1981: 90.

stage of sexual reproduction, are ambiguously gendered'.[94] Impervious to threats from the male domain, they presentify the 'Great Mother', a presence probably underreported in West African ethnography. For instance, when marching against the state, Cameroonian women 'consider themselves kings of the earth and architects of life', but may have to shield younger, fertile women from the dangers inherent in FGP:[95] 'With their very bodies, the women throw down the gauntlet of judgement and challenge to spiritual combat those who would dare defy them.'[96]

Suspicions of witchcraft are never far away from such displays of embodied spiritual power. Margaret Drewal interprets the *gelede* festival as the means by which Yoruba society honours and assuages these 'Mothers': the rather playful masquerade 'seduces' them in order to channel their extraordinary power (*asè*) towards blessing.[97] For *asè* also has the connotation of witchcraft. Among the Ebira, witchcraft is considered a female occult and threatening force, and masquerades are deemed to follow an ancestral precedent to assuage this female mystical 'energy', amounting to 'a dramatic male pretence against a covert female reality'.[98]

A gentler aspect of the female body highlights the same equation: male mask = female body. Among the Fodonon, a Senufo subgroup, a woman's funeral society is called the *tyekpa*, 'women's *poro*'. It is a peculiar institution, resembling a declaration of independence on the part of the Fodonon women.[99] At a funeral celebration the women dance with sculptures on their heads, sizeable statues representing women seated in serene beauty.[100] Like the *sowei* of the Mende, these Senufo women dance with an effigy of themselves on their heads – not a bush be-thing but an ideal woman.

Back now to the Sherry Ortner debate. Indeed, women are associated with the domestic domain, and men with the outward realms; this is quite universal. The assumption that the most visual sort of power, the public one, would be the more highly esteemed, is often correct. In many cultures and societies the subordination of women is a reality, sometimes even a severe

---

94 Grillo 2018: 2.
95 Ibid.: 93.
96 Ibid.: 238
97 M. Drewal 1992: 179; Grillo 2018: 43.
98 Picton 1988a: 65.
99 Glaze 1981: 85. We thank Till Förster for putting this custom into perspective.
100 As among the Eagham: 'Women dancing with sculptures on their heads should be perceived as comparable to male masquerade': Röschenthaler 1998: 38. Art as a gender strategy has also been noted among the Wè of Côte d'Ivoire: M.J. Adams 1986, 1993; Verger-Fèvre 2005.

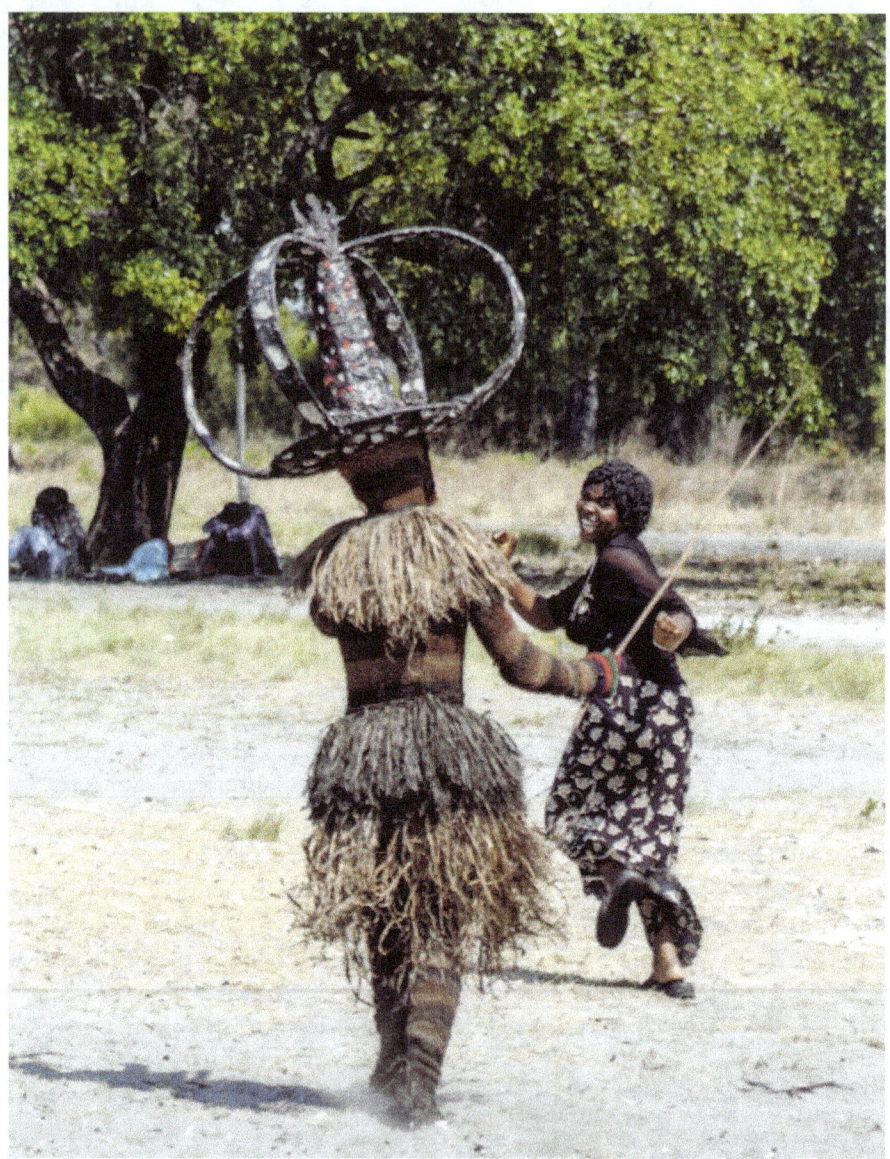

Figure 6.9. A young woman taunting the *kalelwa* mask, an aggressive be-thing that chases away women and uninitiated males during the *Likumbi lya Mise* festival. Luvale, Zambezi, Zambia, August 2003. Photo: Ian Murphy.

one, and male masking may contribute to its more acute realisation; women sometimes are genuinely frightened by mask performances and actually fear the masked men dancing before them.[101] Thus masks may serve as a constructed power base resulting in a skewed gender balance.

However, these very same mask rituals are grounded in the importance of procreation, of bringing children into the world and raising them into adult members of society. The basis of this – admittedly precarious – balance between the genders that the mask rituals operate in, is that children are welcome and even needed, and fertility reigns. So at the very foundation of the mask phenomenon lies its crucial opposition to the female power embedded in her corporal existence. This tension may erupt forcefully in naked marches or gently in the figure of the *sowei* or a dance with beautiful sculptures, but in all these examples the woman in her 'natural state' sets the limits to the presumed omnipotence of the man-*cum*-mask, and she is able to do so because her own body is her mask. Men may have the power of masks; women have their bodies. The power of masks is for the present only, brief and fleeting, but the power of the woman is about the generations to come; she has power over the future. In the gender arena the women have the so-called nuclear option, to be used with the utmost discretion and in extreme situations only, an option men will always have to reckon with. Since masking is about the fragility of the male ego, women realise that theirs is the last word in this struggle.

Conclusion

Most examples in this chapter come from Zones 1 and 2. In Zone 1 the Guro communities are of Type C – the compact village, with some Type D frontier features. The Guro speak a Mande language, and practise shifting cultivation with a variety of crops such as rice, plantain and yams, supplemented by cash crops like coffee, cocoa and cotton. Nowadays they are engaged with palm wine and oil plantations. Their villages have no village head, but they do have male as well as female secret societies that oversee initiations and take charge of masks.[102] Their social organisation is complex[103] with both patrilineal and matrilineal groups, internal division into subunits, and much internal warfare and slavery, in the form of both captives and debt bondage. The

---

101 Binkley 1987: 92.
102 Bouttiaux 2001.
103 Meillassoux 1964.

amount of bride wealth depends on the incidence of patrilineal reckoning, but anyhow most marital gifts comprise luxury goods.[104] Taurine cattle may have been included in these gifts as icons of individual status. Claude Meillassoux interprets the masks as a form of resistance to colonialism, but that is probably a recent function, rather than their origin, which is much older.[105]

Their eastern neighbours, the matrilineal Baule,[106] are closer to Type D, with small, mobile villages of an egalitarian and individualistic character, using individual mobility as a defence mechanism. They have no organised secret societies, neither male nor female, but the collective of men handle the masks, and the collective of masks is the only political force that can impose sanctions.[107] Despite their different organisational structures, Guro and Baule art resemble each other in iconography.

Farther to the west, the Gola, Kpelle, Temne, and Mende are forest farmers who, even though patrilineal, show Type D frontier characteristics, but with a defensive architecture and a plethora of secret societies, both masculine and feminine, that are part of the multiethnic *poro* and *sande* complex which is reminiscent of type C. The Mende have a hierarchical political structure, with a paramount chieftaincy at the top. Among the Gola the *sande* mask is considered the 'husband on the other side' for *sande* women – and is therefore male – while among the Mende the *sowei* represents the Great Mother.[108] The Kpelle mentioned in Chapter 4, though also officially patrilineal, live in typical Type D frontier villages, cultivating dry rice in swiddens. Low populations density offers ample space for opening up new patches of forest, and settlements are dispersed with little centralisation of power; the burden of local organisation lies with the *poro* and *sande* power associations.

The Zone 3 Kete of DRC are a clear case of a matrilineal Type D frontier society, as are the Bemba. The most complex case is the Yoruba in Zone 2, which we will describe in greater detail in the next chapter. All cases mentioned show clear gender arenas, each in its own fashion: the core issue of this chapter.

An intriguing question is whether the use of FGP coincides with the Crescent, since it fits perfectly into our profile of a masking society: the pronatal, important position of women, their separate domain, and the association with witchcraft. Grillo's overview mentions only West Africa,

---

104 Fischer 2008.
105 Meillassoux 1964: 206–220.
106 Étienne 1967, 1971, Guerry 1971.
107 Vogel 1997a: 206.
108 D'Azevedo 1994: 351.

and that is exactly where we too have found FGP cases, not so much in Zone 3. Though reports are still thin on the ground, the phenomenon seems somewhat larger than the Crescent, occurring also in Togo and Benin, where there are no masks. On the other hand, the core of the Akan territory seems to be devoid of them; at least Grillo mentions no cases in Ghana. As we shall see at the end of Chapter 7, there seems to be ample reason for Ashanti women not to use their body as a means of demonstration. Our tentative conclusion is that FGP is relevant to both Type C and D communities; it seems to be based upon similar social conditions to mask rituals, occurring in social formations with definite gender arenas; in fact it is the gender arena in action. Thus, one can assume that FGP operates in most masking cultures, as well as in some societies belonging to Type B where the gender arena is present but where political structures do not resonate with masking. In short, FGP is the ultimate female mask.

7

Masks and Politics

'In the forest, when the branches quarrel, the roots embrace.'

(West African proverb: Fölmi 2015: 228)

Masks for father

In a suburb of Abeokuta, in Yorubaland, the sound of drums heralds the approach of a masquerade.[1] From all houses people emerge to see the parade, and children start dancing in anticipation of the spectacle. When the procession turns the corner, the mask comes into full view, surrounded by a host of excited people. Jumping to the rhythm of the drums, the mask with its finely carved wooden headpiece swings its long robes so that the layers of cloth become visible, layer upon layer. During the procession the mask is in the thick of things, surrounded by people and with drummers following it closely, and among the many attendants one elderly man is dressed in his finest gown. He is Ade, the pater familias of the Akinyode family, and clearly in charge of the whole feast. Women from his household sing in praise of the egungun, *thus honouring also Ade Akinyode's late father, in whose remembrance the masquerade is being organised. They halt at the house of Chief Biobaku, where special songs are intoned to honour Akinyode's daughter, who is married to the chief. But it is Ade Akinyode himself who is central, for all people relate to him: the divining priest, the carver and the tailors, the herbalist, and finally the leader of the* egungun *cult.[2] As a successful businessman in town and a prominent member of the* egungun *association, Ade is grateful to his late father for assisting him in setting up shop, and thus he has every reason to organise this masquerade.*

Masks and the history of the patriline

The masking model that we have adopted implies that mask rituals find a favourite niche in societies where the power balances between men are under periodic redefinition and rely upon competing power bases. In such

---

1   Based upon Drewal and Pemberton 1989.
2   Ibid.: 57.

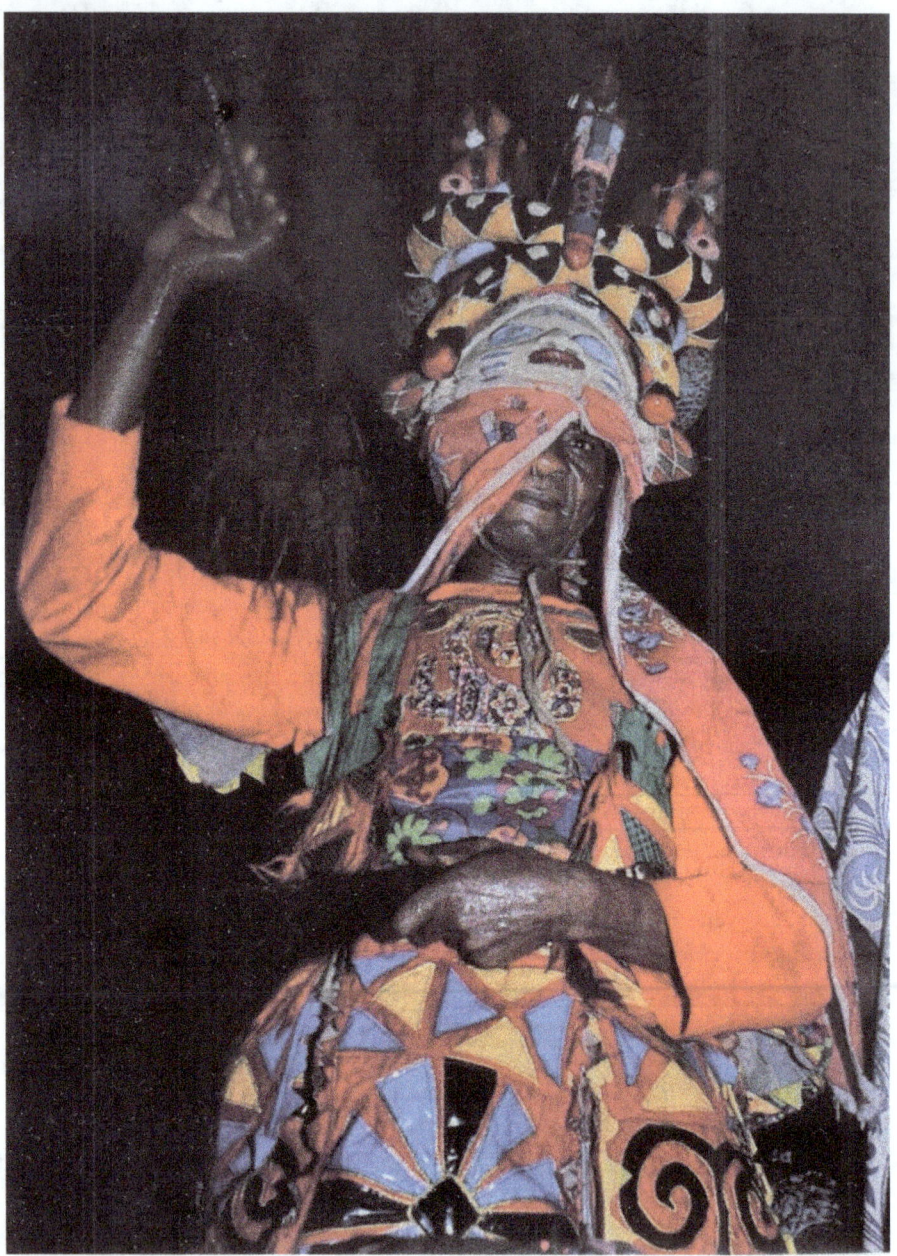

Figure 7.1. Before the foreign photographer, the *oro egungun* mask playfully reveals itself. Cové, Benin, 1984. Photo Edna Bay.

an open arena mask, rituals constitute a power source on their own that in principle is accessible to all males, so the core question is this: Who controls the masks and their rituals?

In this *oro egungun* performance of the Nigerian Yoruba, it is not the bush that enters the town; this full-cloth mask is quite urban, predominantly human, and points at relations between humans much more than it points at the wilderness. Although different areas in Yorubaland possess different masquerades with varying appearance, headpieces, music, and songs, these *egungun* masquerades are tangible expressions of the relationships among the living members of a patrilineage and their link with the ancestors.[3] So there are three issues here: the ancestors, the owner, and the issue of the patri-lineage – and in the Yoruba case these are linked in a special historic way.

Ancestors are assumed to protect their offspring against dangers such as witchcraft, and generally they should be concerned with the well-being of their progeny; on the other hand, they keep close tabs on their offspring, checking whether the latter comply with all the rules and regulations the ancestors have so assiduously left them – if not, the dead are quick to punish the living for transgressions. As with all ancestors, the first burden of their care falls on the lineage heads themselves, aided by associations for ancestral commemoration, among which is the *egungun* association. Its main perfor-mances enliven the annual festivals on behalf of the ancestors, but masquerades may also be called for during a crisis in a family or lineage, such as on the death of an elder, or when an epidemic or cases of witchcraft accusation threaten the community. Then, more than ever, the life-sustaining power of the ancestors is needed, a power that is as supportive as it is corrective.

Usually, the *oro egungun* honours one specific ancestor of a lineage. Not everyone becomes an ancestor after his death; only those who have lived successful lives, fathered children, and enjoyed the respect of their fellow men will be awarded that status. Akinyode's father was a well known and capable hunter in his lifetime; he died at a respectable age and is now considered an ancestor, who would certainly come to the help of his descendants whenever they need it. He really deserves this accolade by his descendants.

The *oro egungun* is by far the most 'textile' mask in Africa. Dressed in layers of precious cloths, often damask, and covering the masker from top to toe, the outfit is designed to express the prestige and wealth of the family in an urban community. Underneath is an indigo and white striped cloth resembling the shroud in which the dead are wrapped, which completely

---

3   Aremu 1995.

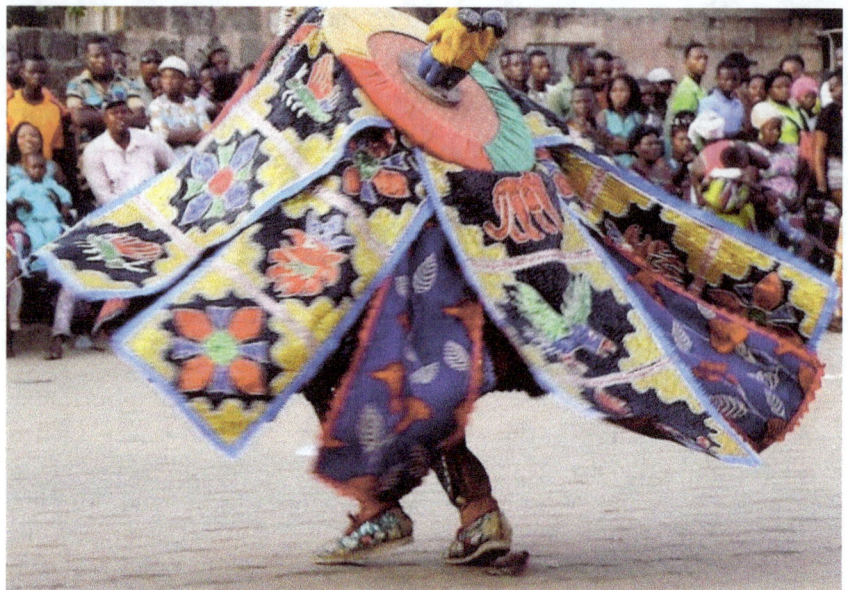

Figure 7.2. Its lappets swinging, the *egungun* represents the past-in-the-present. Yoruba, Benin. Photo: Henri Drewal.

covers the masker's body, except for a netting that one can see through. Layer upon layer of damask lappets are sewn on top of this undergarment, or are attached to a wooden frame; each time the mask is inherited, the new owner adds a layer of cloth or just a lappet, a strip that can flare out during the swirling dance. Many lappets are decorated with patchwork patterns, braids, sequins, tassels, and amulets holding medicinal preparations for protection against enemies – the dancers are vulnerable. With all new generations adding their lengths of cloth, the result is an impressive but very heavy mask that takes a good, strong dancer to perform in; it demands skill-*cum*-force, for the mask must swirl with the lappets flying in order to create a 'breeze of blessing'. Henry Drewal once analysed a particularly old *egungun* estimating it to be at least 150 years old, with the oldest lappets on the inside and the outer layers more recent;[4] the 'breeze of blessing' is indeed a whiff from the past.

The term *egungun* has a wide range of meanings:[5] ancestors, bones, burial shroud – but also indicates the mask as such, plus the whole masquerade.

---

4   Drewal and Pemberton 1989.
5   The Yoruba word *gun* seems to hint at possession: Willis 2018: 10, 60.

The support of the patriline is evident, but patriliny is not a given: in effect *egungun* masks may have been instrumental in the move of Yoruba society from a matrilineal to a patrilineal descent system in the eighteenth and nineteenth centuries.[6] In his recent historical study of the Yoruba,[7] Akinwumi Ogundiran posits as a possible origin of *egungun* the northeast of Yorubaland, close to the Niger-Benue confluence, where today the mask is still of the standard fibre-with-carved-top type. With its historic expansion towards the southwest the mask changed, which may have coincided with a shift in descent reckoning.

Such a transition in kinship usually occurs in the direction of patrilineal descent, at least in recent times, and the reasons for this are reasonably clear and well documented.[8] In an economy turning to cash crop production, fathers and sons generate new wealth together; and the more they earn, the more the fathers want to endow their sons with the wealth they created. Other factors point in the same direction, such as mining, the impact of colonisation, and Christianity. The formation of centralised polities can be a force toward patrilineality too, through the formation of dynasties; with rulers being habitually male, the tendency toward patrilineal dynastic formations has led to incursions into the matrilineal basis in several societies.[9] Descent is never carved in stone.

Historically at least part of Yoruba society had a flexible system of kinship attribution, in the form of cognatic descent; in the Ijebi and Ondo kingdoms in the south this is still the dominant form;[10] in other areas localised patrilineal descent groups populated the cities, usually confined to the city limits and with considerable recognition of female lines – plus a generational kin terminology, which does not stress linearity.[11] On the basis of cognatic descent it is rather easy to create a small patriline, and a masquerade like the *egungun* can be a handy tool: an insistence on patrilocal residence and a symbol for the line suffice to emphasise the father–son bond. As a result of their move towards the southwest, Yoruba society encountered the Atlantic

6   See https://www.dailymaverick.co.za/article/2021-07-11-a-long-view-sheds-fresh-light-on-the-history-of-the-yoruba-people-in-west-africa, consulted 27 December 2022.

7   Ogundiran 2020.

8   The Chewa in Zambia are switching to patrilocality and are increasingly tracing patrilineal descent: Yoshida 2006: 222. On the tenacity of matrilineality, though, see Douglas 1967.

9   Examples are Nupe in Nigeria, and the Zambian Nkoya: Van Binsbergen 1992.

10   Lloyd 1966.

11   Schwab 1955, 1958.

trade system, and grew wealthier. Consequently, the *egungun* morphed into an icon of wealth, showing off its imported silk lappets as symbols of a successful patriline. This also fitted in with urbanisation. Yorubaland is among the most urbanised areas of Africa, and *egungun* is both an expensive and a very urban mask form. All in all, the *oro egungun* performance, in its many forms and fashions, reinforces the main trends and values in Yoruba society: it stresses patrilineality, showcases individual achievement in a modern urban setting, and offers men and women their own important roles in society, all the while being the past-in-the-present.

The intricate political system of the Yoruba, with its many contesting kingdoms throughout the centuries, also provides a good example of the use of masquerades as political instruments at higher echelons. In his study of the history of the *egungun*, John Willis shows how mask rituals formed a crucial factor in the struggle for legitimacy between competing polities, just as they could boost the economic position of a whole city.[12] In 1854, during a period of strife and internal conflict, the Nigerian city of Otta mounted a tremendous mask festival, which served two purposes: internally it occupied the minds and hearts of the populace so that many conflicts evaporated, while for outsiders the town showed itself a safe haven for commerce, inviting foreigners to establish their businesses. Women traders particularly considered Otta a safe city to be in – and one to forge marital relations with.[13]

For the Yoruba in their rapidly changing and globalising world, *egungun* is a powerful point of reference for their collective identity and a constant reminder not to let the values of the past flounder. Recent years have shown more and more public *egungun* festivals, large-scale celebrations that transcend the family and increasingly serve as a cultural core of identity formation (the topic of Chapter 9). Especially in Benin, these festivals have gained massive popularity. Also, the *egungun* has become part of dynastic struggles and conflicts over titles; masquerades are powerful as a means of showing visual support, and since present traditional rulers rely heavily on state theatrics, masks can easily end up in the thick of politicking – and its fall-out.[14]

---

12 Willis 2018.

13 Ibid.: 110. However, three years later, in 1857, a group of masqueraders attacked and executed an uncle of the royal pretender to the throne of Otta (ibid.: 113).

14 See for mask-related violence: https://guardian.ng/news/one-dead-others-injured-in-egungun-festival-violence (consulted 3 May 2023) about a clash in Oyo in July 2017. We thank Ivor Miller for this information.

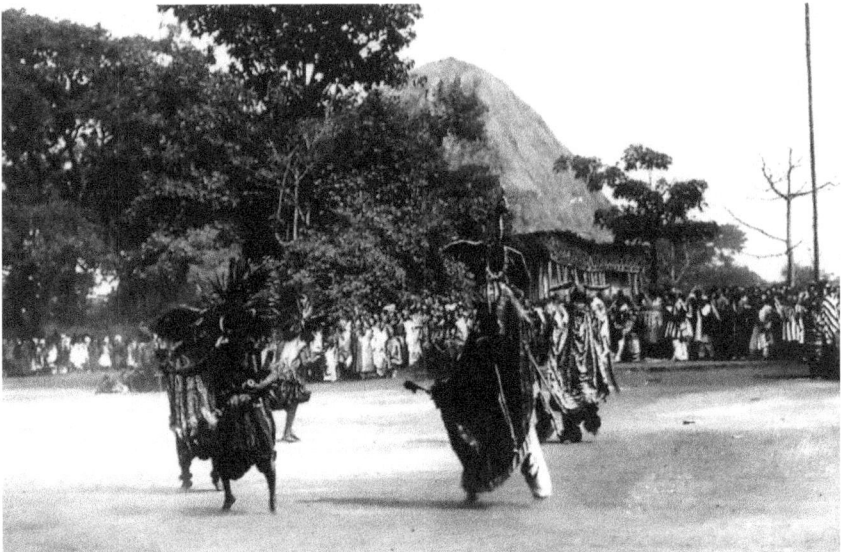

Figure 7.3. The bird masks dance at the *nya* in front of the Basel Mission. Foumban, Cameroon, 1912. Photo: Marie-Pauline Thorbecke.

Feasting the sultan

For a closer look at how these dynamics between masks and chieftaincy operate at the highest political echelon, we turn to western Cameroon. There is good early information on the Bamum festival of *nya* in Cameroon in photographs from 1907 and 1908 and descriptions from 1912, when missionaries reported on this huge and spectacular feast. The highlight of the feast was a long line of masks parading in front of the palace. Over a hundred masks filed by the palace that day, where sultan Njoya, the queen mother, and a crowd of spectators, including Marie-Pauline Thorbecke from the mission station, watched the proceedings. The masks were worn by the retainers at the royal court, most of them the sultan's sisters' sons, wearing cloth costumes and headpieces representing buffaloes, crocodiles, rams, and elephants, plus a host of human faces. The buffalo opened the procession; all other headpieces could be worn by anyone. When the whole mask troupe had passed, the sultan himself followed, dancing slowly and with dignity without a mask, while a crocodile mask kept up with his paces; behind them came the councillors of the land and the princes descended from kings of old. Finally came the princes of the royal household and the crowd of onlookers. All entered the central ground for a festive dance to the tune of the flutes and to the rhythm of the drums and rattles played by the royal family itself. The next morning Njoya poured libations on the graves of his ancestors at the royal graveyard.[15]

There were many festivals with masks at the court, but this *nya* feast was a huge one, calling for the most extravagant outfits. Not only did sultan Njoya himself wear a multicoloured robe, but he had also a courtier wear and display the official royal costume, which consisted of a cloth over ten metres wide, set with jewellery. The German anthropologist Bernhard Ankermann needed a double camera shot to take it all in, and in the book that describes the festival, it takes a double spread.[16] Claude Tardits, the principal ethnographer of the Bamum, calls the *nya* a harvest festival,[17] while the Bamum themselves fondly remember it as 'the day of beauty'.[18] In any case it was a fabulous display of royal riches, of wealth beyond imagination. For instance, the crown of the sultan was so large and heavy that it had to be held by a courtier standing behind the king. During the festival, Njoya's throne – a work of art that has become world famous, made of life-sized carvings completely covered in beads – was placed in front of the palace. As a gesture for Kaiser Wilhelm II's birthday in 1908, Njoya had presented a similar splendid specimen – the throne of his father – to his German 'colleague'; the throne is now one of the highlights of the Ethnological Museum at the Humboldt Forum in Berlin.

Bamum was a military society, a kingdom that thrived on continuous expansion by warfare – for instance, the war leader at his installation wore a mask with a crest depicting a warrior riding a leopard, and his clothing shows the spots of the leopard. In Africa that is as fierce and kingly as one gets. The Bamum realm represented an African polity at its apogee, coinciding with the first arrival of the Europeans – in this case Germany as a coloniser. This was one kingdom that the Germans did not subjugate but rather co-opted, and that they have always respected. But most important, this was not just any African ruler; this was nobody less than sultan Njoya, and no Cameroonian ruler can stand even in the shadow of his fame. After the long and successful reign of his father, Nsangu, Njoya was the seventeenth in a long succession of kings, acceding to the throne in 1886. He witnessed the coming of the Germans and maintained good relations with them throughout. Notably, Njoya recognised the importance of European

---

15 Geary and Njoya 1985: 110–111.
16 Ibid.: 99–100.
17 Tardits 1980: 790–798.
18 Geary and Njoya 1985: 105.

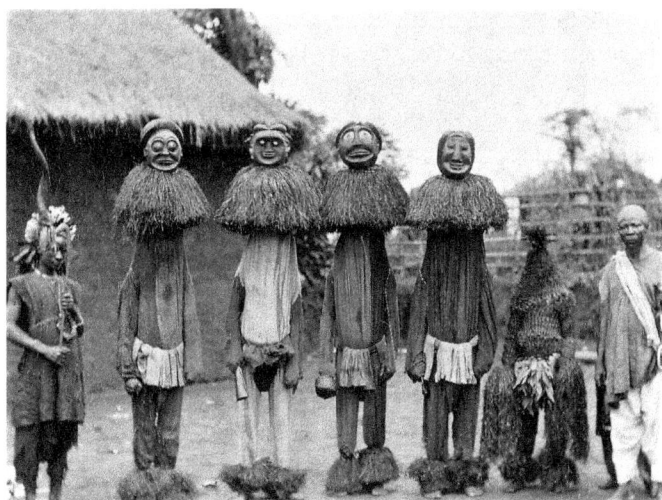

Figure 7.4.
The delegation
of the kingdom
of Pet with
their masks.
Foumban,
Cameroon,
1912. Photo:
Maria
Thorbecke.

script and thus had his sages develop a proper Bamum script, a syllabic one; he even had them write books of Bamum history in that same script. On top of that, Njoya constructed his own written religion, producing a holy text in that script, freely incorporating extracts from the Quran and the Bible into a Bamum syncretic religion. Though not all his spectacular enterprises proved a success, this was an exceptional monarch who later had the misfortune that the French, who succeeded the Germans after World War I, were less enthused about his close German connections and more or less disbanded the sultanate. Although Njoya died in 1933 in Yaoundé, removed from his own Foumban, present-day Bamum is still a thriving sultanate led by one of his grandsons and enjoying huge status in modern Cameroon.

Yet, despite his solid position and huge reputation, the masks that paraded by the palace were not under the command of the sultan. Masks belonged to the secret societies. Njoya and his retinue joined in as sultan, wealthy and powerful but human. His was a power over men, not over the bush. However, his position was so strong that he dominated the secret societies, who paid homage to his exalted status with the masquerade. Beyond the palace masks, Bamum also had masquerades in the villages, of roughly the same genres, but these performances in no way detracted from the centrality of the dynasty.[19]

In effect, masquerades could be a signal of dominance. In the seventeenth century, the king of Bamum had conquered neighbouring Pet, but

[19] Wittmer 1979.

he granted them the right to maintain their own masquerades; and as a homage to his superior, the king of Pet would visit Foumban with a group of masks and perform for the sultan of Foumban; the masks themselves are a variant of the huge human figures that performed there, and hint more at human power than at the otherworld. In any case, having one's own masquerades defines identity, and performing in honour of a superior is a strong visual signal of fiefdom.[20]

A recurring issue of the power arenas in the Mask Crescent is the tension between political centralisation and the power of the secret societies. Whereas the Bamum sultan trumped the power of the secret societies, in the adjoining chiefdoms of Cameroonian Grassfields that is by no means the case; this area houses a host of complex little kingdoms, in which the position of the king varied.

The small mountain realm of Oku forms a counter-example to the Bamum sultanate. Here, the king is the central icon of the society, all-important, powerful, and 'dangerous' because of the many medicines he has been endowed with, a person no commoner may address or touch, and often may not even look at. Extreme deference is shown to him, and he is the only one who may adorn himself with the insignia of animals: teeth, pelts, or images. His palace is the pivot of society; he is the main officiant for the principal sacrifices, and any mask dance will pay elaborate homage to him as king. One of his privileges is that he does not have to pay bride wealth for his spouses, and the important families of the realm will be proud to hand him one of their daughters.[21]

This may sound like a real monarch, but the ethnographer Hans Koloss insists that, in fact, the king is very much hemmed in by all the prerogatives and offices that surround him. Though the source of ultimate power, he is inaccessible and out of bounds to all commoners – for instance, he may never show up at the weekly market. The real power is in the hands of the most important secret society, called Kwifon, which consists of the heads of the various lineages, the king kimself plus numerous other dignitaries and titleholders, up to 230 persons. Princes of the royal clan are banned from this august body; it is just the king who is a member, and the Kwifon shows little subservience to him. Their decisions are binding, also for the king. And it is the Kwifon that commands the masks, the very same masks that honour the king profusely in their dancing. The kingdom knows many

20 Geary and Njoya 1985: 117.
21 Based upon Koloss 2000 and 1992.

types of masks and performances, as we shall see in Chapter 10, that are officially in honour of the king, but behind the scenes are commanded by the Kwifon. For its functions the latter need the cooperation of the king, since he forms the major link to the otherworld, but the king alone has little mandate; so king-without-masks and Kwifon-with-masks hold each other in a tight power embrace. In Koloss's account of Oku, this balancing between king and Kwifon seems to result in a steady state, but more historical analyses point at ever shifting power equations, in which masquerades may reinforce either side of the political coinage, and in so doing flourish. This past-in-the-present even thrives in present rebellions in the Grassfields.[22]

In many other cases we see masks appear at the enthronement rituals of chiefs and kings that are simultaneously an honour and a reminder of the other power structure; the curious brass-covered tops of the Limba are an example.[23] But usually it is during the rulers' funerals that they turn out in the greatest numbers, so the honour is ambivalent anyway. All in all, masquerades have a dialectic political position: in the public eye the masks' support for the ruler is a very visible one,[24] while the power behind the throne aims at staying inconspicuous.

Power in Africa always has an element of sacredness, and the notion that the king has a special connection with otherworldly power comes easily. When the countervailing force of secret societies is absent, the link between king and sacredness becomes dominant, as can be seen in the next case.

The mask as king

Kuba is the name that the Europeans gave to a cluster of kingdoms in what is now Kasaï-Occidental in southern DRC. Most of the descriptions stem from the largest of these kingdoms, the Bushong, and the ethnographic accounts dwell mainly on the royal masks, which form just a part of their masking scene. Few masks in Africa are as colourful and exuberant as these *moshambwooy*, and few are as richly symbolic and 'kingly'.[25]

---

22 Ian Fowler, personal communication.
23 Hart 1988: 60–62.
24 Such as the anniversary celebration of the Fon of Mankon; see https://www.youtube.com/watch?v=E0odgKEgyT0, consulted 19 July 2020.
25 Blier 1998. The Kuba are not the only ones whose chief dances with a mask at his investiture; the chief of neighbouring Luntu does likewise: Petridis 1999: 43–44.

As always, the origin of the *moshambwooy* is mythic; one version refers to the *ngesh* spirits living in the forest, especially near rivers, lakes, and pools, who have the power to make women fertile, cure the sick, and give success to hunters. The myth is important here, since it links mask and king.

> Once upon a time a spirit called *Moshambwooy* haunted the waters of the land and caused many disasters for the people, such as blindness and fatal diseases. During the reign of King Bo Kyeem, a hunter went into the forest and met the spirit. Terrified, he returned home and informed the king of his adventure. When the king asked him to describe the spirit, the man said that he was unable to do so, but he could try to show it. On the king's request the hunter built a little shelter far away from the village and with strips of bark, the skin of a bat and feathers, constructed a strange-looking costume, which he painted yellow, black and white. When the king saw the costume, he got an idea. One day he disappeared from his palace, unnoticed. Not much later a strange be-thing entered the town, that was dressed in that very costume, an imitation of the spirit *Moshambwooy*. Unrecognised by his people, the king danced and caused great fear among all spectators. The masked king returned to the forest where he hid the costume, and when he returned to the palace the next day, he feigned great concern when he heard of the mysterious visit. However, he told the people that he knew of its origin, and that this spirit *Moshambwooy* had caused the diseases and that it had come to see if the women were quarrelsome, and if the young folks were disobedient, so that he could beat them. He, the king, would solve this problem. This is how the costume of *moshambwooy* was born.[26]

As an origin myth of masking, the tale closely resembles other mask myths we have encountered thus far, but with a twist: here it is the king himself who is at the centre of the action, and he has even replaced the spirit itself, which enters the village only in the form of the kingly dancer (Figure 7.5).

This highly symbolic costume consists of a tunic, a costume of bark cloth and textile, to which scores of attributes are attached. Important are a leopard skin and a great number of monkey skins, plus beads and cowries everywhere; the headpiece is sculpted but covered with decoration, a host of cowry shells, and with animal hair suggesting a beard. But most prominent is the crown of eagle feathers, a kingly prerogative. If it represents anything other than itself – always the first meaning of any mask – it portrays the king himself, as an esoteric version of the ruler.

---

26 Cornet 1982: 256.

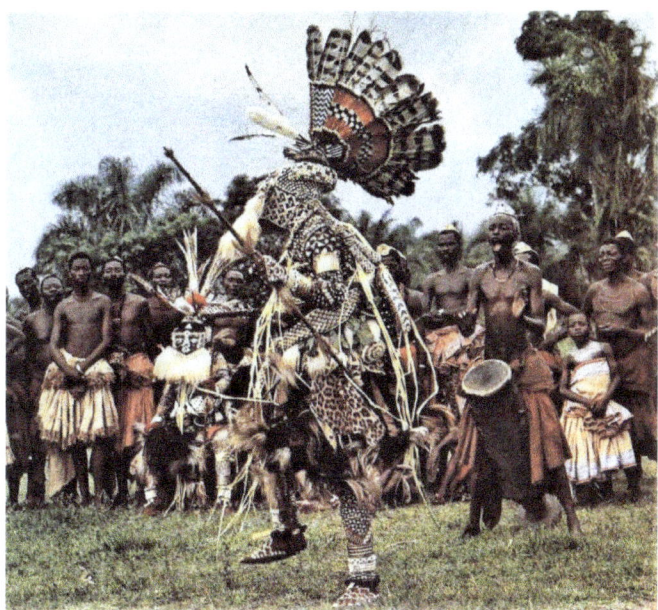

Figure 7.5.
The royal mask
moshambwooy.
Note the eagle
feathers, the
leopard skin,
and the second
dancer sitting.
Mushenge,
Kuba/Bushong,
DRC, 1980.
Photo: Angelo
Turconi.

It is the king who will commission a new mask, which he must then inaugurate in a special dedicatory ritual. This great event starts in the evening with various songs, rendered by the king's wives to procure strength for the king. The next morning the ritual continues in the forest, where the king dances the mask for the first time; he must be guided, since the head cover has no eyes – so, 'led by the spirit', the king dances in his splendid new self. In the afternoon a procession of officials carries the king, fully clothed in his mask, in a palanquin from the forest to the palace, where all the masked men of the community await his arrival. It is here that the king dances with the new mask in public for the first time, led by one of the princesses. From the palace the new mask passes through the main street of the capital city, and at another spot he is received by the officials of the palace. Again the king dances with the newly dedicated mask, the heavy costume making for a slow and dignified dance, as if the mask is an old and wise man, reminiscent of *Woot*, the mythical founder of the Kuba.[27]

Kings and chiefs never walk alone, nor do they dance alone. So the king (also in Figure 7.5), is accompanied by a *bwoom* mask with a sculpted wooden head cover, suggesting a legendary Tshwa pygmy. As for the origin

27 T. Phillips 1995: 278.

of *bwoom*, in one myth king Miko mi-Mbul ordered the children of his predecessor to be killed, but after that he became mentally deranged. He was cured, but he discovered that every time he danced the *moshambwooy*, his disease reappeared. Then a Tshwa pygmy called Mbo Mbakam revealed to the king the shape and details of this new genre of mask, to heal this affliction. The king tried it on and considered it worthy to be treated as a royal mask, and thus it was adopted by the Kuba.

Figure 7.6 shows how much the *moshambwooy* mask looks like the king and vice versa. Not only does the general habitus of the costume, top-heavy with its rich decorations, look like the mask, but even the crown of eagle feathers on his head is identical. Now, why do Kuba kings dress and dance in masks that look like themselves? And why does the king need masks at all?

Central African political organisation tends to be based upon the House, as Jan Vansina calls it: the local residential unit centred around a successful male.[28] Through varying dynamics of cooperation, conquest, trade networking and individual prowess, these units coalesced into larger polities in very different ways. Central Africa harbours a surprisingly wide array of matrilineal political systems, all based upon the autonomous local unit of the House. Kingdoms were just one form, but even as centralised polities they were not states. From a relatively small territorial core around the capital, the king's authority radiated out over ever widening geographical circles, his control diminishing with distance; this constituted the warrior state as mentioned before. The first circle consisted of people who benefited from the court through crafts and trade; the next one just paid tribute, while the outlying area was only under threat of incidental military intervention from the capital. Beyond that outer circle, only the reputation of the king bound the people to the core of the realm. These rulers did not occupy their territory since they had no standing army beyond the palace guards, and the lands were thinly populated anyway, but occasionally visited their realm in military expeditions. The religions of the various groups differed in many ways, but they shared notions such as the close connection with the otherworld and the fundamental human nature of the beings that populate it, which underpinned the pivotal place of the king.[29]

The Kuba have elaborated on this pattern and managed to bind their kingdom together in three ways. First, an intricate system of councils – consisting of a crowd council, a daily council, and a general council with

28 The analysis stems from Vansina 1978, 1992a, 1992b.
29 Biebuyck 1992.

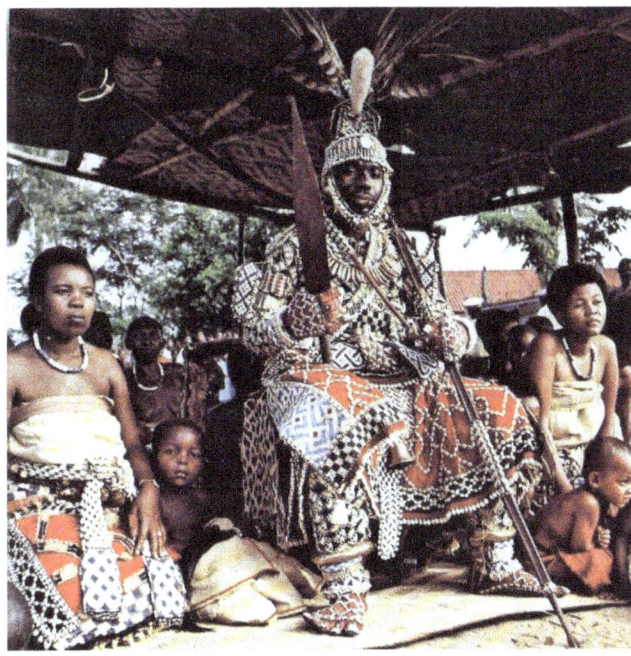

Figure 7.6. The
king of Bushong
in full regalia
with some
of his wives
and children.
Mushenge, Kuba/
Bushong, DRC,
1980. Photo:
Angelo Turconi.

overlapping membership, plus a set of courts – created a system guaranteeing
the balanced representation of litigants in judicial matters; Vansina called it 'the
most sophisticated judicial system in Central Africa'.[30] Second, and important
to the inner circles of the administration, was the title system. Each position
in the realm bore a title, with its accompanying emblem, slogan, history, and
particular privilege. Feathers indicated the rank, with the eagle plumage at
the political apex, while lower ranks were allowed other feathers in a well-
defined order – for instance, the chief of the initiation rituals wore owl
feathers: the owl was seen as the ruler of the forest and the night sky. Titles
were the essence of political life and descended from the king to the lowest
echelons of Kuba society, involving most men in the kingdom; we saw Kuba
initiation bent on reproducing this hierarchy. The emphasis on competitive
titleholding and the subsequent prestige that accrued to titleholders was, and
in many ways still is, a dominant aspect of Kuba culture.[31]

Underscoring this political edifice was a strong ideology of kingship:
the king was sacred and essential to social life, since as a 'god on earth'

---

30 Vansina 1992a, 1992b, 1992c.
31 Darish and Binkley 1995: 161.

he represented the high god and the spirits. He was enveloped in ritual, hemmed in by taboos, and to a large extent controlled by the many councils; yet he still presided over life and death, was the source of fertility, and embodied the realm. His palace grounds housed a huge court, where his queen mother, his many wives and children, and his sisters' sons – his eventual successors – resided with him. As the richest man of the realm he was a prime patron of the arts, since in Africa wealth and power must be seen in splendour and in full public view. Such an ostentatious system made the production of art essential, and the inauguration rituals of the king were replete with the most spectacular art the continent has to offer – for instance, the king in full regalia sitting on the throne was a spectacle many European travellers commented upon with due awe.[32] Public rituals, with all titleholders wearing all the accoutrements of their office, continually reinforced the vision of a strong polity in a visual and ritual overstatement of reality that in the end worked as a self-fulfilling prophecy: the performance produced power, and the virtual world became real.

This visual wealth was backed up by a discourse on supernatural power, on the kinship of the king with the deity and the main bush spirits, as the direct representative of *Woot*, the first human being on the face of the earth.[33] In Africa there is always a flipside to power, for power goes both ways: life and fertility versus punishment and death; indeed the king was also considered the master witch and sorcerer, dangerous and unpredictable. All this resulted, however, in one of the most stable polities in Central Africa. Since its foundation in the seventeenth century, some 125 kings have ruled the Bushong kingdom in succession.

The term theatre state, mentioned in Chapter 1, in many ways holds for the Central African kingdoms in general, but especially for the Kuba. As Geertz defined it: 'The driving aim of higher politics was to construct a state by constructing a king. The more consummate the king, the more exemplary the centre. The more exemplary the centre, the more actual the realm.'[34] If any African kingdom thrived on visual signals, it was the Kuba realm. For the spectator, the king exuded status, both in outfit and in motion. He not only looked like an out-of-this-world being, he also had to perform his own exaltation – and this is where the masks came in. As part of the duo of mythical royal characters, the king danced his own self-definition as part of the show that generated the state. More than in

32 Vansina 1992a, 1992b.
33 Vansina 1978.
34 Geertz 1980: 124.

most other masking cultures, these masks are tied to the founding myths of the Bushong, and the king's performance, in the disguise of the first king, reestablished his kingship repeatedly. Being king was a performance, and staying king demanded a good show with a large cast of officials all performing their ritual and esoteric status: Kuba was the African epitome of a theatre state.

A theatre state where power is shown in exaggerated displays of wealth needs to be founded on some material basis, which in the Kuba case was its monopoly on trade. All major trade was controlled by the palace, which enabled the king to show his largesse. Thus, the king supported subjects who were poor with gifts from his collections, but also engaged numerous artists who created exquisitely made objects (cups, tobacco pipes, clothes, masks, tapestry). The king himself was the wealthiest man of the kingdom, functioning as the core of a redistribution network that linked his subjects to him personally thanks to the gifts and taxes (paid *in natura*) of textiles, masks, ivory tusks, leopard skins, and earthenware; sharing this wealth with his subjects increased his prestige and power.

The Kuba have other masks as well, including the mask of a woman, which, as tradition holds, was commissioned by a queen and seems to presentify the sister of *Woot*, the founder, but also his wife, an incestuous relationship that created the Kuba people. Stories of incest are almost standard in founding myths,[35] and in a matrilineal society, sisters are of utmost importance because they bear the heirs of their brothers, so this bond is very strong; consequently, brother–sister incest is a common theme in their myths. Though this incest would be the solution to the matrilineal puzzle – the men's sisters' sons would be their own sons as well – in all these societies such incest is forbidden in the strongest of terms; for instance, in the *chisungu* girls' initiation of the Bemba group, this was the most absolute of all prohibitions.

Nonetheless, myths sometimes reflect hidden and forbidden wishes. So in Kuba culture, with its rather close connection between mask and myth, this female mask may well express not just the power of women but also the forbidden dream of men to father their own sisters' sons – that is, to have their sons inherit. In fact, the Kuba king's enthronement ritual features such a symbolic incestuous union with his sister. The male fantasies of male-only fertility in patrilineal groups seem to mirror the suppressed hope in the matrilineal Kuba for a father–son dynasty. Masks are a dream of male power,

---

35 Belcher 2005.

but they also show the power of the male dream: the Kuba theatre state has persevered through the ages. If the king can dance himself, his realm is safe, and any struggle for succession will have to wait until his death.

So far, we have shown the position of masks in the power arena in places of increasing centralisation, Yoruba – Oku – Bamum – Kuba. The Oku case shows a rather pervasive trend, that of balancing secret society and king, in fact a real arena in which the outcome of the strife differs in time and place. In quite a few cases the power of the king is pitted against that of the secret societies, and the following examples show how the masks limit the reign of the king, with the first one, the Mundang of Cameroon, introducing a surprising new topic: the death of the king.

Initiation, masks, and regicide

A legend among the Mundang in Cameroon tells of a girl who was fascinated by masks. Her name was Sarkuyo, and did she love masks! Her parents had singled out a groom for her, but she refused him and instead fled into the bush, where in the sacred forest she wanted to spy upon the masks. Almost immediately the boys in the camp grabbed her and brought her before the elders, who summarily executed her. However, that was not the end of her, for the girl was transformed into a mask,[36] effectively the *ma-bi* mask, the most powerful of its genre. In the end the initiated girl, after being killed, became the most powerful mask, so the story goes.

Another legend in the same Mundang country recounts the tale of Prince Gando of the dynasty of the king of Léré, who had a similar craving. He had often seen masks coming into and leaving the village, and he wanted to know everything about them, longing to see how they dressed in their costumes and shed them again; in short, he wanted to be initiated. So he went into the sacred forest and arrived at the mask hut where the costumes were kept, at the very moment when the initiands were dressing and practising their dance steps. Gando grabbed a fibre skirt, tied it on, went back to the village, and danced before the women and uninitiated children. Of course, the initiands immediately came from the bush, caught this 'naked mask' – he had no headcovering – and presented him to the mask elders. With the consent of the king, they killed him. This story does not end well, because he stayed dead and nothing good came of it.

---

36 Adler 1989.

Why is the transgression of a girl like Sarkuyo ritually more productive than that of a prince? Straddling the border between northern Cameroon and Chad, the Mundang are a special case in these savannah regions. Kingship is unusual in this area, since most local cultures are acephalous or have petty chiefs. The Mundang, however, exhibit a clear case of sacred kingship, like the Mbum, who live to their south and with whom they have a historical relationship. In contrast, the Guisiga to the west, from whom the Mundang claim descent, have no kings at all and no masks. All ethnic groups in the area suffered greatly from the Fulbe predations in the nineteenth century, including the Mundang; but whereas other groups eventually had to submit, the Mundang were able to withstand the Fulbe military's might and were never conquered. One reason is that the Mundang had developed a cavalry on a par with the Fulbe, which is rather uncommon.

The difference between the two stories is illustrative. The individual who in most cases would be closest to the masks, young royalty, is actually removed further from them than the one who is the classic opposite of a mask: a young nubile woman. The point is that in Mundang culture, masks and royalty are diametrically opposed, two forces that do not mix and may even annihilate each other: a real arena. Quite a few rituals show this opposition, but the clearest is initiation – at least formerly. In these modern days, as Alfred Adler, the main ethnographer of the Mundang, reports,[37] boys' initiations are performed individually per house, without involvement of the king. Why this is so will become clear.

Formerly, initiation was a grand, collective affair that had to be started by the king. Some three or four years after his enthronement he had to initiate the proceedings – in fact when his reign showed that he could procure rain. The initiation itself was performed almost completely without him or his royal clansmen, for all men of his huge clan were banned from this rite of passage, as indeed the second story made clear. The format of the initiation is quite classic, with the boys ushered into a bush camp, where they are circumcised. After healing they return for a moment to the village, to be snatched up again for the initiation proper, again in the camp. There they meet the masks and learn the 'secret' of the mask, being ultimately reborn between the legs of the mask after a lot of beating. The masks themselves are of the fibre kind, also with fibre tops, in several different forms, each with its own name. The most important mask genres are the *mundere*, the male one of the bush, and the female *muyu*; the one that the girl Sarkuyo

---

37 Adler 1998.

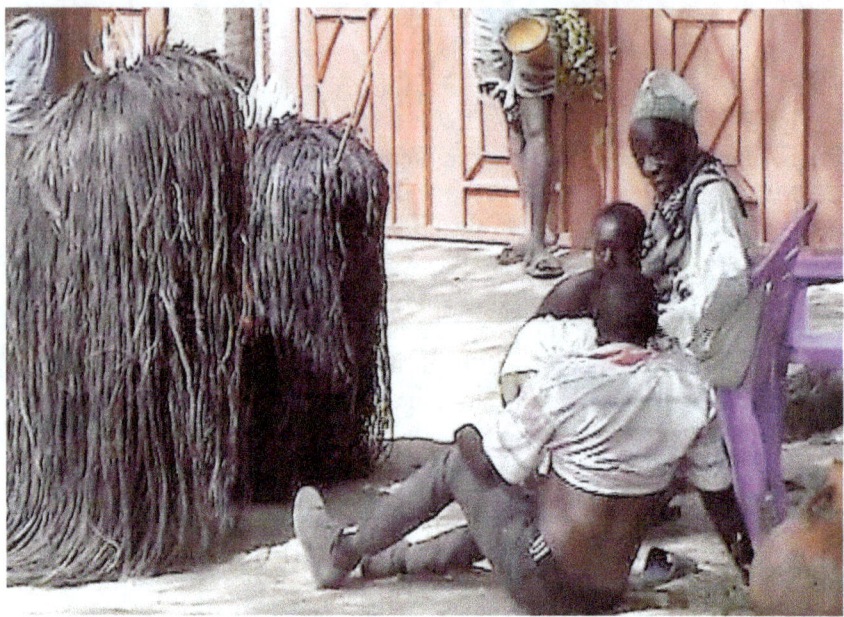

Figure 7.7. Two *muyu* masks address spectators at the market. Lara, Mundang, North Cameroon, 2018. Photo: Michel Dama.

turned into is a variant of the latter. In the bush the initiands learn a secret language, engage in plaiting the fibres into masks skirts, are taught about proper manners, and above all instructed in keeping the secret of the masks from non-initiates.

The princes of the royal clans, who are quite numerous, participate in the first part, the circumcision, but not in the second part, the rebirth through the legs of the masks. They are not 'eaten by the mask'; that final rite is just for the boys of commoner clans. The king at some point enters the camp but is then treated as a nobody; he is even beaten like a neophyte. Although nominally all proceedings are under the tutelage of the monarch, the king and his large family are not welcome. Whereas the huge royal clans pervade the whole Mundang country[38] and might be represented in almost any village, in crucial instances such as the initiation – and the funerals! – the royals are conspicuous by their absence. Indeed, women in the village are much closer to the masks; not only is one of the main mask types considered to be female, but post-menopausal women are on

38 Adler 1982; Taïno Kari 2015.

good terms with masks. A mask may even be allowed to sit on their lap; old women are the familiars of the mask in a way that the king's wife or mother may never be.

The ethnographer Alfred Adler analyses this quite unusual situation from a fundamental opposition between kingship and the clan system; the patrilineal clan system forms a countervailing power against the king, and in initiations and funerals this comes to the fore – because these rituals form the stronghold of the clan elders, not of the king. At the basis of this divide is their link with the earth. It is the commoner clans that have the shrines for the earth, since they belong on the spot; they are the firstcomers, a crucial notion in West Africa. In Mundang culture, the founder of the royal clans came later, from the neighbouring Guisiga, so they are considered strangers. This theme that the king is an immigrant in the country is a dominant motif in Central African kingdoms[39] and is important here also. In Mundang the masks reinforce the link of the clans with the soil and thus with the locality, through their sacred forest. Although the king dominates the annual festivals in the agricultural cycle, initiations and funerals are out of bounds for him.

Despite the king's absence from initiations, he must take the initiative in the next instalment, which should be held once a decade. Since the king was never 'eaten by the mask' as a young prince, he has a vestigial femininity in his body, and following Mundang cultural logic, can supervise only one initiation during his reign. Thus, the king must die before the next one, in about ten years; a longer period without initiation would let the country fall into ruin.[40] So not only is the power of the king curtailed by the mask rituals, but also his life span; while the three huge royal clans permeate the whole residential and political structure of Mundang society, the mask rituals define the essentials of life as being out of reach to the king.

One paradox for the king is that he holds no sway over the earth, but he does over rain. Adler provides the structural reasons for this: the otherworld in the form of the high god is far away and does not intervene in this world, but the king is one of the natural forces under him. The king should intervene, directly and clearly, and his principal task is to procure rain: 'The deeds of the king do not demand interpretation nor any deciphering of a sign: people know that the rains are those of the king of Léré.'[41] The king

---

39   De Heusch 1994; and a core element of Type B.
40   Taïno Kari 2015: 80.
41   'l'Action du roi n'exige nulle interprétation, nul décryptage de signe: on sait que la pluie est celle du roi de Léré' (Adler 1982: 213). Translation by the first author.

has no excuse; if things go wrong and drought hits the area, his life must end. Without rain, he must go. And with drought and famine there is no debate possible. Also Taïno Kari, himself a Mundang, is emphatic about the reality of regicide – albeit in the past.[42]

The two reasons for the king's demise converge and reinforce each other. The king's ritual realm has an inbuilt drought risk; and when new human life must be generated, his position is also weak, for then the other clans hold sway – with masks. Not only are the clans the real autochthones, the masks are just as rooted as spirits of that bush, of that lake, of that mountain, right in the heart of Mundang country. Of importance here is that these are patrilineal clans, fully rooted in the soil, with a strong internal organisation and full corporate functions. Clans-*cum*-masks perform an equilibrium act with the royal clan-*cum*-king. The masks are counter-hegemonic to the throne, and it is the commoner who 'owns' the bush, who speaks the language of the masks – a language the king will never learn.

Becoming king, therefore, involves a clear and reduced life expectancy. Older sources indicate that a Mundang king who overstayed this period of ten years had to be strangled,[43] and that is indeed the dominant tale. One can imagine why in modern Mundang the initiation has been fragmented, allowing the king to live much longer; but the theme of regicide does illustrate the dialectics of masks versus political power, and is not confined to the Mundang. Within the Mask Crescent stories of regicide occur in the northeastern part of Zone 2, from the Jos Plateau in Nigeria to the north of Cameroon where the Mundang are situated. Meek, one of the oldest major sources on northern Nigeria, mentions it for the Jukun;[44] Jean-Claude Muller has reported regicide for the Rukuba of the Jos Plateau,[45] and in Cameroon the Mbum have practised it.[46] Living in the same general area of Cameroon, all have kings with fixed (though less stringently defined) termination dates based upon the cycle of initiation. The Mundang form the best-documented case and highlight the competing principles in the balance of power.

Though in Africa tales of king-killing repeatedly surface, cultural anthropology has learned to be wary of these exotic stories; the dominant view is that they form a discourse expressing structural conflicts inside a polity. It

---

42   Taïno Kari 2015.
43   Lembezat 1961.
44   Meek 1931.
45   Muller 1987, 1994, 1998.
46   Lembezat 1961.

is not the place here to elaborate on the topic, however fascinating, just to gauge the role of masks in this complex of regicide. The inevitable question is whether kings really were killed, and the just as inevitable answer is: 'It depends.' In cultures with a sacred ruler any notion that the well-being of the people depends on the health of the ruler comes easily. So when he grows old and impotent – fertility remains crucial – the country is deemed to go into decline, so he has to be replaced, and not by a peaceful succession; there has to be some violence as his death is considered a sacrifice to expiate for the country.[47] This, all in all, is quite general and constitutes 'the sacred ruler complex', the subject of one of the oldest theories in anthropology.[48] One major task of African sacred rulers is indeed to provide rain, like the Mundang king, which puts the ruler in an awkward position. Given the vagaries and unreliability of precipitation, at some time or other the king will inevitably fail – so his is a fragile throne.

A short expiration date for a king is found not just in Mundang culture. In a fascinating article, Jean-Claude Muller[49] compares the Mundang with their southwestern neighbours the Dìì (also known as the Dourou), and with the Chamba on the border with Nigeria. In all three groups, the bodily health of the chief is important for the well-being of the society, and in all three the collective boys' initiation is a risk for the chief, even to the point that there is a discourse on his death just before or after the initiation.[50] Sacred rulers do not die in their beds, but Muller indicates a number of options for their demise, all of which have been realised at some place and time: (1) a rebellion can end the king's reign, under the cloaking discourse of ritual regicide; (2) the king may be allowed to escape into exile to another community; (3) he can be killed virtually, either by the ritual killing of a substitute (e.g. a slave) or by his undergoing ritual renewal/rebirth;[51] (4) he may be killed just before undergoing a natural death – sacred kings should never die a natural death; (5) he might actually be killed by his own people, in a 'real' regicide.

47 Simonse 2018.
48 James Frazer's *The Golden Bough*, which starts from this complex, is an all-time classic: Van Baal and Van Beek 1985.
49 Muller 1997a.
50 Ten years in Mundang, but the number seven seems dominant, as De Heusch (1987) has argued.
51 Among the Dourou or Dìì this option is realised: a ritual rejuvenation of the ruler (Muller 1997a) that wipes his slate clean, and has him installed for a second – and final – term.

In all cases the official discourse can be the same: the king has been 'killed'. In fact this distinction might not even be particularly relevant, since to a large extent it is the discourse that counts; how exactly he 'dies' is secondary. Sacred rulers can exist well without masks – the Nilotic region has no masks but is full of tales of regicide – but in Zone 2, where masks form the core of the initiations, this version of the sacred ruler complex defines mask rituals as a threat to the king, limiting the length of his realm and possibly of his life.

Masquerades and modern politics

In the power exchange between the king and the populace, masks enter the political arena as a third force: that of the 'outside' or the 'bush', or spirits, and the question is: Whose side are the masks on? Four crucial factors inform their role in the political balance: the scale of the political system, the role of secret societies, primacy of occupation, and wealth. In principle, mask rituals are part of the grass roots organisation, of local communities and associations, and as such tend to distribute political power over a larger part of the community; masks are primarily non-hegemonic and usually provide a check on the centralisation of power, because their otherworldly grounding and performative appeal make them hard to control from the political centre.

Masks are a convenient tool for political contestation. Leon Siroto describes how one mask seemingly ran amok in a Kwele village, killing all the domestic animals. In fact this was part of a festival requiring extensive slaughter for meat, and the mask took the blame for the killing – a standard issue in sacrifices, since a killing must be excused. Although this made for a harmonious feast, gradually the mask performance was used against rival war leaders, shifting the focus from village harmony to intervillage competition.[52]

The Tiv form an example too. This central Nigeria group has a segmentary lineage system, which the main ethnographers describe as a system of 'predatory expansion'[53] in agricultural terms: this patrilineal set-up induces people to explore new terrain, pushing their frontiers ever farther. Thus, as a Type A society, the Tiv indeed do not have masks, at least historically. The Tiv were aware of masks existing among their neighbours, and some of their segments that intruded into Jukun territory seem to have adopted them, of

52 Siroto 1972: 64.
53 Bohannan and Bohannan 1953; Abuku 2008.

the Jukun kind. However, masks are as useful as they are seductive. In 1920 a rebellion in Tiv land against colonial rule triggered a masquerade under the name *akume* (revolution), a name close to that of the Jukun mask, which was called *akuma*. The mask in question was simple: an inner covering of cloth, shirts, and trousers sewn together with eye-holes cut out, plus a raffia outer cover in blue, white, and black.[54] The performance was for men only, part of the political rebellion, and was suppressed by the administration. A few decades later another masquerade developed called *ajigbe*, through entertainment groups by young men. This money-making mask was also just raffia, but in all possible colours, and added roughly carved headpieces; one of them was made from a broken calabash with three holes for eyes and nose. *Ajigbe* continued as a show and is still alive, though transformed.[55] In the 1960s a performing artist and sculptor, Atem Ikye, created *ijov-mbakuv*, a raffia mask with a terrifying face cover,[56] to discipline the local children. It caught on and was used to maintain law and order; masks run either way: discipline or rebellion. The current major Tiv masquerade is the *mamiwata* mask, which they took from the Igbo.[57]

In more modern political surroundings, masks also play a role in the competition for power, since their high visibility render mask performances a prime tool for election struggles and faction feuds. Thus, in urban situations masquerades dot local politics; whoever wants to be elected, organises a mask festival. Charles Gore remarks on Benin: 'Rather than a mode of representing and constituting community, it is now often a site for contestation between different local factions with incommensurate claims to modernity', and the performances offer 'counter-narratives to modernity'.[58]

In order to perform a masquerade, one must own it, and in the urban environment this is not always clear. A fascinating Yoruba court case in 1996 featured a specific *egungun* mask, which claimed to be the oldest one in the city of Otta so that it could take the place of honour at major feasts. The case had to be decided on witness testimonies, and the main and most reliable witness proved to be an elderly woman, described by the judge as 'oldest masquerade chief' and a 'witness of truth'. What distinguished her in court was her detailed account of the migration histories from the Oyo

---

54   The Jukun *akuma* has similar characteristics.
55   Abuku 2008; see https://www.facebook.com/ajigbepiece/, consulted 26 April.
56   See https://www.youtube.com/watch?v=cyYDUkC8v1o&app=desktop, consulted 26 June 2020.
57   Nevertheless called an indigenous African masquerade by commentators.
58   Gore 2008a: 6, 7.

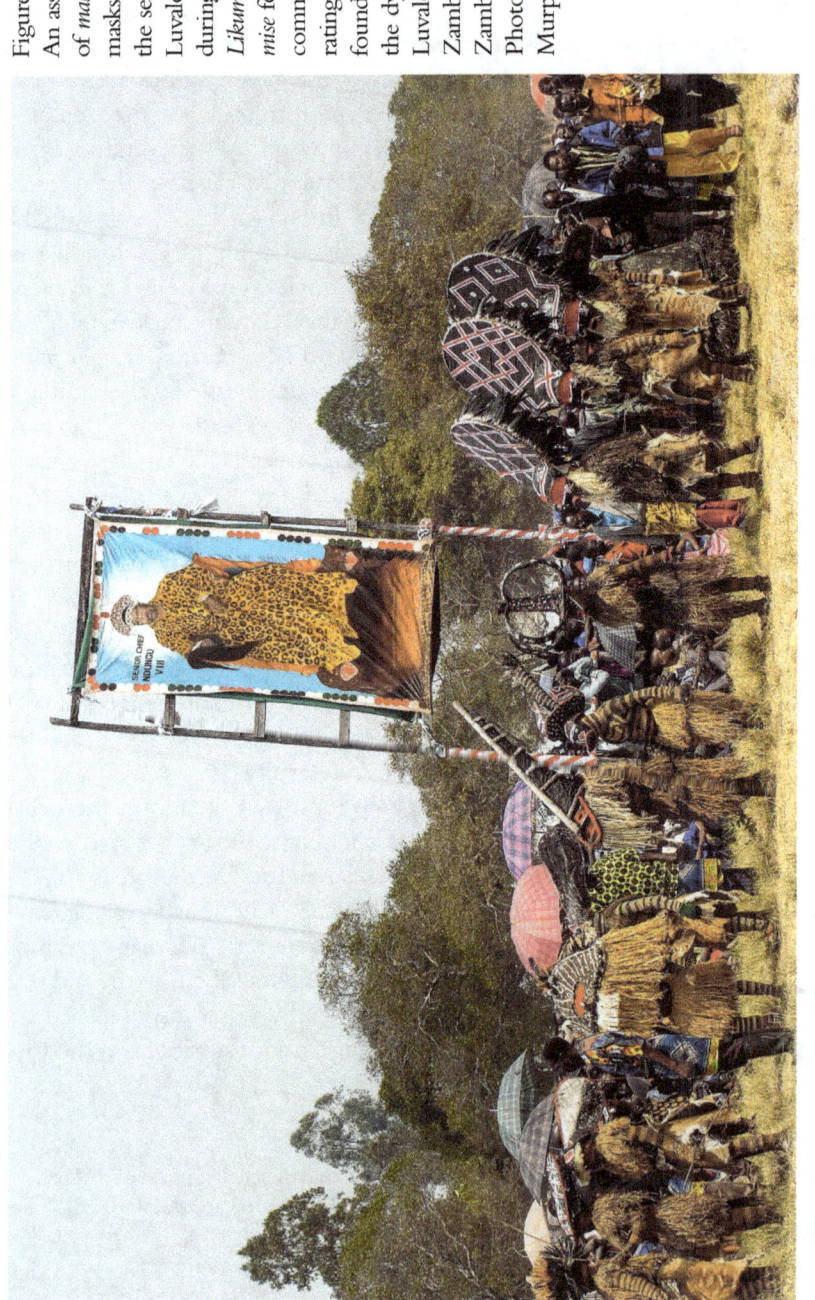

Figure 7.8. An assortment of *makishi* masks escorts the senior Luvale chief during the *Likumbi lya mise* festival, commemorating the founding of the dynasty. Luvale, Zambezi, Zambia, 2017. Photo: Ian Murphy.

realm to Otta at the time of Oyo hegemony; she knew all the relevant details, texts of songs, and particulars about the persons in question – in fact, for John Willis's book she has been just as important. So here was a woman who was an acknowledged expert in matters of masking, testifying from a position of authority in a male-dominated court, about issues that are considered completely within the male domain. She won the case.[59]

In the political sphere, mask rituals accentuate a multilayered society with overlapping principles of division, rendering the battleground between king and subjects opaquer and more nuanced, and operating in a faceted political field that the masks themselves help to generate. In addition, in their performances masks do the opposite again: they unite all participants, performers, and onlookers in one major happening with a large communally staged feast. So masks divide and then unite; they create difference and communitas at the same time. Mask rituals reproduce a society that has open power arenas with multiple players, and hence may support opposing candidates in a political struggle. The battle in the arena, however, is peaceful and highly engaging, through the performance of a unifying spectacle based upon a public secret.

Conclusion: The Akan Gap

We started out this chapter with the Yoruba. In the text we traced some parameters of their society and our typology clearly does not cover them, since for most of their history they have been town people in well-structured realms. This huge, diversified group inhabits a rich ecosystem and has created a complex society owing to its many craft guilds, priestly cults, and formerly echelons of slavery. Their vibrant masking tradition addresses the strong position of women in the economy, in the family, and even in politics;[60] the *gelede* spectacle of Chapter 6 was a showcase of the precarious balance between the genders: women were admired, lauded – and feared. Patrilineality is an issue in Yoruba social organisation, never self-evident – cognatic descent seems an option in many instances – and always hemmed in by politics, religion, and the borders of the locality.[61] Politically they are organised in many kingdoms, which shows an intricate balance between the *oba*, king, and an array of councils based on lineages and crafts; as is common in African

---

59 Willis 2018: 175–176. For the Chokwe, similar reports have been made: Bastin 1982, 1984, 1992.
60 R.S. Smith 1988: 95.
61 Lloyd 1966.

kingship, the king has a ritual position and serves as a point of redistribution, partly in a political arena with many other players, including women.[62] Despite this rather unique configuration, the fields of politics and gender clearly show up as arenas, driving the masquerades that remain important today.

But it is an obvious absence of masks that draws our main attention here. Zone 1 and Zone 2 are separated by a sizeable portion of West Africa without mask rituals, most of Ghana, Togo, and Benin, the 'Akan gap'.[63] These Akan-speaking groups in southern Ghana are clearly matrilineal, herd no cattle, and surely have excellent sculptors,[64] so why do they not have masks? The ecologies of the coastal parts of the Gap are different from the northern areas, so we need to look at two strains of explanation.

In our masking model in Chapter 1 it is factor 3 that puts marriage systems at the centre of the explanation. Southern Ghana shows a peculiar rule of marital residence[65] called duolocality, in which husband and wife do not cohabit but continue to live apart, each with his or her matrilineal relatives. Usually the spouses live at close quarters, and the wife can visit her husband at night. Anthropology calls this arrangement a visiting spouse system. Marital relations in Africa are expressed by food: in polygynous marriages the wife who cooks has intercourse. In a duolocal system the wife cooks for her husband at her own location, and has his food delivered in the early evening, usually through a daughter. The husband and his brothers combine the meals they receive, and together the mini-matrilineage sits down for dinner. The main contributions of a husband are the school fees for his children and the so-called 'chop money'; the money needed to buy ingredients for the meal – an arrangement open to negotiation and debate.

Katherine Abu analyses why this visiting spouse arrangement suits the Ashanti. According to her it coincides well with strong matrilineages, individual agency, and mobility for the wife when doing business – in which her husband should invest – while it also makes divorce easy.[66] Duolocal residence is quite rare, and occurs only in matrilineal settings where it has the advantage that brothers do not split up, and neither do sisters; brothers work together on their tasks, and women club together over their own chores. This feeds into a strong matriline, since all matrilineal-related males live together in one household. This solution of the matrilineal puzzle comes at the cost of what most cultures would define as the core of the marital union: a nuclear

62   R.S Smith 1988: 91.
63   McNaughton 1991.
64   Cole and Ross 1977.
65   Abu 1983.
66   Hagan 1983; Fortes 1950.

family that lives together. The classic tension in matrilineal systems – that between husband and brother over who controls the woman – is absent here, because the husband simply does not live with his wife; her brother does. As her brother is dependent on his sister to have inheritors, the position of the woman inside these matrilineages is fully embedded and extremely strong.[67] Significantly, in their position as mothers, the women wield considerable power; they have their own place in the palace, and their own ritual seats – the famous stools – while some even earn a reputation in warfare.

The political structure among the Ashanti is clear and unambiguous: in the palace, in the kingdom, in the chiefdoms, down to the individual households, men and women hold undisputed positions within the political system. This stability is based upon the structure of the matrilineage mentioned above and upon the many rituals surrounding the throne. What is also remarkable is the absence of secret societies. Ashanti men were organised in military companies, usually joining their father's company, and had to perform military service entirely within the state system.

Such a hierarchical, matrilineal, and duolocal society lacks the arenas addressed by mask rituals because the indeterminacies that feed masks are simply not present. Domain demarcation between the genders is institutionalised, the power configuration is not up for debate, and the authority of the king remains unchallenged. In such a system, mask rituals are not required to patrol the borders between the domains since the latter are not disputed, while secret societies, with their uncontrollable outside source of power, would be subversive.

Inheritable wealth is another factor. In no small measure the stability of the Ashanti realm is based on wealth, with gold as its shining icon. The chiefs and kings are decked with gold, with the Asantehene as a virtual mountain of gold, loaded with visible riches. Power needs to be visible in Africa, and for the Ashanti the sign of power is gold, coupled with the famous *kente* cloth – the theatre state is never far away. Even today, the Asantehene's influence is enormous and his position in Ghanaian politics is undisputed.[68] The combination of wealth and visibility is a strong one, and gold provides just that for the Asantehene, who goes by the epitaph of *Ote Kokoosuo Nana*, the 'King

---

67 Kwame 1983.
68 There is, however, an object called 'The Ashanti Gold Mask.' It is 29 cm in height, weighs 1.36 kg and is made of pure gold. See https://www.modernghana.com/news/310930/when-will-britain-return-looted-golden-ghanaian.html, consulted 7 August 2020. It is never worn, and viewing its size, never has been. It currently resides in the British Museum.

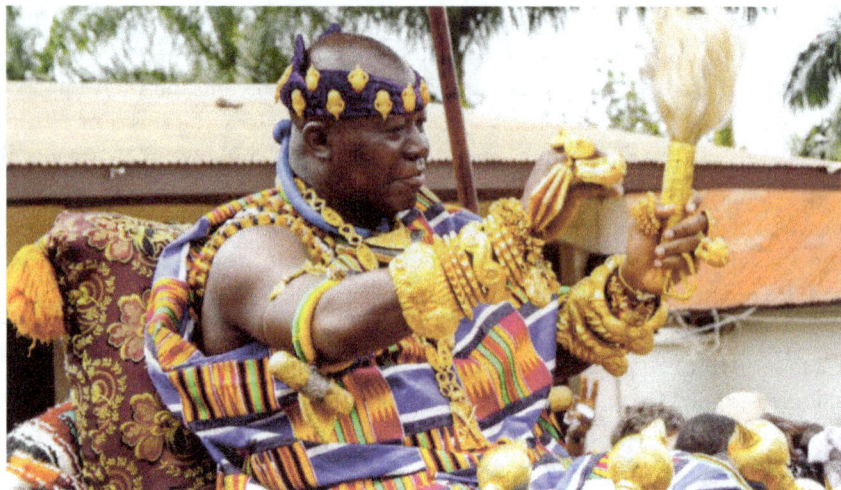

Figure 7.9. The Asantehene Otumfuo Osei Tutu II: no need for a mask. Photo: Common source.

Who Sits on Gold';[69] his wealth shows him to be a legitimate and highly laudable king, the pivot of the realm. Gold is the Akan royal mask.

The absence of masks can have other reasons as well. In the mid-eastern part of Côte d'Ivoire live the Beng, hemmed between masking groups, with a double descent system[70] that could make them ideally suited for mask rituals. However, their ethnographer Alma Gottlieb[71] reports that they do not have masquerades in their ritual repertoire. Why this seeming exception? On closer inspection similar reasons resurface: social organisation and wealth. Beng matriclans are localised, whereas the patriclans are not, and while the latter have religious functions, in daily life the matriclans dominate, and the point is that they are endogamous, meaning that husband and wife should stem from the same clan. This is very unusual in Africa, but maternal first cousins do marry within the Beng matriclan as MSD (mother's sisters' daughter), but at least a generation removed. The patriclans, on the other hand, are exogamous, and these clans are dispersed. Since marriage partners share the same matriclan, the father's relatives may be of a different patriclan, but they still belong to the same matriclan as the mother. Though marital residence is patrilocal, this curious endogamy ensures that the bride still lives very close

69 See https://www.ancient-origins.net/ancient-places-africa/asante-empire-0016395.
70 Gottlieb 1992: 46, 66; See for this case also Gottlieb 1998, 2000, 2004.
71 Alma Gottlieb, personal communication. She mentions the incidental appearance of a Senufo-like mask, which did not catch on.

to her family. Also, in case of polygyny – which is limited – the same would hold: all co-wives are from the husband's and each other's matriclan.

In most societies, African or other, this endogamy would imply marrying a sibling, so would tend to be defined as incest, but in Beng society it is the preferred marriage system. It does have the effect of solving the matrilineal puzzle in another and quite different way: all members of the same matriline live together, so there is no problem around leadership in the community. Indeed, these small-sized communities have 'kings' and 'queens',[72] a political centralisation that comes as somewhat of a surprise considering village size and the mixed subsistence of hunting, gathering, and farming.

Because of this centralisation, gender and power do not form real arenas in Beng society: the relations between men and women are complementary and unambiguous, while the descent system provides a power system without indeterminacy. In addition, there is the rather unexpected factor of wealth: each matriclan keeps a stock of gold, nuggets, coins, and stools as a central symbol of clanship – they have a historic link with Akan groups – but also as a resource in times of need. Guarded by the clan chief, this treasure forms a nodal point in internal clan politics that is held under communal scrutiny. By itself the presence of a small hoard of gold would not be a sufficient condition, since the same custom is present among the Baule,[73] but coupled with the absence of the gender arena it becomes clear why on closer inspection the Beng case fits our theory.

On Map 1 the Akan Gap extends all the way to the north, including most of northern Ghana, Togo, and Benin. This is the area where the West African forest cover shows a significant gap, with the savannah reaching down to the ocean, and with sleeping sickness still extant.[74] Two factors have shaped local societies here. First, the ecology of the region favoured horse breeding over cattle keeping, so the endogenic polities from the Ghanaian middle belt were based on cavalry. Second, the dynamics of Muslim jihadism produced no Fulbe realm in the north of the Gap, owing maybe to the existence of local cavalries, so local realms have dominated each other in this area without incoming warrior states.

This is the region dominated by Type B, the layered community, with a ruler group that is politically dominant over a subjugated one. The rulers in this area often are organised according to the genealogical grid of Type A societies, but they do not command the land; instead, the lower echelon

---

72 See also Stone 2006: 162–168.
73 Weiskel 1978.
74 Morton-Williams 1969: 87. The classical source is Rattray 1956.

holds all the links, especially the spiritual ones, with the land, and is represented by the chiefs of the Earth, the so-called *tindana*. The position of the dominated group varies from being subjects of the warrior groups to being fully integrated in their society, yet still masters of the land.

Earlier ethnographies followed the dominant interpretation in which the newcomers occupied the land settled by earlier inhabitants, but recent studies question such historical charters. The division between the chief and the *tindana* is found all over the area, and may well be a function of internal divisions and inheritance rules, rather than the result of historic contingency. Wyatt MacGaffey[75] notes how the Dagomba charter myth tells how the founder of the state eliminated all *tindana*, yet they are still there, have always been around, and are found everywhere in the wider area. This political situation is quite stable, with a rule-based interaction between the two power bases, power over people versus power over land, which amounts to an inherent balance between two types of capital, social and symbolic, that leads to a clearly defined power field. As predicted by our model, mask rituals are not an evident option in a structure like this. But there are exceptions, for some Type B societies do have rituals including masks and they are important for our analysis.

This border region of Zone 1 offers the most direct tests for our model, since it houses different types of communities in close contact. For instance in northwestern Ghana, on the border with Burkina Faso, the Dagara are described as 'aggressive farmers' in search of new land, using shrines as markers of occupation and ownership of the land; they have the Type A patrilineal segmentary lineage system that goes with such an expansive use of territory. Their Sisala neighbours, on the other hand, have closed villages, local clans, no territorial expansion, and fixed shrines: Type C. Also their bride wealth confers much fewer marital rights and duties than the more substantial Dagara.[76] And, indeed the Sisala (used to) have mask rituals, while the Dagara never did.

But the main socio-cultural dynamics in this region centre on Type B societies. The Mossi or Moose of Burkina Faso have historic links with northern Ghana and show characteristics of the Type B profile, but they do have masks. As with the Mundang, it is not the king who commands the masks but the 'people of the earth', and ownership of masks resides in individual families – which may trace their descent from various other groups; one would be the Kurumba near the border with Mali, who have

---

75 MacGaffey 2013: 1, 71.
76 Lentz 2009. For the disappearing Sisala mask, Nunley 1977.

masks in many forms.[77] There are no secret societies in Mossi, and the masks do not play a part in initiations, but function during the second funerals of important figures, in both societal echelons but not in those of the kings themselves.[78] In appearance most of their masks closely resemble the plank masks of Burkina Faso: the Mossi seem to form a transitional region between the mask-rich area of Burkina Faso, and the maskless Gap: masking remains a cultural and creative choice.

A comparison with the Mundang, discussed above, is revealing. The Mundang have some Type C characteristics: large defensive patrilineal villages with localised circumscripted lineages that have mask initiation, though without secret societies; yet their realm is based on cavalry, and their royalty stems from elsewhere. Compared to Type B, the division of tasks between king and masking society is the reverse: the king is responsible for rain and fertility, and the masks for the next generations. The Mundang balance of power between royalty and general society-*cum*-masks is skewed towards the agricultural basis of society, while in Type B the upper layer dominates politically and the lower echelon dominates in agriculture, as among the Mossi.

Anyway, the dualistic power structure of the layered society does echo the more generalised political see-sawing between king and secret societies. The many forms of centralised kingship, with their clear descent rules, stand in opposition to either the secret society or the institution of the *tindana*, the first with masks and the second usually without. The point is that the latter are grounded not in social but in symbolic capital, dispersed, and in the hands of local communities. So *tindana* and masks both operate as a check against the centralisation of power: they mirror each other, and their parallel functions tend to exclude one another.

Such a balancing act of kingship versus symbolic power is hardly a new development. Around 1350 CE, Ibn Batuta visited Mansa Suleiman, king of Mali, and witnessed masks at his court, when the bards appeared before their king in a feather costume with a bird's head.[79] The voyager of Islam thought their outfit ridiculous – masks and Islam are uneasy companions – but he did furnish the earliest ever description of African masks. In his account the masks recited history, and it was explained to him that these 'poets' had a message for the ruler to heed to the rules of nobility established by his predecessors. Today such recitations, in which the bards deliver the epic of Sunjata, the forefather of the king in question, are well known.

77　Schweeger-Hefel 1980, Schweeger-Hefel and Staude 1972.
78　Izard 1985, 1992, 2005, Luning 2010, 1991.
79　Ibn Batuta 2005, Book II, Chapter XIV: 411.

About this tale and its dedicated performers, *jeli* in Mande, a massive literature has developed that sheds light on the incident.[80] The standard interpretation of this epic is as a poetic rendition of a historical ruler, Sunjata Keita, founder of the Mali empire and forefather of the king whom Ibn Batuta encountered. However, Sunjata expert Jan Jansen argues that Ibn Batuta witnessed a mask performance that mirrored the Komo initiation – see Chapter 4 – and that in fact a Komo performance underlies this epic story.[81] In that case, local masks must have preceded the court masquerade, which fits into our model. But with such a large time gap one should beware of an overly presentist interpretation, so we will just note that masks were present at the fourteenth-century Malian court, and did advise the ruler.

If masks are indeed a counter-hegemonic check on central power, the Kuba case is exceptional. The Kuba realm is itself an outgrowth of a Type D society, in which a stable hegemonic polity has been formed based on trade monopolies, periodic reconquest, and state shows. Their forest ecology mirrors that of other groups in Zone 3, but here the House has managed to acquire a religious grounding through masking that seems out of the reach of other realms. Vansina shows that some masks may be borrowed from the neighbouring Kete, and traditions attribute some mask types to a legendary queen, while anyway the relation between the initiation masks and the kingly ones is not overly clear.[82] The point is that the mask strengthens the king directly by linking him to the bush – in fact through a pygmy, a man of the deep bush. Though kings in Africa habitually hail their provenance from outside the ethnic group, the bush usually is the reserved area for masks, not kings.

All in all, the relation between power and masks is quite dialectic: even if masks are hard to control from the centre, in the end they tend to bolster the forces that be, either the power associations or the kings. And they do add to the state spectacle. Just as wealth must be seen, power should shine in public displays, so masquerades serve as an independent visual force that the king may support, enjoy, or even try to own, but even if he does not control the masks, his position is at least periodically bolstered in state-affirming rituals. Masks may be a check on the king's power, but they also construct the theatre state.

80 For instance Bulman and Vydrine 2017, Conrad 2004.
81 Jansen 2018b. See also Jansen 2000.
82 Vansina 1978: 215–217.

8

Masks and the Order of Things

'May the gods, the masks and the statues keep us together.'
(Manthia Diawara, in Fölmi 2015: 258. See also Diawara 1998)

Masks in the field

They are easily the most elegant of all mask tops, and anyone interested in African art immediately recognises them: the stylised antelopes called *ciwara*. As icons of African art they had a lasting influence on European avant-garde artists such as Braque and Picasso. These headpieces are part of the culture of the Bamana, the dominant group in Mali. Nowadays this *ciwara* is considered a national emblem, and images of the antelope headpiece are routinely mis-used commercially. These striking tops come in many variations and styles, and are arguably among the most intensely studied headpieces of the Mask Crescent. We would not dream of publishing a book on African masks without giving them the attention they so well deserve, and yet they form a curious footnote in the story of masquerading on the continent.

The scene is the village of Dyele in the south of Mali, where the anthropologist Jean-Paul Colleyn has brought a film team to 'his' village for a *ciwara* ceremony.[1] It is the end of March, dry and hot, and the first rains are not due for another three months, but this is the ritual season, and the season for an agricultural rite.

Late on the night of 23 March, the musicians begin to arrive in the village square, which in Bamana culture means quite an ensemble: a huge xylophone, a grating instrument, and four drums of different sizes, plus an iron bell. At the side of the square they start playing, and a group of girls joins them in song: 'The animals of prey are coming, let

---

1   The film *Chronique d'une saison sèche. Le Ty-wara* resulted from this field trip, later to be featured in the exposition *Ciwara. Chimères africaines*, at the Branly Museum in Paris, 23 June–28 December 2006. The description is based upon Colleyn 2006.

*them come, give wide berth to the power (*nyama*) [...] the wild animals will swing around'.*[2] *Suddenly two masks emerge from the dark, dancing to music and songs. Clothed in raffia, their headdresses show the features of the 'antelope cheval',*[3] *the male mask's horns long and high, those of the female mask shorter. The leading male mask dances with two sticks covered in old sacrificial blood. Their first dance is short, just an introductory appearance, and then they sit down at the side. With a crowd gathering and the girls singing, one elder, a dancer of old, takes one of the sticks from the male's hand to serve as a recipient for the coming sacrifices. Following their age grades girls take turns in singing in groups, with the masks jumping up for occasional performances during the night.*

The next morning sees action in the court of the ciwara *sanctuary, where the adepts of the* ciwara *society bring along antelope horns to be refilled with magical black paste, while young boys who want to be initiated come with 200 cowries and two chickens. The core act of this morning is a series of sacrifices on the altars of the sanctuary, involving small handfuls of millet, the essence of the* ciwara *cult, plus a paste made of millet, millet cream, and beer. Assisted by the 'sister of the* ciwara*', the officiating elder pronounces an invocation to the mask: 'Ciwara, here's your beer. This is given for you to keep the children healthy, you get this beer, so give us good luck in the dry season and rain later. Give us children and give us women [...]'*[4] *– and proceeds to ask for health, plenty of food, and prosperity for the village. The terminology used refers to a marriage, of the village to the* ciwara*; the cult is considered to come from another village 'in marriage' to Dyele town, and the sister of the mask represents this union. The long text invokes the role of the blacksmith, as origin of the tools for agriculture: 'Here your water [beer] to buy the millet, the cultivator has taken credit with the smith, give him millet to reimburse his debt.'*[5] *The officiator douses the altar with beer, kills the chickens and throws them on the floor, watching how they die; they should end up on their backs. The young initiates gather some sacrificial blood in their horns, the elders rub the blood of the altar onto the mask stick, and the general drinking and eating session starts – the essence of all African sacrifices. The whole session is interspersed with songs, led by an experienced singer with a choir of girls.*

It is time now for the masks to dress again, so hidden from spectators the 'wearers of raffia' – which is what they are called in the ritual – put on their costumes with the headpieces on top and follow the musical ensemble; the troupe keeps dancing and playing while the masks move first to the sacrificial place and then to other spots where

---

2   'Les fauves (*waraw*) vont venir! Laissez le passage, laissez le passage pour le *nyama* (la force) qui vient [...] le *ciwara* va se dandiner.' Colleyn 2006: 66–67.
3   *Hippotragus equinus.*
4   Colleyn 2006: 68.
5   Ibid.: 69.

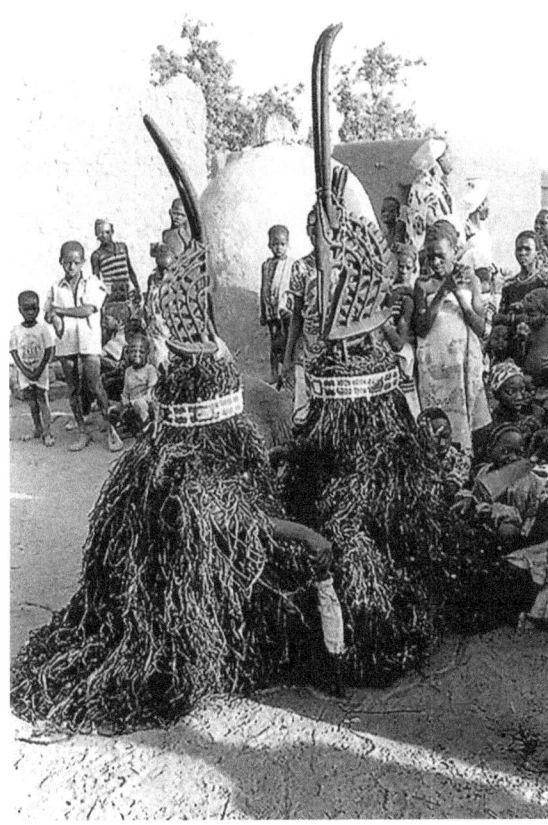

Figure 8.1. Two *ciwara*, one male and one female, perform their 'wedding'. Dyele, Bamana, Mali. Photo: Catherine DeClippel, 1985.

the ancestors have left protective devices for the village. At each spot the two dancers squat down and engage in a gentle chanting exchange that symbolises their wedding (see Figure 8.1), interpreted by Colleyn as a union between the two basic principles in the world, male and female, which underly fertility in the world. Their ensuing promenade sanctifies the fields that the founders of the village have taken from the bush.

Bamana society has a caste of jesters, people who may comment freely and mock others, and these now join the fray, dancing seductively at this 'wedding'. Then the officiator, an old dancer himself, shows the dancing steps that evoke the agile feet of antelopes, while the women present give cowries as offerings to the masks, that are seated at the side. The ciwara *are repeatedly thanked for a good season and the promise of babies and health. From time to time, and at the end of the afternoon, the two masks dance again, longer now and with movements that imitate the act of cultivation. Leaping like proper antelopes, they bend over and scratch the earth with their horns and their large stick; the female usually dances behind the male, fanning him as if spreading his powers into the gathered community.*

On the final day of the feast, 25 March, the chief of the ciwara *society leads all visitors in a series of sacrifices of chickens and goats, while behind a low wall some youngsters help the dancers put on their costumes. Women come in with food, and some join in with the songs of praise for the* ciwara, *the chief, ancestors, and the jesters – 'the first people in the world were jesters'. Some women take a surreptitious peek at the mask preparation, for the gender taboo around the* ciwara *is light. Called by the frenetic rhythm of the musicians, the masks emerge again for the last time and dance around the area, this time swirling around. After this final performance, they disappear into the sanctuary, the drums fall silent, and the festival is over:* ciwara *has been honoured and the next season guaranteed, for both crops and people. As masks they are the true agricultural champions, as anthropologist Stephen Wooten analyses them, the embodiment of the central values of a society dedicated to cultivation.*[6]

There are other instances where the *ciwara* masks come out, but this is the most important one, and they should always appear in pairs, one with a male and one with a female headdress, the male more vertical, the female more horizontal and often with a foal. The *ciwara* society has its own niche in the whole Bamana roster of secret societies. *Ciwara* means 'animal that cultivates the soil', and the mimetic part of the dance echoes its founding myth. *Ciwara*, so the tale goes, was half-man and half-animal, son of a snake and the first woman, Mousso Koroni. With his horns and staff he cultivated the soil and transformed herbs into millet; in fact, he was so successful that his human pupils neglected their own agricultural work, and *ciwara* fled to the heavens. To entice him back, the people built an altar and danced with the masks in his likeness, to remember his teachings and to have a good harvest.

All in all, this *ciwara* ritual is remarkable, since very few mask rituals address this basis of life: the growing of crops.[7] Mask rituals are usually well distinguished from sacrificial complexes. The Mundang king showed as much, but the same holds for the Bobo, Dogon, Dan, Nupe, Senufo, and many others. The ritual distinction between the yearly cycle of rain and agriculture, and the life cycle, is remarkably consistent: masks feature in initiation and death rites, and not in cyclical rituals, which often feature sacrifices. After all, most agriculture is in the hands of women, which is one of the starting points of our theory, so in the fields, masks are on women's terrain. The specific position of the *ciwara* shows in the details of its ritual.

6   Wooten 2000.
7   Another case is the *koui* mask among the Wè in Côte d'Ivoire, Guyblehon 2013.

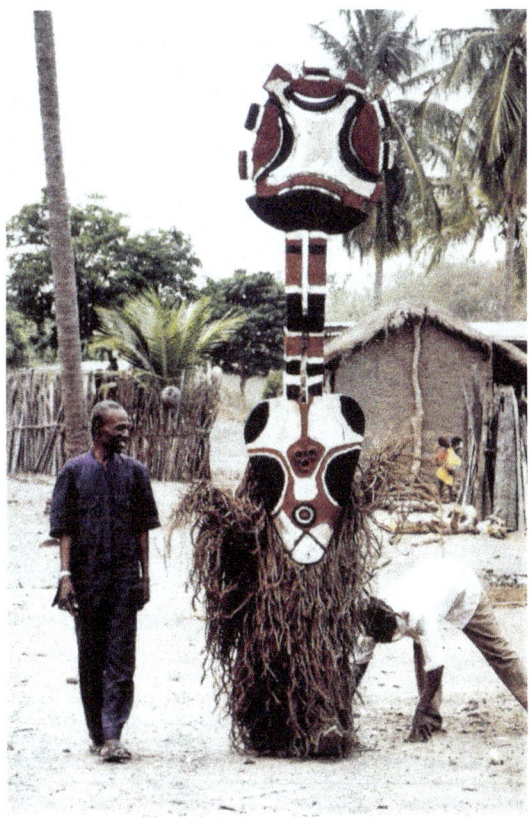

Figure 8.2. *Bedu* mask
(*bedu sosoonro*, the tall *bedu*).
Daribin, Côte d'Ivoire,
1994. Photo: Karel Arnaut.

Usually masking performances consist mainly of coming on stage, dancing, and interaction with the public, yet the *ciwara* couple take part in what is essentially a community sacrifice. Also their performance is shot through with reminiscences of wedding and fertility, and when they really dance at the conclusion of the festival, the basic gender taboo is almost lifted.

The *ciwara* involvement with cultivation is rare but not unique. Mette Bovin reports that Mumuye masks play a role in preparing the cultivation cycle.[8] In Cameroon the Dìì masks make an appearance as part of a harvest ritual at the start of the dry season.[9] In the end, the men burn the fibre costumes and scatter the ashes over the dancing ground. They tell the women that they are sowing ground peas, in the expectation that when women walk over them the next morning they will conceive more easily.

8 Bovin 1966: 81.
9 Muller 2002.

Similarly, the *bedu* mask of Côte d'Ivoire marks the seasons and supervises the making of the first fire in the fields, prior to the communal hunt.

Though the *ciwara* case does not stand completely on its own, the relation between masks and cultivation is far from evident. One reason is that masks are routinely defined as creatures of the dry, and in opposition to rain, and often also to lakes and streams. Masks belong to dry land and they dominate all rituals of passage that take place during the dry season. For the Dogon, dryness is an essential symbol in their masks, lauded in the accompanying songs. A wet mask is not a mask at all; in fact a wet mask would be ridiculous, losing its powers – and its colours. Their mask festival is held at the very end of the dry season, and must be finished before the onset of the rains, which may be a close call. The elders in charge of the *dama* may be pressured to finish the whole sequence before the first raindrops fall.

All over the Crescent, rain and mask are defined in opposition to each other in a complicated relationship. Among the many rituals to procure rain in Africa, very few involve masks – a revealing observation. Muller reports of the Dìì that when rain is lacking masks may dance to chase away the evil force causing the delay; but that dance addresses witches, which masks combat anyway.[10] Rain is the essence of life, and masks are a life-sustaining power, so why are they not related? The reason resides in a cosmological rationale. Rain comes from on high, from the heavens, from deities; masks stem from the bush. Masks and bush spirits are essentially in the human plane of existence as a wild circle around the human village, whereas the realm of rains-*cum*-deity is up high and distinct. The two do not mix; the Mundang example was chrystal clear in this respect. The fundamental opposition, therefore, is between the vertical axis of earth and sky, and the horizontal axis of village and bush. Although mask rituals may just precede the rainy season, calling for rain is not mask business at all. If rains fail, people do not call in the masks but address the king, or make sacrifices on their shrines to deities and ancestors. The latter is revealing: even if ancestors are routinely associated with masks, they seldom really *are* masks, so asking ancestors for rain means relying on them as intermediaries with the deity who is the source of rain. When ancestors are approached for rain, they are addressed as halfway heaven, not as halfway bush.

This chapter starts not with a typical case but with an exception, since these *ciwara* promote cultivation, unusual for masks. Many masquerades occur during annual festivals, which usually occur during the dry season at

10   Muller 2001: 64.

a time when cultivation is not on the agenda.[11] Obviously, this designated time has a sound logistical reason – the moment people have enough time for extensive rituals – but the gentle opposition of mask versus cultivation is notable; and exceptions, to be expected in any theory, highlight this contrast. Powerful as masks are, one would think their help in cultivation would be called in much more often, but such is not the case.

Masks and the adjudication of law

Whoever has power must use it. As powerful be-things, masks form an obvious tool to keep dissenters in check and to enforce behaviour that conforms with the norms. In societies with weak socio-political structures – which are apt to have mask rituals – masks are welcome as agents of order, and in dealing with purported transgressions, masks embody the values that hold society together. Thus, the general relationship of masks with established norms and rules – or to use a more formal term, law – is at issue here. In his foundational volume on indigenous law, Edward Hoebel speaks of laws or 'law-ways',[12] since most of the rules and norms are not codified but are transmitted orally and case by case. Maintaining these norms is a quest in which four elements can be discerned: (1) a normative element; (2) regularity; (3) courts; and (4) enforcement. 'A social norm is legal if its neglect or infraction is met, in threat or in fact, by the application of physical force by an individual or group possessing the socially recognised privilege of so acting.'[13] Formulated otherwise, law adjudication entails a 'court'[14] pronouncing a verdict – a court that has both the right to issue it and the power to make it stick. So the court must have an enforcing body at its disposal.

It is only at the end of the judicial procedure that we see masks operating, when after accusation and fact-finding the judgement must be announced. Rendering a verdict requires both knowledge and authority, and these come naturally to masks. The example comes from the Dan in Liberia. The judgement mask of the Dan is called *gle wa* and is owned by the *go* association, which is responsible for peacekeeping in the village.[15]

---

11   The *ikeji* harvest festival among the Aro in Nigeria, in a more urban environment, has morphed into a festival of collective identity: Bentor 1994b: 325.
12   Hoebel 1976: 35.
13   Ibid.: 28.
14   Pospisil 1974.
15   Based upon Reed 2003.

Two families in a community are at loggerheads with each other and mediation has failed, so the judgement mask is called in. Through its accompanying elders, the mask summons the two factions to a public square and takes a seat between them. Each faction then narrates, once again, its grievances against the other. After hearing out the litigants, the mask will determine which side is right and which is the guilty party in the conflict. The winning side expresses its gratitude to the mask and celebrates its victory by presenting the mask with a white ox, a white ram, and strips of white cotton – white being the colour of righteousness. The losing party acknowledges the mask's verdict, is expected to say it is happy that the conflict has been resolved, and also presents the mask with the three white sacrificial gifts. The mask orders the animals to be slaughtered and cooked, and all villagers are invited to eat from the meal as a token that they too accept the verdict.

Here the mask is clearly in the role of the court, as an otherworldly presence presumed to 'know' the truth and communicate it. But it is very expensive. Dan is an agricultural society in which oxen are extremely costly, and completely white ones are extra hard to come by. However, a verdict should demand a major sacrifice from the claimants because only a costly verdict will be accepted as a true one; real justice cannot be cheap. This means that the mask is called in only for the larger cases, conflicts between major parties and rich litigants over serious questions: consulting the mask is a last resort. Of course one must visualise a hidden court of well-informed elders behind most utterances of the mask, for the masker is briefed beforehand by the elders of the community; even during the session he keeps in contact with the backstage, the ones who guide and lead him. Masks never operate alone.

What the mask achieves is three-fold. First, it concentrates all attention on the case in question, since its appearance marks a definite liminal time; the daily world has stopped for a moment when the mask pronounces its judgement on the conflict. The more special the judging moment, the less the parties tend to come back to the issue at hand. Second, the mask is the symbol of the community's unity, a symbol that is beyond criticism or reproach. Third, in the absence of formal political and judicial structures, the mask bundles the various power positions in the village into one whole through its performance. Acephalous societies such as the Dan are based upon rather diffuse age and kin relations, and in order to make and enforce decisions, the mask sides with the community elders by reinforcing a weak judicial moral order. Raphael Njoku poses the question what would happen when the mask verdict is incorrect, since that may turn out to be the case.

The answer is that since the mask itself cannot make mistakes, it must have been the drummer who led the mask on erroneous pathways by his music.[16]

As Hoebel formulates it, in judicial processes power must be 'transpersonalised'.[17] Courts tend to symbolise this transpersonalisation quite visibly – the wigs in British courts spring to mind, as do the ubiquitous gowns – justice demands a theatre. By clear visual and symbolic means, the verdict is divorced from the person delivering it, and the figure of a mask rendering final judgement in a difficult and protracted court case is as theatrical as can be. In Africa such a separation is even more important because of the close ties of kinship and mutual obligations between all parties:

> In the process of enforcing rules, the masked spirits must punish, or be able to make fully credible a threat to punish all wrong-doers, regardless of family allegiances, ages, or social status. […] Since the mask is conceived as a spirit, there is no person to blame and no recrimination or retaliation within the community.[18]

In the adjudication of law, masks enable the feeble forces of a society to lift its rules to a higher plane, tying mundane personal relations to powers beyond human control. Masks are not justice as such and neither do they represent the law, however conceived, but they bolster the authority responsible for the application of law – and by incorporating the theatrics of the judicial process, they 'perform' law.

Within the Ibibio group in southeastern Nigeria, Joseph Akpan reports, the masking societies form such a judicial body, but this increases their power. Since masks experience few restrictions in their performances, they must control each other in order to remain within acceptable limits. Only together as a body are 'their actions […] specifically directed towards the maintenance of law and order', and they need authority to legitimately incur fear: 'The masks must be frightening in order to invoke the threat of force and authority necessary for the masked characters to maintain order.'[19] The law needs teeth, the Romans knew, and for the masks this holds just as well.[20] Societies with more fixed political structures do not involve masks in courts; they clearly do not need them – and control of them would be

16 Njoku 2020: 41.
17 Hoebel 1976: 277.
18 Siegmann 1980, quoted in Reed 2003: 84.
19 Akpan 1994: 53.
20 For Njoku (2020), this forms the basis of masking.

difficult – and thus the judicial function of masks is more or less limited to acephalous societies, well represented in the Crescent.

The discourse on witchcraft

The scene is a Fang village in Gabon before the Second World War. At the sound of the drums, a mask came into the village and immediately drew everybody's full attention, because they thought it was 'monstrous'. To the ethnographer this was not immediately obvious: the raffia costume sported a white wooden face cover set with feathers, waving in the dance: 'Despite the serene appearance of his mask the intimidating emissary emitted terrifying raucous noises and was identified with punishment and retribution.'[21] Through its demeanour and soundscape the Fang identified this *ngil* mask as a frightening monster,[22] who had come into the village to hunt down and punish evildoers. *Ngil* or *ngi* means both a powerful medicine and a male association, two closely related notions in this part of Africa. The *ngil* association was especially powerful at the end of the nineteenth century, with an authority that went way beyond the clan. Its leader, *nnom ngi*, had the power to police the community, and travel from village to village with impunity because he was recognised as a peacekeeper. His main task was to combat witchcraft, assisted by prominent individuals such as family heads, pursuing and eliminating presumed witches. When disaster struck the village in the form of illness or death, especially after a few unexplainable departures, the villagers organised *ngi* ceremonies to detect the 'culprits' and punish the witches and sorcerers they considered responsible.

Trilles's iconic photo – one of the oldest ones in our book – shows it less prominently, but the main counterintuitive aspect of *ngil* mask faces seems to be their elongation,[23] a trait that Europeans would indeed find serene – suggesting even a comparison with a Modigliani; the small photo shows as much. But for the Fang this deliberate anatomical distortion transforms it into a terrifying semi-human being, scary enough to confound the sorcerer

---

21 LaGamma 2007: 300.

22 The headpiece was imbued with death. The initiation rites of the *ngil* association occurred in a secret enclosure with a large recumbent figure made of earth, in which the bones of prisoners of war were buried – nameless bones, not those of deceased lineage members.

23 For instance, the famous *ngil* headpiece of the Branly Museum in Paris. See https://commons.wikimedia.org/wiki/File:Fang_mask_Louvre_MH65-104-1.jpg, consulted 25 April 2023.

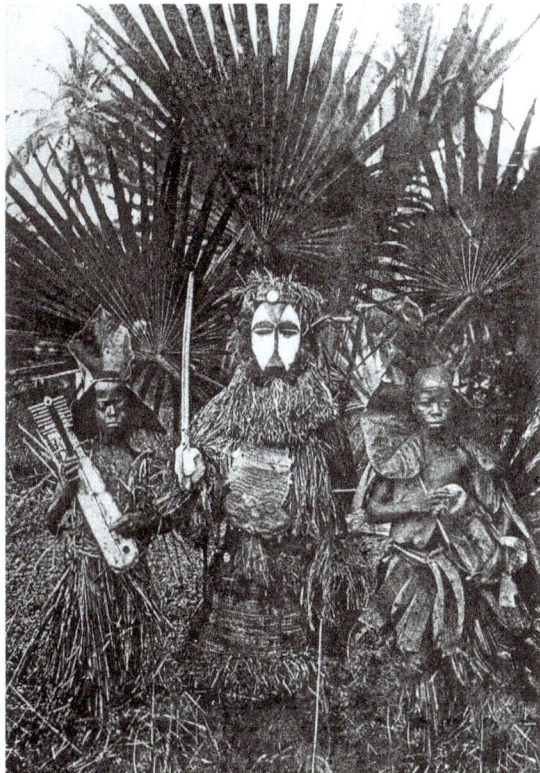

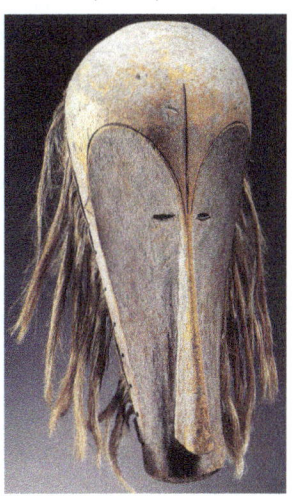

Figure 8.3a (left). *Ngil* mask and neophytes. Gabon, 1899–1901. Photo: Henri Trilles.
Figure 8.3b (below). *Ngil* headpiece. Denver Art Museum, USA, 2021.

or the witch, hunt down the social deviant, and punish the criminal.[24] Such a punishment was required when disaster struck, but also when *ngil* adepts behaved badly in the community; the *ngil* group would then appear in public with the mask in question, often at the request and expense of petitioners, to frighten anyone who had caused the unrest or had evil intentions.[25]

When public order is on the masks' agenda, the struggle against witchcraft is always number one, and many publications mention this function.[26] For instance, in the *sigma* mask societies of northwestern Ghana that are found among several Gur-speaking groups, the masks proceed against witches in several ways.[27] At an unexpected and untimely – and thus suspect – death, the elders of the *sigma* society perform divination in order to choose between three

24 Perrois 2006: 324. See also Perrois 2008.
25 T. Phillips 1995: 324–325. See also R. Phillips 1975.
26 For instance Danfulani 1999b.
27 Poppi 2013.

options. First, the deceased might have been a witch who was executed for that reason by the *sigma* mask. In that case several masks were called in, who dragged the naked body to a shallow grave lined with thorns; the deceased would never be mentioned again, and his property would be incorporated into the *sigma* society's shrine treasures. The second option was that the death was the result of witchcraft, in which case the society tried to identify the culprit witch, who would then be clubbed to death by the masks. The third option was that the death was natural, termed a 'God death', and a full proper burial could be undertaken. If the deceased in question was an initiated *sigma* member, a large first funeral would be held immediately, with the masks featuring prominently. A few years later a second, even larger funeral would establish his place among the ancestors.

Death by witchcraft is the epitome of a wrongful death, both for the one who died and for the purported witch. Given the strong and enduring association of the masks with death, their preoccupation with witchcraft is understandable. But there are more and deeper reasons why masks are so rabidly anti-witch, and these lie in the contrast between their ethical side and the purported nature of the witch. The otherworld is ambivalent, it is people who can be right or wrong. Some people are considered to have a shadow or spirit that is harmful, leaving the sleeping owner to create havoc in the night – flying out to attack the shadows of other people, often little children, who then fall ill.[28] Such a bad shadow or spirit belongs to a witch, and a belief in and discourse on witches is called witchcraft. Definitions vary in Africa, but ever since the pioneering work of Evans-Pritchard on the Zande, it has proven productive to distinguish witchcraft from sorcery.[29] Sorcerers perform magic, manipulate things, and utter spells to achieve clear ends – either harmful or beneficial, but in any case, a voluntary act that can be controlled by the person in question; sorcery can be learned. Witchcraft, on the contrary, is thought to be involuntary, difficult to contain, inborn, and always harmful; it is usually seen as an inherited trait triggered by greed or jealousy. Witches are considered simply evil in themselves. Some African cultures suppose there is some 'stuff' inside the body of the witch, only visible after dissection.

This is the bleak side of many African indigenous religions, since supposed witches can seldom be 'cured' and may be persecuted or banished. What is discernible for any observer, of course, is just the discourse: people whisper, gossip, and speak about 'witches', mostly in general terms but occasionally directed at specific individuals, a discourse that becomes fully overt when

---

28 Bowie 2009: 222–223; Olsen and Van Beek 2015.
29 Evans-Pritchard 1937.

people accuse witches. It is these accusations that cause trouble and suffering, for accusations usually focus on the weak in society, following society's fault lines; structural conflicts at the grass roots level, such as between co-wives and half-brothers, are common reasons for witchcraft accusations. Sometimes the accused have the option to cleanse themselves – for the moment – or make themselves 'inactive' as a 'witch', but often they must flee and find sanctuary. Witch hunting creates havoc and suffering. Historically, also among the Fang, witch hunts instigated waves of anti-witchcraft movements, over time generating ever new versions of the witch-finding rites.[30]

All this questions the very existence of witches, and most scholars studying witchcraft – which is by no means exclusive to Africa – share the authors' conviction that the content of the belief is erroneous. But the point is that people believe it and act accordingly, and the impact of the belief in witches on individuals and society is what constitutes the problem. There is a scholarly quandary here. One cannot really understand and write about these discourses on the occult without feeling some empathy toward what it would mean to believe in them. On the other hand the suffering through accusations, persecutions, and killings is very real,[31] and blaming the victims is poor justice in any system. For instance, when young street children in Kinshasa are persecuted for being witches and the cause of problems that are actually endemic to the city,[32] the devastating effects of the discourse are glaringly obvious, and an academic distance is no longer possible. With children accused, convicted, and abandoned, empathy disappears and the evil of witchcraft accusations appears in full view.

The notion of witchcraft may also have a less deleterious side, since it includes an aspect of maintaining order. People who behave abnormally, who are out of order, or who stand out too much among their peers, run the risk of being accused of witchcraft. In Bemba society, someone with a better harvest than his neighbour has been lucky; if the same happens the following year, he is an astute farmer; but the third bumper harvest in a row makes him a witch. All this induces people to share generously,[33] and the witch discourse can be a leveller in society.[34] More important still, the process of finding and dealing with the supposed witch unites society, for all find each other in the belief that together they have solved the problem. Scapegoats are innocent in themselves, but their sacrifice is a

30 Fernandez 1982: 222.
31 Geschiere 2017.
32 Ter Haar 2007: 16.
33 A. Richards 1982.
34 Geschiere 1997: 10.

powerful tool for unity.[35] That being so, the problem is two-fold. First, any unity deriving from a scapegoat sacrifice – which the public persecution of a witch represents – can only be a fleeting one, since the root causes of the problem are not addressed; it is a pseudo-solution. Second, this way of maintaining order and unity is extremely costly in human suffering, which can be ignored only by defining the 'culprits' as non-humans.

Why is the discourse on witchcraft so widespread? The main issue is the notion that any adversity must have a reason, and the idea that a witch caused the problem is the most facile explanation of all. A specific mishap at this moment must be the work of an evil person who is close at hand, so someone in the immediate environment must be the culprit; witchcraft looks for the enemy within the gates. In this way, the witchcraft discourse offers a ready-made explanation for each individual problem, since it answers the question: 'Why is this happening to me, and why now?', finding the answer in a relation gone wrong, and these are always at hand. Given the premise of such a mystical connection, the witchcraft discourse constitutes a closed but faulty reasoning that is hard to disprove, and works by heaping blame on the heads of the weak. The witchcraft discourse is a 'meme', an idea that is easily picked up and is difficult to unlearn – a cognitive virus that blames victims and, in the end, weakens society.

Masks versus 'witches'

The witchcraft discourse is almost pan-African, so it also occurs in the Mask Crescent. But there is a more structural reason why a confrontation between masks and presumed witches is inevitable: societies that are prone to witchcraft accusations share important characteristics with those that harbour mask rituals. Cultures in which social relations are under constant negotiation house mask rituals, but they also offer a fertile ground for witchcraft accusations; thus, for instance, in matrilineal societies we see a flurry of these accusations since they tend to follow the lines of ambivalent relations. African societies with clear-cut social structures seem to suffer less from such accusations. Masks and witchcraft discourse are two sides of the same coin. Notions of witchcraft vary from a vague notion of threat to precise accusations of personal evildoing,[36] but the fact remains that societies with weak socio-political structures generate an intense witchcraft discourse, as well as providing a haven for masking rituals.

[35]　Girard 1989.
[36]　See the cases in Geschiere 1997, 2017, and the schema in Van Beek 2007.

Masks and witches may be thrown together by social dynamics, but they are always in opposition: masks are against witches and are never equated with them. Witches, in African reasoning, are seen as pure, unadulterated evil, while masks may be ambivalent: they are never evil but always a social asset. As part of secret societies, masks are highly ethical and educational, teaching proper behaviour and speech throughout the liminal period, bolstering the major societal values; masks are instruments of social norms. A curious example is found in the border region between Senufo and Bamana, where masks helped a hunters' association to become hunters not of game but of thieves.[37]

So masks are the structural opposite of witches. A witch is a human being who looks normal but has a hidden evil streak; a mask is a be-thing that performs in public. A man is initiated in order to become a mask, but witches are supposed to be born that way. Witches operate alone and out of sight; masks perform before an audience, either in groups or alone, but always accompanied. Masks have an overwhelming auditory presence; witches are considered to work in absolute silence, undetected. The two are each other's absolute antithesis, which we summarise in Table 3.

Table 3. Differences between witches and masks.

Witches	Masks
Human	Non-human
Predominantly female	Predominantly male
Suspect femininity	Laud motherhood
Normal form	Strange form
Hidden faculty	Overt power
Invisible	Highly visible
Harmful	Do not harm
Protection needed	Sought after
Absolutely evil	Highly moral
Threat from inside	Outside force
Accused has no defence	Performed by the powerful
No organisation	Core of organisation
Perform no ritual	The essence of ritual
Operate alone	Perform most as a troupe
Silent throughout	An auditory explosion
Cannot be learned	Core of extensive teaching

[37] Gagliardi 2010: 17

Clearly masks are the obvious tool to use against presumed witches, and for this function in the occult world they often protect themselves magically. When a Baule masker dresses himself, he must sprinkle a herbal concoction over his body, place amulets around his wrists and ankles, and tie some protective devices onto his chest, such as razor blades, while the leader of the troupe warns the participants in the performance of the threat of witches.[38] The masks designed to combat witchcraft in Oku, Cameroon, have special costumes densely covered with all sorts of amulets. The ethnographer Hans Koloss noted with surprise that this mask had no elaborate headdress, but wore a simple head cover of cloth and feathers: to combat witches one needs protection by amulets – aesthetics are less important.[39]

African societies are used to whisperings, offhand remarks, or gossip about presumed witches, a discourse that is tolerable as long it is subdued. When accusations run wild, masks may be called in to find out who the culprits are, either by 'sniffing out' witches – they are often considered to be smelly – or by performing divination in order to discover who the supposed evildoers are. Then, by whatever means they have been 'found out', the masks chase witches and sorcerers out of the village in a cleansing ritual.[40]

During a Yoruba masquerade to honour the ancestors, a specific mask, the *agba egungun*, appears in town in order to cleanse the town of criminals, witches, and other dangers. This powerful and frightful *egungun* figure is dressed in a shapeless mass of cloths and rags, and its head carries a tray with monkey skulls, animal bones, and other objects-with-power covered with blood and the remnants of sacrifices – in short, a frightening, thus powerful, mask. It is said that the *agba egungun* carries an invisible bird on its shoulders that enables the mask to defeat the witches.[41] If needed, several *egungun* combine in a show of force, one of which has a headpiece showing a hare. For some observers, its long ears and teeth symbolise the powers that effectively attack the witches, but others see them as the signs of the ancestors, who hear all that is said and done by their descendants.[42] Symbols, especially in masks, are polyvalent, but they all combat 'witches'.

---

38 A-M. Boyer 2008: 58.
39 Koloss 2012: 117, with a very convincing picture. Medicines, in this case meaning amulets, are crucial in endowing power to Oku masks anyway.
40 The *obasinjom* mask of the Ejagham in Zone 2 performs divination to identify witches; Röschenthaler 2004; see also Röschenthaler 1993.
41 Witte 2002, 2004.
42 Drewal and Pemberton 1989: 183.

Their peculiar solution of the matrilineal puzzle makes the Ivorian Beng a maskless society, as explained above, but it comes at a price. Since witchcraft is widely considered to be inherited matrilineally, a marriage system that is confined to the matriline easily generates notions of potent witchcraft. For the neighbours of the Beng, used to masks as a deterrent for this inheritable evil, the absence of masks implies that there is no check on this occult aggression, so throughout their region, the Beng are considered powerful witches, feared by their neighbours.[43]

As modern witchcraft studies have shown,[44] the discourse on presumed witches is more than just a case of blaming the victim: it also has a definite political side. By no means is the witchcraft discourse limited to rural 'traditional' societies; it is very much a feature of modern political life in Africa. If anything, witchcraft is a perceived form of power and may reflect people's view of their political elites: powerful, dangerous, unaccountable, and without morals. Power is always ambivalent, and political supremacy and witchcraft may easily be conceived as two sides of the same coin – since the powers from this world and the otherworld are deemed to go hand in hand. An example is the *ndakò gbòyá* mask of the Nigerian Nupe, the mask consisting of a huge tent-like cloth cylinder of Figure 2.5. Their mask societies came down heavily on purported witches, and they even toured the whole area demanding large payments from accused witches and from villages to be cleansed. Nadel reports that in 1920 their tours became so oppressive for the villages that the government had to ban all mask performances.[45] But the witchcraft discourse itself can have political overtones, as a voice from the grass roots against oppression by illegitimate rulers. Although overtly against the weak in society, much of the witchcraft discourse in Nupe served as a meta-commentary against the rich and powerful.[46]

Anti-witchcraft cults are notoriously unsuccessful in the long run, and cleansings by masks also have only a temporary effect. Even the most powerful performances never succeed in eradicating witchcraft as such. After all, religious measures against witchcraft accusations and discourse strengthen belief in the reality of the phenomenon, so eventually these well-meaning

---

43 Even the researchers were considered at ease with witchcraft, and therefore very powerful: Gottlieb and Graham 1993: 60.
44 Geschiere 1997, 2017.
45 Nadel 1954: 197.
46 See https://www.researchgate.net/publication/24115257_On_the_Articulation_of_Witchcraft_and_Modes_of_Production_among_the_Nupe_Northern_Nigeria, consulted 1 November 2020.

movements usually peter out. The Nupe themselves avow that the masks can cleanse a community from presumed witches only for a moment; what they do is restrain witches from being too active. As Nadel comments: 'If the Nupe knew our saying about poverty they would no doubt say that witchcraft, like the poor, will always be with us; all man can hope to do is to keep it within reasonable bounds.'[47]

Combating witchcraft may have such a high priority that people adopt a mask complex just for that reason. The Irigwe, one of the many small groups on the Jos Plateau of Nigeria, were vexed with the colonial measures against their witch hunting. Surely, this meant that the witches would be out of control, so to forestall an explosion of witchcraft they imported a masking cult, the *dodo*, from their neighbours, the Chawai; the Jos Plateau harbours cultures with and without masking traditions. These masks visited the village, danced for the whole community with all women and girls in attendance, and inquired into any problems the village attributed to witches; these were speaking masks communicating in a disguised voice directly to the audience.

For the elders who called in the masks, there was another issue: the institution of 'secondary marriages'.[48] On the Plateau, quite generally, young women can marry more than one husband – up to three in fact. Although the wife lives with only one husband at a time, when she has problems with her first husband, she is quite free to move to one of her other partners; weaned children stay behind with the husband who has paid the bride wealth. This curious form of polyandry offered women quite some social leverage, but it was considered a severe strain by the husbands, who lacked control over their wives; the contours of the gender arena are very clear. In most of the Plateau groups this female mobility was in male eyes almost a corollary of witchcraft, so it too was addressed by the masks.[49] For instance, young men of the Abisi group, neighbours of the Irigwe, adopted the new mask cult, not so much against witchcraft as to marry earlier and have more control over their wives.[50] The arenas of power and gender keep being mixed.

The *dodo* masks were made of plaited raffia, in form-fitting costumes that covered the head, often with a special crest, and each of these mask types had a different name. This area is culturally highly fragmented, but the various ethnic groups on the Jos Plateau share the same mask types

---

47 Nadel 1954: 201.
48 M.G. Smith 1959.
49 Sangree 1974; Isichei 1988, 1991.
50 Chalifoux 1981.

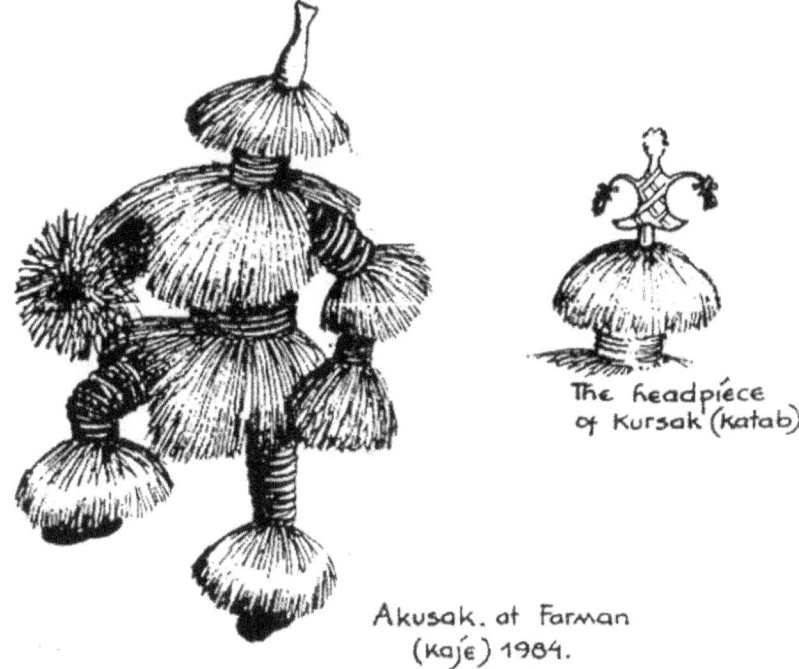

The headpiece
of Kursak (katab)

Akusak. at Farman
(kajé) 1984.

Figure 8.4. The *dodo* mask of the Jos Plateau. Jos Plateau, Nigeria. Drawing Elizabeth Isichei.

and organisation; at least, they did so if they adopted the new mask cults at all, since not all of them did.[51] Some groups seem to have had the masks for much longer.[52]

With the mask the Abisi immediately adopted the whole masking complex, including the secrecy plus the usual silent complicity of the women. The women were not actually always completely silent, since a young Abisi woman remarked to the researcher: 'People say that the *dodo* is a spirit, but as for me, I know when it is my husband who is masked. I have been living with him now for five years, and I can well see that the dancer limps like him.'[53]

51 Muller 1987, 1997b. For the drawing in Figure 8.4, see Isichei 1988: 49, 51. The drawing is made from archival photos in the Jos archives.
52 Isichei 1988: 48.
53 Chalifoux 1981: 61.

'Uncovering witchcraft': A mask performance abroad

If masks combat witchcraft, how exactly do they do it? For an in-depth description we turn to Daniel Reed's study on Dan mask performances,[54] and the vignette of the Introduction, the appearance of the *gegbadë* mask. Through its leader, Oulai Théodore, the group had acquired such a reputation that their services were called on outside Dan country, on the coast where the Dida live, who have no masking tradition of their own. Because of a series of unexpected and untimely deaths in her family, a Dida woman of status called in the Dan mask troupe, since she thought that her Christian church did not have the means to combat this evil.[55]

The setting of the séance in question was fraught with uncertainties, small conflicts, and misunderstandings,[56] highlighting the inherent strangeness of the situation: a major Dan mask troupe operating in a culture without masks. The witch-finding session was dominated by Théodore; the *gegbadë* mask itself had a subdued role. The drums, bells, and flutes started the session, with the mask sitting at the side, and Théodore launched into a series of orations directed to the sizeable audience. Since the spirits speak Dan, the orations were in Dan, translated into French.

The woman who hired him explained what her problem was, and then he guided the mask and the whole crowd into the woods, singling out a tree where he said the witches had gathered and had built a mystical compound. Everyone had to gather leaves from the spot and take them home. Back in the compound, with the help of some stuff used to discover hidden things, he singled out a certain hut: that was the suspect one. He entered it, came out, entered it again, and had his assistant fill a bucket with water-*cum*-medicine. Two Dida youngsters had to undress – to show that they had no 'stuff' on them – and all entered the hut now. With the bells ringing at a frenetic pace, one of the drummers fired a gunshot in the air. Inside the hut the men dug a hole in the ground and uncovered a buried 'fetish', which was considered invisible, seen only by the one inspired by the mask spirit, Théodore. He grabbed 'it' from the air in full flight, put it in the water, which made it visible, and his aides covered it with leaves. All emerged from the hut with the bucket, and Théodore took out the 'fetish' and placed it on the ground for all to see. Immediately a penetrating stench

---

54 Reed 2003.
55 Reed speaks of 'sorcery', reflecting the French usage of *sorcellerie*, which means witchcraft as well as sorcery, without the distinction made above.
56 Reed 2003: 161–162.

filled the courtyard, like that of a 'cadaver of spoiled meat': the thing was difficult to identify, was covered in a slimy black substance and purportedly had snail shells, ballpoints, and padlocks inside.

The mask troupe did not identify any guilty parties, assuming the guilty sorcerer/witch would now come forward and confess; also, direct accusations would have provoked fights, which would be dangerous in a foreign evironment. The woman in question thus had to wait for the final closure. Reed reports that one more person in the family died not long after the session, bringing the total number of casualties to nine(!). The woman's faith in the mask was as strong as ever: 'I like the mask because it's something that cannot be wrong.'[57] Probably, following witchcraft logic, that last death was counted as that of the culprit witch/sorcerer, thus settling the issue. In such cleansing rituals the future defines what has happened in the present.

This is not a standard situation and may not have been a routine performance, but there are few standards for this kind of performance – and they are never routine. One of the peculiarities, perhaps novelties, of this case is the marginality of the mask itself, which did not do the talking but served as the presumed connection with the otherworld – the *fons et origo* of the hidden information needed for the séance. The mask was simply there, being transformed from a questioning individual into an all-knowing mask, its presence highlighting the performance's inspired nature. Of course, it also operated as a safety device, since as an incarnated spirit the mask could not be protested or argued against. In séances inside Dan territory to uncover witchcraft, the music and the movements of the mask are said to indicate whether someone is guilty. It is important to note here that not just guilt can be discovered; innocence can be established as well. In another case, an accused woman was found innocent by the mask, and the dancing apparition became a comforting presence for that woman. That ultimate verdict came in a song that was specially geared to pronouncing innocence.

So this case was different, especially the stinking fetish. Throughout Africa, anthropologists have witnessed healing rituals during which objects suddenly appeared; observers have seen all sorts of things 'extracted' from patients' bodies – bones, splinters, stones, etc. The first author witnessed a woman healer 'extract' a dozen small frogs from the swollen belly of a child, without leaving any trace whatsoever on the taut belly skin.[58] Clearly, such unexpected objects are crucial for the believing client and any admiring

57 Ibid. 168, 169.
58 Van Beek 2015.

audience, and like the stinking fetish they are too helpful as theatrical props to be left to chance. Nobody saw the thing in the ground, it seems, and only after Théodore plucked it from mid-air and put the invisible version in a bucket of water did it really 'appear', as part of the theatricals that characterise anti-witchcraft rituals.

This healing function of masks is sometimes mentioned but seldom described in detail. For the *egungun* it is said that their aim is 'to wipe away death, pestilence, convulsion and many mishaps',[59] but also to bring children into the world; there is no shortage of claims about masks. When masks are reported to heal, they do not manipulate herbs, nor make incisions in the skin of the patient; they just do what they are best at: they appear, are present, and dance. Of course, divining masks may use their skills in unearthing hidden realities, as any diviner does, and speak in an obscure language, but in the huge complex of African divination the role of the masks is restricted.[60] So among the Ebira of Central Nigeria the healing role of their *eku* mask is all the more remarkable, since the healing advice is spoken and sung, with the masks as such out of sight of their female 'clients' and often not 'fully dressed'.[61] Overall, healing seems not a core role of masks, but a tangential function derived from their central position in other rituals.

Since masks are ambivalent at their core, they can be both healing and harmful. Lorenz Homberger describes a case of healing by a mask in Tibeita, Côte d'Ivoire, in 1983.[62] The wife of Irie bi Nanti had fallen ill with dysentery, and local medicine had not helped. The diviner indicated that neglect of the *zauli* mask was the main cause, so the husband arranged a sacrifice to the *zauli* shrine, a bundle of herbs covered with sacrificial blood, with the mask present. It made its usual forceful appearance, and then silently sat down for the sacrifice.

Figure 8.5 shows the introduction of the *zauli* shrine. During the actual sacrifice the mask was covered with a white sheet and did not budge. In this case the mask functioned like the ancestors, viz. as a be-thing from the otherworld demanding the attention of its people, for after all the mask had caused the problem itself; whoever calls a mask in to help knows he is hard put to control his helper. In many other cases mask healing is mentioned as an oblique way of referring to the mask's conflict with witchcraft.

59 Poynor 1976: 67.
60 Peek and Van Beek 2013.
61 Picton 1988b: 199.
62 Fischer 2008: 256–259.

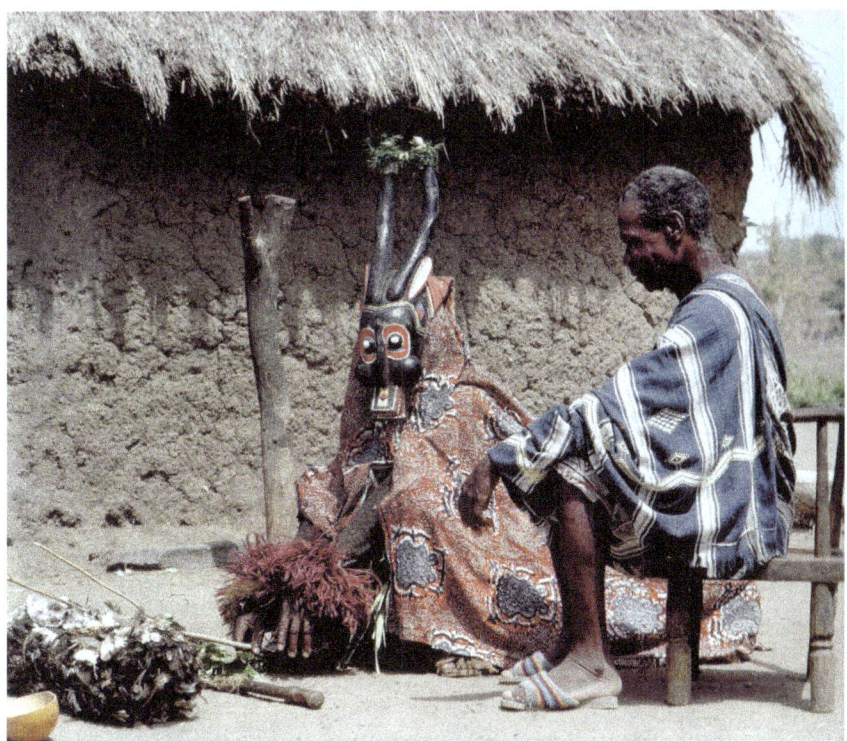

Figure 8.5. Irie bi Nanti directs a sacrifice, made in the presence of the mask, to cure his wife's illness. Guro, Côte d'Ivoire, 1983. Photo: Lorenz Homberger.

'War masks'

A major corollary of power is war, and the mask literature makes occasional references to the use of masks in wars. Africa has known many wars, generated by expanding empires, slave raiding, and many intervillage and interethnic skirmishes. Since most anthropologists came after colonisation, which also involved pacification – often after a colonial war – they have encountered local wars mainly through oral history. These tales are very much alive, and function as heroic accounts of an insecure past, great for telling over a fresh pot of beer. Similarly, many tales about masks and war appear to be tall tales about the role of masks, meaning that the information on war masks tends to be rather unreliable.

A typical story comes from the Dan, where Himmelheber reports on the *bu gle*, the warrior mask, its headpiece covered with crusts of sacrificial blood and topped with eagle feathers. During the precolonial intervillage skirmishes this mask would bless the men before they left for the fight, and then accompany them into the battle. It was believed that the mask itself would shoot arrows, not against the enemies, but against invisible powers and witches that might harm its fellow combatants. The power of the mask was believed to permeate the leaves of the costume. Any feather lost during the dance was collected by one of the masker's assistants, lest anyone would use its power to harm other people.[63] That was the story; however; the actual performance of the mask was quite different. When approaching the village from the forest, it strode majestically, but once between the houses it moved intermittently, stopping abruptly as if looking for an enemy, then jumped up and hurried through the village; it was a commentary more on fear than on actual fighting. The capstone of the performance was a group of women who approached the mask, greeted it, and bade it welcome in their village. So much for its heroism.

Oral Yoruba tradition has warriors wearing the charms belonging to the masks into battle, or has a column of warriors preceded by an *egungun* mask full of amulets paving the way for a good fight. Other accounts relate how some warriors carried the *egungun* to the rim of the battlefield, where the masks had the task of executing war captives after the battle – a function also reported from the Cameroonian Grassfields.[64] Masks would claim results long after the hostilities, but many of these traditions that place the *egungun* on the battlefield itself, are relegated by Willis to 'later inventions'.[65]

One major, and well-researched, example of these tall tales is the so-called war mask of the Bwa, of northern DRC.[66] In a penetrating article in *African Art*, Rik Ceyssens[67] traces the earliest reports of two Bwa war masks in the Tervuren Museum. He shows how the idea that these masks functioned in wars came into being, and how it developed through time. The first rumour was that this mask functioned specifically in a skirmish between the Bwa and colonial troops; reports contradicting that notion were ignored, even by later scholars, gradually producing the image of the Bwa as extremely fierce fighters, whose medicine men even wore masks to the battlefield. More reliable witnesses at that time never mentioned them, and Ceyssens' conclusion is that this whole idea of making war in masks is a fabrication, with two goals. The idea originated from the neighbouring Zande, who wanted to keep the white people out of Bwa territory in order to secure

---

63 Himmelheber 1979: 4.
64 Chem-Langhee and Fanso 2011.
65 Willis 2018: 85, 143.
66 They are often refered to as Boa, to distinguish them from the Bwa of Burkina Faso.
67 Ceyssens 2007.

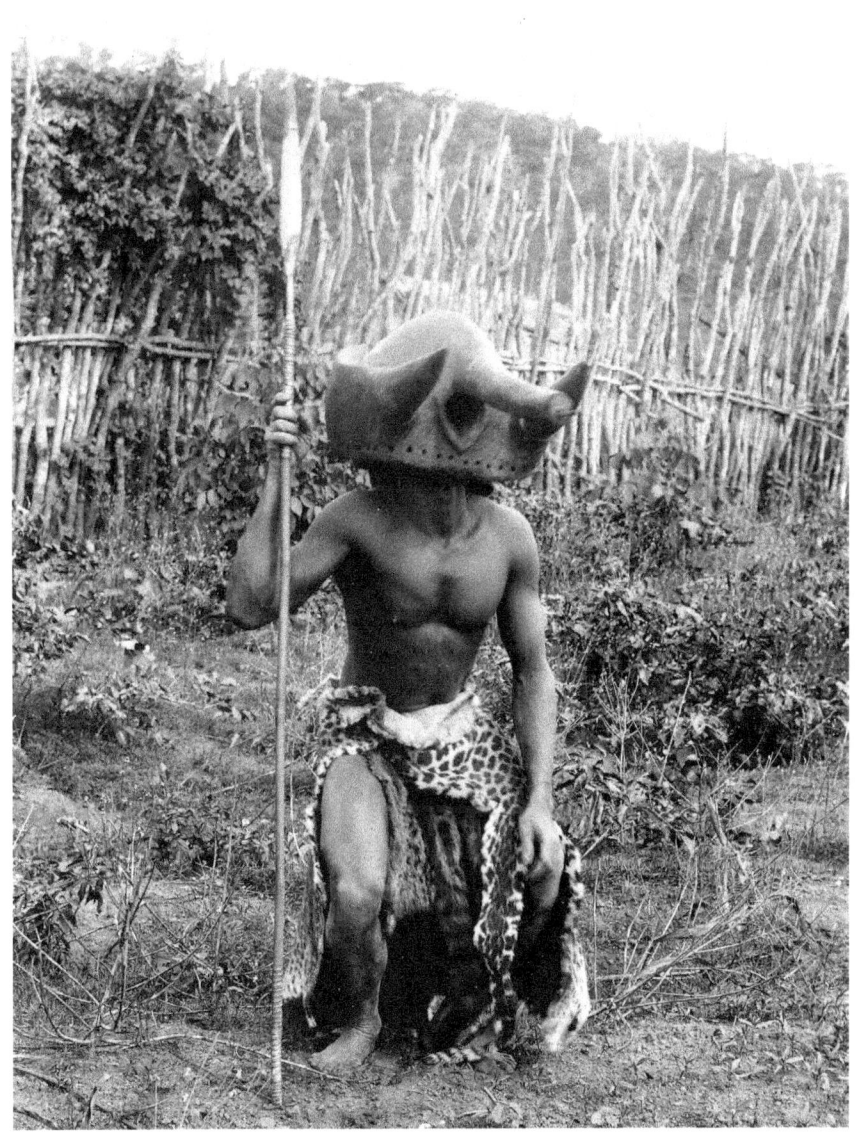

Figure 8.6. A so-called 'war mask', nicely posed and full of internal contradictions. Pweto, Lake Mweru, DRC. Photo Franz Michel 1898.

their own position as middlemen in a lucrative trade. The second dynamic, on the white side, is the notion of 'othering', the depiction of the colonised other as a fierce savage; the combination of medicine men, war, and masks is a heady cocktail of exotic ingredients.[68]

Since masks are costumes with face covers, wearing one on the battle field is a recipe for a quick death, but in novel situations masks may be of use. When the Baule confronted a new enemy in Africa, the French colonial army, they reasoned that this unknown enemy required a powerful response, so they sent their *je i* masks.[69] History shows the ploy did not work; the French won the battle as well as the whole colonial war, and simply 'collected' the *je i* masks – meaning, they seized them; four of these masks are now in the Musée Branly in Paris.[70] In his book on Makonde masquerades in Mozambique, Paolo Israel mentions another, quite inventive, way of using a mask against a foreign invader: as a decoy. During the Portuguese conquest of the Makonde Plateau in 1917 the colonial soldiers were approaching the area when suddenly the 'mask with the great ears' appeared before the marching column, dancing forcefully in front of the flabbergasted soldiers. Then, from the sides, the Makonde attacked with their arrows and arquebuses.[71] But even this military diversion-by-mask could not prevent the occupation.

More plausible is the part masks might play as a magical preparation for war. Africa knew many kinds of war before colonisation, and magical preparation for these was almost routine. The main reports we have on internal wars mention individual preparation in the sense of rubbing ointment on the body to make the skin impermeable, benedictions and spells, and often sacrifices on special altars. Amulets abound to deflect arrows and spears, or just to provide luck. In this amalgam of measures, masks may well have served to support the group preparation, to strengthen

---

[68] Figure 8.6 claims to be a genuine picture of a Bwa medicine man/warrior mask. However, there is no real mask costume, not even a fibre in sight, just the chief's leopard skin, another exotic African icon! The photo, taken by a Belgian colonial called Franz Michel in 1898 actually shows how early colonials were preoccupied with the construction of the 'exotic other'. The headpiece on the photo is called *bwile*, and was collected near Lake Mweru, far to the South of the Boa/Bwa area. The so-called Bwa war mask is the *pongdudu*, usually with large ears. Together with similar mask tops that accrued the epithet 'war mask', this shows that the whole notion of war masks was very much a colonial fantasy, and not just in the case of the Boa/Bwa.

[69] Vogel 1997b; see also A-M. Boyer 2008.

[70] One was captured during a revolt at the village of Lomo Sud (southern Warebo region) before 1900, and donated by Maurice Delafosse, who called it *kaka guie*.

[71] Israel 2014: 47–48.

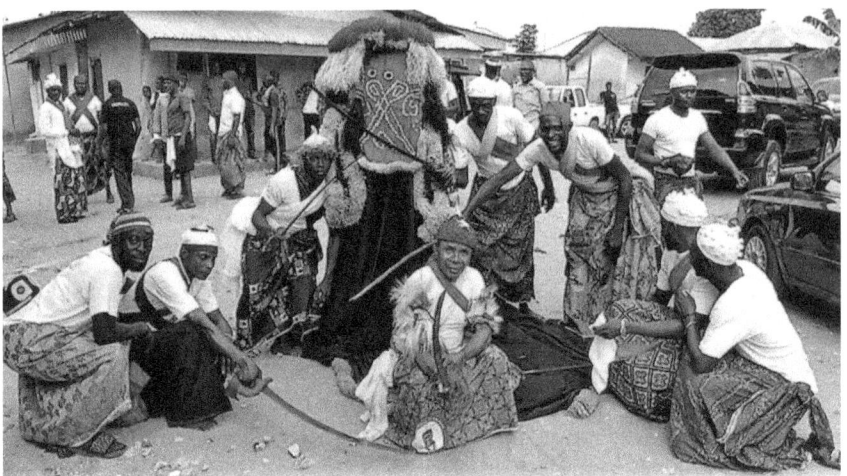

Figure 8.7. War as theatre: a Nigerian *ukwa* 'war mask' with its dancing troupe. Calabar, Nigeria, 2019. Photo: Ivor Miller.

morale, and perhaps to confound the enemy; after all, power stems from the bush and masks channel it; but the enemy had the same option.

One rare mention of masks fighting comes from Nigeria. Joseph Akpan reports on an Ibibio boundary dispute between two *ekpo* secret societies. One mask drew a line in the sand and challenged the mask from the other side to cross it. All secret society members on both sides laid down whatever weapon they carried, sat down, and watched. The actual battle was a wrestling match, a very popular sport in the region. Whoever threw his opponent to the ground and removed his head cover won; the loser had to surrender the headpiece or hand over some money to get it back. The victorious village revelled in the humiliation of its thoroughly shamed neighbour: they had 'taken a head'. A captured headpiece was put on display in the shrine of the secret society – out of the sight of women, of course. Akpan adds: 'Head taking has occurred frequently within the past ten years.'[72] This curious instance of fighting masks portrays them as a champions' duel in a kind of sports setting, a kind of judicial fight, with surprisingly little magical preparation.

In the expansion of African empires, war masks are absent. For instance, in the history of Bamum expansion no mention of them is made[73] – and the Bamum do have masks. Nor, for that matter, are they mentioned in the prevalent mode of war in Africa: slave raiding. Not only has slave raiding been

---

72 Akpan 1994: 51. For other intricate transactions regarding masquerades, see Fenton 2019.
73 Tardits 1980, 1992, 1996.

to a large extent the occupation of the Muslim realms of West Africa, which never sported masks, but also the constant threat of insecurity among the raided peoples precluded any systematic preparation for battlefields. The same holds for the immense number of captives who were taken from their home grounds to be shipped across the Atlantic. This traumatic period in African history may well have generated the local conditions for mask rituals, but these masks were not meant for the war, but to enable life in a situation of great insecurity.

Consequently, the description of the Baule and Makonde incidentally countering a completely foreign enemy with masks is far more plausible than 'war masks' as such. Thus, the irony is double: colonial reports constructed the Bwa mask as a 'war mask' because the West tends to paint the 'African other' in strong exotic colours, while the Baule and Makonde's use of masks stemmed from a defence against colonial invasion. Whatever war masks may have been, they are for a major part our own construct.

Conclusion

The Jos Plateau houses a plethora of small ethnic groups, like the Rukuba, Irigwe, Abisi, Anaguta, Chawai, Kofyar and many others, that are represented on the map of Zone 2 by the Irigwe and Rukuba. They form a rather clearly circumscribed, inaccessible cultural area that sits right inside the territory of the nineteenth-century Fulbe jihad of Usman dan Fodio, which radiated out from Sokoto. The hills formed a defence for the local groups, while the marauding jihadists considered the Plateau as a slave reservoir. These groups are typical Type C communities, villages depending on the terrain as well as on architectural features for their defence. The mountain slopes are intensively cultivated with sorghum, millet, and maize, and supplemented with small crops, resulting in a sustainable self-sufficient agriculture feeding a dense population. Many villages used to tend some taurine cattle, but these have been dwindling.

The clearly recognisable villages are patrilineal and patrilocal, with segmentary systems that do not transcend the village boundaries. Age is scarcely organised and there are no secret societies. Most of these groups do initiate their youngsters, and circumcise boys. This ethnically fragmented area harbours many languages, and relations between villages and groups are tense. Though the power field is not an obvious arena, the gender one is: marriages are brittle – as shown by the secondary marriage system – while the level of bride wealth varies. As can be expected from our masking profile, such a situation is moderately conducive for masking, and indeed some of the groups have masks, while others have none. This is the area with most reports on bought or stolen masquerades owing to their cultural similarity, and the small distances between the groups.

Côte d'Ivoire, right in the centre of Zone 1, is full of masquerades, and as a nation it is proud of them. Why do the Dida, living in the central southern part of the country, have no masks of their own, while their neighbours to the west and the south are avid maskers? The Dida peoples live in a densely forested environment, where their hunting and gathering is complemented by what their ethnographer, Emmanuel Terray, calls nomadic agriculture.[74] The small villages shift over time to new clearings, and in this mixed economy the contributions that men and women make to acquiring food and income are well balanced, with the tasks divided clearly along gender lines. Descent is patrilineal, marital residence is patrilocal, and the patrilineal system throughout is of a segmentary kind – Type A – but with some peculiar characteristics. The main relation that the lineage holds is not so much with land as it is with the huge nets they use for communal hunting – their lineages are even called 'nets'. Not only are segmentary systems not conducive to masking, but the low population density of the Dida invites a comparison with the Central African Gbaya, who have no masks either.[75]

---

74 Terray 1969.
75 Burnham 1975, 1980.

9

Masks and Modernity

'The mystery of the world is the visible, not the invisible.'

(Oscar Wilde, *The Picture of Dorian Gray* 29)

Playful sharks in the Delta

The Ijo group in the Niger Delta[1] have a masking myth that tells of Kperighada, a fisherman. He wanted to explore new fishing waters far from home, so he joined other fishermen in an expedition all the way to Cameroon. There, suddenly, he disappeared, and his colleagues were unable to trace him. After seven days he reappeared. Asked about his experiences, Kperighada told them that he had been kidnapped by water spirits and taken to their underwater world, where he was taught how to dance a masquerade. Back home in his village he called all the elders of his town together and told them he would die if they did not accept the masquerade called ofurumo *(shark). The elders agreed and since then the shark masquerade is performed in all Ijo towns.*

In this origin story the usual female protagonist is lacking, but also the ritual itself has special characteristics. A mask with a mullet headpiece runs through the village as his assistants sing: 'Sharks are coming! Run and hide!' Villagers hasten to the riverside to watch a canoe tow a raft with the shark mask upriver, while crew members and supporters sing and drum his praise. The mask carries a large horizontal headpiece in the form of a shark, and has a costume made of head ties, wrappers, and trousers. A man and his wife circle the raft in a canoe as if they are stalking their prey. When the man throws his spear, the canoe capsizes and the pair end up in the water. This refers to a well-known song: 'Anyone who spears this fish will upset his canoe.' On land all start to dance, and the drummers accompany the mask with songs, such as 'Force someone to give him food' and 'To remove all the

---

1   M.G. Anderson 2002.

fish and give fishless soup to one's husband', songs criticising antisocial behaviour.[2]
The masquerade ends with a pantomime in which the fishing couple reappear,
dragging their canoe around as if they are still paddling and chasing their prey, even
occasionally pretending to capsize. Finally, the fisherman spears ofurumo *and hauls*
him into his canoe, where he 'kills' the spirit.

What is special here is the light tone of the performance. Sharks are
dangerous enough and quite plentiful in these waters, but the Ijo call these
masquerades 'plays' and speak of masking as 'playing'. As they see it, water
spirits initiated masquerades largely because they enjoy the artistic aspects
of these 'plays', very much as humans do, as well as the camaraderie evident
during these events. The spirits even 'pay' the performers; a musician, so
the story goes, saw his drumming rewarded by the water spirits when the
next morning he found very many fish on the water surface, ready to be
caught. In fact the masks neither presentify nor embody the water spirits;
they simply imitate them, and in this theatrical performance everybody is
welcome. But then, these water spirits are quite nice, living in spectacular
underwater towns as beautiful, light-skinned beings with long, flowing hair,
like wealthy foreigners. Preferred offerings are dolls, cloth, and white saucers
with corned beef, and Coca Cola; they are fully modern spirits.

So the Ijo play their masks as a form of entertainment and tend to
downplay any ritual significance.[3] Masking is 'for fun', even if the undertone
of serious concern is not that far away; after all, the Ijo are faced with the
real-life dangers of shark and saw-fish, so treading on these daily menaces
lightly in the mask play might be a sensible adaptation.

Theatre is an integral part of any masquerade,[4] and this Ijo case shows that,
even without a clear religious aspect, masks can still perform. This side of
masking, the public show, seems to be thriving, especially in a rapidly changing
Africa. Increasingly, Christianity and Islam dominate the religious spectrum,
leaving less and less room for masquerades. Initiation rituals are still around
in many places, but have been abandoned in others, leaving these icons of
'paganism' behind; funerals stage fewer masquerades, second funerals morph
into memorials. With the establishment of postcolonial African regimes, the
role of secret societies is shifting, and though their appeal can still be considerable, their power position vis-à-vis the state is eroding.

2   Alagoa 1967: 155.
3   Horton 1963; M.G. Anderson 2002: 160.
4   The point Victor Turner already made in 1974, referring to a larger body of rituals:
V. Turner 1974.

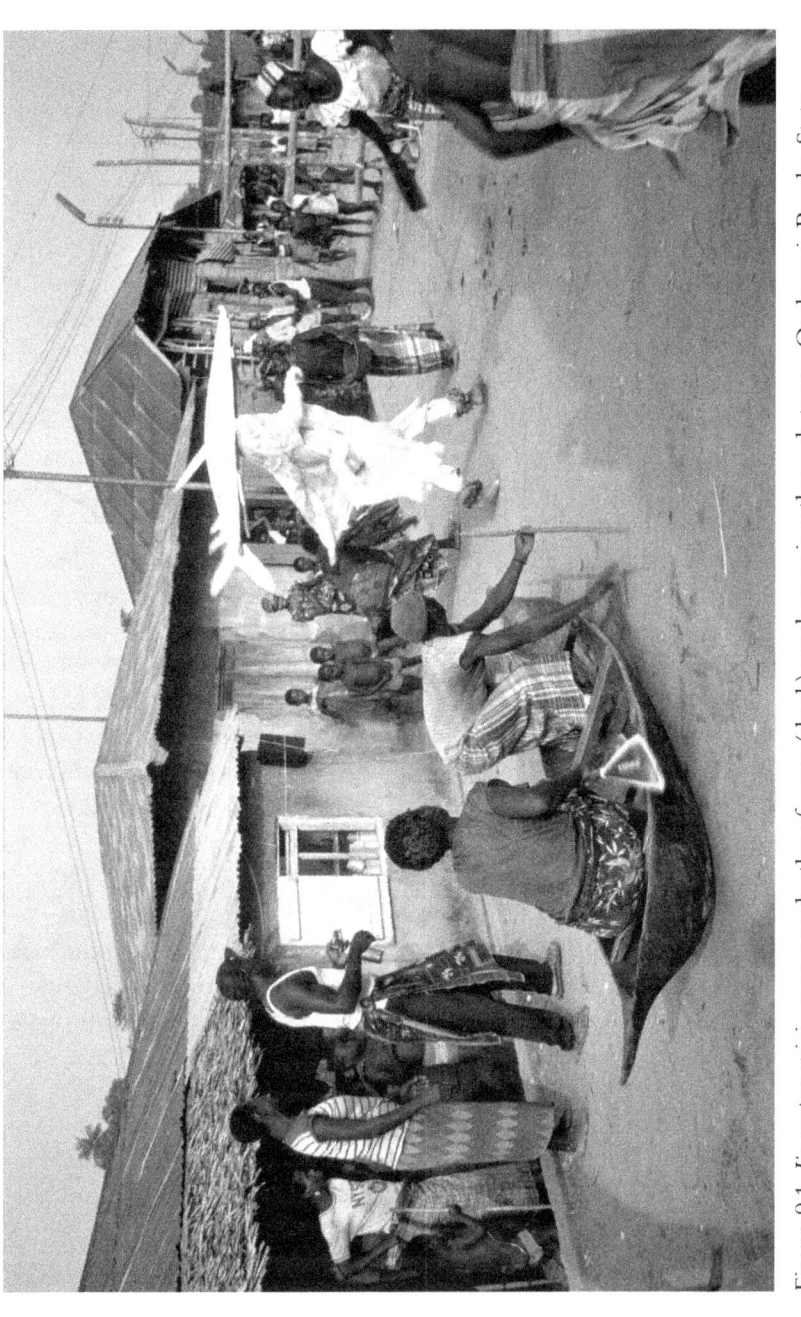

Figure 9.1. *Ijo* water spirit masquerade: the *ofuruma* (shark) mask running through town. Ondewari, Bayelsa State, Nigeria, 1992. Photo: Martha G. Anderson.

So mask rituals show a general shift towards festivals, from experience to spectacle, and thus from internal arenas to the arena of social identity. Masks become the core of theatre-like productions serving as showcases for wealth, as icons for heritage, and as political instruments. The emergence of mask rituals as such can still be explained by our theoretical model, but the application of masks in other settings has broadened. Mask performances, whatever their *fons et origo*, are becoming tools in higher-echelon politics and in the encounter of the modern nation state with the traditions of its component groups, leading the process of local as well as supra-local identity construction.

Three dynamics in the encounter of masks with modernity form the core of this chapter: theatricalisation, commoditisation, and iconisation, which are all building blocks of identity. As for the first, the thespian side is essential in regular masquerades, as the next two examples testify, but theatricalisation accrues its own dynamics when mask festivals are organised specifically for entertainment, either for tourists or for general public enjoyment. Growth in public masking highlights fads and fashions in masks with new forms being added to or replaced by others over time, a dynamic that is natural in stage productions, to which masks seem to adapt rather easily.[5]

This Ijo theatre is still linked to ritual and may be viewed as a first step on the pathway from ritual to theatre. The next example explores a masquerade, also within a local setting, that is predominantly theatre: the Afikpo group on the western shore of the Cross River in southwest Nigeria.

Theatre at Cross River

At the call of the stage leader two masks appear in front of the musicians and chorus, one with black raffia clothing and the other with lighter-coloured fibres, both with human-faced headpieces, a husband with his wife. Ostentatiously the wife takes her husband by the wrist and leads him to a house shrine (represented by a pot), holds an egg over his head and tells him: 'If there is any title-taking in which you are involved and if you have not finished preparing soup for me before you go, this god will kill you.' The husband bends down before her, and she waves the egg around his head, puts it in the pot, and walks away.[6]

---

5   The counter-implication is that they are also vulnerable to political change: see Bentor 2005.
6   This case is based upon Ottenberg 1975.

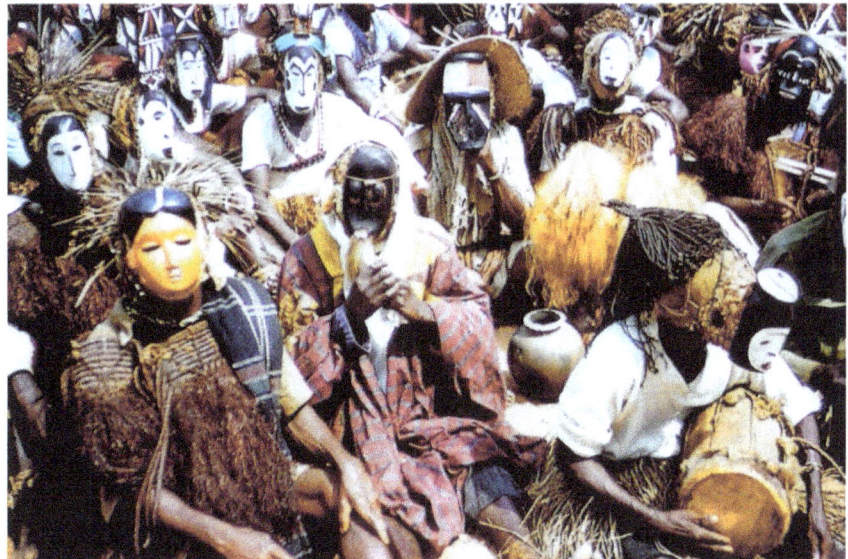

Figure 9.2. Masked chorus and musicians accompanying a mask performance. Afikpo, Cross River, Nigeria, 1970. Photo: Simon Ottenberg.

The gesture with the egg is clear for all spectators: the wife commands the husband and even has magical means at her disposal. In this way the usual gender roles are completely reversed; the egg and the pot hint at sacrifices that are always performed by men, just as soup is prepared by women. For the Afikpo audience this is highly amusing, since the role reversal is quite complete: title taking is an important part of male secret society life and thus out of bounds to the woman. Such a typical henpecked husband is the laughing stock of everyone. Similar skits follow in this vein, each with the wife taking on male roles over a docile, feminised husband. Hilarious accompanying songs comment on this male weakness, which is quite recognisable for all; afterwards the stage leaders explain the skit to the audience anyway.

A series of other skits follows, focusing on tight-fisted chiefs (generosity is a core value in Afikpo), conflicts with other villages, uppity women who want to meddle with the boys' initiation, and many other themes of daily life, as well as events from the past year. Together, these plays, songs, and parades fill a whole afternoon, keeping the village spellbound, all sitting at the rim of the main square. People targeted by songs and skits should take the satire in good spirit and show that they harbour no hard feelings toward the originators, even if they might feel otherwise.

All participants are masked, and this is immediately visible at the first appearance on stage when the whole troupe walks in full dress to the playground: all musicians, players, the chorus, and the leaders in front wear masks – 'an impressive sight, with some one hundred or more masked and costumed men moving en masse', writes ethnographer Simon Ottenberg.[7] The skit players with male and female roles are recognisable by their different costumes, as are the dancers and the chorus. Two stage leaders carrying wide floppy hats keep moving around, directing, urging, never dancing, often at the side but always present. Finally, the musicians are crucial: one with a basket rattle, one with a wooden gong, three drummers, and the sixth with a single iron gong. With their raffia skirts and a variety of head tops they fit in well with the troupe, but they remain seated in front of the chorus for the whole duration of the play. The fact that these musicians also wear masks characterises the whole performance as a theatrical one. Often they stem from other villages, selected for their musical excellence, since much of the success of the *okumkpa* depends on the quality of their performance; singing and dancing are not so much accompanied by the music as led by it.

Masking is also part of an intricate ritual cycle in Afikpo; after the yam festival and the rainy season festival, masks turn out at the start of the dry season for a variety of other festivals, marking a ceremonial season that lasts until July. Yet the *okumkpa* performances are special. The villages coordinate their productions to some extent, and no more than three or four of them are likely to produce such a play in the same year. This creative event depends on a central organiser, someone who likes to stand out as an initiator but is not usually among the ruling senior men of the village – men of prestige and wealth 'have buried their own nonsense'. Yet, despite being not overly 'serious', theatrical skill and performative excellence are very much admired, and with such a production one does gain renown inside the village. The organiser and his assistant start at least nine months before the dry season, working on song lines, selecting issues in the village to be commented upon, devising skits, and recruiting two associate leaders and – very important – musicians, plus of course singers and actors. In the meantime the elders of the village order all younger age classes of the secret society to be ready to participate in the play, for it is a village affair and the secret society represents the whole village; the youngest age class mainly provides the dancers, and finally over a hundred players ready themselves for the event.

Some ritual elements remain, however; for instance, the major actors should refrain from sexual intercourse the nights before the performance,

7   Ibid.: 91.

lest they 'become weak, their voices [...] falter and they dance poorly'.[8] A small sacrifice to the spirit of the secret society just before the play, plus an amulet and other charms, should assure the two organisers a good performance, a strong voice, and a fleet-footed dance. Putting on a mask allows a person to behave differently from normal, since it turns him into a *mma* (spirit), not dangerous or threatening but 'a positive force of an active nature'.[9] Such a licence to act beyond one's personal stature is crucial for a convincing performance.

Okumkpa is the epitome of a mask performance accruing a dynamic of its own, a village theatre that is still recognisably local, one that the village 'owns' and in which it can play out its views on the world and provide meta-commentaries on fellow men – still shielded by the essential anonymity of the mask, within a liminal setting that provides social immunity. This is not the bush entering the village; this is the village playing itself, and otherworldly forces are distant here.

The king of masks, the elephant of masks

The general trend toward masks-as-show is visible in one of the largest and complex of all masks, and surely one of the heaviest: the *ijele* mask of the Igbo. This contraption is a huge construction that can be worn only by very strong and firm-footed dancers. This is neither a mask of the bush nor a mask of the king, but it is the mask of masks, showing the whole repertoire of Igbo forms, a moving theatre of masks with few links to the otherworld.

The mask consists of a wide cylinder hung with expensive fabrics, topped by a round open structure set with a plethora of figures, all in gaudy colours, with flagpoles sticking out in all directions. The two parts are separated by the image of a huge flecked python. Although all is made of light bamboo poles, it is still very heavy for a one-man mask, and consequently the pride of any youngster who succeeds in moving gracefully with it.[10]

The central square in the town is alive with hundreds of expectant people, closely watching the matted enclosure in one corner, where hidden from prying eyes the *ijele* is dressing. The people have already seen some other smaller masks perform, and appreciated them, but mainly as a prelude for the big mask. The musicians start playing, and the line of flautists, drummers, gong players, dancers, and singers makes one round over the square, counterclockwise,

8   Ibid.: 90.
9   Ibid.: 11.
10 Based on Aniakor 1978.

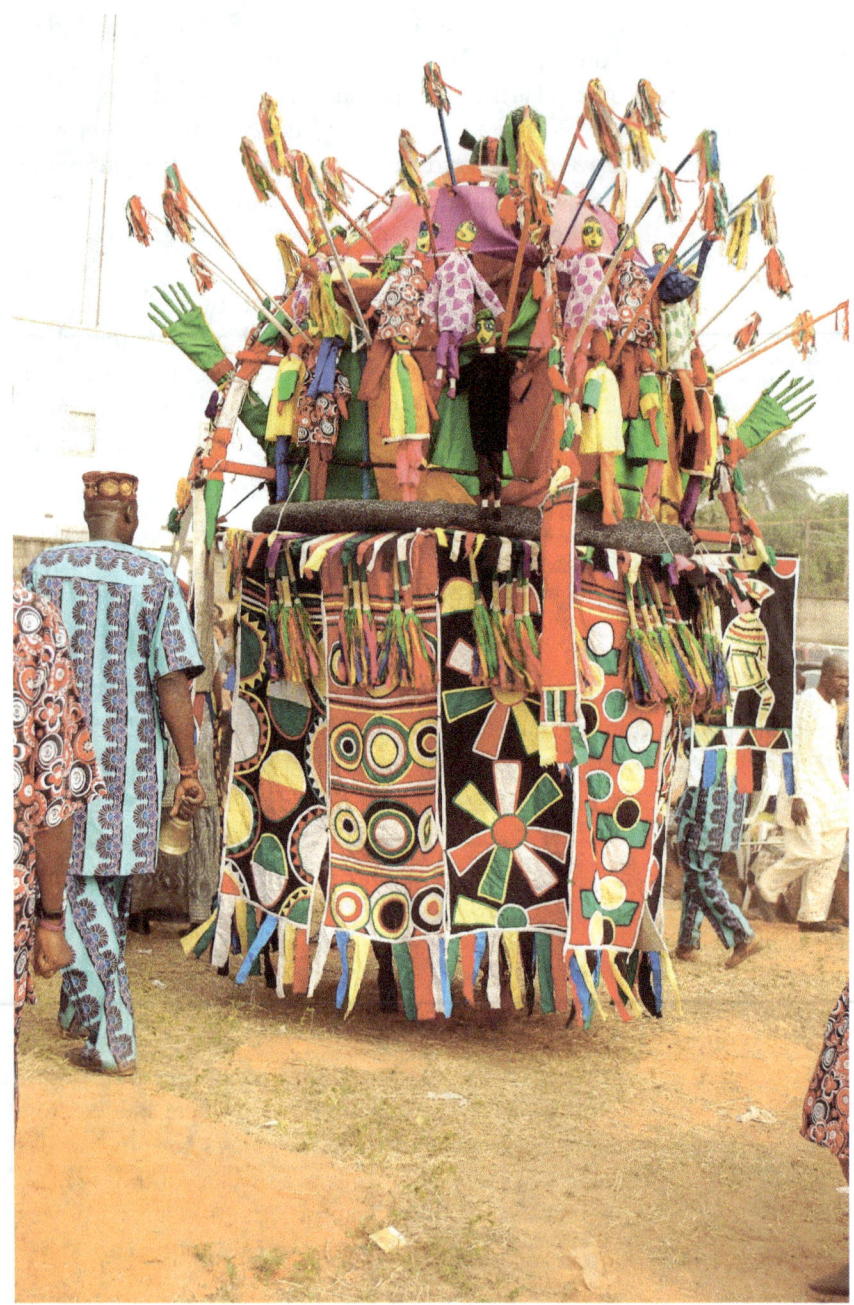

Figure 9.3. The *ijele* mask in full glory. Igbo, Nigeria. Photo: Chike Aniakor.

calling the *ijele* into the enclosure by the sheer volume of their sound. The onlookers see the top of the mask move above the enclosure, hesitantly at first to gain a proper balance, and then emerge from it slowly, led by one experienced dancer and escorted by many. Gaining more confidence the whole apparition starts to dance, moving its huge frame forward and backward, then sideways, and finally begins to rotate in half-turns.

> The cloth hangings sway in rhythmic response, the numerous symbols on the headdress seem to tilt from side to side, the decorative mirrors glint in the sun, and the open headdress seems to revolve in shifting scenes of colour and design.[11]

And a majestic dance it is, as behoves the king of masks. Then, at the sign of the music, the mask picks up speed, going into full motion with small, swift steps while the musicians pull out all the stops in a polyphony of sound, providing the enthralled audience with an impressive visual spectacle of volume-*cum*-agility in a deafening soundscape. Slowly, the whole spectacle circles the town square, and at last the music dies down and the mask disappears again into the enclosure. The dance does not last long – how could it? – but it leaves a lasting impression on anyone who has witnessed it. It will return another day, for another breathtaking performance.

The Igbo call *ijele* the 'elephant of masks', not only because it is the largest of all, but also as it conforms with a common African belief that the elephant in essence is an accumulation of all the wild animals of the bush; an elephant is all beasts together. Similarly, the *ijele* combines elements of all other Igbo masks, so in Igbo eyes is the most beautiful of masks for a compelling reason: wealth. It has the greatest number of figures and images in all possible colours, the gaudiest of masks. But more important, it is the most expensive mask and can be commanded only by someone extremely rich: this is the Ferrari among masks, and in Nigerian eyes price makes beauty. The intricate cloths hanging from the cylinder are all extremely costly and thus splendid, calling into mind the *egungun* mask with its many lappets; in the *ijele*, the link with the ancestors is remote. Its top part, mounted on two perpendicular giant arches, shows a host of multicoloured figurines; the greater the number and the gaudier, the more beautiful. Chike Aniakor highlights this aspect of Igbo aesthetics: 'If beauty is related to size and social status, then *ijele* embodies the best of art.'[12] In all their art, the Igbo admire complex forms and elaborate surface decorations. And colour, much colour.

---

11   Aniakor 1978: 47.
12   Ibid.: 43.

The twelve appliquéd velvet panels of 1.80 x 1.20 m are prestige items, one of which shows the 'face of *ijele*', with two outstretched arms, about the only hint at the spirit associated with the mask. Many of the motifs on the cloths stem from house decorations, so in a sense the dancer wears his house around him. Most of the figurines are human, picturing people in their daily activities: a man with a hoe, a soldier, a woman with a child on her arm, a well-dressed gentleman showing his wealth. They are surrounded by several domestic animals and a few wild ones, such as the leopard and – obviously – the elephant. History is present as well in a colonial officer or a turbaned Hausa horseman from the north, but modern authority is amply represented by images of a dozen policemen directing traffic. Often a replica of a stilt mask, as the highest one among many other masks, tops the whole structure. There is also a mirror with the power to draw in and punish evildoers; anti-witchcraft is never far from masks.

Ijele is a showcase for the super-rich, used whenever a wealthy Igbo aims to convert his economic capital into social capital, which in Africa is actually a good investment. In the past it was a rare occurrence, but these days *ijele* is turning into a city event, so these great apparitions have not grown rarer; on the contrary, especially in the north of Igbo country with its less egalitarian social structures, it has become a regular feature, stimulated by the fact that the *ijele* has been listed by UNESCO as intangible cultural heritage – it has accrued status. Of course, performing the mask is also a means to gain renown as a dancer; *ijele* mask carriers, chosen by ballot, seclude themselves for three months, feeding on a special diet to build the strength necessary to properly dance this giant mask.

We mentioned three processes of identity construction: theatricalisation, commoditisation, and iconisation. With their visual appeal and association with hidden layers of meaning, mask performances are well suited for the second dynamic, commoditisation, and one industry expertly focusing on this aspect is tourism. Tourists form a relatively new audience for masks; and here we turn to the Dogon.

Masks for new audiences

The sun has set behind the cliff when Abojo, the village crier, climbs toward the 'rock of the voice' just above the Dogon village of Tireli. His voice echoes off the cliff behind him, so all can hear his message loud and clear: 'Tomorrow afternoon a group of tourists will come, and the masks will dance. All youngsters have to come and participate.' The message invites no

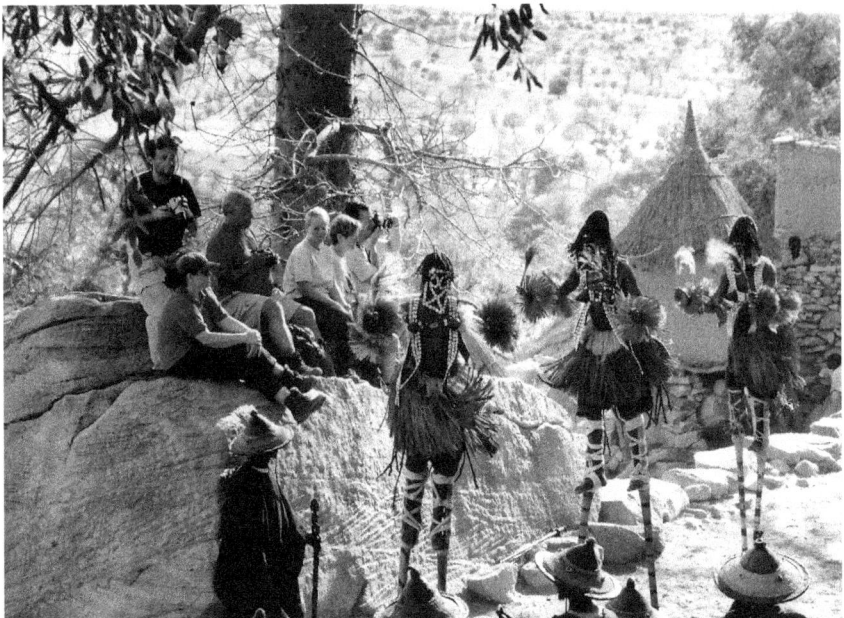

Figure 9.4. Dogon stilt masks dancing for tourists as part of a larger troupe. In the foreground the elders address the dancers in the mask language. Tireli, Dogon, Mali, 1995. Photo: Walter van Beek.

reaction, but the point is well taken. In fact, such messages have become standard procedure in the village for the last few years.[13]

In the early afternoon of the next day a lonely drum starts beating on the dancing ground, the first call for the masks. The young men finish their work and retrieve their costumes from the dark of their hut, or from one of the many small caverns on the hillside. An hour later the appeal is repeated and toward 4 pm, when the dancing ground is in the cliff's shadow, the men gather at the *toguna*, the men's house just above the dance square. Five pots with beer have been brought, the standard bonus for the dancers. One by one the masks gather there, fully clothed as mask, complete with headpiece, indigo trousers, cowry shell shirts, beads, and dancing sticks. The old men who are to lead them are also in full dress: dark indigo gown, large hat, stick in hand. Two expert drummers and an elder with an iron bell, the lead

13 The description stems from 2010 from the first author's fieldwork. Similar instances are found in Doquet 1999 and 2022. See Hollyman and Van Beek (2001) for a pictorial essay on such a performance.

instrument in Dogon, warm up at the dancing ground just below the men's house, while the performers take an initial sip at the men's house above. Meanwhile a small group of tourists make themselves comfortable on one of the rocks alongside the dancing place, cameras at the ready. After a short time – the real drinking is to come later – musicians, elders, and the masks file down from their hiding place. The beating of the drums, led by the shrill tones of the bell, guides the dancing masks, who echo the music with their high-pitched animal cry: *hè hè hè*. The dance has started.

The programme of the dance is taken from the third day of a Dogon *dama* (the second funeral, depicted in Chapter 5), since the elders use this 'meeting the foreigners' day as the basic format for show dances. Initially the fact that they were funeral dances presented a problem: how to deal with objects of power outside their ritual context? In Tireli there were lengthy debates on this issue. The elders knew that elsewhere such show dances had been performed for several years; in those villages the leaders had decided to make copies of their masks for tourism, so they now had two sets of masks: masks for tourists, and those for the rituals. This was a good example to follow, but still there was some apprehension: masks are special objects anyway, whatever the audience or the occasion. So the young men who were to dance for the tourists were frightened. They acquiesced when the elder in charge of the masks promised that he would perform some extra sacrifices on the mask altar and purify all dancers after each performance. Still, the ones who participated in that first performance do remember being very nervous when coming onto the stage.

In due time, these show dances would generate a considerable income for the village and the dancers, and villages such as Tireli became quite willing to accommodate their guests; this was 'amusement'. How amusing it was became apparent when a group of Japanese tourists wished to view the dance at the top of the cliff against which Tireli is built. The Dogon willingly obliged, at double the usual price of course. So twenty masks, twelve elders with two drums and a few bells – plus the inevitable anthropologist – jokingly climbed the hill to give their usual show on top of the cliff. But a surprise awaited them there. The Japanese women were shielding themselves from the sun with parasols, but two young ladies went one step further: they not only had a little umbrella and a hat, but also wore a complete face mask. The Dogon elders tried to keep a straight face, but many of them had to turn away to hide their mirth. One stilt mask had to seek support against a tree, almost falling over with laughter. And indeed, the spectacle of masked foreigners looking at masked Africans was unforgettable.

After decades of intense tourism, the political troubles since 2013 have rendered the area too dangerous for tourists, and this part of the Dogon economy has collapsed. It will take time to regain some degree of political stability in the region, but if that happens, tourism is a resilient industry that may bounce back. This kind of commoditisation of performances has often been decried as a cultural sell-out, but that is not the way the Dogon saw or see it. They are intensely occupied with their own culture and with their masks in particular, and the tourist fascination with these masks feeds into their own valuation of that tradition. More masks than ever are (were) being made, and older types that had disappeared were revitalised. The sizeable influx in money generated some difficulties and conflicts,[14] but it also assured that mask performances remained important.

Not only tourists form the new target audiences of mask dances; increasingly, urban Africans have become the public for their own mask festivals, a process that has been going on for some time already. Such masks perform during commemoration feasts and village festivals, on annual holidays such as New Year's Day, and during visits of government officials. Even in the early years of the twentieth century, enterprising Guro dancers in Côte d'Ivoire wanted to adapt old forms of dance and music, and had new masks made for themselves; their headpieces are now in museum collections, dating back to the 1920s. The dancers themselves spread stories about the origins of the masks and the dance. Some said they were hunting in the bush when they came across a group of dancing chimpanzees. When they were about to run away, the chimps called them back and taught them the dance, and also gave the young men magic substances in order to protect them against witchcraft during performances.[15] The new myths and the masks themselves, costumes as well as headpieces, were clearly inspired by existing Guro masquerades, variations aimed at garnering the appreciation of a conservative public. Thus, the new dancers linked their performances to established masquerades, calling them 'daughters' or even 'granddaughters' of *zamble* and *gu*, the prototypical mask couple of the Guro.

They were probably not the first, but will certainly not be the last of a series of masks devised by young Guro, each with their own performances. Each set of masks flourished, and when after a few decades they lost public appeal, new forms followed. During the middle of the twentieth century for example, the *seli* or *sauli* mask became very popular, spreading throughout

---

14 Van Beek 2012.
15 Fischer 2008: 265.

Guro land, but after some decades fell into oblivion and then developed into the *uale* masquerade, which still later produced the *fiali* version.[16]

The costumes do not change much – they are still based upon the prototypes – but the headpieces do change, and they define these masks as both fully modern and public. Not just elephants, snakes, and birds appeared on the dancer's head, or a hunter attacked by a leopard or a weaver at his loom, but also football players in front of a goal or two boxers fighting. Intriguing are the rainbow mask and the mask called *mamiwata*, the lady of the waters, the Indian icon that is expanding all over Africa.[17] The state became present in masking in the image of the late president Houphouet-Boigny of Côte d'Ivoire, who appears to steer two elephants.[18] These festivals can be attended, watched, and enjoyed by all members of the community without restrictions, even by fundamentalist Christians who are forbidden to watch 'pagan festivals'; by playing with prototypes, these masks became denomination-neutral.

The Baule, neighbours of the Guro, chose a different path and created a new category of masks: the *goli*, a new prototype. A Baule *goli* group consists of four pairs of masks, who perform after each other. First on stage is a pair of disc-masks, called *kplekple*, in which young dancers cavort to the amusement of the audience; their costume of fibres and darker skin is bushy enough, but their face cover is funny: a wooden disc with eyes and mouth, and two little horns on top. The 'father', *goli glin*, depicts a mixture of animals in a costume of fibres plus leaves, on his back the skin of a cob antelope, and with a highly impressive headpiece. A therianthropic mask pair, *kwam kple*, follows with a human face topped by horns, and finally one in full human splendour, with a knitted fibre costume. This 'queen of the *goli*' depicts a beautiful young woman, her face as serene as those of the Baule statues, with a leopard skin on its back as a sign of power and chieftainship. The very beauty of the mask is such that 'women let their dishes burn', because they watch its performance while cooking; the mask is often brought to the dancing place on the back of an assistant, to avoid soiling the feet, and dances just for half an hour, the embodiment of what Baule call 'sweetness'.[19]

Earlier in Ivorian history the French colonials recruited a *goli* performance for their feast of Quatorze Juillet,[20] as a sign of the ascendancy of the colonial

---

16   Fischer 2008: 311. In a *sauli* masquerade the dancer took off his mask, including the head cloth, and handed it to his attendant, who danced with it, thus defining the theatre as a modern, public one.

17   Ibid.: 72.

18   Steiner 1992a and 1992b.

19   A.-M. Boyer 2008, Vogel 1997b.

20   The national holiday of France.

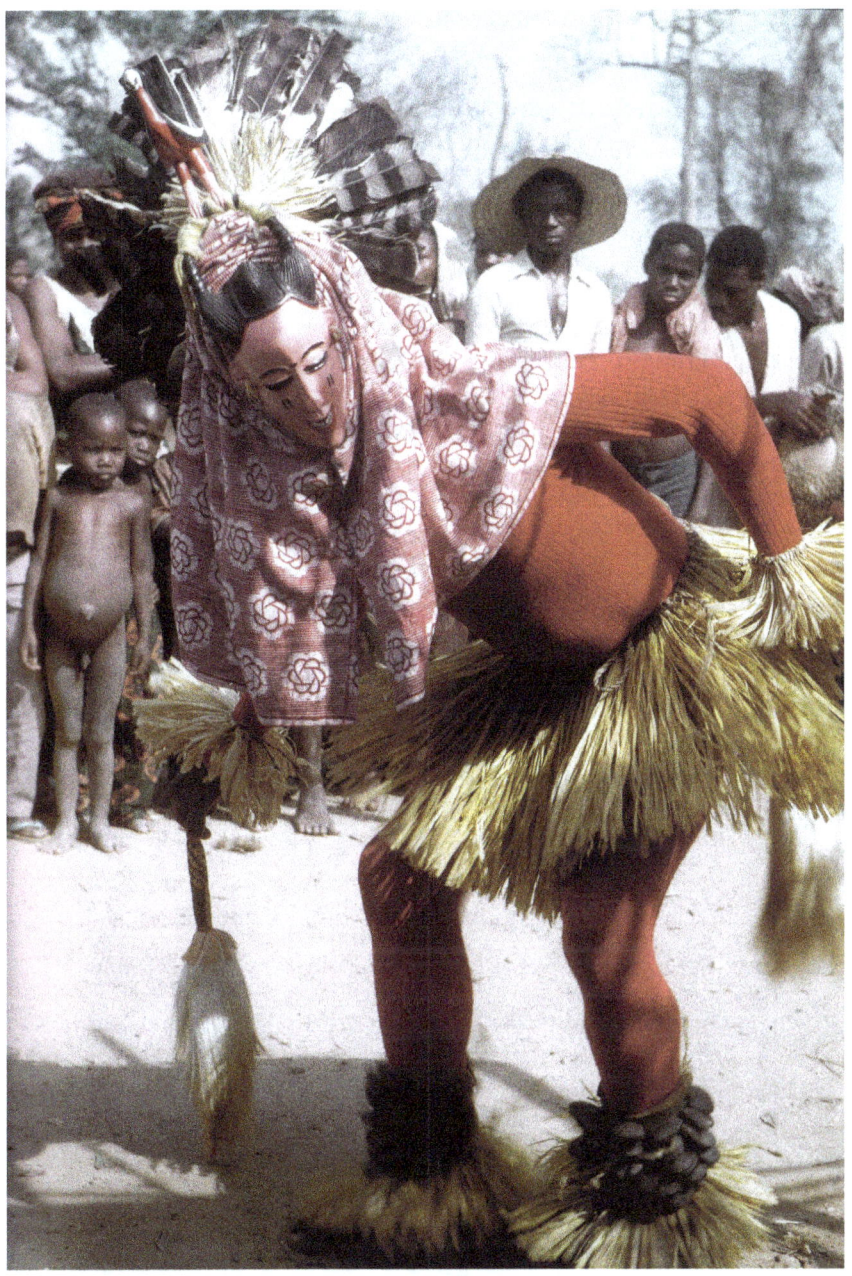

Figure 9.5. The *fiali* masquerade. Zuenoula, Guro, Côte d'Ivoire, 1975. Photo: Hans Himmelheber.

occupation.[21] From that moment onward the *goli* flourished. But whatever their function, masks as objects of power always have a serious undertone:

> The adoption of Goli at a time of social anxiety and political reversals, and the dancing of Goli and of the Mblo dance Gbagba for funerals, are connected to their value as distractions offering psychological relief in times of stress [...] Even if these dances have no particular religious role, the very presence of the masks in the village imparts a general sense of security and well-being.[22]

Each of the three groups – Dogon, Guro, and Baule – thus had its own creative adaptation to the new demand for public mask performances; building upon the corpus they already had, they either copied a separate set of the pieces themselves, expanded upon an already existing category of masks, or devised a new one, each according to its own cultural logic. In all three cases, new performances followed preexisting ritual formats, and origin myths popped up whenever needed. The Dogon were used to having a large array of different masks performing in ritual, so a separate set of masks fitted in well. The Guro already had a quite clear distinction between the initiation masks and those for public performances, so they expanded on the latter category, which was already visually different. Baule masks for initiation and for public feasts cannot be distinguished on sight; the function of their masks cannot be deduced from their countenance. Boyer stresses this as a crucial feature of their masking: 'Depending on the circumstances the same object can fulfil two different functions.'[23] So the Baule had to create a separate category.

That does not mean that old closed systems of masking were transformed into new open ones; in principle mask systems in most cultures have always been open, changing and adapting to historical circumstances, and it was this very openness and flexibility that has helped in expanding the public side of their heritage; the spectrum from ritual to theatre has always been present in masking traditions. Some are broader than others, some are more inclusive, but masking traditions tend to cover the whole scale from 'extremely secret' to 'completely public' in one way or another. After all, the secret and the public form a continuum, not a dichotomy, and they always need each other; the cases just elaborate the public side, stimulated by new political realities and commercial motives.

---

21   A.-M. Boyer 2008: 41.
22   Vogel 1997a: 140.
23   A.-M. Boyer 2008: 47.

Not only are the masks adapted in theatricalisation, so are the performers. In many areas mask dancers organised themselves in professional dancing troupes who tour the region for a living, such as among the Makonde, on the border between Tanzania and Mozambique. From their basis in traditional Makonde masking, these troupes developed new costumes and headpieces and introduced completely new elements in the shows; one of these is a mask on wheels, a masked player performing on a bicycle. The ethnographer Paolo Israel gives the following description:

> The dancers and the mask positioned themselves at a long distance from the iron bar strikers. The drummer played the mask call. Responding from afar, Naupanga jumped on a bicycle and rushed at breakneck speed toward the drummers; as it was about to reach them, it peeled out and turned, kicking away the bike and standing on its feet. Then more mimetic styles came. When the drum called the end of *nshakasha* [the performance] Naupanga jumped again on its bike and vanished in a cloud of dust and stupefaction.[24]

This professionalisation of masking may loosen the link between mask and ritual, but it heightens the audience's role. When masquerades are commoditised, audiences become a market.[25] This is a common phenomenon and should not elicit negative responses from the scholarly field, since it is the way masks will keep dancing. Also, this process inverts one divisive element in masking: the power difference between the elders and the youngsters. As long as masks are under the control of elders, often through secret societies, the performances bolster their authority vis-à-vis the young men, even becoming exploitative at times. Public shows, on the other hand, highlight the central position of the young, who must after all perform these strenuous dances; in dancing troupes such as Makonde ones, the next generation takes over. Power configurations change when masks are preempted by another echelon in society: masks remain an internal power factor.

Masks as icons of ethnic identity

When masks perform outside their natural habitat, they enter a different arena from the ethnic setting that gave birth to them. A foreign audience has no access to any inside references and will miss out on symbolic clues that are obvious to a home crowd. Consequently, the masquerades shift meaning and

---

24 Israel 2014: 236. As Dutchmen, the authors can sympathise with a biking mask.
25 For an example, see Weil 2005.

become emblems of a group or a nation, a process we call iconisation.[26] This can happen at several levels. For an ethnic group the masks may serve as ethnic identity markers, or as a focus of regional pride; they may also become national emblems, or even signs of Africa as such. In short, they become heritage.

Heritage is the new buzz word in African cultural matters, and masks feed right into it. Often local societies are fascinated by this expressive part of their own culture, and thus develop what has been called 'cultural self-confidence',[27] feeling that their culture matters a lot: an important attitude in a changing world. They cherish this cultural heritage as a contribution to the world, and in many ways derive their identity from their masks. At a higher echelon, masks have risen to the forefront of what Africans see as their common cultural heritage, and performances are seen as manifestations of both ethnic identity and national culture. The fact that most countries are now predomi- nantly Christian or Muslim adds weight to masks as prime objects for cultural identification, and as instruments for identity construction at higher levels.

In many West African countries ethnic groups tend to self-organise, creating ethnic associations geared to preserve and promote their specific cultural heritage. However, this ethnic card is ambivalent, since official politics may prohibit any association that calls itself 'ethnic'; after all, govern- ments avow that the times of 'tribalism' are over, and stress national identity over any ethnic identity. For instance in Senegal these organisations are not permitted to use the term 'ethnic' or 'cultural' association, since the country wants to be seen as one undivided nation. So other terms are needed, such as 'association of people coming from',[28] and they must portray themselves mainly as mutual support associations, not as representing a culture that diverges from the Muslim Wolof mainstream. Other countries, such as Mali and Burkina Faso, have fewer qualms and freely allow *associations culturelles* to exist and flourish.

Usually it is not the dominant ethnic group that organises itself this way, but minority ones who feel the need to maintain a clear sense of self-worth and appreciation of their own culture. The Dogon are one such group, and indeed they have an active cultural association called Ginna Dogon (big house, lineage). Since 1997 they have organised cultural festivals every other year in the various major towns of the Dogon country, but since the jihadist troubles they have changed this into a yearly *semaine culturelle* (cultural week) in Bamako, Mali's capital, inviting groups from all Dogon

---

26 Blier 1988.
27 Van Beek and Schmidt 2012.
28 'les ressortissents de'; see Van Beek 2013.

villages to represent themselves with their specific expressive cultural forms. These include songs, women's dances, performances of youth groups, a feast of clothes, hairdos, dancing, and – indeed – masks, illustrating the viability of Dogon culture as well its variability. The association also organises mask dances at national festivities and even engages in scholarly research on Dogon cultural heritage, including masks.

Multiethnic festivals represent masking cultures nationally and even internationally. A spectacular one is right in the heart of Zone 1 in Dedougou, inside Bwa territory. Since 1996 the Association for the Protection of Masks (ASAMA)[29] in Burkina Faso has organised a biannual festival, where all masking cultures in the wider region join in a week-long celebration of African culture, the FESTIMA. In 2016 this feast of 'all masks of Africa' welcomed hundreds of masks from six countries – Benin, Côte d'Ivoire, Mali, Togo, Senegal, and fifty villages of Burkina. In 2018 Nigeria joined, and other cultural items, such as leatherwork, pottery, and sculpture, were added. ASAMA director Ki Leonce told the press:

> There are two aspects about masks [...] One is cult and the other is culture; there might be a religious conflict for people who venerate masks, but there is no conflict from the cultural point. It is our cultural heritage, every African, every Burkinabe shares it and we cherish it.[30]

In 2018 the official opening was performed by the Burkina Faso prime minister, with the ministers of culture from Benin and Côte d'Ivoire present; it had grown from a private initiative into a regional pride. During the first day hundreds of masks dominated the streets of Dedougou in the Grand Parade, of course with their musicians, assistants, and elders; among the most spectacular were the large leaf masks of the Bwa themselves. The event drew thousands of visitors, mainly from Burkina Faso itself, for masks remain an important African fascination.

Like our typology the organisation distinguishes types of masks based on the costumes: leaf, bark, straw, cloth, and feathers.[31] A separate category for the organisers are the night masks – often made of cloth – since they have a different stage for performance. Women are welcome in the audience, as are the omnipresent eager young boys; this is theatre, not ritual. Nevertheless,

---

29 L'Association pour la Sauvegarde du Masque. Recent turmoil in the Sahel ended these events.
30 See Loov 2016. Leonce hinted at an Islamist attack in the capital Ouagadougou some weeks earlier.
31 We have conflated fibre and bark, and consider feathers as an addition to cloth.

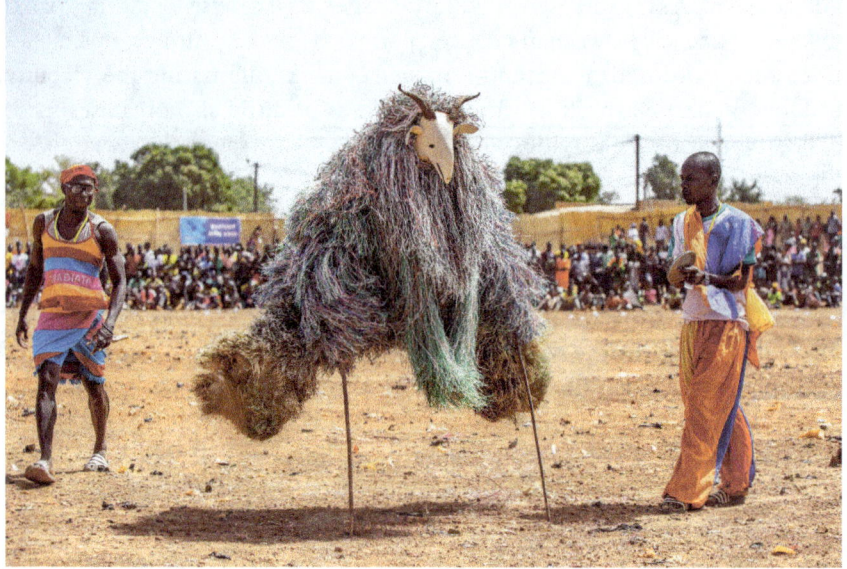

Figure 9.6. Goat mask performing at the FESTIMA in Dedougou. Bwa, Burkina Faso, 2020. Photo: Elena Borkova/Alamy stock.

the power of the masks is never far away, as one Malian musician explained to a photographer: 'Of course, these masks are not given full power during the festival. Otherwise, you would not even be able to photograph them; nothing would show up in the picture.'[32]

   At such a festival the masks serve as ethnic markers, as expressions of local cultures, which gain both exposure and respectability from this festivalisation. In monoethnic feasts such as that of Ginna Dogon, individual villages stand out through their mask performances, while in the multiethnic ones, the ethnic groups profile themselves as such with their most spectacular mask dances. Here any ritual is far away, and all performances must be cut down to a manageable troupe and to a length that is convenient for a foreign audience. The focus at the festival is not on content and interpretation, but on visual variety as a stepping stone for ethnic identity. So the festivals highlight African culture as a feast of diversity, a kaleidoscope of ethnic identities, but also as variations on a theme, on a central mode of expression that is considered African to the core.

[32] Characteristically, the Malian spoke not about sacredness, but about power.

Heritage, icon, and commodity

Heritage in these festivals means intangible heritage. In Africa the term heritage is viewed as a synonym for ethnic culture, but with one major difference. A cultural item called heritage accrues international respect and recognition, far beyond any quaint and curious local custom; the quest for recognition is 'an expansive force built upon the confidence of nation-building and sustained by a sense of loss'.[33] The fact that in UNESCO parlance the idea of heritage implies scarcity and being under threat does not seem to be at the forefront of people's minds; for Africans calling a mask performance 'heritage' puts it in the realm of internationally accredited cultural masterpieces, rather than positing it as a fragile remnant of the past. However, it also implies a process involving both a strong selection and streamlining of the traditions, since such a distinction is available for a few performances only.[34]

This is not the place to delve deeply into the dynamics of heritage nominations,[35] but for the future of many masking traditions it is relevant. Heritage is an important stimulus, but one that does carry some risks and costs. Defining a culture as heritage tends to freeze it at a particular point in time, through both its recognition process and sponsored performances. In doing so the notion of tradition is also essentialised, becoming identical to a particular cultural expression, which risks hampering the very dynamics generating such expression. Preservating intangible heritage should aim at keeping alive the processes that spawned that heritage, but this is often very difficult. What exactly constitutes this safeguarding differs from case to case, but since national identities are high on the political agenda in Africa too, heritage will continue to increase in importance. For masquerades, at least, recognition as heritage equals respectability, and though deemed heretical by fundamentalist religious groups, either Islamic or Christian, these performances do become permitted and respected; the definition as heritage serves as a shield against religious fervour.

The selectivity of heritage recognition leads to iconisation, the process by which a single visual sign becomes a central emblem for a society. An icon is culture reduced to a recognisable visual form, a simplified sign that stands for the whole cultural conglomerate. The link between that sign and its meaning is one-dimensional: an icon stands for a specific cultural unit. The process of iconisation reduces both the complexity of the sign and

---

33   Rowlands and De Jong 2007: 17.
34   Rowlands and Warnier 1996, 2002.
35   See De Jong and Rowlands 2007.

the breadth of its interpretation: a single standardised form refers to one specific referent, a shortcut in meaning construction.

As standardised symbols icons are easily communicable. Writing as Dutchmen, we recognise that for foreigners the icons of the Netherlands are the tulip, the windmill, and wooden shoes (clogs) – indeed, tourism is a prime iconising industry. Thinking of Paris, one immediately visualises the Eiffel Tower; and just as almost no Dutchmen wear wooden shoes, most Parisians never go up the Eiffel Tower. But this is what iconisation does; icons are memes, images that are easy to learn, quick to transfer, and almost impossible to forget.

The young nations of Africa need icons as national emblems in order to forge a unity that is difficult to obtain otherwise, emblems that come in handy when representing oneself to the outside world and to themselves. Masquerades become prime actors in the process of heritage definition because they form such a separate category of apparitions. In a mediatised modern environment, masks are immediately recognised as such, and the relative strangeness of their appearance can serve a whole array of functions: local villages can identify with them and so can ethnic groups or even cultural regions, but also a whole nation can include masks as icons for its identity politics; identity is always a nested phenomenon based on contrast. Masks can even become an icon for countries that have no masks, evoking a generalised Africanity.

At the 2015 Biennale in Venice, Kenya was represented by a dozen artistic masks, even though the country harbours no masking tradition to speak of. This iconic role of the mask was even more poignant when it appeared that of the eight artists representing the country, six were neither Kenyans nor even Africans, but Chinese who had never set foot in Kenya. A huge outcry arose in the country, and the jury's selection was called shameful and symbolic of the dispossession of the country. But these made-in-China masks had been commissioned by Kenya, and without any qualms were accepted by the Italian jury.

Masks have become the hallmark of the post-colony in Africa. Côte d'Ivoire advertises itself as a country of masks, both the Guro *zauli* and the Baule portrait masks. The Bobo plank masks are important in the international presentation of Burkina Faso. In Mali, the Dogon *kanaga* mask has become almost a brand, as has the Bamana *ciwara*. Evidently, UNESCO recognition does stimulate this, as is shown by the Likumbi lya Mise festival of the Luvale in Zambia,[36] and by the *gelede* masquerade of the Yoruba, which are now a recognised world heritage, but are attributed to Zambia and Nigeria as a whole.

Since icons are images distilled from the past that define modern identities, any fully modern event can be spruced up by iconic masks. For instance, in December 2006 the Senegalese Draughts Federation organised one of the largest mind sports events ever held on the African continent, the World Cup of Nations in International Draughts. As part of the opening ceremonies a *kumpo* mask came out and danced before the authorities and officials in front of the hotel where the competition was held. The all-fibre mask performed its swirling dance without any sound, even drumming, and without any explanation afterwards to the guests. Bereft of its usual musical accompaniment and assistants, the performance seemed to the European guest[37] rather perfunctory, eliciting more a gentle chuckle than awe at the apparition of a power figure. But at least it was African, completely African, and the Senegalese organisers were very proud. The fact that the mask had danced was sufficient to define the whole endeavour as 'African' vis-à-vis the guests from other continents, and as such the opening ceremony could proceed inside the modern hotel, without the mask.

But it is another Senegalese mask that was pushed to the forefront of publicity, one that seems even less suited to this role. Ferdinand de Jong describes how the *kankurang*[38] mask, which functions in Manding initiations, received UNESCO recognition as a masterpiece of intangible cultural heritage.[39] This mask is of the 'wild man' type, performing with a show of violence by both the mask and its attendants, and it received recognition in 2005 as part of the Manding initiation rites. In the urban context these rites had already been routinised, from once per five years to every year, which generated complaints about the 'loss of the secret' and 'banalisation' of the ritual. The quest for official recognition changed the place of the mask even further, for the mask morphed from an object the audience was forbidden to look at into an object of public contemplation and a commodity. De Jong defines this process also as a change from restoration to reinvention: the elders wanted the secret restored, and UNESCO's recognition led to the mask passing into the hands of the youth.

---

36 Ellert, Murphy and Ball 2004: 38–63.
37 The first author was present as vice-president of the African Draughts Confederation.
38 This extended case is based upon De Jong's description (2007a).
39 De Jong 2007b. The same mask performance had already developed into a national icon for The Gambia. See for a different mask trajectory De Jong 1999.

A curious example of this national iconisation is the *zangbeto* mask in Benin, which participated in the FESTIMA and also performs in other settings. For instance, in 2017 the *zangbeto* masks from the south of Benin opened the twenty-third annual Pan-African Festival of Film and Television in Ouagadougou; Burkina Faso has a thriving film industry and hosts the major film festival in Africa south of the Sahara. These *zangbeto* masks have become the prime representation of Benin national culture and sometimes serve as icons for all West African culture.

The *zangbeto* mask, however, is an unusual case. It is found as a rather standard all-fibre mask among the Ogu or Egun peoples of Benin and Nigeria,[40] but another version has caught the national imagination in the form of a cloth-covered cone with some specific features at the top.[41] This particular rendition of the mask seems to stem from a small fishing group in the very southeastern corner of the country, the Kpla or Hwepl, where the mask is the guardian mask of the village, keeping villagers safe from harm, enemies, and the ubiquitous 'witches'. Nowadays these cone-shaped *zangbeto* masks are found all over the country, performing at public functions. They operate in foursomes, carefully herded by assistants in female wraparound skirts, and their essential dance is to swirl around, fast and furiously – what else could they do? However, the apogee of the performance – and here we are in the sphere of the festivals – is when after elaborate theatricals the assistants lift the cone to show that it is empty, thus 'proving' that it is the spirits who made them dance.

Clearly, this revelation is the exact opposite of the one at the heart of initiations, where boys may have thought masks were spirits, but learn the human truth inside them. Whereas initiation is about internal demystification kept hidden from outsiders, *zangbeto* relies on public mystification. This trick has made the *zangbeto* very popular, and nowadays many such groups tour the country to make a living, each group even more expert at the masking illusion.[42] Such an illusionist show as the *zangbeto* mask may well be an apt emblem for Benin;[43] after all, one major scholarly definition of the nation/ state is an 'imagined community',[44] so what better icon for whatever national identity than an expertly performed illusion […]?

---

[40]   Noukpo 2020.

[41]   For a similar cone-shaped mask, see the Mende: Jedrej 1986.

[42]   The authors have no idea how they do it, but as Westerners used to illusionists who make scores of pretty girls vanish and return unharmed, it is not difficult to suspend judgement.

[43]   Of course, tourists are quick to attribute this to 'African voodoo', for Benin is the heart of the Vodun religion, the *fons et origo* of Haitian voodoo.

[44]   The seminal work of Benedict Anderson, 2006 (1983).

Conclusion

Cross River societies figure prominently in this book. Efik, Ekpeye, Ejagham, Yakö, Ekoi, and Afikpo form an area of ethnic splintering east of the large Igbo cluster, from which the Cross River separates them. These Cross River cultures share many features of Type C: autonomous villages, varying in size, often with double descent, all with a history of defence against slave raiding; age is important, as are internal title systems. Secret societies have flourished for a long time already, as a response to a male power vacuum. This is the area where secret societies branch out into a franchise system, linking the small ethnic groups in larger cultural areas. Their relation with the Igbo has been politically tenuous, but culturally close.

As for our masking model, the case of the fishing Ijo is remarkable, for the other fishing communities mentioned do not have masks. Most of the latter are river fishers, like the Wagenia of the Congo River, and the Bozo of the Bani River in Mali. Such fishing communities tend to disperse over the fishing grounds, and the division of tasks among men and women is highly complementary; the genders seem not in competition. So river fishing seems to preclude masking, even if they have neighbouring groups – even joking partners[45] – that mask. But the Ijo fish both the river and the ocean, like the Kpla, and live in permanent settlements where masks may find a niche. However, viewing the role of women in the Ijo 'shark-theatre', the genders seem well matched, and indeed the gender and power arenas are not evident in the proceedings. Consequently, the masquerade is more a theatre than a ritual.

Makonde masking groups root in a strong local tradition. Living on the Negala Plateau in Tanzania and the Mueda Plateau in Mozambique, this patrilineal society shows Type C characteristics with large defensive villages. They cultivate maize, beans, and cashew, and have neither cattle nor goats, but raise pigs in abundance; the strong position of their women is renowned in northern Mozambique.[46] Helped by their inaccessible habitat, they have a long history of successful resistance to Arab-induced slave raiding and to colonial armies, especially the Portuguese. Though now predominantly Christian, their initiation – with masks – is still vibrant, as a major hallmark of an ethnic group renowned for their fighting skills in the civil war, with a reputation of being aided by strong magical means.

---

45 The Dogon as a group have an institutionalised joking relation with the Bozo as a group.

46 We thank Augusto Jaime, himself also Makonde, for this information.

10

Memories of Power, Power of Memories

'History does not repeat itself, but it often rhymes.'

(attributed to Mark Twain)

Arrest that mask!

The scene is the Basse Casamance in Senegal, south of The Gambia, a region dominated by two ethnic groups, the Manding and Jola; the setting, surprisingly, is a court room. The case involves a confrontation between the state and a mask and occurred in 1988 in Sédhiou, a town on the Casamance River. A kankurang mask[1] that accompanied a dancing crowd happened to annoy the Assistant Prefect – it actually annoyed him quite seriously. The official was vexed to the point that he had the police arrest the mask and take it to the police station, where the police, as the anthropologist Ferdinand de Jong put it,[2] 'took the unprecedented step of undressing him'. Word got around and the next morning an angry crowd gathered at the football stadium and decided to send a delegation to the police station, demanding the immediate release of the mask. As fate would have it, the Assistant Prefect arrived with his car at that time, and a riot ensued; the car was set on fire, police officers were stoned, guns were fired, and the crowd attacked the homes of the policemen.

The story was also that, adding insult to injury, the police asked two girls to identify the masker [...] girls! The meeting in the stadium was for initiates only, and many showed up bare-chested, as if in the sacred forest. In the ensuing debates among the many Manding involved, one policeman who was Wolof gradually became the scapegoat; after all, the Assistant Prefect was a fellow Manding and initiated. The case was tried quickly, to appease a thoroughly incensed populace, and the rioters who stood trial received light suspended sentences. The officials in question were transferred to other

1 The same mask that received UNESCO recognition, mentioned in the previous chapter.
2 Based on De Jong 2007a: 139.

towns, a clear measure to defuse the situation. So in the end the cultural obligation to defend the secrecy of the mask was more or less confirmed and sustained by the state.

This clash shows the power of a local group with masks vis-à-vis the state, through a series of factors. One major issue is secrecy, a discourse shared to some extent by the government. Another point is the value of masks as a self-regulating force for order, but such a local order does not always run parallel to public priorities, at least as defined by national functionaries. Also, the masquerading appeared to have been an unscheduled one, and in the aftermath of this high-profile case the elders imposed some self-regulation on mask appearances, a way to adapt the masks to the exigencies of the modern public space.[3]

Looking back on this scene, one wonders about the heavy-handed approach of the state representative. If initiation teaches one thing to boys, it is how to handle masks when confronted with them: appropriate greetings, signals of being initiated oneself, and at least a certain self-confidence in approaching masks – these are the first lessons the initiates learn. Although the *kankurang* is an aggressive mask, surely there were more flexible responses possible. The Assistant Prefect must have severely misjudged the situation, overrating the strength of his own position as a major administrative figure, perhaps piqued by the mask's lack of deference. The subsequent transfer of the administrators to other towns showed a wiser response from the higher echelons, who used the same kind of countermeasures that the former colonial government would have taken: riot control and personnel transfer. Devolving the blame to a non-initiate seems an injustice, but conforms to local law enforcement. We saw as much in the previous chapter; setting up a scapegoat is not exactly administering justice, but it is effective in saving the moment.

Clearly, when masquerades enter the public space of the African state, the very ambivalence of the powerful masks may pose a challenge to state hegemony. Modern African states have an ambiguous relation to local power, especially to the tradition-honoured position of secret societies as represented by masks. Another court case of the Jola in Senegal shows a more serious challenge and one with a grave accusation: double manslaughter.

Solo had arrived in the Basse Casamance as a refugee from Guinea-Bissau but had settled well in his new country.[4] In 1987, as a part of Manding initiation – which occurs at long intervals – a *kankurang* mask encountered Solo on the town street; for some unknown reason the two came to blows. As noted, the *kankurang* is a mask with a violent demeanour, so it was acting its character; however, Solo was neither amused nor, as non-Manding,

---

3   Ibid.: 142.
4   De Jong 2007a: 133–136, 138–140. We use the most plausible variant; see page 134.

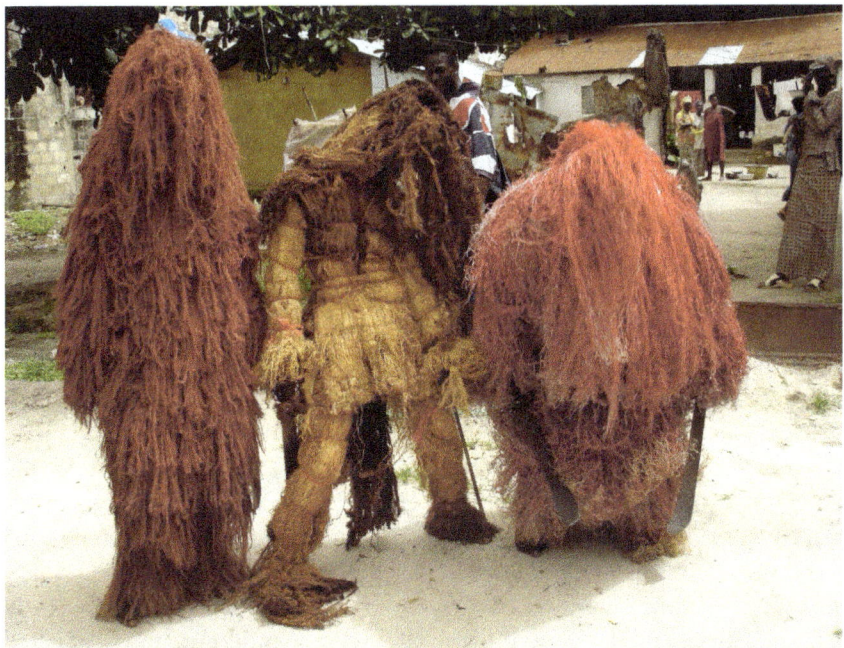

Figure 10.1. *Kankurang* masks. Jola, Senegal, 1999. Photo: Ferdinand de Jong.

overly impressed with the mask. Strong as he was, Solo easily overpowered the apparition, partially undressed it, and took the mask's machete to the *souspréfet*, the local administrator. The mask fled to the sacred forest where the initiation was being held. The next morning a group of men came after Solo, set fire to his house, and beat him up when he came out. His uncle came to his assistance, and both men were clubbed to death.

Similar gruesome stories are often told as cautionary tales during initiation, in order to imprint novices with the executive power of the secret society, and many of these are just that: tales. But this was real. Although this kind of revenge must have occurred in the past as well, this killing occurred in full view of the modern state, including press coverage. Clearly the state of Senegal could not tolerate such an execution, so the police acted and no less than twenty-eight people were arrested and charged.

The case took an extremely long time – nine years, in fact – to be brought to trial, and of all the people arrested only five were prosecuted. On trial should have been the mask itself, but that is an otherworldly entity that cannot be summoned; and it was not the mask that committed the manslaughter. The case received overwhelming public attention and massive press coverage, with all the Manding population clamouring that Solo's desecration of the mask had been sufficient reason for his severe punishment. In the event, the five accused got off lightly: three received suspended sentences, and two were discharged. Even the state had trouble upholding its laws against the discourse of secrecy; the mask's iconic position as the emblem of Manding society, plus the fact that the crime was committed during the liminal time of the initiation, made stiff sentences even more difficult.

The anthropologist Ferdinand de Jong analyses this complex case in terms of the power position of the young men in the society, their command of this masking society, and their resentment of immigrants. Of course, the defence line was that 'the *kankurang* avenged the sacrilege', and their lawyer got a lot of mileage out of the secrecy issue, capitalising on the mystery that pervades any *kankurang* masquerade: 'Who can know what happened? Does anyone know?' Although the Senegalese state could not tolerate this violation of the state monopoly on violence, the prosecutor shied away from mentioning that the mask was a man in disguise: 'The discourse of secrecy was not ruptured in court.'[5] Secrecy can be a very effective defence against a hegemonic power.

Senegal has a relatively strong state with a predominantly Muslim population. If clashes were to continue, it is difficult to see how in the long run masks could hold out against a reasonably powerful state. Also, in these *kankurang* conflicts one perceives an awkward truce between the two powers: the local one empowered by secrecy and the machinery of the modern political establishment. One additional issue was that the Basse Casamance at the time harboured a separation movement, which made the government skittish over any unrest.

Many nation states in Africa are not as strong as Senegal and hardly penetrate the countryside beyond the major cities or even the capital, and recent conflicts in the Crescent do little to tilt the balance of power toward central governments. So in the short run these clashes between local organisations and national presences can be expected to continue, if only because these local institutions and the performances of secrecy can be hijacked by external forces, such as separatism, jihadism, or outright banditry. In any case, these *kankurang* incidents show how tenacious the combination of a secret society with masks can be in the face of modernity; secrecy is a highly effective tool of local self-organisation, underscored by the deeply

5   Ibid.: 142.

ambivalent power of the wilderness as manifested in the masks: a power that is not at all annulled by the modern state.

Clashes with modernity are not rare. In Nigeria, for example, where sentiments often run high on religion, masks have been reported to target evangelical churches, which define anything related to traditional religion as evil. In September 2012 a group of masks invaded a Christ Apostolic Church in a small town in Ondo State, where the congregation was busy with a meeting to 'exorcise evil'. The masks beat up the pastor and some of the members and then quoted the Bible to justify their action.[6] So modernity has many faces, including the masks themselves, who nowadays 'know their Scriptures'.

Satire, the weapon of the weak

Against the modern state masks will be the weaker force in the long run, but that is not an unusual position for masks to be in. Also in more rural settings masks often function as 'weapons of the weak', tools for the subjugated to get back at their dominators, turning the tables of inequality in discourse and performance. One way to deal with past inequities is to turn former power holders into a laughing stock, and satire is the obvious means to do so. Humour is a great leveller, invariably depicting the powerful as stupid, since these dumb usurpers cannot even grasp how they are being turned into fools. Mask performances can be very effective in cutting foreign dominators down to size, for masquerades are full of hidden codes and oblique references that are accessible only to the initiated.[7] However, also without masks these tactics can be efficient.

In the early 1960s Kwame Nkrumah decided to make a visit to Winneba, a fishing town some five kilometres from the main road.[8] As instructed, all the schoolchildren of Winneba were lined up along the whole length of the road to welcome the president. But presidents in Africa are not the most punctual of potentates, so he was late – quite late, in fact. The schoolchildren had been taught a welcoming song with *Akwaaba*, a widely known Twi word meaning 'welcome'. However, with the sun shining and the hours passing for the girls in their dainty but warm school uniforms without any shade or water available, their teachers made a slight modification to the

---

6   Njoku 2020: 156.
7   See for examples Okagbue 1997 and Jordán 1993.
8   Story by the second author.

text: the word *Akwaaba* morphed into *Abwaba*, a word in Effutu, Winneba's own language, and this meant 'fool'. So when Nkrumah, who did not speak Effutu, finally arrived, he enthusiastically waved to all those dear girls who sang out loud to him '*Abwaba*'. He probably never knew, but then he overestimated his popularity anyway.

Clearly, authority figures are the main targets of fun, and masks are prime vehicles for carrying messages of resistance. Given the inherent conservatism of masking rituals, many codes of resistance have remained inside the masks' repertoires, so part of the performances can be read as satirical plays on enemies of old. For the Dogon, for instance, those enemies were the raiders of yore, the Fulbe, pastoralists who founded their emirates in the region in the eighteenth and nineteenth centuries. Like most Muslim polities at the time, these realms were inveterate slave raiders, and the horticulturalists in the savannah always had to be vigilant against their marauding cavalries. The cliffside habitat of the Dogon, now famous for its splendid views and picturesque villages, was in fact a defensive bulwark against mounted raiders.

It was in their masquerades that the Dogon retaliated, with the weapon of the weak: satire. Second funerals, like the one described in Chapter 5, often feature a Fulbe man or woman. The man is the easiest to recognise; with a gown as a costume, often topped with a whitened face, the mask sports a wooden stick horse. Its dance mainly consists of stumbling around with the horse; it tries to mount it, the stick between its legs, and then trips over the 'war horse'. This caricature of a formidable enemy of old elicits a good laugh from the audience, and the same holds for the Fulbe woman, who pretends in her dance to scoop up dung for her fire, always looking for more droppings.

The mask *samo* (Figure 2.7) features the Samo, neighbours of the Dogon, also a slave-raiding group. Despite its threatening mien, it has a major weakness: it cannot speak well, and does not even know how to greet properly. Dogon masks do not usually speak, but this one does, and is quite bad at it; instead of forming words like a normal human being, it fumbles its speech, mixing half-words into a failed greeting. Since greeting defines someone in Dogon as human, the mask characterises itself as sub-human. Why fear someone who cannot even speak properly?[9]

Mask satire targets not only enemies or authorities, but also people in the group who do not behave properly, like the chiefs in the Afikpo masked theatre, who were held to the yardstick of proper behaviour. Guro youth associations perform masquerades with ape-like masks figuring as tricksters

---

[9] One Nyau mask depicts a slave hunter suffering from syphilis! Curran 1999: 74.

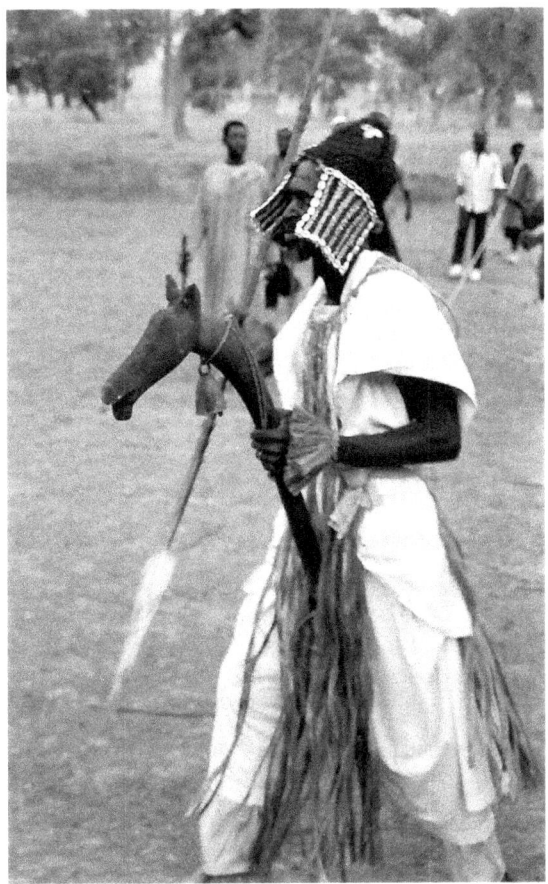

Figure 10.2. Dogon mask
of a Fulbe man, half-
dressed between perfor-
mances. Amani, Dogon,
Mali. Photo: Walter van
Beek, 1989.

in commentaries on societal issues.[10] In 1992 a pair of masks called *powin*[11]
represented an old but worthy and dignified-looking man, plus his ugly and
grotesque counterpart, one with a frill of raffia fibres around its head, sometimes
portrayed as leprosy-infected. The 'ugly old man' in pantomime represented 'an
elderly man who does not keep to his (social) place but takes a very young
wife'.[12] Not only was this the dance of a youth association, but young men
are the main dancers in any masquerade; eager to marry as they were, they
saw the marriage market spoiled by rich old men who could easily afford
another young wife. Specific ugly Yoruba masks are, as Marilyn Houlberg

10 Himmelheber 1960: 153–155.
11 Bouloré 1995; Himmelheber 1960: 314.
12 Haxaire 2011: Figure 3.

noted, 'convenient for satirising foreigners, such as Hausa, Nupe and European, as well as for ridiculing socially undesirable characters within Yoruba society: buck teeth, eavesdroppers, greedy, dumb, gossip, drunk, and glutton'.[13]

A central satirical figure in African oral literature and myth is the trickster. Folk tales of the continent are replete with these figures, and in masquerades they easily translate into jester masks, the essential anti-authority figures. Used as they are to trickster stories, Africans easily attribute hidden dimensions to a jester, such as the Senufo *yalajo* mask described in Chapter 5, which is both a buffoon and extra-human.[14] In Nigeria one Edo mask serves as a messenger for all other masquerades, a figure that creates havoc in order to extract meaning and sometimes order.[15] The *zauli* mask of the Guro has a similar function. Fundamentally ambivalent, most masks have elements of a trickster, which merge in the impersonation of the jester[16] – or, in the words of the Bamana, 'The trickster is the first person in the world'.[17] Masks-as-jesters fit in well with what Mikhail Bakhtin called the grotesque, characterising it as 'a world of inversion, reversal, and degradation that confronted the inequality [...] of the official power structures with an anarchic double of [...] irreverence and radical egalitarianism'.[18] In this vein, mask humour is not just liminal, but represents the ever-present contradictions in the lived world, their satire stipulating that in the end people are equal – meaning equally weird.

One obvious authority figure in Africa is the white man, who is portrayed with an ambiguous mix of satire and appreciation. For the many groups in the zones that have suffered deeply from slave hunting, colonialisation may have implied loss of autonomy, but brought a measure of safety and stability they never had before. The white man ended slavery, both external and internal, and ended tribal wars – which is still widely appreciated. But at the same time he demanded labour and taxes, levied for soldiers in colonial times, and throughout remained strange and weird. So this white man – white women are almost never depicted – forms a ready target for some gentle fun.

As a major tourist attraction the Dogon have been exposed to a long parade of white people coming into their country, so they portray the European in their masquerades. Clothed in trousers and shirt, crowned with a fiery-red wooden top and sporting an unruly beard and flowing hair – Europeans are

---

13   Houlberg 1978: 59.
14   Glaze 1981 plate 11 and page 118.
15   Borgatti 1988.
16   Like the Likoma jester mask, which the Makonde took over: Bouttiaux 2009a: 70.
17   Colleyn 2002f: 77. 'Le bouffon est la première personne du monde.'
18   Cited in Argenti 2007: 196.

both sunburned and hairy – the mask performs in three versions. Dancing is not something a European usually excels at, so the mask walks around, and in the first version distributes small written notes and collects money: the colonial officer trying to collect taxes. The second version is armed with a wooden 'camera', bends over backward to get a good view, and shoves people out of the way to get a closer shot: the tourist. The third one is good for reflexivity: the mask sits on a stool, flanked by two Dogon sitting in the sand, notebook and ballpoint in the hand, points at the dancers, and asks the most stupid questions imaginable: the anthropologist! The first author collected such a headpiece, which, as his informants immediately pointed out, was made in his very own likeness.

This satirical side of masks is even more convincing since it is set inside a general theatrical spectacle in which a host of characters are portrayed. Some of them are to be laughed at, others are there to admire. Chapter 6 focused on mask portraits of women, which should be icons of beauty; when such a mask is on stage, Chokwe women in the audience are highly critical if the appearance is in any way substandard:

> Women may accept this male concept of the ideal female if they feel the performance honours them, but they may 'chase away' a performer whom they feel is not up to their standards. Often, the best female dancers in the community dance alongside [the mask] to test the skill of the impersonator.[19]

The Guro of Côte d'Ivoire with its sophisticated sculptural tradition[20] carve their *fiali* (girl) mask tops with flair and confidence, and the local carvers sometimes use specific women of the village as their inspiration. The resulting headpieces thus become paragons of female beauty, not only enhanced but also individualised. Each *fiali* mask is recognisable, and sometimes the woman who served as an inspiration for the carver is indeed known. This should not be mentioned too clearly, of course, for the gentle taboo still holds. And the consequence is significant: whenever the inspiring beauty is too well known, the mask must leave the village to perform in another village.[21]

Drama demands contrast, so after the beauty comes the beast: the ugly human. Quite a few mask tops portray heads with distorted faces, tops that are

---

19 Jordán 1982: 68. If this mask appears during a boys' initiation, it is considered a ghost of exceptional beauty for the boys to dream about; aesthetics count!
20 Fischer 2008.
21 Bouttiaux 2013a: 133.

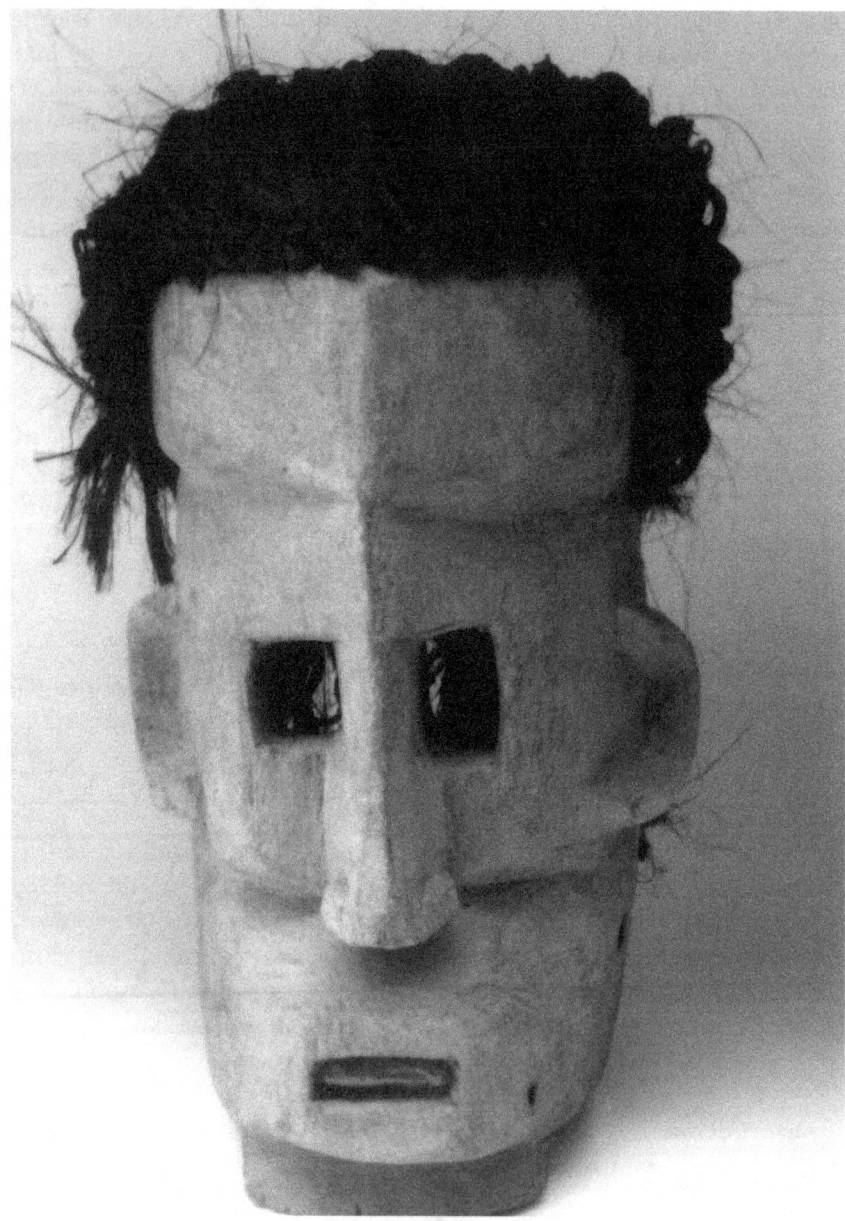

Figure 10.3. The *èmna anyara*, white man's mask, in the likeness of Walter van Beek. Tireli, Dogon, Mali, 2008. Photo: Museum of World Cultures, Amsterdam.

sometimes called 'illness masks'.[22] Are they? Africa is no stranger to diseases, but the problem is one of interpretation: why would carvers make headpieces that seem to resemble people struck by afflictions? In his overview of Afikpo masks, Simon Ottenberg provides a series of such masks,[23] called *okpesu umuruma*; he even ordered some himself from a well-known carver. These masks are made 'ugly' in the eyes of the Afikpo on purpose, in the various ways that people can be ugly. The carver did not mention illnesses, and neither does Ottenberg. African art being quite figurative, with a keen eye for detail the carver has used deformed faces from his own village as inspiration for his ugly tops. Suzanne Blier explains the contrast between 'beauty and the beast' as one of an aesthetic contrast that translates onto the stage.[24] They are part of a storyline featuring the young and beautiful as opposed to the old and ugly, or the generous and well-liked as opposed to the greedy and stingy. Stage logic dictates that the latter should be portrayed as ugly, since social qualities should match physical ones. When the association between masks and ancestors is strong, like in the Annang society of southern Nigeria, the ugly masks presentify those ancestors that are malignant, whereas the beautiful masks call to mind good spirits that have made a successful transition from living person into benevolent ancestor. In their *ékpó* performances the first category appeared in dark outfits, dancing towards their left and gesturing with their left hand, while the beautiful ones, clothed and painted in light colours, directed their dancing towards their right-hand side.[25]

This stage logic moves into satire when deformations are considered funny. For instance, the Dogon have a mask called *èmna ojogoro* (goitre mask), featuring a woman with (indeed) a goitre, an abnormal enlargement of the thyroid gland. Dancing with a hoe in its hand, the mask tries to cultivate the earth; but the large swelling under its chin, part of the face cover, prohibits it from bending over, so the 'woman' just cultivates in mid-air.[26] For the

---

22 Many of these stem from the Cross River Region. The Dutchman T. Vossenaar (1989) made a collection of these 'strange' headpieces. As a pathologist he recognises in these masks a series of medical afflictions, such as *gangosa* (Burkitt lymphoma) – with a fascinating story of its discovery – acute nephritis, and a paralysis of the *nervus facialis*. He thought the masks were aimed at warning the public about the wrath of the ancestors, when the former transgressed the ancestral prescriptions. This interpretation tells more about European stereotypes than about the masks, but his identification of the specific illnesses as models for 'uglification' is relevant.

23 Ottenberg 1975: 44–47, 56.

24 Blier 1976; see also Nunley 1977 and 1981.

25 Pratten 2007: 31–32.

26 This mask always depicts a woman.

Dogon, this expression of a common ailment – iodine used to be rare in the area – is always good for a hearty laugh.[27] In the *uale* masquerade of the Guro, where caricatures are standard, a distorted black mask represents a leprosy patient, which is for the Guro just as amusing as goitre is for the Dogon.[28] An ailment can be funny for the spectator if the affliction is not too severe, and leads to comical behaviour.

In the global north, laughing about 'funny illnesses' would be politically incorrect, but this is seen differently in Africa; the sense of humour varies among cultures and historical periods. Amusement, mirth, and indeed laughter are an integral part of the array of emotions that together make up a good mask performance. But, more important, laughter is an existential weapon in the struggle for life on an unforgiving continent. For Africans these masks are a funny way of expressing a character in a play, good for a nice frisson and a gentle laugh in acknowledgement of shared existence in a world beset with mixtures of good and evil, of comfort and threat, of wealth and poverty – all portrayed in the mask by a form of strangeness that all recognise.

Some rare masks may even directly portray all the afflictions human flesh is heir to, such as the *mbangu* mask of the Pende in the Tervuren Museum.[29] Zoë S. Strother describes this mask[30] as a theatrical warning that anyone may fall prey to misfortune, which is unevenly allotted in life.[31] The mask dances to the song 'We look [unable to help], the sorcerers have bewitched him', and it wears a humpback in its costume from which extrudes an arrow, like the invisible arrows sorcerers are reputed to send. Its face evokes the scars of someone who fell into the fire, an eyelid with traces of small pox plus facial nerve paralysis, a composite sign of all eventual mishaps. The Pende interpreted this mask with: 'Do not mock your neighbour. Do not laugh at your brother [...] Anyone may fall prey to misfortune. It could happen to you.'[32]

In mask satire the transcendent and the mundane are inextricably intertwined, with jesting at moments of intensity: 'The gravest things and the most trivial are sometimes so analogous that we cannot tell them apart.'[33] A

27 These days commercial iodinated salt has become common, so the ailment is rare, as is the mask.
28 Fischer 2008: 314.
29 Verswijver et al. 1995: 116 (plate 83). The caption reads: 'Mbangu mask, Central Pende. Bandundu, Zaire.' The description can be found on page 314. The registration number is EO 1959.15.18, entered in 1959.
30 Collected by Emile Torday in 1909.
31 Strother 2008: 27, 28.
32 Strother 2008: 29.
33 Bouttiaux 2009b: 247.

good satire goes both ways, to the other and the self, and these masks are the materialisation of *la condition humaine*, the existential realisation of human inadequacy. In portraying the ridiculous authority or the aberrant other, funny masks embody human frailty, and have the audience not looking at strangers but viewing themselves. As tools of estrangement, as in any good theatre play, masks impose a different view of familiar surroundings, generating another experience of self in a self-conscious audience.[34] Masks are powerful theatre and serious fun, all under the shielding umbrella of the otherworld.

Masquerades and the slaving state

Writing on masks and modernity in Benin, Charles Gore remarks: 'The masquerade remains a vital medium of creativity and performances that offers counter-narratives of modernity, locality and the translocal.'[35] In an important study of *mapiko* masking in Mozambique, Paolo Israel shows how both masking and songwriting for the Makonde population form an adaptive response to the vagaries of their recent political history, scarred as this history is by revolution and civil war. In these performances the local becomes liveable through a running commentary on outside happenings, offering both an emotional refuge and a safe zone of creativity for people whose recent history has been anything but benign.[36] To dance is to live, to sing is to think, and to mask is to communicate all of this safely.

No inequality or historical trauma in Africa has been as dominant as slavery, and no institution has marked Africa's past more than the enslavement, trade, and exploitation of millions of Africans, as well as the death of as many millions in raids, transportation, and hardship. Not only have the centuries of intense slave raiding across the Atlantic traumatised Africa deeply, the even longer history of slave raiding by African empires, many of them Muslim, has left deep scars in the present as well, intensified through the concomitant domestic slaving that fed into these huge extractive markets.

Though colonisation put an end to slavery, the trauma of slavery has not been forgotten, as is shown in an example from West Cameroon, the small mountain realm of Oku. Situated in an inaccessible and forested region around Mount Oku, the realm never opted for predatory expansion, but through an internal meshwork of social and political organisations, focused

34 Strother 2008: 12.
35 Gore 2008a: 6.
36 Israel 2014.

on stability – but a stability with provisos. We noted in Chapter 7 that the king of this Grassfields realm saw his power curtailed by the Kwifon, the central secret society, and vice versa; together they constituted a balanced duo-institution ruling the Oku polity. The king was the pivot of the collective identity, but the Kwifon was the power behind the throne; whenever the many masks danced, they glorified the king, but obeyed the Kwifon.

There is a flipside to this picture of political balancing, since the relationship of this combined ruling elite with the populace appears much less harmonious. Below the surface, a major tension between generations is discernible. Masking tends to be in the hands of the elders: age structuring favours the settled generations, and initiation creates a distance between the newly initiated young and the advanced initiates higher up on the ladder of age-*cum*-revelation. Plus, in the Grassfields full adulthood often depends on positional succession, meaning a man must own specific titles in order to be eligible for death celebrations that promote him to ancestral status; such a pathway is not for everyone, so generates losers in life – men who never attain full masculine adulthood, 'perpetual youth'.[37] So, whatever power balance may be achieved, it is always under siege.

In his restudy of Oku masking, Nicholas Argenti traced these contradictions between the palace and the subjects in palace masquerades. In 1993 a Kwifon member suffered a premature death, making for a highly charged funeral for which a sizeable crowd had gathered. At the palace grounds a dark apparition emerged from the gate, and in one great sprint stormed toward the group of mourners in the far corner of the yard. The barefooted mask was surprisingly quick, and in their panic the mourners scattered into the bushes, with the fierce mask in pursuit. Shaking spears at them, the mask even inflicted cuts and bruises, while the people fled like 'so many chickens before a diving hawk';[38] the metaphor refers to the costume of the mask, a cloth costume set with stiff brown raptor feathers. The headpiece shows a human-like face worn as a crest.

This is *mabuh*, one of the masks of a Kwifon masking group, in an advanced 'hot' state because of the death. Outside the palace yard one cannot look at it, but should quickly hide in the undergrowth at the wayside. In this performance there is no music, though the mask is followed by several acolytes; in other performances, when the mask is feeling 'cool', a musician with a double bell may accompany it.[39]

---

37 Ian Fowler, personal communication.
38 Argenti 2007: 60.
39 Ibid.: 62.

In Chapter 7 we saw how a Bamum mask could only be restrained by breast milk. In Oku a similar mask is called *nkok* and it also appears in the palace yard; again, this mask has no music, its soundscape consisting mainly of the shrieks and shouts of the audience when they flee before its attacks. This formidable mask is clothed in rags and tatters on a rough black gown that covers all but its hands and feet; however, its defining feature is an enormous black headdress 'from which great hanks of black webbing and ragged bedraggled cloths hang recklessly to the ground, dragging through the rainy-season mud like the decomposing flesh of the amphibious otter on its monstrous back'.[40] Two assistants hold ropes to its elbows, while the mask wields its roughly hewn bludgeon with great force; the restraining just underscores its super-wildness. The human element is far away; the dead otter is called 'the child', worn like a mother bears her child on her back – but this child is both amphibious and very dead. So the mask crosses several boundaries at the same time: bush and village, living and dead, palace and populace, the sacred – otters are benign, sacred creatures in Oku – and decay. Restraining it seems not to have been on the ritual agenda.

Argenti describes other instances of mask violence, and wonders why people come to watch such violent spectacles that stage them as victims. As it happens, his informants admire the performance, the sudden rapidity of the mask's movements, its breach of social norms, and its display of raw power, even if they are targeted themselves; a nice shiver makes for good amusement as well, just like watching a horror film, 'laughing nervously and shouting exclamations of almost adulatory disbelief as they run from it'.[41] But there seems to be more to this strangely captive audience at a mask performance. Why all this aggression toward the audience? The *kankurang* mask in Senegal behaved in a similar way, but that was against uninitiated outsiders, while here the aggression is directed at a mandatory audience that is integral to the whole performance.

From the perspective of the local youth Argenti interprets these performances as counter-history, a reaction to the intensive slave raiding and the deep insecurity that two centuries of slaving have generated,[42] his principal argument being that many of the regimes in these fertile hills were complicit in this very trade. First, raiding for slaves was considered a major and normal occupation for kings; and the Bamum kings in their expansionist wars routinely hunted and captured slaves. Second, local kings like the Oku one

40 Ibid.: 66.
41 Argenti 2007.
42 For a recent overview, see Nortey et al. 2021.

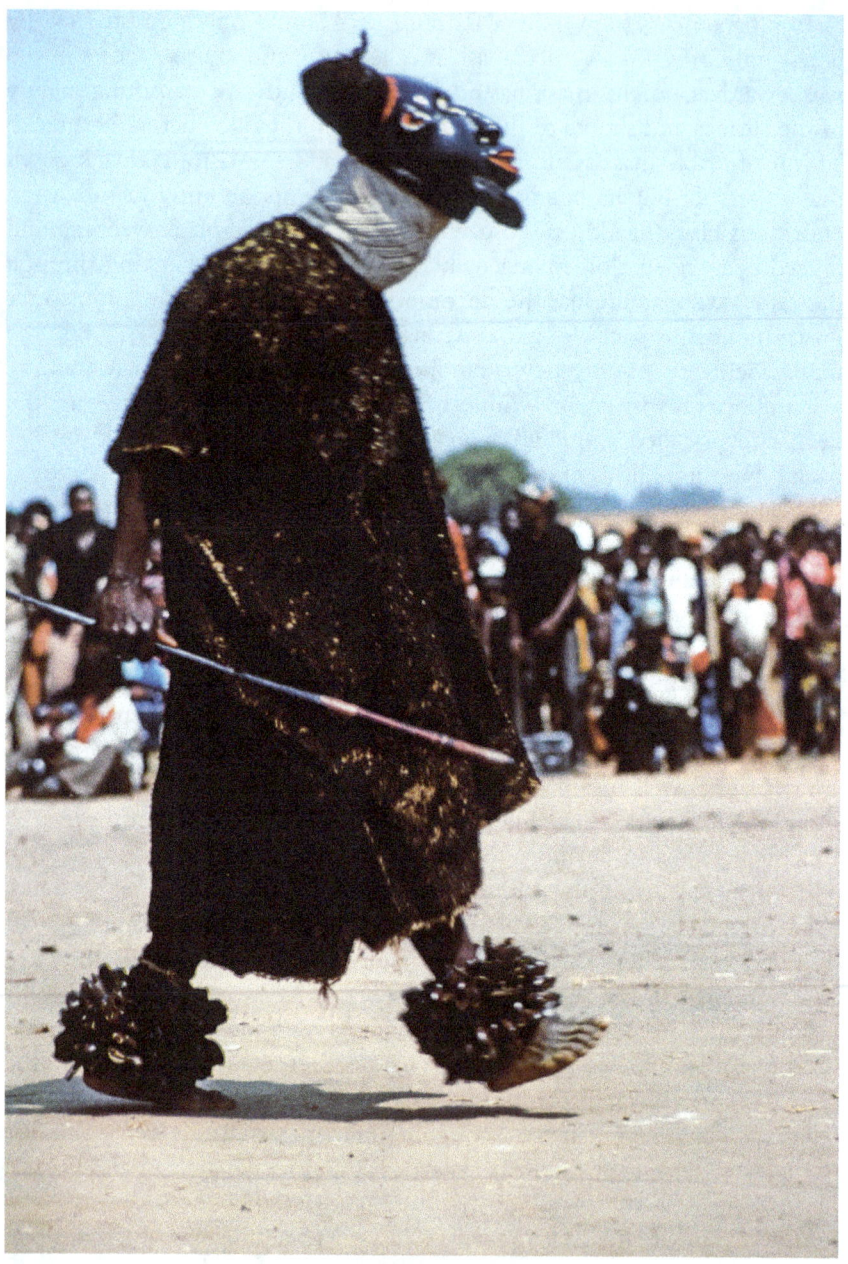

Figure 10.4. Mask of the Oku secret society strutting around the dancing place. Oku, Cameroon, 1977. Photo: Hans Knöpfli.

also sold their own population as slaves, targeting youngsters without power or kin relations to be sold to the traders. The very same palace that portrays itself as the protector of its people and the source of all health and wealth, in the past seduced and betrayed its own young populace in order to gain money for luxury items and weaponry. In Argenti's eyes this duplicity is illustrated in those masquerades storming from the palace, all imbued with threat and danger. These masks are thought to embody a disempowered populace in the hands of the palatial elite, meaning that the mask appearances reflect a cultural memory that is both repressed and denied.[43]

Violence in masquerades is a regular feature in the Grassfields, and in fact is found in all our three Zones. In this case the untimely death triggered aggression and violence, for the more important the death, the stronger the violence that is to be expected. To this day, if a member of any royalty dies somewhere in the Crescent, immigrant labourers leave for home, to return after the succession ceremony. The combination of the king and the Kwifon in the institution of the palace can generate a serious political imbalance between palace and population. In 1979, Elisabeth Tonkin argued that in many cases the opposition between king and secret society at a higher level gives way to a complex and hegemonic political system.[44] Yet we noted in Chapter 7 that mask performances show egalitarian tendencies, so they could be pitted against such a hegemony as well; and indeed they are. Oku is replete with masks, and one crucial masquerade is the village lineage mask dance. This complex performance features cloth masks with carved wooden tops, representing men or animals, and involves both youngsters and women in a series of joyous celebrations. Gender is central here as in so many local mask rituals, but history is never far away either, since some song texts obliquely refer to slavery. So the young generation uses slavery references as a meta-commentary on palace domination. Argenti notes that the palace looks askance on these performances, which means that they are effective, and symbolically form a cathartic answer to power differences.

Thus, not only can masks be players in the power arena, but can themselves be the arena, the symbolic meeting of an inflexible hierarchy with a countervailing force. All this underlines the crucial role mask rituals play in power

---

43 This interpretation has triggered considerable debate: Mentan 2009: 499, Bay 2009: 94, and Fowler 2009: 430. We agree with these critics that explanation by repressed memory, such as Argenti uses, is not the strongest of paradigms, even if it is not to be ruled out. Memory as such, of a less repressed kind, is not unusual in masquerades. For instance, among the Luba of DRC masks refer to dynasties and kings of old, in general to old glory: Nooter and Roberts 1996, Nooter 1992, Vecsey 1983, and O'Reefe 1981.
44 Tonkin 1979: 245.

configurations, either in evening out distinctions or in accentuating and highlighting them, while the polyinterpretability of masking guarantees diverging readings of the same performance. Indeed, a masquerade is not observed from one spot only, as Danfulani (1999) has remarked.

From Africa to the African diaspora

Many people who were shipped to the Americas stemmed from masking groups, and some of these masquerades, against all odds, survived the Middle Passage. In his study on these transnational connections of masks, Raphael Njoku provides a host of examples of other African-derived masquerades in Latin America and the Caribbean;[45] and the tide of cross-Atlantic studies is still coming in. One major message of his book is that despite the historical links and the commonalities in form, the Caribbean masks are not a replica of the Old World; they are transformed. In the New World these masquerades function in the shadow of dominant political and religious systems and have never accrued the power base that characterises them in Africa. That is precisely what traditions do; they adapt to ever new circumstances and provide for new needs. Authenticity, as Njoku rightfully stresses, is a problematic concept anyway: 'Authentic is something adapted from another past.'[46] This very flexibility and adaptability of masking traditions come to the fore in a well-documented case, the link between Nigeria and Cuba.

It starts with a secret society, in this case the *èkpè*. The Cross River Region in Nigeria, its main city the port of Calabar, harbours an ethnically and linguistically fragmented population with as their central socio-political institution the *èkpè* power association; they have hardly any other kind of political power.[47] This male power association can be found over a wide circle of ethnic groups, providing both the administration of justice inside the villages and the major link between villages and linguistic groups. Miller and Ojong claim that this system of village-based lodges developed right inside this Cross River Region and then spread out over the larger forest area, up to southern Cameroon.[48]

The *èkpè* society conferred citizenship inside the village, had the power of meting out disciplinary punishment for antisocial behaviour, provided entertainment through feasts, and served as an initiation platform. As is

45 Njoku 2020. See also Ogundiran 2014.
46 Njoku 2020: 189. See the debate on authenticity triggered by Strother 2012.
47 See Afigbo 1987 on the dominant role of these societies in the nineteenth century.
48 Miller and Ojong 2012: 267. See for a general overview Miller et al. 2017.

usual in secret societies, the system sported a series of initiation grades with titles, nine grades in all and each with three tiers, thus making for twenty-seven different titles one could attain; in a culture without wealth, titles are the things to strive for, to be earned by organising feasts with handouts. Masks, the dearest child of the secret society, abounded: each grade and tier had its own masquerade. The various *ékpè* masks were first and foremost considered to be emissaries of the *ékpè* lodges themselves, combining the power of the bush with the bonds of secrecy. The mask itself looked indeed like a ferocious animal, and with its all-cloth costume and characteristic large breast part, it was often equated with a lion; yet the name *ékpè* means leopard, the general African symbol of power and chieftaincy. The *ékpè* mask has been studied by the Efik themselves in some detail. 'Engineer' Bassey, one of the initiates who wrote extensively on *ékpè*,[49] expressed the emic viewpoint on what constitutes a mask: the costume, including the dancing paraphernalia, is central, and the association with any specific animal referent is secondary to the fact that a mask is, above all, a mask. Masks are be-things who are themselves.

Secret societies are prime instruments for political and social resistance, and the victims of the Middle Passage reinstalled *ékpè*-like lodges in Cuba some time in the 1830s, serving as a mutual aid society to cope with the hardships of slavery. They too produced masks, even if the Roman Catholic Cuban society was against them, calling them *diablitos* (little devils).[50] These lodges are well documented now[51] and found their inspiration in one specific African *ékpè* mask, the *ebongo*, characterised by a high conical headpiece, a rather unusual feature in mask tops. The Cubans made a similar headpiece, in a process of gradual reinvention of a home culture that they still remembered after the trauma of slavery.

For some time the notion of an African legacy had fallen out of fashion in anthropology. Many Caribbeanist scholars viewed links across the Atlantic with some misgivings, since for them the 'black cultures' of these descendants of slaves, even the Maroon cultures stemming from runaway slaves, represented new cultural creations generated by the particular history of the area rather than by their roots in West Africa. But recently ever more surprising and detailed instances of cross-oceanic cultural inheritance have popped up, and in the Cuban–Calabar mask connection we have a strong, well-evidenced case of such a deep long-distance connection.

49   And a major informant of Ivor Miller.
50   Miller 2005: 193.
51   Miller 2011.

The Cuban societies and their masks are called Abakuá, and the linguistic link across the ocean was easily found, since a branch of Ejagham speakers, one of the many groups in the Calabar region, is known as Abakpa. The Cuban mask in Figure 10.5 is remarkably like masks belonging to a functioning *ékpè* initiation grade in Calabar. The mask, called *ebongo*, according to *ékpè* elders refers to a state of spiritual transcendence, but with a definite feminine slant, since '*Ebongo* represents the universal mother who makes initiated reborn as *eyeneka*, children of the same mother, a term used both in Calabar and Cuba'.[52] This similarity is just one in a long list of striking cultural and linguistic parallels, especially convincing in its minute details and specific names.

These transatlantic links were easily recognised by participants from both sides of the Middle Passage, the Nigerians and the Cubans, underscoring the connections found by scholars. In a rare series of cross-Atlantic encounters, the two cultures of Cuba and Calabar met through the mediation of the anthropologist Ivor Miller. For the first time ever, in 2001 in Calabar, masks from across the ocean met: the Efik of Nigeria and the Abakuá of Cuba.[53] A series of further encounters followed in Michigan (2003), Calabar (2004), and Paris (2007). These meetings were for a large part brokered by the sizeable Calabar community in the United States, and the most recent meeting between Cuban Abakuá and its 'home country' in the form of this expatriate community was on 29 July 2019 in Boston. Miller describes these meetings as immensely joyful, 'electric', and with an immediate mutual recognition of both kinship and tradition, shown in splendid galas of shared culture.[54]

Of course, many things have changed since the infamous era of the Middle Passage, also in Nigeria. The *ékpè* as a secret society still exists, but its function has shifted in modern southeastern Nigeria; though it is still important at the local village level and still admits new initiates to its ranks, it no longer admin-isters justice or serves as a *de facto* government. Contrary to the Senegalese case of the last chapter, there seems to be little confrontation between the masking society and these Nigerian states, let alone the Federal State of Nigeria, and the masquerade has evolved into a public spectacle.

Calabar was no stranger to the slave trade; in fact, it was a major slave hub in the eighteenth and nineteenth centuries, and for many of the captives

---

[52] Miller 2011: 197. For a more general view of the Cuba–Calabar relationship, see Miller 2016.

[53] Miller 2011. Sponsored by the Efik National Association at the Pratt Institute, Brooklyn, NY.

[54] See http://www.afrocubaweb.com/efik.htm, consulted 7 August 2019.

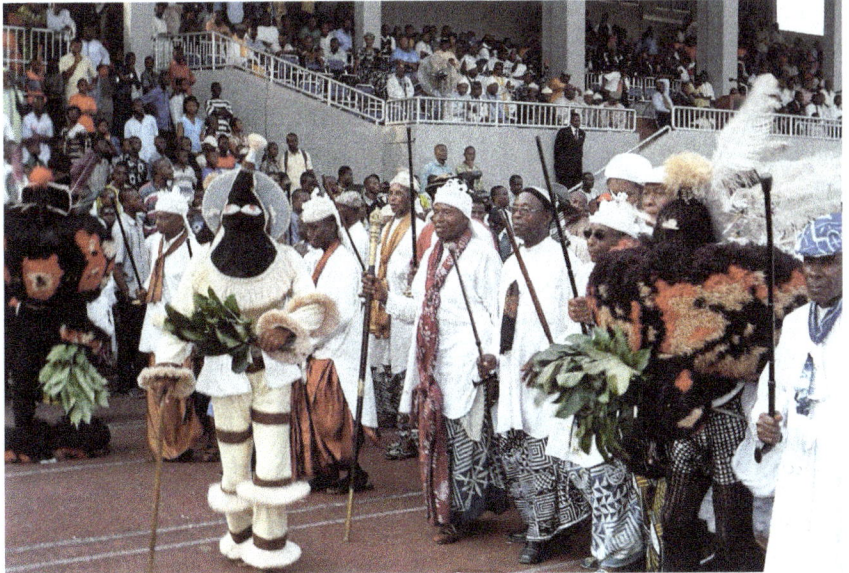

Figure 10.5. The Cuban mask in front, the Nigerian masks at the sides. Calabar, Nigeria, 2004. Photo: Ivor Miller.

from Oku, the port of Calabar must have been their last view of Africa. The slave trade was a huge and complex process. The coastal groups were deeply implicated in this whole machinery of extraction, and so were the elites of the hinterland; the constant demand for humans transformed these slaving coasts into a series of war zones reaching deep into the African interior, with African slave hunters, slave holders, slave merchants, and corridors of slave transport.[55]

All of this was highly profitable, with raiders and traders growing rich, and city populations growing accustomed to European luxury items. Through the import of European weapons, local rulers became potentates themselves, and thus the slave trade profoundly shaped these parts of Africa. The masks became icons of wealth; the earliest pictures of *ékpè* masks have less elaborate breast parts than Figure 10.6, for instance, where a show of riches has become essential. Consequently, the masks turned into items of conspicuous ownership and display, growing breast parts of almost unmanageable proportions, showing off huge wealth and ponderous power in the city parades. In Africa in general and certainly in Nigeria, wealth must be seen and one's possessions must be on display. Nigerian culture values visible wealth as good and, by definition,

55 Lovejoy 2012.

beautiful – as in the *ijebi* masquerade – and it considers exuberance to be excellence. So the urban masks morphed into symbols of fortune.

These festive occasions in New York, Michigan, Calabar, and Paris had several levels of meaning, and were more than just a parent culture that embraced its emigrant child, for the irony of history intervened. Their present form and substance both derive from the slave trade, but from opposite sides of the same coin, and festive though it surely was, in the encounter the progeny of former slave traders met the descendants of former slaves.

That might well have been awkward, but for two reasons. Cuban participants may never have realised that there were descendants of enslavers present; for most it was mainly a homecoming, a feast of mutual cultural recognition. The second reason, however, is a little more cynical. The Calabari elite received the Cubans in Nigeria, and at these meetings the Efik and the Cuban Abakuá got along famously, because the Efik were amazed how well the Cubans knew their culture, a joyful 'reunion' since their legacy was alive overseas. However, when Ivor Miller tried to inspire a Calabar return visit to Cuba, that never took place. Why? The response of the ninety-year-old *ékpè* expert, Bassey,[56] was that the elite Efik still considered the Cubans to be slaves, and 'why would they want to see slaves?' Miller remarks: 'That is a harsh reality about the elite political class in Calabar, who would rather go shopping in Dubai, London or New York!'[57] In fact, the meetings outside Africa featured only people from the Calabar region who had already emigrated – that is, the expats; no Nigerians travelled for these encounters.

Nonetheless, when Africans realise that the present population descends from both perpetrators and victims – like for instance in northern Cameroon, where this slaving history is more recent and where descendants of both parties live together – they seem to manage this awkward part of history with some ease and grace.[58] One way is to joke about it, in the many joking relationships that the continent harbours; people call each other 'my slave' and 'my slaver' and have a good laugh; or they both call each other 'slave'. When properly responded to, even slaving history can be an enrichment of the social encounter.

---

56   The author of Bassey 1998/2001.

57   Ivor Miller, personal communication. The leaves in Figure 10.6 are of *Newbouldia laevis*, used throughout the region in rituals. We thank Ivor Miller for the photo and the information.

58   The study of José van Santen shows well how, in the process of islamisation in the Mandara Mountains, informants take this aspect of their history in their stride: Van Santen 1993.

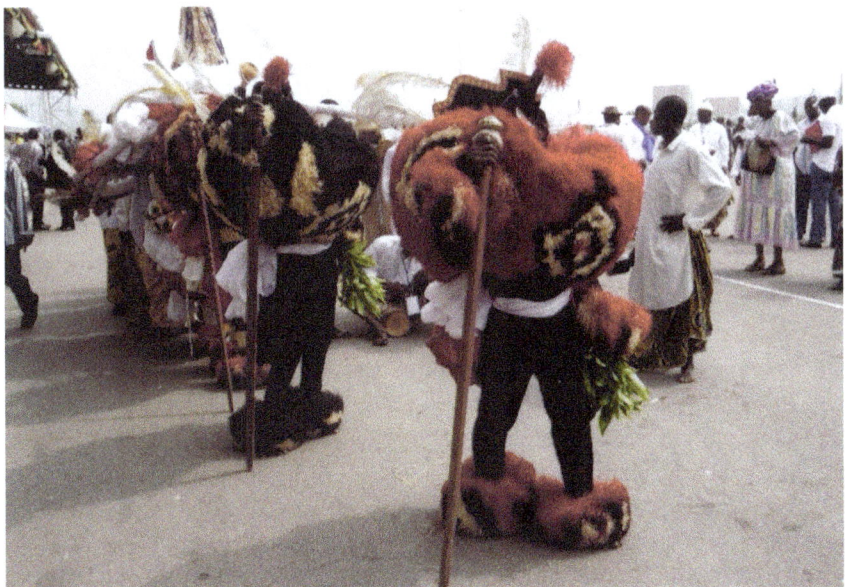

Figure 10.6. *Ékpè* masks on parade. Note the bundle of leaves in their left hand. Calabar, Nigeria, 2004. Photo: Ivor Miller.

Anyway, the Cuban case clearly shows the tenacity of that old masculine ruse of organised secrecy, of the binding force inherent in a secret society either as a power house or as a counter-society against an oppressive system. In the face of domination, mask rituals are a prime instrument for cultural survival; bonding in secret and then flaunting the existence of that very secrecy in public shows, one can regain the personal and group agency needed for a meaningful life. Rituals can fight back, and mask rituals do so effectively.

Conclusion

Northwest Cameroon is one of the core cultural areas in masking, and crucial to this book. Its rich green hills with fertile volcanic soils have long been inhabited,[59] resulting in the old cultural landscape of the Grassfields, the habitat of, among others, the Bamenda, Bamum, Bamileke, Tikar, Bafut, Kom, Bali, Nso', and Oku. The large population shows very diverse forms

---

59 Warnier 2011, Hurault 1962, Kafko Fokou 2014.

of political organisation, ranging from acephalous societies to sacred kings.[60] These polities consist of elaborate patrilineal or matrilineal systems, with secret societies of all kinds and flavours, including some female ones, as well as systems of sacred kingship in all possible varieties. In the course of history this became the area of the Fons, sacred kings with a retinue of intricate palace organisations, supplemented – or thwarted – by secret societies. Most of these polities are small – Bamum is an exception – and quite a few are fragmented, but all are complex, and show competing power systems enmeshed with each other. Their expressive material culture has become famous in studies on African art – with masks as an important element of the local craft production. The level of ethnographic reporting is high, since the area has been a core research area for British social anthropology since its inception, while Cameroon's colonial history also brought French and German scholars to the area.

Our masking profile focuses on local communities, while the ethnographic emphasis in the Grassfields is on the palace cultures, as elaborate constructions around sacred rulers. Yet in many ways these realms are local communities writ large, with similar arenas of gender and power. Women in the Grassfields are supremely important in providing for the family, as elaborated upon in Chapter 1, and some classic studies have been instrumental in mapping this gender arena. But it is the power arena that stands out: the dynamics between secret-societies-with-masks, and the Fon-without-masks, reverberate through all descriptions.

Slavery was a major theme in the Grasslands, but even more so at the Calabar coast in the southeast of Nigeria. Tied into secret societies, masks became a major outlet for politics-*cum*-wealth on the coast, showing that the other end of the enslavement chain, the perpetrators of the trade, could be conducive to masking as well. The city of Calabar – as distinct from the Kalabari – is a case in point, with its local masquerades as showcases for wealth. Masking responds to the power arena irrespective of the forces inside it.

60 Fowler 2011: 292. See also Fowler and Fanso 2009.

11

Conclusion

The cultural niche for masquerades

A long book needs a short conclusion. Reviewing the dynamics of the masquerades in the various fields and overviewing the concluding sections in each chapter, we come back to the first part of our theory test: what is the socio-cultural niche for masking?

The answer resides in a network of related factors. The population density should be above a certain threshold, because the cultures housing mask rituals must have a socio-ecological basis with a certain permanence, not continuously moving, and of sufficient complexity. People have a definite pronatal attitude, children are welcome.[1] In the horticultural system, root crops have an important place, and women shoulder a large responsibility for food production, a crucial role in subsistence that offers them a strong social position relative to men. This position is reinforced through lasting bonds with their kinsmen, while society also tends to matrilineal kinship reckoning and has a high local endogamy; bride wealth is relatively low. In these societies men do not form strong corporate groups, have little inheritable wealth, and must negotiate for their socio-political positions. Kinship lines are shallow and tend to be limited to the village. Cattle are absent – at least the cattle complex is not there – and the same holds largely for camels and horses.

Thus, the position of the men is to a high degree defined by what they do not have – wealth, power, and authority over women – while the women's position is painted in what they do have – fertility, production, and family. The male power base is one of indeterminacy, open to constant debate and negotiation, while the female power base is solidly inside the domestic unit, plus in her body. In the economy labour forms the main capital, one reason for the desire for children, which fits in with the horticultural food production. That, in short, is the common element inside

---

1   For a thorough analysis on this phenomenon, see Brand 2004.

the Mask Crescent, and when overviewing profiles the societies housing masquerades are shown to comply with this profile, even with the leeway that can be expected from a probabilistic theory. So we can conclude that this gender-*cum*-power factor is the first step in the explanation for the highly peculiar distribution of masquerades on the continent.

The second phase of explanation concerns how masquerades address these two basic arenas. The mask rituals as discussed in this book form a balancing mechanism in the hands of men, becoming their ritual tool to address quandaries of the social formation. The underlying worldview is that power is considered to stem from the bush, a major theme in masking: masks form an independent power base that originates in the wilderness and is founded on the fusion between man and bush. Presentifying more than representing, the masks are first and foremost regarded as a category in themselves; and second, they relate to spirits of the bush, the ancestors, or stereotypes in village life.

Masquerades as a power factor depend on performance: the power of the bush is on show, and the staging of the masks for their targeted audience forms the main dynamic of the ritual. All over the Mask Crescent mask performances are quite recognisable – in fact, variations on a limited number of themes: the grand entrance, dance, assistants, music, audience separation between initiates and non-initiates, with speech as a rare element; the reasons for the performances vary more than the elements of their staging. By their very nature, masquerades are fleeting, calling up an evanescent world that is ephemeral, and in principle so are the masks themselves, both the costumes and often also the tops, even if carved. What these performances stage is power, so the masked performance of power generates the power of the performance, an impact enhanced by aesthetic appreciation. Life needs high points, and mask rituals are incomparable at providing them.

Masks feature in rituals, but in specific rituals only, a limitation that is highly relevant for our theoretical stance: masks are important to initiation in its many forms, death rites, and displays of power, and are in principle absent in other types of rituals.

Initiations featuring masks follow a distinct pattern in which the mask revelation forms the core element of the liturgy, and in this way, masks give content and substance to a rite of passage that provides a clear demarcation line between boyhood and adulthood. Since masks are male tools in the local gender and power arena, they are important instruments in the construction of masculinity. Often it is the encounter with the mask itself that marks the border with adulthood, defining masculinity as familiarisation with the thoroughly unfamiliar, the spirit side of the bush, thus constructing a polarity between those in the know and the ignorant – a division based upon a presumed difference in knowledge that in fact hardly exists. This is more than just a charade played by all participants, since in the performance of the public secret the reality and even materiality of the otherworld become both evident and convincing. The mundane and the arcane merge in an experience of otherworldly power, mediated through an orchestrated mutual secrecy.

A second major border between boy and man is circumcision, a continent-wide marker for coming of age. Circumcision leads to a definite rhythm inside the initiation camps and thus to a time period that must be filled for initiates. Although the term bush school is often used, learning is primarily experiential, with the initiands drilled on secret keeping and linguistic proficiency, sometimes including an initiation language. For the construction of the male power base in masks, the creation of the secret as a virtual field of knowledge is essential, a field that on closer inspection shows up empty. Both signposts of manhood, masks and circumcision, occur independently of each other, but where they interact, they tend to mitigate each other. Among the four models for masculinity that we identified, the twin signs of masks and circumcision allow for an antagonistic definition of masculinity in opposition to femininity, modelled not on marriage but on wildness, not on gender complementarity but on overbearing male power.

The power base constructed by masks is a high-profile one, demanding a high investment from the men. Mask rituals stimulate internal male organisation, and easily lead to – or result from – mask-oriented organisations such as secret societies. It is in these power associations that the notion of initiation, and thus of masks as proponents of male power, comes into full force, ritualised as a series of subsequent initiations. However, it is mainly in the lower echelons of these initiations that masks are important, since their revelatory moment cannot be repeated indefinitely. All in all, the first initiation of a boy into a secret society is remarkably like one without such a power association, save that he enters a structured male world which is inaccessible to females; also, the mask tops play a larger role as objects of power, more central in the cults.

The more secret they are, the more masks seem to morph into sound, becoming just an acoustic presence, highlighting the difference between the initiates and non-initiates, and thus between genders. The institutionalisation of secrecy guarantees that the occasional mask events become permanent, since in the minds of all parties these happenings are continuously evoked in the strongly regulated discourse between the initiated and non-initiated: masks come and go, the discourse of secrecy remains. With their stronghold in masked performances, secret societies form the main support of the male social position in these societies; in some cases, they form the political structure itself, not as a countervailing force but as the power house proper. When masks really organise, they take over society. But in that case women may well do the same and form their own associations, so the challenge of balancing power remains on the table.

Initiation is such a core action for masks that they pursue it into death, but masquerades perform different functions in the three phases of farewell. In the first phase they accompany the deceased on his second initiatory journey, using much of the symbolism of initiation in order to redefine him as a person of the bush. Such a repeated initiation means that the masks take the deceased into that part of the otherworld that is situated around the daily world, not above or below it; the deceased becomes bush, not heaven. The masks' engagement with the corpse stipulates that the deceased no longer belongs to the family, but has become the property of the village or secret society, in order to be dispatched to the otherworld where it henceforth belongs. The second phase, the waiting and mourning time, is not for masks, but in the final phase of the second funeral they come out in full force and glory. Their performance terminates the material memorabilia of the deceased and revitalises the village in a display of male creative power. For the duration of these mask rituals, male (pro)creation dominates over the female variant. Thus, second funeral masquerades ritually overshadow female human creation, and virtual fertility tops biological fertility, at least for a fleeting, liminal, but magnificent moment. When the imported religions enter the scene, ancestors may come to the fore, another male force balancing female fertility.

Masks hinge on women, the chapter on women is right in the middle of the book. Their distance from masking is evident, and so is their complicity in keeping the public secret from being exposed. Masks seemingly oppose them, but dance for them and exist thanks to them. Gender forms the pivot of our masking theory, and the relationship of women with masks is much more complex than the simplistic notion that masks just scare or dominate them. Masquerades form a constructed tool for balancing male and female power, but the male supremacy that mask rituals seem to emanate, ultimately goes only as far as the women will allow. Secrecy, ritual domination, male ascendancy, and power associations form the clubbing characteristics of the male of the species, but the basic power – the real mask, so to speak – resides in the bodies of the women; in the final analysis the men are hemmed in by their absolute need for progeny. In one part of the Mask Crescent women organise themselves into parallel associations and have taken masking into their own hands, with the full support of their husbands. But in a much wider swath of the Crescent, when men cross the line, women call them back with symbolic actions that cannot be misunderstood. The fact that the ultimate mask stemmed from a woman, as stated in many origin myths of masks, points to such a solid biological basis: she finds the mask because her body is the mask.

It is not just power between the genders that is negotiable, so is power between men. As an independent power base mask rituals can work in several ways, either underscoring the power structure or forming a counter-vailing force. Masks can highlight male kinship reckoning at the grass roots level, and masquerades can be a tool to shift descent reckoning at societal level. Also, a strong ruler can encapsulate mask rituals and appropriate their organising capacity into his own reign, using them as an additional legiti-mation of his realm. When mask and king become one and the same, this results in a theatre state where masquerades form the visual highpoint of kingly powers. But a more general trend is for mask rituals to be anti-hegemonic, since their link with secret societies is very strong and these are not easy to control for a monarch. The ritual power of masks may well conflict with the power of ritual kingship, and thus mask rituals feed into the old anthropological debate on regicide; chances are that the two powers, that of masks and of sacred kingship, will be in competition with each other.

From here the power base of masks branches out into various applica-tions of power, all concerned with maintaining the status quo. Masks seem to be inherently conservative, not only balancing various powers but also reinforcing the desired situation – occasionally in agriculture, sometimes in administering justice, but generally in guarding against the presumed ravages of witchcraft. Rituals are not ethical per se, but mask rituals are very ethical; they are expressly pro-community, pro-order, and anti-witch. Policing is a task that comes easily to them, though this is always a guarded action, even when keeping order is a central focus for mask actions. *Quis custodiet ipsos custodes?* – the old Roman wisdom holds well: 'Who guards the guardians?' – and the masks serve well as instruments of social control in the hands of elders or secret societies, who as the guardians' guardians can thus remain anonymous, or at least inconspicuous; but controlling the masks themselves is a continuous challenge. Masks transpersonalise the juridical procedure, and bolster a weak social authority by adding otherworldly authority to their verdicts. The masks' antithetical relation with presumed witchcraft highlights this process; as the very opposite of 'the witch', the mask combats its virtual antipode simply by being there, by roaming, by loud noises, and by showing off, thus overwhelming the covert, silent evil with the boisterous spectacle of dancing ethics; at least for a time.

Our theory situates mask rituals primarily inside their local settings, relating the performances to the social realities on the ground. The dynamics of gender division and power indeterminacy find their prime playing fields at the grass roots level, and the model seems to work well at that level. But how do masks fare at higher echelons? All over the world, rituals are used for political aims, to establish and construct identity or simply for entertainment, and mask performances are eminently suited for these purposes. The series of brushes with modernity in which the theatricalisation of masks went from coping with everyday danger through the confrontation youth versus elders to a tourist attraction, showed that mask performances are very adaptable, and easily move into new fields of action. The greater the cultural distance between performers and audience, the more the masks distance themselves from their ritual context and from the societal dilemmas they embody. But even if the dynamics of identity construction and iconisation take over, the masks do not completely shed their gendered nature, nor their relation with wildness; the attribution of external power does remain their forte. Even if they gradually morph into icons for identity at various societal levels as well as into signs for cultural difference, they remain based upon a local masking culture. As past-in-the-present masquerades can become a major source of national inspiration for the heritage movement, but only when solidly rooted in a prototypical past.

A larger political framework also indicates a longer time frame, for mask performances increasingly link cultures over time and space. Their relation with the larger dynamics such as state formation and the deep history of slavery in Africa, is ambivalent. On one side mask performances have an inherent democratic value, anti-hegemonic as an alternative power base that is managed at the grass roots. One mechanism for this is the use of humour and satire as levelling mechanisms, which are solidly founded in the masks' precious anonymity. But on the other side masks can presentify historical inequalities; either way, mask performances carry deep memories. Especially when combined with their twin organisation, the secret society, masks and their songs survived even the Middle Passage surprisingly well.

All in all, we think that with this eco-sociological approach to masquerades we have solved in the first place some puzzles – that of their presence as well as that of their absence – and in the second place identified the social and symbolic mechanisms through which the African masquerades address the

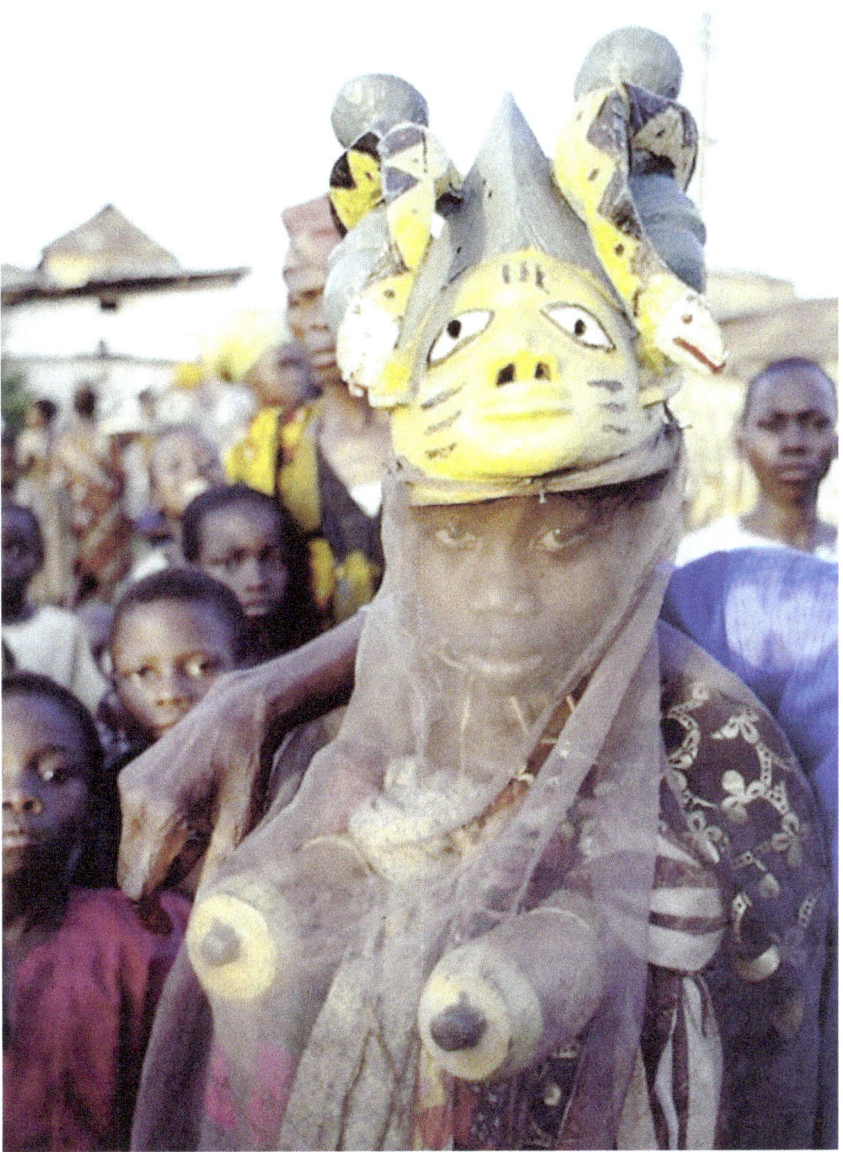

Figure 11.1. *Gelede*, a young one, and no question about gender. Ilaro town, Egbado area, Yoruba, Nigeria, 1977. Photo: Margaret Thomson Drewal.

contradictions inherent in the social formations from which they stem.[2] This great tradition of masking appears to founded on specific configurations of the African way of life, rooted in both its ecology and its turbulent history.

A future for masks?

Is there a future for masks in Africa? In order to answer this question it might be helpful to take a glimpse at their past as well: How long have mask rituals been around in the continent?[3] Obviously the answers to both questions are speculative, but based on the sources and our masking theory we will formulate some informed guesses.

Historical sources scarcely mention masking in Africa; Ibn Batuta's account is by far the earliest one. Apart from his report, there is little inside information on Africa before the arrival of the European slave traders on the coast, and the formation of Muslim realms in the Sahel, towards the end of the fifteenth century. Other early European and Islamic contacts hardly ever mention masks, contacts that increasingly turned to slave trading, which is not very conducive to empathetic understanding or intercultural exchange. Probably the earliest report of a secret society is by Alvaes d'Almada from 1594, while Olfert Dapper (1668) mentions the *poro* society as 'Belli-Paaro'.[4]

The headpieces themselves hardly ever precede the eighteenth century. In Bassani's book on pre-1800 European collections, only one mask top is provided: a horned headpiece that probably stems from the Casamance (1751–1800).[5] In 1996 a *sande* mask was put up for auction in Paris, allegedly collected in 1786.[6] The National Museum in Mali houses a terracotta face mask, but without clear provenance and with diverging thermoluminescence dates,[7] and this seems to be a death mask rather than a dancing one. All other headpieces in collections are from the eighteenth century and after.

---

2   Note for instance internal contradictions as a constant in Gore 2008b.

3   Here we omit shamanic masking, as hinted at in rock paintings (e.g. Samorini (1992)), as well as the death masks of Egyptian pharaohs.

4   Van de Raadt 2023: 62.

5   Fayolle collection, Musée de l'Homme, no 34.33.38, Bassani 2000: 282. The author compares this with a drawing in Froger 1698: 42. We thank Rogier Bedaux for this information.

6   Van de Raadt 2023: 62.

7   Sidibé et al. 2006: 27. But the general dates of these Djenné-Djenno terracottas, around the 14th century, do coincide with the Ibn Batuta story. See for this mask the film 'The African King', by Nigel Evans.

Archaeologically the continent is still under-researched, and especially in the wetter parts – our three zones – the ecology tends to erase most marks of history, and rituals leave few traces. Masquerades are ephemeral to begin with, even the carved headpieces, while the oldest forms of masks are just bush: fibres and leaves. Also, data on historical demography, on the impact of new food crops and new diseases, on the historical development of cattle husbandry, and on historical settlement patterns – all of these are relatively scarce.

Oral history is largely silent on masks. The long epical tales such as the Sunjata epic, do not mention them explicitly,[8] while historic song cycles only mention them in passing, such as the Dogon *baja ni*.[9] On the other hand, local traditions are full of myths on the masks' provenance. Myth is not history, but apart from the female presence one other element stands out in these origin myths on masking. Africa is a continent of migrations, and most peoples have tales about their provenance from elsewhere – yet most masking myths have the masks appear after their own group has settled in their present habitat. Viewing the close link between masks and bush this makes perfect symbolic sense, and myths can easily be adapted; but whenever specific places of origin are indicated, they tend to be close at hand.[10] Masks come from around the corner – meaning, from the bush that belongs to the village – and are not relegated to any far-off place the group stems from. Although myths are, like rituals, 'instruments to erase time'[11] making any historical interpretation tricky, the order of arrival – group first, masks later – is a dominant pattern and thus might serve as an indication for a limited timeframe of masking. The historical depth of masks in the three Zones probably differs, but for the whole of masking it seems clear that masks may have been around for a long time on the continent, but definitely not for ever: there must have been a long era without masks in Africa.

According to our analysis mask rituals depend on a specific village-based social configuration within definite ecological parameters, so masking probably started when this kind of village life came into being. The Congo Basin gap indicates that demography is a crucial factor: human population density needs to be sufficiently high for the kind of villages that generate masking traditions to develop; the Vansina rule of four people per square kilometre comes to mind here, as a minimum requirement for any form of

8   Jansen 1995, 2018b.
9   Van Beek, Ongoiba and Saye 2022.
10   For instance, the Dogon trace themselves from Mande, but their masks from a mountain in their present habitat, after their arrival at the cliffside.
11   'Machines à effacer le temps', Lévi-Strauss 1979.

sedentarisation and political centralisation. It is beyond our scope to trace the pathways of this 'villageisation' in Africa, which will differ for the various regions of the continent, but in all probability these conditions arose during the second millennium CE, first in Zones 1 and 2 and later in Zone 3.

Descent has been shown to be a crucial factor. However, the various ways of tracing descent not only coexist side by side and are interchangeable, but also have been invented and reinvented repeatedly; for matrilineality in Zone 3 this has been amply demonstrated.[12] Also, as we have shown, they morph into one another. Some ideas seem to be within easy grasp; descent is one, but masking, as the old trick of mankind, is another such idea. Map 1 could easily be read as a distribution history from at least three points of origin, while it is almost impossible to derive a monogenetic hypothesis from it. Masks probably originated independently in various parts of the Crescent, so we expect masking to have emerged independently in the three zones, and at different times. The whole complex of secrecy and initiation, together with gendered masking, seems a logical gravitation point for rituals in the village cultures we have sketched, so with masks this complex probably came into being as a coherent whole.[13]

The role of women in subsistence was always high throughout Africa's prehistory, but their position was probably strengthened by the intensified root crop cultivation that followed the influx of the American cultivars, such as cassava and sweet potatoes, brought to Africa by European slavers in the sixteenth century. Especially cassava, the more important of the two, has a long growing cycle, since its cultivation takes over a year[14] and demands a rather stable location; it is a typical village crop. Cultivated by women who have accrued enough expertise to deal with the plant's toxic qualities, this crop underwrites the gender division of our masking model.[15] For instance, the importance of cassava shows in a Kuba oral tradition that relates how the founder of the reigning dynasty journeyed to the Atlantic coast, where he became familiar with such new cultivars; he then introduced cassava into his kingdom, so the start of the Kuba kingdom coincides with the Columbian exchange.

---

[12] Vansina notes that matrilineality has been invented multiple times in Equatorial Africa (1990: 152).

[13] This is in line with the way spectacular and infrequent rituals tend to cluster in religions based on imagistic religiosity, Whitehouse 2004. Mask rituals, as argued, form a major example of this religious phenomenon.

[14] See https://www.thespruce.com/growing-cassava-plants-5087849, consulted 7 March 2022.

[15] We thank Ton Dietz for drawing attention to this fact.

From the seventeenth century onward, outside influences must have favoured the rise of masking rituals. The slave trade itself increased during the seventeenth and eighteenth centuries, at the apogee of the Atlantic triangle. The continuous pressure on these societies in the hinterland of the slavers did much to produce and reproduce exactly those social and ecological conditions that are conducive to masking rituals. With the nineteenth century intrusion of the colonising forces, the incentives for masking may initially have increased, both because of the physical encounter with these European strangers, and because of Africans' loss of agency over their own societies. So it was probably during the early days of colonialism that masking found its most exuberant expression, with the secret societies blossoming both as a reaction to foreign hegemony and as filling in a political vacuum, thus providing a hothouse for masks.

The Abrahamic religions came in waves: from the eighth century onward Islam advanced in Zone 1, and may have triggered the earliest forms of masquerades at the start of the second millennium. Christianity has an ancient presence in the Horn of Africa but gained influence in most of the continent, at least in the Crescent, only with the advent of the coloniser. Overall, the encounter with Islam did not directly affect masking cultures – the Mali example is telling in this respect – but zebu, horse, and Islam did move together. In West Africa this led to a clear division between Muslim pastoralists and the cultivators they encountered, which in fact stimulated defensive village formation, and therefore masking, among the latter. In East Africa cattle husbandry has never been dominated by one ethnic group, but pastoralism as such cut through the eastern side of the matrilineal belt and must have transformed local masking cultures into societies based upon mixed cattle husbandry – and thus into maskless cultures. The isolated masking societies in Zone 3 are probably what is left from a much larger array of masking cultures in those regions less accessible to the zebu, remnants of masking traditions relying on the staying power of secret societies.

The post-colonies have seen a general reduction in masking; reports abound on masking traditions that have floundered, are on the verge of disappearance or have disappeared completely. One major reason for this are the socio-economic changes brought about by the intrusion of a cash economy, seasonal labour migration and urbanisation. Life is always changing in Africa. The structures responsible for masking, such as the combination of lineages and age-sets, became less relevant, and gender arrangements shifted. Also, in many societies in the Crescent ongoing Christianisation has reduced masking, especially with the rise of the more evangelical churches. The main mechanism for such a disappearance is the halting of boys' initiation ceremonies; whenever this age-old tradition is deleted from the cultural agenda, masking does not really survive. The same holds for societies in the sphere of Islam; the recent rise of radical Islam forms a major threat for masking. These trends are not new, and it has been noted before that cultures on the border of Islam tend to reduce the flamboyancy of their cultural expressions.[16]

Masking thus belongs to a specific episode in African history, with a long gradual build-up from early in the second millennium – at least in Zone 1 – towards a culmination during a rather recent period, the eighteenth and nineteenth centuries. However, its final days might well be shorter: the future for traditional masking looks rather bleak. It is difficult to imagine that ongoing modernisation, urbanisation, and the continuing march of the Abrahamic religions will not reduce this expression of African culture. The local village basis for masking is eroding; indigenous religions are being phased out, secret societies must vie with the modern state, and more and more initiation rituals with masks are disappearing, while the population continues to move toward the cities.

Nevertheless, history tells us of flexible and adaptive masking traditions that translate their masking past well into a viable present. In all these local histories the interplay among European intervention, local political dynamics, and regional events merge into the invention of new masking types, changes in genre, or the formation of a new power association with the masks. As Jan Vansina notes, 'art cannot be understood at all without history',[17] which surely holds true for masking. However, history does not end in the present, and one should never underestimate African creativity.

As Chapters 9 and 10 argue, masquerades find new fertile grounds, and masks may well thrive in four diverging fields. One is political: in cities, boys' masquerades pop up as part of a developing youth culture,[18] political figures appropriate masks for their own goals, and resistance movements rely on the equalising power that masks still possess. Contestation comes easy to masks, but also comes with a risk, when masquerades are equated with only one part of a political see-saw.

Second, the developing theatre world in many African countries has already embraced the legacy of masking, and masquerades form the high point of many performances and festivals, an arts scene that is expected to grow.[19] For a range of cultural expressions, organising public festivals appear

---

16 Imperato 1980: 83.
17 Vansina 1992b: 23.
18 As in Freetown, Nunley 1987.
19 Cissé 2022.

to be a viable way into the future; it is simply a matter of finding new reasons for celebrations. Festivalisation of religious events has been going on all over the world. Another theatrical podium is tourism, the ultimate iconisation industry, and the outsider's gaze on Africa will continue to demand not just the Big Five in wildlife, but also masks. Although some scholars may be of two minds about the influence of tourism on local communities, we as authors will rejoice the day when the Crescent will again be 'safe for tourism'.

Third, masks increasingly function as emblems and icons of identity, at levels ranging from that of the ethnic group to the nation, occasionally even extending all the way to the whole continent. Important in this field is the present heritage movement, which is conducive to a new flourishing of masks in media, as visual representations of African-ness. The challenge is to integrate mask performances into new historical commemorations, since the young African nations will need the power of memory to forge their new collective identities. The question is how much of their cultural heritage they can include into their modern definition of self.

The fourth field is the scholarly community, which faces a challenge in recording, understanding, and preserving African masquerades. This field consists of the researchers, artists, sculptors, dancers, and museums in Africa, together with the northern museums, researchers, and lovers of art – in short, all those who appreciate the expressive forms of African masquerades. Obviously, this must be very much a joint endeavour between African museums – which in many parts of Africa are just starting – and the northern countries to which most of the cultural heritage has been shipped off, both museums and private collections. Restitution and repatriation of cultural objects are very much on the agenda these days, and masks will have to be considered in this groundswell. We can only hope that the move back to the areas of origin will also reinstate the masks in their full glory, costumed and in motion, grounded in the societies they originated from. UNESCO recognition will undoubtedly help – like in the case of the *gelede* – but regarding masks, the distinction between tangible and intangible heritage is not particularly relevant. Ultimately, masks are like ancestors: they remain important as long as they are not forgotten, so part of their future lies in our own hands.

So, at the end of this anthropological quest for the socio-political embeddedness of masquerades, we come back to art-historical themes: aesthetics, artistic creativity, visual appeal, and histories of local traditions, insights that triggered our search and that we have gratefully used. It is through our solution of part of the African masking puzzle that we wish to contribute to the joint quest for meaning that is the driving force of both disciplines, art history and anthropology. We hope this book will serve as a bridge between the two academic communities, which have been apart for too long, for we all feel the lure of the mask and perceive the threat to this deep African heritage, realising that only together we can hope to understand the 'puzzle inside a riddle, wrapped in an enigma'[20] which is the African masquerade.

[20] Quoting Churchill on Russia, in a radio speech in October 1939.

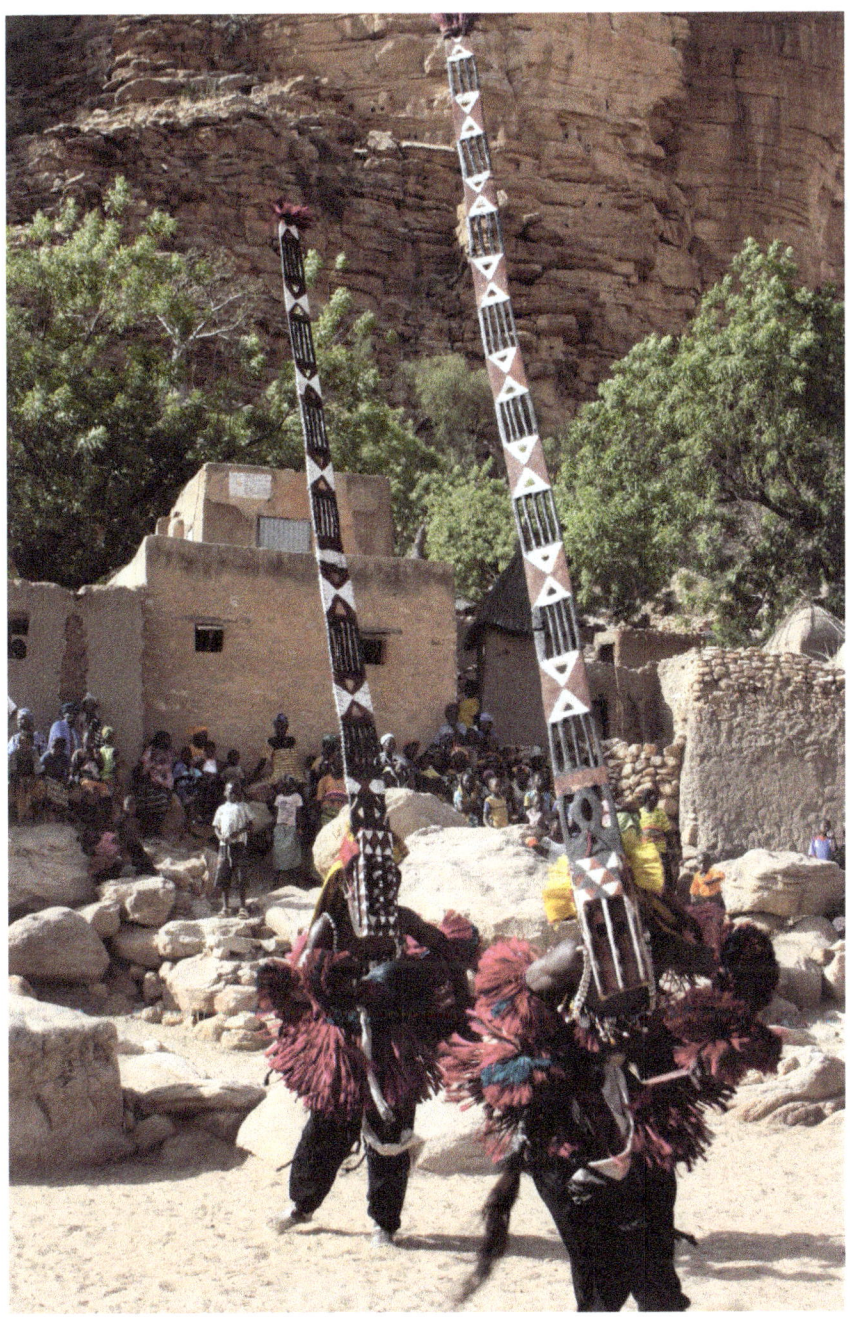

Figure 11.2. Two *èmna tiû*, tree masks, signify the arrival of the bush in a show of strength and athleticism. Tireli, Dogon, Mali, 2008. Photo: Walter van Beek.

Bibliography

Adams, Marie J. 1983. 'Current directions in the study of masking in Africa', *Africana Journal* 14, 2/3: 89–114.

Alsan, Marcella. 2015. 'The effect of the tsetse fly on African development', *American Economic Review* 105, 1: 382–410.

Amadiume, Ifi. 1997. *Re-inventing Africa: Matriarchy, religion and culture*. London: Zed Books.

Anderson, Benedict R. 2006 (1983). *Imagined communities. Reflections on the origin and spread of nationalism*. London: Verso.

Ardiner, Shirley. 1975. *Perceiving women*. London: Malaby Press.

Arnoldi, Mary-Jo, Christraud M. Geary, and Kris L. Hardin (eds). 1996. *African material culture*. Bloomington: Indiana University Press.

Arweck, P. 2004. *Materialising religion. Expression, performance, and ritual*. London: Ashgate.

Bacquart, Jean-Baptiste. 2004. *The tribal arts of Africa*. London: Thames & Hudson.

Barley, Nigel. 1995. *Dancing on the grave. Encounters with death*. London: Abacus.

Barrett, David W. 2007. *A brief history of secret societies*. London: Robinson.

Barth, Fredrik. 1987. *Cosmologies in the making: A generative approach to cultural variation in inner New Guinea*. Cambridge: Cambridge University Press.

——. 1973. 'Descent and marriage reconsidered'. In Jack Goody (ed.) *The character of kinship*. Cambridge: Cambridge University Press, 3–20.

Bassani, E. 2000. *African art and artefacts in European collections 1400–1800*. London: British Museum Press.

Belcher, Stephen. 2005. *African myths of origin*. London: Penguin Books.

Bell, Catherine. 1997. *Ritual: Perspectives and dimensions*. New York: Oxford University Press.

Belting, Hans. 2013. *Faces: Eine Geschichte des Gesichts*. Munich: C.H. Beck.

Bernardi, Bernardo, and David I. Kerzer. 2009. *Age class systems: Social institutions and polities based on age*. Cambridge: Cambridge University Press.

Biebuyck, Daniel P. 1992. 'Central African religion'. In Erna Beumers and Hans-Joachim Koloss (eds) *Kings of Africa. Art and authority in Central Africa*. Berlin: Museum für Völkerkunde, 27–29.

Blake, Barry L. 2010. *Secret language. Codes, tricks, spies, thieves, and symbols*. Oxford: Oxford University Press.

Bleakley, Robert. 1978. *African masks*. London: Thames & Hudson.

Blench, Roger. 1998. 'Le West African shorthorn au Nigeria'. In Christian Seignobos and Éric Thys (eds) *Des taurins et des hommes, Cameroun, Nigéria*. Paris: Orstom, 249–292.

Blier, Suzanne Preston. 1998. *Royal arts of Africa: The majesty of form*. London: Laurent King.

——. 1988. 'Words about icons: iconology and the study of African art', *Art Journal* 47, 2: 75–87.

——. 1976. *The beauty and the beast: A study in contrast*. New York: Tribal Arts Gallery.

Bloch, Marc. 1992. *Prey into hunter. The politics of religious experience*. Cambridge: Cambridge University Press.

——, and Jonathan P. Parry. 1999. *Death and the regeneration of life*. Cambridge: Cambridge University Press.

Bouquet, Mary. 2001. *Academic anthropology and the museum: Back to the future*. Oxford: Berghahn.

Bourdieu, Pierre. 1992. *Language and symbolic power*. Cambridge: Polity Press.

——. 1990. *The logic of practice*. Cambridge: Polity Press.

Bouttiaux, Anne-Marie (ed.). 2013a. *La dynamique des masques en Afrique occidentale*. Tervuren: Royal Museum for Central Africa.

——. 2013b. 'Guarantors of continuity and permeable to change. Masks and their dynamics in West Africa'. In Anne-Marie Bouttiaux (ed.) *La dynamique des masques en Afrique occidentale*. Tervuren: Royal Museum for Central Africa, 7–35.

——. 2009a. 'Masks of Africa: Identities hidden and revealed', *African Arts* 42, 3: 62–71.

——. 2009b. *Persona: Masks of Africa: Identities hidden and revealed*. Tervuren: Royal Museum for Central Africa.

Bowie, Fiona. 2009. *The anthropology of religion: An introduction*. Oxford: Blackwell.

Boyer, Pascal. 2001. *Religion explained: The human instincts that fashion gods, spirits and ancestors*. London: Heinemann.

——. 1990. *Tradition as truth and communication*. Cambridge: Cambridge University Press.

Brain, Robert. 1980. *Art and society in Africa*. Longman: London.

Brand, Saskia. 2004. *Mediating means and fate: A socio-political analysis of fertility and demographic change in Bamako, Mali*. Leiden: LOVA.

Bravmann, René. 1974. *Islam and art in West Africa*. Cambridge: Cambridge University Press.

——. 1973. *Open frontiers: The mobility of art in Black Africa*. Seattle: University of Washington Press.

Brown, Judith. 1963. 'A cross-cultural study of female initiation', *American Anthropologist* 65: 837–853.

Buckley, Thomas, and Alma Gottlieb. 1988. *Blood magic. The anthropology of menstruation*. Berkeley: University of California Press.

Caughlin, J P, and A.L. Vangelisti. 2009. 'Why people conceal or reveal secrets: A multiple goals theory perspective'. In T. Afifi and W. Afifi (eds) *Uncertainty and information regulation in interpersonal contexts*. New York: Routledge, 45–53.

Cole, Catherine M., Takyiwaa Manuh, and Stephan F. Miescher (eds). 2007. *Africa after gender?* Bloomington: Indiana University Press.

Cole, Herbert M. 1989. *Icons: Ideals and power in the art of Africa. Washington. DC*: Smithsonian Institution Press for the National Museum of African Art.

Colleyn, Jean-Paul. 2011. 'Les masques et le rapport à l'invisible'. In Paul Marathan (ed.) *Arts d'Afrique. Voir l'invisible.* Bordeaux: Musée d'Aquitanie, 19–22.

Coombes, Annie E. 1994. *Reinventing Africa. Museums, material culture and popular imagination.* New Haven: Yale University Press.

Coquet, Michèle. 1996. *Arts de cour en Afrique noire.* Paris: Adam Biro.

Cornwall, Andrea A. 2003. 'To be a man is more than a day's work: Shifting ideals of masculinity in Ado-Odo, Southwestern Nigeria'. In Lisa A. Lindsay and Stephan F. Miescher (eds) *Men and masculinities in modern Africa.* Portsmouth: Heineman, 230–248.

Crapanzano, Vincent. 1981. 'Rite of return: Circumcision in Morocco'. In Werner Münsterberger and L. Bryce Boyer (eds) *The psychoanalytic study of society,* vol. 9: 15–36.

Danfulani, Umar H.D. 1999a. 'A masquerade is not watched from one spot. Reassessing the study of African religion', *Scripta Instituti Donneriani Aboensis* 17, 2: 43–67.

D'Azevedo, Warren L. (ed.). 1979. *The traditional artist in African societies.* Bloomington: Indiana University Press.

De Garine, Igor, and Geoffrey A. Harrison. 1988. *Coping with uncertainty in food supply.* Oxford: Clarendon Press; New York: Oxford University Press.

De Heusch, Luc (ed.). 1995. *Objects, signs of Africa.* Tervuren: Snoeck-Ducaju & Son.

——. 1994. 'Myth and epic in Central Africa'. In Thomas D. Blakely, Walter E.A. van Beek, and Dennis L. Thomson (eds) *Religion in Africa: Experience and expression.* London/New York: Currey & Heinemann, 229–238.

——. 1987. 'Introduction'. In Luc de Heusch (ed.) *Chefs et rois sacrés. Systèmes de pensée en Afrique Noire,* 10. Paris: CNRS, 7–34.

De Jong, Ferdinand, and Michael Rowlands (eds). 2007. *Reclaiming heritage. Alternative imagineries of memory in West Africa.* Walnut Creek, CA: Left Coast Press.

De Wolf, Jan. 2006. 'Ethnographic confrontations: The anthropology of initiation among Gisu and Bukusu'. In Geert L.A.M. Mommersteeg and Anthony Robben (eds) *Een handvol kolanoten.* Maastricht: Shaker Publishing, 83–110.

Descola, Philip. 2021. *Les formes du visible. Une anthropologie de la figuration.* Paris: Seuil.

Diawara, Manthia. 1998. *In search of Africa.* Cambridge, MA: Harvard UP.

Douglas, Mary. 1973. *Natural symbols. Explorations in cosmology.* New York: Vintage Books.

——. 1967. 'Are matrilineal societies doomed?'. In Mary Douglas and Phyllis Kaberry (eds) *Man in Africa.* London: Tavistock, 121–136.

——. 1966. *Purity and danger. An analysis of notions of pollution and taboo.* New York: Penguin.

Droogers, André. 1974. *De gevaarlijke reis: Jongensinitiatie bij de Wagenia van Kisangani (Zaïre).* Amsterdam: Vrije Universiteit Amsterdam.

Edwards, Tim. 2006. *Cultures of masculinity.* London: Routledge.

Ekoué, Léokadie, and Judy Rosenthal. 2015. 'Aze and the incommensurable'. In William C. Olsen and Walter E.A. van Beek (eds) *Evil in Africa. Encounters with the everyday.* Bloomington: Indiana University Press.

Ellis, Stephen, and Gerrie Ter Haar. 2004. *World of power. Religious thought and political practice in Africa.* London: Hurst.

Ember, Melvin and Carol R. Ember. 1971. 'The conditions favoring matrilocal versus patrilocal residence', *American Anthropologist* 73: 571–594.

Evans-Pritchard, E.E. 1937. *Witchcraft, oracles and magic among the Azande.* Oxford: Clarendon.

Fabian, Johannes. 1983. *Time and the other: How anthropology makes its object.* New York: Columbia University Press.

Fagg, William. 1980. *Masques d'Afrique dans les collections du Musée Barbier-Müller.* Paris/Lausanne: Fernand Nathan/LEP.

Ferrandìz, Francisco, and Anthonius C.G.M. Robben. 2015. *Necropolitics: Mass graves and exhumations in the age of human rights.* Philadelphia: University of Pennsylvania Press.

Ferry, Marie-Paule. 2013. 'Masques chez le Bedik du Sénégal oriental'. In Anne-Marie Bouttiaux (ed.) *La dynamique des masques en Afrique occidentale.* Tervuren: Royal Museum for Central Africa, 67–78.

Finkenauer, Catrin. 1998. *Secrets: Types, determinants, functions, and consequences.* Unpublished PhD thesis, Louvain University.

Fölmi, Danielle, and Oliver. 2015. *Moments of mindfulness. African wisdom.* New York: Thames & Hudson.

Forge, Anthony. 1973. 'Introduction'. In Anthony Forge (ed.) *Primitive art and society.* London: Oxford University Press, xiii–xxii.

Fortes, Meyer. 1969 (1945). *The dynamics of clanship among the Tallensi: Being the first part of an analysis of the social structure of a trans-Volta tribe.* Oosterhout: Anthropological Publications.

——. 1957 (1949). *The web of kinship among the Tallensi. The second part of an analysis of the social structure of a trans-Volta tribe.* London: Oxford University Press.

Fraser, Douglas, and Herbert Cole (eds). 1972. *African art and leadership.* Madison: University of Wisconsin Press.

Frijns, Tom, 2004. *Keeping secrets: Quantity, quality and consequences.* Unpublished PhD thesis. Amsterdam: Free University Amsterdam.

Froger, F. 1698. *Relation d'un voyage fait en 1695, 1696 et 1697, aux Côtes d'Afrique, Détroit de Magellan.* Paris: Brunet.

Geertz, Clifford. 1980. *Negara: The theatre state in nineteenth-century Bali.* Princeton, NJ: Princeton University Press.

Gell, Alfred. 1999. *Art and agency. An anthropological theory.* Oxford: Clarendon Press.

Geschiere, Peter. 2017. *Witchcraft, intimacy and trust: Africa in comparison.* Chicago: University of Chicago Press.

——. 1997. *The modernity of witchcraft: Politics and the occult in post-colonial Africa.* Charlottesville: University Press of Virginia.

Gewald, Jan-Bart. 1999. *Herero heroes: A sociopolitical history of the Herero of Namibia 1890–1923.* Oxford: James Currey.

Gilmore, David. 1990. *Manhood in the making: Cultural concepts of masculinity.* New Haven: Yale University Press.

Girard, René. 1989. *The scapegoat.* Baltimore: Johns Hopkins University Press.

Goffman, Ervin. 1971. *The presentation of self in everyday life*. Harmondsworth: Penguin.

Goody, Jack (ed.). 1973a. *The character of kinship*. Cambridge: Cambridge University Press.

——. 1973b. 'Polygyny, economy and the role of women'. In Jack Goody (ed.) *The character of kinship*. Cambridge: Cambridge University Press, 175–190.

——. 1971. *Technology, tradition, and the state in Africa*. London: Oxford University Press.

——, and Stanley Tambiah. 1973. *Bridewealth and dowry*. Cambridge: Cambridge University Press.

Gore, Charles. 2008a. 'Masks and modernities', *African Arts* 41, 4: 4–7.

Grand-Dufay, Charlotte. 2016. *Les Lumbu: Un art sacré = Bungeelë yi bayisi*. Paris: Gourcuff-Gradenigo: Galerie Bernard Dulon.

Green, Sandra E. 1996. *Gender, ethnicity, and social change on the Upper Slave Coast of the Anlo-Ewe*. Portsmouth, NH: Heinemann.

Grillo, Laura S. 2018. *An intimate rebuke. Female genital power in ritual and politics in West Africa*. Durham, NC: Duke University Press.

Grimes, Ronald. 2000. *Deeply into the bone. Reinventing rites of passage*. Berkeley: University of California Press.

——. 2014. *The craft of ritual studies*. New York: Oxford University Press.

Hahner-Herzog, Iris, Maria Kecskési and László Vajda. 1989. 'I am not myself'. In Herbert M. Cole (ed.) *Icons: Ideals and power in the art of Africa*. Washington, DC: Smithsonian Institution Press for the National Museum of African Art, 1–29.

Hallam, Elizabeth, and Tim Ingold. 2007. *Creativity and cultural improvisation*. Oxford: Berg.

Harris, Marvin. 1981. *Cultural materialism: The struggle for a science of culture*. New York: Random House.

Hertz, R. 1907. 'Contribution à une étude sur la epresentation collective de la mort', *Année Sociologique* 10: 48–137.

Hobsbawm, Eric, and Terence Ranger (eds). 1983. *The invention of tradition*. Cambridge: Cambridge UP.

Hodgson, Dorothy L. 2003. 'Being Maasai men: modernity and the production of Maasai masculinities'. In Lisa A. Lindsay and Stephan F. Miescher (eds) *Men and masculinities in modern Africa*. Portsmouth. Heineman, 211 229.

Hoebel, Edward A. 1976. *The law of primitive man: A study in comparative legal dynamics*. New York: Atheneum.

Holbeke, Mireille (ed.). 1966. *Het object als bemiddelaar*. Antwerpen: Hoogma.

Holden, Clare J. and Ruth Mace. 2003. 'Spread of cattle led to the loss of matrilineal descent in Africa: a co-evolutionary analysis', *Proceedings of the Royal Society of London* 270, 1532: 2425–2433.

Holy, Ladislav. 1996. *Anthropological perspectives on kinship*. London: Pluto Press.

Homberger, Lorenz (ed.). 2008. *Cameroon. Art and kings*. Zürich: Museum Rietberg.

Horton, Robin. 1993. *Patterns of thought in Africa and the West: Essays on magic, religion and science*. Cambridge: Cambridge University Press.

——. 1976 (1971). 'Stateless societies in the history of West Africa'. In J.F.A. Ajayi and Michael Crowder (eds) *History of West Africa*.Volume 1, 2nd edition, 72–113.

Howson, Richard. 2006. *Challenging hegemonic masculinity*. London: Routledge.

Huet, Michel. 1995. *Africa dances*. London: Thames & Hudson.

Ibn Batuta. 2005. *Travels in Asia and Africa, 1325–1354*. Abingdon, Oxon: Routledge Curzon.

Ingold, Tim, 2011. *Being alive. Essays on movement, knowledge and description*. London: Routledge.

——. 2000. *The perception of the environment. Essays on livelihood, dwelling and skill*. London: Routledge.

Jackson, Michael. 1982. *Allegories of the wilderness. Ethics and ambiguity in Kuranko narratives*. Bloomington: Indiana University Press.

Janssen, Diederik F. 2007. 'Male initiation: Imagining ritual necessity'. *Journal of Men, Masculinities and Spirituality* 1, 3: 215–234.

Jaulin, Robert. 1971. *La mort sara: l'ordre de la vie ou la pensée de la mort au Tchad*, 2e éd. Paris: Plon.

Jay, Nancy. 1992. *Throughout your generations forever. Sacrifice, religion and paternity*. Chicago: Chicago University Press.

Jedrej, M.C. 1980a. 'A comparison of some masks from North America, Africa and Melanesia', *Journal of Anthropological Research* 36, 2: 220–230.

Jones, G.I. 1985. 'A memoir of early field photography', *African Arts* 18, 4: 64–67.

Jones, Graham. 2014. Secrecy. *Annual Review of Anthropology* 43: 53–69.

Jónsson, Kjartan. 2006. *Pokot masculinity: The role of rituals in forming men*. Reykjavík: University of Iceland.

Kaberry, Phyllis. 2005. *Women of the Grassfields. A study of the economic position of women in Bamenda, British Cameroons*. London: Routledge.

Kapferer, Bruce. 2013. *Ritual practice and anthropological theory*. New York: Berghahn.

——. 2004. 'Ritual dynamics and virtual practice: Beyond representation and meaning', *Social analysis* 48, 2: 33–54.

Kasfir, Sidney L. 1998a. 'Elephant women, furious and majestic: Women's masquerades in Africa and the diaspora', *African Arts* 31, 2: 18–27, 92.

—— (ed.). 1988b. *West African masks and cultural systems*. Tervuren: Royal Museum for Central Africa.

——. 1984. 'One tribe, one style? Paradigms in the historiography of African art', *History in Africa* 11: 163–193.

Kecskési, Maria and László Vajda. 2007. *African masks*. Geneva: Barbier-Mueller.

Keesing, Roger. 1975. *Kin groups and social structure*. New York: Holt, Rinehart & Winston.

Kelly, Anita E. 2002. *The psychology of secrets*. New York: Kluwer & Plenum.

Kerchache, Jacques, Jean-Louis Paudrat and Lucien Stephan. 2008. *Art Africain*. Paris: Citadelles.

Kingdon, Zachary. 1995. 'Lega'. In Tom Phillips (ed.) *Africa. The art of a continent*. Munich/New York: Prestel, 300–301.

Kopytoff, Igor. 1987. *The African frontier: The reproduction of traditional African societies*. Bloomington: Indiana University Press.

Kreamer, Christine M. 2010. 'Impermanent by design: The ephemeral in Africa's tradition-based arts', *African Arts* 43, 1, 14–27.

La Fontaine, Jean S. 1985. *Initiation. Ritual drama and secret knowledge across the world.* Harmondsworth: Penguin.

Last, Murray. 1974. 'Reform in West Africa: The jihād movement of the nineteenth century'. In J.F.A. Ajayi and Michael Crowder (eds) *History of West Africa,* vol. 2. Harlow: Longman, 1–47.

Lembezat, Bertrand. 1961. *Populations païennes du Nord Cameroun.* London: International African Institute.

Lévi-Strauss, Claude. 1979. *La voie des masques.* Paris: Plon.

Lewis, John L. 2013. *The anthropology of cultural performance.* New York: Palgrave Macmillan.

Leyten, Harrie. 2015. *From idol to art. African 'objects-with-power': A challenge for missionaries, anthropologists and museum curators.* Leiden: ASC.

Lifschitz, Edward. 1988. 'Hearing is believing: Acoustic masks and spirit manifestation'. In Sidney L. Kasfir (ed.) *West African masks and cultural systems.* Tervuren: Royal Museum for Central Africa, 221–230.

Lindsay, Lisa A., and Stephan F. Miescher (eds). 2003. *Men and masculinities in modern Africa.* Portsmouth: Heineman.

Loov, Jacob Balzani. 2016. 'In Burkina Faso: FESTIMA, a festival of African masks', *Aljazeera,* https://www.aljazeera.com/gallery/2016/3/13/in-burkina-faso-festima-a-festival-of-african-masks/, consulted 25 May 2023.

Lovejoy, Paul. 2012. *Transformations in slavery: A history of slavery in Africa.* Cambridge: Cambridge University Press.

Luhrman, Thomas M. 1989. 'The magic of secrecy'. *Ethos* 17, 2: 131–165.

Lusty, Natalya, and Julian Murphet (eds). 2014. *Modernism and masculinity.* New York: Cambridge University Press.

Middleton, John. 1987. 'Secrecy among the Lugbara'. In Kees W. Bolle (ed.) *Secrecy in religions.* Leiden: Brill, 25–43.

McClusky, Pamela, and Erika Dalya Massaquoi. 2015. *Disguise: Masks and global African art.* Exh. cat. New Haven: Yale University Press.

McCormack, Carol P. and Marilyn Strathern. 1980. *Nature, culture and gender.* Cambridge: Cambridge UP.

McNaughton, Patrick. 2008. *A bird dance near Saturday City: Sidi Ballo and the art of West African masquerade.* Bloomington: Indiana University Press.

——. 1992. 'From Mande Komo till Jukun Akuma. Approaching the difficult question of history', *African Arts* 25, 2: 76–85, 99–100.

——. 1991. 'Is there history in horizontal masks? A preliminary response to the dilemma of form', *African Arts* 24, 2: 40–53, 88–90.

MacRae, Graeme. 2005. 'Negara Ubud: The theatre-state in twenty-first-century Bali', *History and Anthropology* 16, 4: 393–413.

Maples, Amanda M. 2018. 'Unravelling political and historical threads: Youth and masquerade mobility in Freetown', *Social Dynamics* 44, 3: 487–509.

Martin, Jean-Hubert and Étienne Féau. 1997. *Arts de Nigeria: Collection du musée des Arts d'Afrique et d'Océanie.* Bordeaux: Réunion des Musées Nationaux.

Memel-Fotê, Harris. 1980. *Le système politique de Lodyoukrou: une société lignagère à classes d'âge à Côte d'Ivoire).* Paris: Présence Africaine.

Metcalfe, Peter, and Richard Huntington. 1991. *Celebrations of death. The anthropology of mortuary ritual*. Cambridge: Cambridge University Press, 2nd edition.

Meyer, Birgit. 2015. *Sensational movies: Video, vision, and Christianity in Ghana*. Oakland, CA: University of California Press.

Michaels, Axel. 2006. 'Ritual and meaning'. In Jan Kreinath, Jan Snoeck, and Michael Stausberg (eds) *Theorising rituals: Issues, topics, approaches, concepts*. Leiden: Brill, 247–263.

Miescher, Stephan, and Lisa A. Lindsay. 2003. 'Introduction: men and masculinities in modern African history'. In Lisa A. Lindsay and Stephan F. Miescher (eds) *Men and masculinities in modern Africa*. Portsmouth: Heineman, 1–30.

Mohan, Urmila, and Laurence Douny (eds). 2021. *The material subject. Rethinking objects and bodies in motion*. London: Routledge.

Molendijk, Arie L. 2010. 'The notion of the "sacred"'. In Paul Post and Arie L. Molendijk (eds) *Holy Ground. Re-inventing ritual space in modern Western culture*. Leuven: Peeters, 17–54.

Moor, Nienke. 2009. *Explaining worldwide religious diversity. The relationship between subsistence technologies and ideas about the unknown in pre-industrial and post-industrial societies*. Nijmegen: ICS.

Moore, Henrietta L. 1994. *A passion for difference: Essays in anthropology and gender*. Cambridge: Polity Press.

Murdock, George P. 1959. *Africa, its peoples and their cultural history*. New York: McGraw-Hill.

Napier, A. David. 1988. 'Masks and metaphysics: An empirical dilemma'. In Sidney L. Kasfir (ed.) *West African Masks and Cultural Systems*. Tervuren: Royal Museum for Central Africa, 231–240

——. 1986. *Masks, transformations and paradox*. Los Angeles: Berkeley University Press.

Needham, Rodney. 1967. 'Percussion and Transition', *Man* 2, 4: 606–614.

Newell, Sasha. 2013. 'Brands as masks: Public secrecy and the counterfeit in Côte d'Ivoire', *Journal of the Royal Anthropological Institute* (NS) 19: 138–154.

Neyt, François. 2010. *Congo river. Arts of Central Africa*. Paris: Musée du quai Branly.

Njoku, Raphael C. 2020. *West African masking traditions and diaspora masquerade carnivals: History, memory, and transnationalism*. University of Rochester Press.

Nortey, Samuel, Edwin K. Bodjawah, and Kwaku B. Kissiedu. 2021. 'African masking systems: An archive of social commentary', *African Arts* 54, 4: 52–63.

Noukpo, Patrick. 2020. *Les masques africains: des patrimoines identitaires dans la diversité culturelle entre espaces profane et sacré au Bénin*. Thesis Université de Lorraine.

Ogundiran, Akinwumi O. 2014. *Materialities of ritual in the Black Atlantic*. Bloomington: Indiana University Press.

O'Hern, Robin, Ellen Pearlstein, and Susan Gagliardi. 2016. 'Beyond the surface: Where cultural contexts and scientific analyses meet in museum conservation of West African power association helmet masks', *Museum Anthropology* 39, 1: 70–86.

Olsen, William C., and Walter E.A. van Beek (eds). 2015. *Evil in Africa. Encounters with the everyday*. Bloomington: Indiana University Press.

Oppong, Christine (ed.). 1983. *Female and male in West Africa*. London: George Allen and Unwin.

Ortner, Sherry B. 1974. 'Is female to male as nature is to culture?'. In Michelle Rosaldo and Louise Lamphere (eds) *Woman, culture, and society*. Stanford: Stanford University Press, 67–87.

Ottenberg, Simon. 1982. 'Illusion, communication and psychology in West African masquerades', *Ethos* 10, 2: 149–185.

——, and David A. Binkley. 2006. 'Introduction: An overview'. In Simon Ottenberg and David Binkley (eds) *Playful performers. African children's masquerades*. New Brunswick: Transaction publishers, 1–46.

Paige, Karin E., and Jeffry M. Paige. 1981. *The politics of reproductive ritual*. Berkeley: University of California Press.

Paulme, Denise. 1973. 'Adornment and nudity in tropical Africa'. In Anthony Forge (ed.) *Primitive art and society*. London: Oxford University Press: 11–24.

Peek, Philip M. and Walter E.A. van Beek. 2013. 'African dynamics of divination'. In Walter E.A. van Beek and Philip M. Peek (eds) *Reviewing reality. Dynamics of African divination*. Berlin: LIT Verlag, 1–24.

Pernet, Henry. 1992. *Ritual masks: Deceptions and revelations*. Columbia: University of South Carolina Press.

Phillips, Tom (ed.). 1995. *Africa. The art of a continent*. Munich/New York: Prestel.

Pospisil, Leo. 1974. *The anthropology of law: A comparative theory*. New Haven: HRAF Press.

Post, Paul. 2007. 'A symbolic bridge between faiths', *Yearbook for Liturgical and Ritual Studies* 23: 171–201.

Pratten, David. 2007. *The man-leopard murders: history and society in colonial Nigeria*. Edinburgh: Edinburgh University Press.

Purpura, Allyson. 2010. 'On the verge: ephemeral art, part II', *African Arts* 43, 1: 12–13.

Rappaport, Roy A. 1999. *Ritual and religion in the making of mankind*. Cambridge: Cambridge University Press.

Ravenhill, Philip. 1996b. 'The passive object and the tribal paradigm: Colonial museography in French West Africa'. In Mary-Jo Arnoldi, Christraud M. Geary, and Kris L. Hardin (eds) *African material culture*. Bloomington: Indiana University Press, 265–282.

Rowlands, Michael. 2002. 'The power of origins: Questions of cultural rights?'. In V. Buchli (ed.) *The material culture reader*. Oxford: Berg, 115–134.

——, and Ferdinand de Jong. 2007. 'Reconsidering heritage and memory'. In Ferdinand de Jong and Michael Rowlands (eds) *Reclaiming heritage. Alternative imagineries of memory in West Africa*. Walnut Creek, CA: Left Coast Press, 13–30.

——, and Jean-Pierre Warnier. 1996. 'Magical iron technology in the Cameroonian Grassfields'. In Mary-Jo Arnoldi, Christraud M. Geary and Kris L. Hardin (eds) *African material culture*. Bloomington: Indiana University Press, 51–72.

Samorini, Giorgio. 1992. 'The oldest representations of hallucinogenic mushroom in the world (Sahara Desert, 9000–7000 B.P.)', *Integration* 2 & 3: 69–78.

Schechner, Richard. 2003. *Performance theory*. London: Routledge.

——, and Victor Turner. 1985. *Between theater and anthropology*. Philadelphia: University of Pennsylvania Press.

Schildkrout, Enid (ed.) 1989. *Wild spirits, strong medicine. African art and the wilderness*. New York: Center for African Art.

Schneider, David. 1961. 'The distinctive features of matrilineal descent groups', In Kathryn Gough and David Schneider (eds) *Matrilineal Kinship*. Berkeley: UCLA Press: 1–29.

Segy, Ladislas. 1976. *Masks of black Africa*. New York: Dover Publications.

Seignobos, Christian, and Éric Thys. 1998. 'Introduction'. In Christian Seignobos and Éric Thys (eds) *Des taurins et des hommes: Cameroun, Nigéria*. Paris: Orstom, 9–14.

Setlhabi, Keletso G. 2014. 'I took an allegiance to secrecy: Complexities of conducting ethnographic research at home', *Africa. Journal of the International African Institute* 84, 2: 314–334.

Shakespeare, William. 1997. *Macbeth: The New Cambridge Shakespeare*. Albert R. Braunmuller (ed). Cambridge: Cambridge University Press.

Shefer, Tamara, Kopano Ratele, Anna Strebel, Nokuthia Shabalala, and Rosemarie Buikema. 2007. 'From boys to men: an overview'. In Tamara Shefer et al. (eds) *From boys to men: Social constructions of masculinity in contemporary society*. Landsdowne: Juta Company, 1–12.

Sheridan, Michael and Celia Nyamweru (eds). 2008. *African sacred groves: Ecological dynamics and social change*. Oxford: James Currey.

Sidibé, Samuel, Salia Malé, Annette Schmidt, Rogier Bedaux, Kléna Sanogo, and Mohamadou Dembélé (eds). 2006. *Le Musée National du Mali. Catalogue de l'exposition permanente*. Bamako and Leiden: Musée National du Mali et Musée National d'Ethnologie.

Simmel, Georg. 1950. *The sociology of Georg Simmel*. New York: Free Press.

Simonse, Simon. 2018. *Kings of disaster. Dualism, centralism and the scapegoat king in Southeastern Sudan*. Kampala: Fountainhead Publishers.

Smith, Jonathan Z. 1987. *To take place: Towards theory in ritual*. Chicago: Chicago University Press.

Sparks, Logan and Paul Post (eds). 2015. *The study of culture through the lens of ritual*. Amsterdam/Groningen: NSRL 15.

Sperber, Dan. 1974. *Rethinking symbolism*. Cambridge: Cambridge University Press.

Staal, Frits. 1989. *Rules without meaning: Ritual, mantras and the human sciences*. Bern: Peter Lang.

——. 1975. 'The meaninglessness of ritual', *Numen* 26, 1: 2–22.

Steiner, Christopher B. 1992a. 'The invisible face: Masks, ethnicity and the state in Côte d'Ivoire, West Africa', *Museum Anthropology* 16: 53–57.

——. 1992b. 'Fake masks and faux modernity', *African Arts* 25, 3: 18–20.

Stepan, Peter. 2005. *Spirits speak*. New York: Prestel-Munich.

Stewart, Pamela J. and Andrew J. Strathern. 2014. *Ritual: Key concepts in religion*. London: Bloomsbury.

Stone, Linda. 2006. *Kinship and gender. An introduction*. Boulder: Westview Press.

Strother, Z.S. 2012. 'Iconoclash: From "tradition" to "heritage" in global Africa', *African Arts* 45, 3: 1–6.

Taussig, Michael. 1999. *Defacement: Public secrecy and the labor of the negative.* Stanford: University Press.

Ter Haar, Gerrie 2007 (ed.). *Witchcraft beliefs and accusations in contemporary Africa.* Trenton NJ: Africa World Press.

——, and Stephen Ellis. 2009. 'The occult does not exist. A response to Terence Ranger', *Africa. Journal of the International African Society* 79, 3: 399–412.

Thompson, Elizabeth. 1997. 'Masters, masks and myths: reflections on the masculinities in the Southern Africa colloquium', *Agenda* 13: 35: 83–85.

Thompson, Robert F. 1974. *African arts in motion. Icon and act.* Los Angeles: University of California Press.

Tonkin, Elizabeth. 1988. 'Cunning mysteries'. In Sidney L. Kasfir, *West African masks and cultural systems.* Tervuren: Royal Museum for Central Africa, 241–249.

——. 1979. 'Masks and power', *Man* 14 (2), 237–248.

Turner, Edith. 2012. *Communitas. The anthropology of collective joy.* New York: Palgrave/MacMillan.

Ugwu, Chidi. 2017. 'The "native" as ethnographer: Doing social research in globalising Nsukka"', *The Qualitative Report* 22, 10: 2629–2637. Available at http://nsuworks.nova.edu/tqr/vol22/iss10/7, consulted 16 April 2022.

Van Baal, Jan and Walter E.A. van Beek. 1985. *Symbols for communication: Religion in anthropological theory.* Assen: Van Gorcum.

Van Beek, Walter E.A. 2011. 'Cultural models of power in Africa'. In Jan Abbink and Mirjam de Bruijn (eds) *Land, law and politics in Africa: Mediating conflict and reshaping the state.* Leiden, Brill, 25–48.

——. 2007. 'The escalation of witchcraft accusations'. In Gerrie ter Haar (ed.) *Imagining evil: Witchcraft beliefs and accusations in contemporary Africa.* Trenton, NJ: Africa World Press, 293–316.

——, and William C. Olsen. 2015. 'African notions of evil: The chimera of justice'. In William C. Olsen and Walter E.A. van Beek (eds) *Evil in Africa: Encounters with the everyday.* Bloomington: Indiana University Press, 1–26.

——, and Annette Schmidt. 2012. 'African dynamics of cultural tourism'. In Walter E.A. van Beek and Annette Schmidt (eds) *African hosts and their guests: Dynamics of cultural tourism in Africa.* Oxford: Currey, 1–33.

Van der Geest, Sjaak. 2000. 'Funerals for the living. Conversations with elderly people in Kwahu (Ghana)', *African Studies Review* 43, 3: 103–129.

Van Gennep, Arnold. 1960. *The rites of passage.* Chicago: University of Chicago Press.

Van Santen, José C.M. 1993. *They leave their jars behind: The conversion of Mafa women to Islam (North Cameroon).* Leiden: VENA.

Vansina, Jan. 1992a. 'History of Central African civilisation'. In Erna Beumers and Hans-Joachim Koloss (eds) *Kings of Africa: Art and authority in Central Africa.* Berlin: Museum für Völkerkunde, 13–18.

——. 1992b. 'Kings in tropical Africa'. In Erna Beumers and Hans-Joachim Koloss (eds) *Kings of Africa: Art and authority in Central Africa.* Berlin: Museum für Völkerkunde, 19–26.

——. 1990. *Pathways in the rainforests: Toward a history of political tradition in Equatorial Africa.* London: Currey.

Vàsquez, Gabriel. 2011. *More than belief: A materialist theory of religion.* Oxford: Oxford University Press.

Visonà Blackmun, Monica, Robin Poynor, and Herbert M. Cole. 2000. *A history of art in Africa.* London: Thames & Hudson.

Wagner, Roy. 1981 *The invention of culture.* Chicago: Chicago University Press.

Warren, Carol, and Barbara Lasslet. 1977. 'Privacy and secrecy: A conceptual comparison', *Journal of Social Issues* 33, 3: 43–51.

Wassing, René S. 1970. *The arts of Africa.* London: Thames & Hudson.

Wegner, Daniel, Julie Lane, and Sara Dimitri. 1994. 'The allure of secret relationships', *Journal of Personality and Social Psychology* 53, 1: 5–13.

Weinhold, Ulrike, and Kevin Cook. 2000. *Het eeuwige gezicht: Afrikaanse maskers en de westerse samenleving.* Berg en Dal: Afrika Museum.

Whitehouse, Harvey. 2004. *Modes of religiosity: A cognitive theory of religious transmission.* Walnut Creek: Altamira Press.

Wilde, Oscar. 2007 (1890). *The Picture of Dorian Grey.* London: Vintage.

Wilson, Godfrey 1939. *The constitution of Ngonde.* Livingstone: Rhodes-Livingstone Institute.

Wismeijer, Andreas and Mirre Bots. 2009. *Geheimen. De psychologie van wat we niet vertellen.* Amsterdam: Nieuw Amsterdam Uitgevers.

Wittmer, Marcilene K. and William Arnett. 1978. *Three rivers of Nigeria.* Atlanta: The High Museum of Art.

Wolf, Eric. 1997. *Europe and the people without history.* Berkeley CA: University of California Press.

Sources for Ethnographic Cases

The section below lists those titles that have served as sources for the ethnographic cases discussed in the book and plotted on Maps 2, 3, and 4. They are listed here either by ethnic group or sub-region. A slash between the labels indicates alternative versions of the name, a comma separate names of related groups in the same cultural area. Within each ethnic group, the entries first focus on the masking traditions, and second on the socio-cultural context.

Ashanti/Asante/Akan

Abu, Katherine. 1983. 'The separateness of spouses: Conjugal resources in an Ashanti town'. In Christine Oppong (ed.) *Female and male in West Africa*. London: George Allen and Unwin, 156–168.

Cole, Herbert M. and Doran H. Ross. 1977. *The arts of Ghana*. Los Angeles: Museum of Cultural History and University of California.

Fortes, Meyer. 1950. 'Kinship and Marriage among the Ashanti'. In Alfred R. Radcliffe-Brown and Daryll Forde (eds) *African systems of kinship and marriage*. London: KPI & IAF: 252–284.

Hagan, George. 1983. Marriage, divorce and polygyny in Winneba. In Christine Oppong (ed.) *Female and male in West Africa*. London: George Allen and Unwin, 192–203.

Kwame, Arhin. 1983. 'The political and military roles of Akan women'. In Christine Oppong (ed.) *Female and male in West Africa*. London: George Allen and Unwin, 91–98.

Morton-Williams, Peter. 1969. 'The influence of habitat and trade on the polities of Oyo and Ashanti'. In Mary Douglas and Phyllis Kaberry (eds) *Man in Africa*. London: Tavistock Publications, 79–98.

Rattray, R.S. 1956 (1916). *Ashanti law and constitution*. London: Oxford UP.

——. 1952 (1914). *Ashanti proverbs*. Oxford: Clarendon Press.

Vellenga, Dorothy D. 1983. 'Who is a wife? Legal expressions of heterosexual conflicts in Ghana'. In Christine Oppong (ed.) *Female and male in West Africa*. London: George Allen and Unwin, 144–155.

Vercruijsse, Emile. 1983. 'Fish mongers, big dealers and fishermen: Cooperation and conflict between the sexes in Ghanaian canoe fishing'. In Christine Oppong (ed.) *Female and male in West Africa*. London: George Allen and Unwin, 179–191.

Baga

Lamp, Frederick J. 2013. 'Communicating body knowledge through regional culture-based performance in Guinea'. In Anne-Marie Bouttiaux (ed.) *La dynamique des masques en Afrique occidentale*. Tervuren: Royal Museum for Central Africa, 79–102.

——. 2011. 'Un symbole de ce qu'il y a de meilleur en l'homme: Le masque baga *d'mba*". In Paul Marathan (ed.) *Arts d'Afrique. Voir l'invisible*. Bordeaux: Musée d'Aquitanie, 29–32.

——. 1985. 'Cosmos, cosmetics and the spirit of Bondo', *African Arts* 18, 3: 28–43, 98–99.

Baka

Joiris, D.V. 1996. 'A comparative approach to hunting rituals among the Baka pygmies'. In S. Kent (ed.) *Cultural diversity among 20th century foragers*. Cambridge: Cambridge University Press, 245–275.

Tsuru, Daisaku. 2001. 'Generation and transaction processes in the spirit ritual of the Baka pygmies in Southeast Cameroon', *African Study Monographs* 27:103–123.

——. 1998. 'Diversity of ritual spirit performances among the Baka pygmies in Southeastern Cameroon', *African Study Monographs* 25: 47–84.

Balante

Mark, Peter. 1987. 'The Senegambian horned initiation mask: History and provenance', *Art Bulletin* 69, 4: 626–640.

Temudo, Marina Padrão. 2019. 'Between 'forced marriage' and 'free choice': Social transformations and perceptions of gender and sexuality among the Balanta in Guinea-Bissau', *Africa. Journal of the International African Society* 89, 1: 1–20.

Bamana/Bambara

Aden, Jonathan E. 2003. *Anvils of blood, oaths of iron: A history of power and association in the Komo complex of the western Sudan (West Africa) from the late nineteenth century to the present*. Michigan: ProQuest Dissertations Publishing.

Arnoldi, Mary-Jo, 1996. 'Material narratives and the negotiation of identities through objects in Malian theatre'. In Mary-Jo Arnoldi, Christraud M. Geary, and Kris L. Hardin (eds) *African material culture*. Bloomington: Indiana University Press, 167–187.

——, and Elisabeth den Otter. 2008. 'Puppet management in Kirango, Mali: Continuity, innovation and changing contexts'. In Stephen Belcher, Jan Jansen, and Mohamed N'Daou (eds) *Mande Mansa: Essays in honor of David Conrad*. Berlin: LIT Verlag, 7–16.

Bulman, Stephen P.D. and Valentin F. Vydrine (eds). 2017. *The epic of Sumanguru Kante narrated by Abdulaye Sako*. Leiden: Brill.

Colleyn, Jean-Paul. 2006. *Fêtes et cérémonies*. Paris: Musée Branly.
——. 2002a. 'Le *Ci-Wara*'. In Jean-Paul Colleyn (ed.) *Bamana. Un art et un savoir-vivre au Mali*. Gent: Snoeck-Ducaju, 201–235.
——. 2002b. 'Le *Kòmò*'. In Jean-Paul Colleyn (ed.) *Bamana. Un art et un savoir-vivre au Mali*. Gent: Snoeck-Ducaju, 175–184.
——. 2002c. 'Le *Kònò*'. In Jean-Paul Colleyn (ed.) *Bamana. Un art et un savoir-vivre au Mali*. Gent: Snoeck-Ducaju, 185–200.
——. 2002d. 'Ntomo et Koré'. In Jean-Paul Colleyn (ed.) *Bamana. Un art et un savoir-vivre au Mali*. Gent: Snoeck-Ducaju, 95–130.
—— (ed.) 2002e. *Bamana. Un art et un savoir-vivre au Mali*. Gent: Snoeck-Ducaju.
——. 2002f. *Bamana*. Milan: Visions of Africa, 5 Continents.
——. 1987. *Minyanka funerals*. Film.
Conrad, David C. 2004. *Sunjata: A West African epic of the Mande peoples; narrated by Djanka Tassey Condé*. Indianapolis: Hackett.
Dieterlen, Germaine. 1988. *Essai sur la religion Bambara*, 2nd edition. Brussels: Institute of Social Anthropology.
Hoffman, Barbara G. 2017. 'The roles of the griot in the future of Mali: A twenty-first-century institutionalisation of a thirteenth-century traditional institution', *African Studies Review* 60, 1: 101–122.
Imperato, Pascal J. 1980. 'Bambara and Malinke ton masquerades', *African Arts* 13, 4: 47–55, 82–85, 87.
Jansen, Jan. 2000. 'Masking Sunjata: A hermeneutical critique', *History in Africa* 27: 131–141.
——. 2018a. 'The next generation: Young griots' quest for authority'. In Toby Green and Benedetta Rossi (eds) *Landscapes, sources, and intellectual projects: Politics, history, and the West African past*. Leiden: Brill, 296–311.
——. 2018b. 'Beyond the Mali empire – a new paradigm for the Sunjata epic', *International Journal of African Historical Studies* 51, 2: 317–340.
——. 1995. *De draaiende put: Een studie naar de relatie tussen het Sunjata-epos en de samenleving in de Haut-Niger (Mali)*. Leiden: CNWS.
——, and Philip Roth. 2000. 'Secrets and lies in the Mande world', *Mande Studies* 2.
McNaughton, Patrick. 2002. 'Introduction'. In Jean-Paul Colleyn (ed.) *Bamana. Un art et un savoir-vivre au Mali*. Gent: Snoeck-Ducaju, 167–174.
——. 1988. *The Mande blacksmiths. Knowledge, power, and art in West Africa*. Bloomington: Indiana University Press.
Schulz, Dorothea. 2000. 'Seductive secretiveness: "Jeliw" as creators and creations of ethnography', *Mande Studies* 2: 55–79.
Wooten, Stephen R. 2000. 'Antelope headdresses and champion farmers: Negotiating meaning and identity through the Bamana ciwara complex', *African Arts* 33, 2: 18–33+89–90.
Zahan, Dominique. 1980. *Antilopes du soleil: Arts et rites agraires d'Afrique noire*. Vienna: A. Schendl.
——. 1960. *Sociétés d'initiation Bambara. Le N'domo, le Koré*. Paris: Mouton.
Zobel, Clemens. 1996. 'Les génies du Kòma: *Identités* locales, logiques religieuses et enjeux sociopolitiques dans les monts Manding du Mali', *Cahiers d'études africaines* 36, 144: 625–658.

Bamum

Geary, Christraud M. 2008. 'Bamum and Tikar. Inspiration and innovation'. In Lorenz Homberger (ed.) *Cameroon Art and Kings*. Zürich: Prestel, 31–60.

——. 1996. 'Art, politics and the transformation of meaning: Bamum art in the twentieth century'. In Mary-Jo Arnoldi, Christraud M. Geary, and Kris L. Hardin (eds) *African material culture*. Bloomington: Indiana University Press, 283–307.

——, and Adam N. Njoya. 1985. *Mandou Yénou. Photographies du pays Bamoum, royaume ouest-africain 1902–1915*. München: Trickster Verlag.

Tardits, Claude. 1996. 'Pursue to attain: A royal religion'. In Ian Fowler and David Zeitlyn (eds) *African crossroads. Intersections between history and anthropology in Cameroon*. Oxford: Berghahn, 141–164.

——. 1992. 'The kingdom of Bamum'. In Erna Beumers and Hans-Joachim Koloss (eds) *Kings of Africa. Art and authority in Central Africa*. Berlin: Museum für Völkerkunde, 43–56.

——. 1980. *Le royaume bamoum*. Paris: A. Colin.

Wittmer, Marcilene K. 1979. 'Bamum village masks', *African Arts* 12, 4: 58–63+92.

Baule

Bouloré, Vincent. 1995. *Les masques baoulé dans la Côte d'Ivoire centrale*. Ph.D. diss., Université de Paris, Pantheon-Sorbonne.)

Boyer, Alain-Michel. 2008. *Les Baule*. Milan: 5 Continents Editions.

Étienne, P. and M. 1971. '"A qui mieux mieux" ou le mariage chez les Baoulé', *Cahiers ORSTOM*, sér. Sciences humaines VIII, 2: 165–186.

——. ——. 1967. 'Terminologie de la parenté et de l'alliance chez les Baoulé (Côte d'Ivoire)', *L'Homme* VII, 4: 50–76.

Evanoff, Elizabeth. 1985. 'Baule'. In Herbert M. Cole (ed.) *I am not myself; the art of African masquerade*. Los Angeles: Museum of Cultural History, 54–59.

Guerry, Vincent. 1971. *La vie quotidienne dans un village baoulé*. Abidjan: INADES.

Memet-Foté, Harris. 1980. *Le système politique de Lodyoukrou: Une société lignagère à classes d'âge*. Paris: Présence Africaine.

Ravenhill, Philip. 1996a. *Dreams and reverie. Images of otherworld mates among the Baule, West Africa*. Washington and London: Smithsonian Institution Press.

Vogel, Susan. 1997a. *Baule. African art, western eyes*. New Haven: Yale University Press/New York: Museum for African Art.

——. 1997b. 'Baule. African art, western eyes', *African Arts* 30, 4: 64–77+95.

Weiskel, Timothy C. 1978. 'The precolonial Baule: A reconstruction'. *Cahiers d'études africaines* 18, 72: 503–560.

Bemba

Richards, Audrey. 1982. *Chisungu. A girls' initiation ceremony among the Bemba of Zambia*. London: Routledge.

Beng (Côte d'Ivoire)

Gottlieb, Alma. 2004. *The afterlife is where we come from: The culture of infancy in West Africa.* Chicago: University of Chicago Press.

——. 2000. 'Secrets and society: the Beng of Côte d'Ivoire', *Mande Studies* 2: 129–151.

——. 1998. 'Do infants have religion? The spiritual lives of Beng babies', *American Anthropologist* 100, 1: 122–135.

——. 1992. *Under the kapok tree. Identity and difference in Beng thought.* Chicago: University of Chicago Press.

——. 1988. 'Menstrual cosmology among the Beng of Ivory Coast'. In Thomas Buckley and Alma Gottlieb (eds) *Blood magic. The anthropology of menstruation.* Berkeley: University of California Press, 55–74.

——. 1982. 'Sex, fertility and menstruation among the Beng of the Ivory Coast: a symbolic analysis', *Africa. Journal of the International African Institute* 52, 4: 34–47.

——, and Philip Graham. 1993. *Parallel worlds. An anthropologist and a writer encounter Africa.* New York: Crown Publishers.

Upper Benue: Chamba, Dowayo, Koma, Dìì/Dourou

Barley, Nigel. 1983. *Symbolic structures: An exploration of the culture of the Dowayos.* Cambridge University Press.

Fardon, Richard. 2007. *Fusions: Masquerades and thought style east of the Niger-Benue confluence, West Africa.* London: Saffron Books.

——. 2006. *History through ceremony in Cameroon.* London: Berghahn.

——. 1990. *Between God, the dead and the wild. Chamba interpretations of religion and ritual.* Edinburgh: Edinburgh University Press.

——, and Christine Stelzig. 2005. *Column to volume. Formal innovation in Chamba statuary.* London: Saffron Books.

Garine, Éric. 1998. 'Les Dowayo et leurs taurins'. In Christian Seignobos and Éric Thys (eds) *Des taurins et des hommes, Cameroun, Nigéria.* Paris: Orstom, 61–122.

Muller, Jean-Claude. 2008. 'Political structure and its ritual expression: The symbolism of initiation rites in two chiefdoms', *Social Evolution and History* 7, 1: 154–165.

——. 2002. *Les rites initiatiques des Dìì de l'Adamaoua (Cameroun).* Nanterre: Société d'ethnologie.

——. 2001. 'Inside, outside, and inside out: Masks, rulers, and gender among the Dìì and their neighbors', *African Arts* 34, 1: 58–71, 95–96.

——. 1997a. 'Circoncision et régicide: Thème et variations chez les Dìì, les Chamba et les Moundang des confins de la Bénoué et du Tchad', *L'Homme* 141: 7–24.

——. 1997b. 'Un système crow patrilinéaire: Les Dìì de Mbé (Adamaoua, Nord Cameroun)', *Anthropologie et Société* 21, 2–3: 125–141.

——. 1993. 'Les deux fois circoncis et les presque excisées: Le cas des Dìi de l'Adamaoua (Nord Cameroun). *Cahiers d'Études Africaines* 33, 4: 132–144.

Paarup-Laursen, Bjarke. 1998. 'Le role du bovin chez les Koma du nord du Nigeria'. In Christian Seignobos and Éric Thys (eds) *Des taurins et des hommes, Cameroun, Nigéria*. Paris: Orstom, 229–248.

Bobo/Bobo Fin

Homann, Lisa. 2020. 'Incremental shifts: The contemporariness of masquerade'. *African Arts* 53 (4): 38–45.

Le Moal, Guy. 2008. *Masques Bobo. Vie, formes et couleurs*. Paris: IRD, Biro.

——. 2003. 'De la brousse au village: Autels de fondation et code sacrificiel chez les Bobo'. In Marcel Detienne (ed.) *Tracés de fondation* 69–84. Leuven: Peters.

——. 1980. *Les Bobo. Nature et fonction des masques*. Paris: Orstom.

Saul, Mahir. 1991. 'The Bobo 'house' and the use of categories of descent', *Africa. Journal of the International African Institute* 61, 1: 71–79.

Bwa/Bobo Oulé, Nafana

Arnaut, Karel. 2013. 'On multiplicity and performance: The complexity of Bedu mask dances in the Bondoukou region (Côte d'Ivoire)'. In Anne-Marie Bouttiaux (ed.) *La dynamique des masques en Afrique occidentale*. Tervuren: Royal Museum for Central Africa, 141–171.

Coquet, Michèle. 1995. 'Des dieux sans visage. De la morphologie des masques de feuilles bwaba (Burkina Faso)'. In Luc de Heusch (ed.) *Objects, signs of Africa*. Gent: Snoeck-Ducaju and Son, 21–35.

Roy, Christopher D. 2007. *Land of the flying masks; arts and culture in Burkina Faso*. New York: Prestel.

——. 2003. 'Leaf masks among the Bobo and the Bwa'. In Frank Herreman (ed.) *Material differences; art and identity in Africa*. New York: Museum of African Art. 123–127.

——. 1987a. 'The spread of mask styles in the Black Volta Basin', *African Arts* 20, 4: 40–47, 89–90.

——. 1987b. *Art of the Upper Volta river*. Meudon: Chaffin Books.

Films

African art in motion. The masks of the Nuna people of Burkina Faso. Christopher Roy, 2002.

African art: Burkina Faso, Christopher Roy, 2003.

Art as a verb in Africa: The masks of the Bwa village of Boni. Christopher Roy, 2005.

Bwa/Boa (DRC)

Ceyssens, Rik. 2007. 'The 'Bwa war masks' of the Middle Uele region: A review', *African Arts* 40, 4: 58–73.

Northwest Cameroon

Argenti, Nicolas. 2014. 'Mascarades d'enfants: Entre guerre et rituel au royaume d'Oku (Cameroun)'. In Michel Coquet and Claude Macherel (eds) *Enfances: Pratiques, croyances et inventions*. Paris: CNRS, 132–147.

——. 2007. *The intestines of the state. Youth, violence, and belated histories in the Cameroon Grassfields*. Chicago: University of Chicago Press.

——. 2001 '"*Kesum-body*" and the places of the gods: the politics of children's masking and second world realities in Oku (Cameroon)'. *Man: Journal of the Royal Anthropological Institute* 7, 1: 67–94.

Bay, Edna. 2009. 'Review of Argenti 2007', *African Arts*, 42, 4: 94–95,

Fanso, Verkijika G., and B. Chem-Langhee. 2011. *Nso and its neighbours. Readings in the social history of the Western Grassfields of Cameroon*. Mankon: Langaa.

Fowler, Ian. 2011. 'Kingdoms of the Cameroon Grassfields', *Reviews in Anthropology* 40, 4: 292–311.

——. 2009. 'Review of Argenti 2007', *The Journal of the Anthropological Institute* 15, 2: 429–430.

——, and Verkijika G. Fanso, 2009. *Encounter, transformation and identity: peoples of the western Cameroon borderlands, 1891–2000*. New York: Berghahn Books.

——, and David Zeitlyn. 1996. *African crossroads: Intersections between history and anthropology in Cameroon*. Providence, Rhode I.: Berghahn Books.

Hurault, Jean. 1962. *La structure sociale des Bamiléké*. Paris, The Hague: Mouton.

Jindra, Michael. 2011. 'The rise of 'death celebrations' in the Cameroonian Grassfields'. In Michael Jindra and Joël Noret (eds) *Funerals in Africa. Explorations of a social phenomenon*. New York: Berghahn, 109–129.

——, and Joël Noret (eds). 2011. *Funerals in Africa. Explorations of a social phenomenon*. New York: Berghahn.

Kafko Fokou, Roger (ed.). 2014. *Les Mbäfeung: peuple des hautes terres de l'ouest du Cameroun: Croyances et pratiques traditionnelles et culturelles*. Paris: L'Harmattan.

Koloss, Hans-Joachim, 2012. *Cameroon thoughts and memories: Ethnological research in Oku and Kembong 1975–2005*. Berlin: Dietrich Reimer Verlag.

——. 2000. *World-view and society in Oku (Cameroon)*. Berlin: Reimer.

——. 1992. 'Kwifon and Fon in Oku. On kingship in the Cameroon Grasslands'. In Erna Beumers and Hans-Joachim Koloss (eds) *Kings of Africa. Art and authority in Central Africa*. Berlin: Museum für Völkerkunde, 33–42.

Mentan, Tatah. 2009. 'Review of Argenti 2007', *African Affairs* 108, 432: 498–499.

Rowlands, Michael. 2007. 'The sound of witchcraft: Noise as mediation in religious transmission'. In David Berliner and Ramon Sarró (eds) *Learning religion. Anthropological approaches*. Oxford: Berghahn, 191–207.

Stelzig, Christine. 2009. 'Cameroon: Art and Kings', *African Arts* 42, 1: 104–106.

Warnier, Jean-Pierre. 2011. 'The history of the peopling of western Cameroon and the genesis of its landscapes'. In B. Chem-Langhee and V.G. Fanso (eds) *Nso' and its neighbours. Readings in the social history of the western Grassfields of Cameroon*. Mankon: Langaa Research & Publishing, 3–22.

——. 2007. *The pot-king. The body and technologies of power*. Leiden: Brill.

Chewa, Mang'anja/Maravi

Birch, Laurel. 1996. *Inscribing the mask: Nyau ritual and performance among the Chewa of Central Malawi*. Freiburg: Anthropos Institute and University of Freiburg Press.

——. 1988. 'Basketry masks of the Chewa', *African Arts* 21, 3: 28–31+86.

Blackmun, Barbara, and Matthew Schoffeleers. 1972. 'Masks of Malawi', *African Arts* 5, 4: 36–41, 69, 88.

Boucher, Claude, Gary Morgan, and Arjen van de Merwe. 2012. *When animals sing and spirits dance: Gule Wankulu, the great dance of the Chewa people of Malawi*. Mua Parish: Kungoni Centre of Culture and Art.

Curran, Douglas. 1999. 'Nyau masks and ritual'. *African Arts* 32, 3: 68–77.

Kubik, Gerhard. 1993. *Makiwi nyau mapiko. Maskentraditionen im bantu-sprechenden Afrika*. Munich: Trickster Verlag.

Yoshida, Kenji. 2006. 'Kalumba and Chisudzo: Boys' and girls' masquerades among the Chewa'. In Simon Ottenberg and David Binkley (eds) *Playful performers. African children's masquerades*. New Brunswick: Transaction Publishers, 221–236.

Chokwe

Bastin, Marie-Louise. 1992. 'The Mnwanangana Chokwe chief and art'. In Erna Beumers and Hans-Joachim Koloss (eds) *Kings of Africa. Art and authority in Central Africa*. Berlin: Museum für Völkerkunde, 65–70.

——. 1984. 'Ritual masks of the Chokwe', *African Arts* 7, 4: 40–45, 92, 93, 95–96.

——. 1982. *La sculpture tshokwe*. Meudon: Alain et Francoise Chaffin.

Cameron, Elisabeth, and Manuel Jordán. 2006. 'Playing with the future: Children and rituals in North-Western Province, Zambia'. In Simon Ottenberg and David Binkley (eds) *Playful performers. African children's masquerades*. New Brunswick: Transaction publishers, 237–246.

Crowley, Daniel J. 1972. 'Chokwe: Political art in a plebeian society'. In Douglas Fraser and Herbert Cole (eds) *African art and leadership. Madison: University of Wisconsin Press*, 21–40.

Jordán, Manuel. 2014. 'Chokwe pwo masks: A note on style', *Tribal Arts* 71: 108–119.

——. 2000. 'Revisiting Pwo', *African Arts* 33, 4: 16–25, 92–93.

—— (ed.). 1982. *Chokwe: Art and initiation among the Chokwe and related peoples*. Munich: Prestel Publishing.

Rodrigues de Areia, M.L. 2003. *Chokwe and their Bantu neighbours*. Zürich: Jean David and Gerhard Merzedes.

Wastiau, Boris. 2008. *Chokwe*. Milan: Visions of Africa, 5 Continents.

Cross River

Afigbo, A.E. 1987. 'Southeastern Nigeria in the nineteenth century'. In J.F.A. Ajayi and Michael Crowder (eds) *History of West Africa*. Volume 2. Harlow: Longman: 429- 484.

Bentor, Eli. 2005. 'Challenges to rural festivals with the return to democratic rule in southeastern Nigeria', *African Arts* 38, 4: 38–45+93.

Berns, Maria C. and Richard Fardon, 2011. 'Central Nigeria unmasked: Arts of the Benue River valley', *African Arts* 44, 3, 16–37.

Ifeka, Caroline. 2009. 'Titi Ikoli revisited. Fetishism, gender and power in transitional forest economies of the upper Cross River borderlands, 1920s–1990s'. In Ian Fowler and Verkijika Fanso (eds) *Encounter, transformation and identity. Peoples of the Western Cameroon borderlands 1891–2000*. New York: Berghahn, 151–168.

Kasfir, Sidney L. 1988c. 'Celebrating male aggression: The Idoma Oglinye masquerade'. In Sidney L. Kasfir (ed.) *West African masks and cultural systems*. Tervuren: Royal Museum for Central Africa, 85–108.

Messenger, John C. 1979. 'The role of the carver in Anang society'. In Warren L. d'Azevedo (ed.) *The traditional artist in African societies*. Bloomington: Indiana University Press, 101–127.

Nichols, Robert W. 2006. '*Omepa* and *onjeweh* children's masquerades'. In Simon Ottenberg and David Binkley (eds) *Playful performers. African children's masquerades*. New Brunswick: Transaction publishers, 129–150.

Nicklin, Keith. 1979. 'Skin-covered masks of Cameroon', *African Arts* 12, 2: 54–59, 91–92.

——, and Jill Salmons. 1988. 'Ikem, the history of a masquerade in southeast Nigeria'. In Sidney Kasfir (ed.) *West African masks and cultural systems*. Brussels: Musée Royale de l'Afrique Central, 123–149.

Rea, Will, 2019. 'The Ẹpa Masquerades of Èkìtì: A Structural Approach', *African Arts* 52, 3: 16–27.

Röschenthaler, Ute. 2011. *Purchasing culture: The transmission of associations in the Cross River region of Nigeria and Cameroon*. Trenton NJ: Africa World Press.

——. 2004. 'Transacting Obasinjom: The dissemination of a cult agency in the Cross River Area', *Africa. Journal of the International African Society* 74, 2: 241–276.

——. 1998. 'Honoring Ejagham women', *African Arts* 31, 2: 38–49, 92–93.

——. 1993. *Die Kunst der Frauen: Zur Komplementarität von Nacktheit und Maskierung bei den Ejagham im Sudwesten Kameruns*. Berlin: Verlag für Wissenschaft und Bildung.

Dan, Kran

Fischer, Eberhard. 1978. 'Dan forest spirits: masks in Dan villages'. *African Arts* 11, 2: 16–23, 94.

——, and Hans Himmelheber. 1984. *The arts of the Dan in West Africa*. Zürich: Museum Rietberg.

Himmelheber, Hans. 1979. *Masken und Beschneidung*. Zürich: Museum Rietberg.

——. 1964. 'Die Geister und ihre irdische Verkörperungen als Grundvorstellungenin der Religion der Dan', *Baesler Archiv NF* 12: 1–88.

——. 1960. *Negerkunst und Negerkünstler*. Braunschweig: Klinkhardt and Biermann.

Reed, Daniel B. 2003. *Dan Ge performance. Masks and music in contemporary Côte d'Ivoire*. Bloomington: Indiana University Press.

——. 2001. 'Pop goes the sacred: Dan mask performance and popular culture in postcolonial Côte d'Ivoire', *Africa Today* 48, 4: 67–85.

Dida

Terray, Emmanuel, 1969. *L'organisation sociale des Dida de Côte d'Ivoire: Essai sur un village Dida de la region de Lakota*. Abidjan: Université d'Abidjan.

Dogon/Samo

Cissé, Lasana. 2022. 'A renaissance of masking'. In Polly Richards (ed.) *Dogon masks in motion*. Glienecke: Galda Verlag, 230–241.

Doquet, Anne. 2022. 'Mask festivals in the twenty-first century'. In Polly Richards (ed.) *Dogon masks in motion*. Glienecke: Galda Verlag, 230–240.

——. 1999. *Les masques dogon: Ethnologie savante et ethnologie autochtone*. Paris: Karthala.

Griaule, Marcel. 1938. *Masques dogons*. Paris: Plon.

Holder, Gilles. 2002. 'De la 'cité-État' en Afrique noire: L'espace et le politique chez les Saman du pays dogon (Mali)', *Cahiers d'études africaines* 42, 166: 257–283.

——. 2001. 'Gens de caste ou "Personnes-Blanches"? Esquisse du statut de l'étranger natif du pays dogon', *Journal des africanistes*, 71, 1: 121–148.

——. 1998. 'Slaves and captives among the Dogon: The Sama slavery society', *L'Homme*, 38, 145: 71–108.

Hollyman, Stepheny, and Walter E.A. van Beek. 2001. *Dogon. Africa's people of the cliffs*. New York: Abrams.

Leiris, Michel. 1948. *La langue secrète des Dogons de Sanga (Soudan français)*. Travaux et Mémoires de l'Institut d'Ethnologie 50. Paris: Institut d'Ethnologie, Musée de l'Homme.

Richards, Polly. 2022. *Dogon masks in motion*. Glienecke: Galda Verlag.

——. 2005. 'Dogon masks in a changing world', *African Arts* 38, 4: 46–53, 93.

Van Beek, Walter E.A. 2022. 'Masks in the Dogon tourist bubble'. In Polly Richards (ed.) *Dogon masks in motion*. Glienecke: Galda Verlag, 196–115.

——. 2018. 'Matter in motion: The Dogon kanaga mask', *Religions*, Special Issue, Albertina Nugteren (ed.), 9, 264; 14. Doi:10.3390/rel9090264.

——. 2013. 'Connecting ourselves: A Dogon ethnic association and the impact of connectivity'. In Rijk van Dijk and Mirjam de Bruijn (eds) *The social life of connectivity in Africa*. New York: Palgrave MacMillan, 243–264.

——. 2012. 'To dance or not to dance: Dogon masks as an arena'. In Walter E.A. van Beek and Annette Schmidt (eds) *African hosts and their guests. Dynamics of cultural tourism in Africa*. Oxford: James Currey, 37–57.

——. 2006. 'Boys and masks among the Dogon'. In Simon Ottenberg and David A. Binkley (eds) *Playful performers. African children's masquerades*. New Brunswick and London: Transaction Publishers, 67–88.

——. 1991a. 'Enter the bush: A Dogon mask festival'. In Susan Vogel (ed.) *Africa explores; 20ᵗʰ century African art*. New York: Prestel-Munich and Center for African Art, 56–73.

——. 1991b. 'Dogon restudied: A field evaluation of the work of Marcel Griaule', *Current Anthropology* 32, 2: 139–167.

——. 1988. 'Functions of sculpture in Dogon religion', *African Arts* 21, 4: 58–66.

——, and Pieteke Banga. 1992. 'The Dogon and their trees'. In Elisabeth Croll and David Parkin (eds) *Bush base, forest farm. Culture, environment and development*. London: Routledge, 57–75.

——, Oumar Ongoiba, and Atimè Saye. 2022. *Singing with the Dogon prophet*. New York: Lexington University Press.

Ebira

Ballard, J.A. 1971. 'Historical inferences from the linguistic geography of the Nigerian Middle Belt', *Africa. Journal of the International African Institute* 41, 4: 294–305.

Picton, John. 2009. 'Cloth and the corpse in Ebira', *Textile: The Journal of Cloth and Culture* 7, 3: 296–313.

——. 1997. 'On (men?) placing women in Ebira', *Annals of the New York Academy of Sciences* 810, 1: 337–369.

——. 1992. 'Masks and identities in Ebira culture'. In Joan Maw and John Picton (eds) *Concepts of the body/self in Africa*. Vienna: Afro-Publishers, 67–86.

——. 1989. 'On placing masquerades in Ebira', *African Languages and Cultures* 2, 1: 73–92.

——. 1988a. 'Some Ebira reflexions on the energies of women', *African Languages and Cultures* 1, 1: 61–76.

——. 1988b. 'What's in a mask?', *African languages and cultures* 3, 2: 181–202.

Sani, H.A. 1993. *Sociology of the Ebira Tao people of Nigeria*. Okene: Habibu Angulu Sani and Sons Enterprises.

Segun, Joshua. 2018. 'Clan politics and violent conflict in Nigeria: The Ebira Tao experience', *African Identities* 16, 1: 35–49.

Fali (North Cameroon)[1]

Gauthier, J.-G. 1988. *Les chemins du mythe*. Meudon: Editions du CNRS.

——. 1969. *Les Fali Hou et Tšalo. Montagnards du Nord-Cameroun*. Oosterhout: Anthropological Publications.

---

1   Different from the Fali in northeastern Nigeria, who have no masks.

Fang

Fernandez, James W. 1982. *Bwiti: An ethnography of the religious imagination in Africa.* Princeton, NJ: Princeton University Press.

Lagamma, Alisa (ed.). 2007. *Eternal ancestors. The art of the Central African reliquary.* New Haven and London: Yale University Press.

Perrois, Louis. 2008. 'Fang masks of Equatorial Africa', *Tribal Arts* 50: 96–113.

——. 2006. *Fang.* Visions d'Afrique series. Milan: 5 Continents Editions.

Fulbe

De Bruijn, Mirjam, and Han van Dijk. 1995. *Arid ways. Cultural understandings of insecurity in Fulbe society, Central Mali.* Amsterdam: Thela Publishers.

Gbaya

Burnham, Philip. 1980. *Opportunity and constraint in a savannah society: The Gbaya of Meiganga, Cameroon.* London: Academic Press.

——. 1975. '"Regroupement" and mobile societies: Two Cameroonian cases', *Journal of African History* 16, 4: 577–594.

Roulon-Doko, Paulette. 2017. 'L'adresse annuelle aux ancêtres chez le Gbaya de Centrafrique'. In Émilie Guitard and Walter E.A. van Beek (eds) *Rites et religions dans le basin du lac Tchad.* Paris: Karthala, 255–272.

Pilo Atta, Silvie. 2017. 'Les rites de procréation chez les Gbaya Yaayuwé'. In Émilie Guitard and Walter E.A. van Beek (eds) *Rites et religions dans le basin du lac Tchad.* Paris: Karthala, 241–254.

North Ghana

Lentz, Carola. 2009. 'Constructing ritual protection on an expanding settlement frontier: Earth shrines in the Black Volta region'. In Allan C. Dawson (ed.) *Shrines in Africa. History, politics, and society.* Calgary: University of Calgary Press, 121–152.

MacGaffey, Wyatt. 2013. *Chiefs, priests, and praise-singers.* Charlottesville: University of Virginia Press.

Nunley, John W. 1987. *Moving with the face of the devil. Art and politics in urban West Africa.* Chicago: University of Chicago Press.

——. 1981. 'The fancy and the fierce', *African Arts* 14, 2: 52–58+87–88.

——. 1977. 'Sikilen: Transformation of a Sisala masquerade', *African Arts* 11, 1: 58–64+92.

Poppi, Césare. 2013. 'The trail of Sigma. Masks and technologies of power in North-Western Ghana'. In Anne-Marie Bouttiaux (ed.) *La dynamique des masques en Afrique occidentale.* Tervuren: Royal Museum for Central Africa, 181–196.

Guro

Aubry N. et al. 1988. *Corps sculptés, corps parés, corps masqués: chefs d'œuvre de Côte d'Ivoire*. Paris: Galeries du Grand Palais.

Bouttiaux, Anne-Marie. 2013a. 'Du divertissement au sacrifice. Danses des masques guro de la région de Zuenoula, Côte d'Ivoire'. In Anne-Marie Bouttiaux (ed.) *La dynamique des masques en Afrique occidentale*. Tervuren: Royal Museum for Central Africa, 115–140.

——. 2001. *La danse des masques, la jubilation des esprits. Masques guro de la région de Zuenoula*. Brussels: Université libre de Bruxelles.

——. 2009. 'Guro masked performers: Sculpted bodies serving spirits and people', *African Arts* 42, 2: 56–67.

Fischer, Eberhard. 2008. *Guro. Masks, performances and master carvers in Ivory Coast*. Munich: Prestel.

Haxaire, Claude. 2011. 'The power of ambiguity: The nature and efficacy of Zamble masks revealed by "disease masks" among the Guro people (Côte d'Ivoire)', *Africa. Journal of the International African Institute* 79, 4: 543–569.

Meillassoux, Claude. 1964. *Anthropologie économique des Gouro de Côte d'Ivoire: De l'économie de subsistance à l'agriculture commerciale*. Paris/The Hague: Mouton.

Igbo, Ibibio, Afikpo, Aro, Igala

Achebe, Nwando. 2003. '"And she became a man": King Ahebi Ugbabe in the history of Enugu-Ezike, Northern Igboland 1880–1940'. In Lisa A. Lindsay and Stephan F. Miescher (eds) *Men and masculinities in modern Africa*. Portsmouth: Heineman, 52–68.

Aniakor, Chike C. 1978. 'The Igbo Ijele Mask', *African Arts*, 11, 4: 42–53+95.

Akpan, Joseph, J. 1994. 'Ekpo society masks of the Ibibio', *African Arts* 27, 4: 48–53, 94–95.

Bentor, Eli. 1994a. '"Remember six foot deep": Masks and the exculpation of/ from death in Aro masquerade', *Journal of Religion in Africa* 14, 4: 323–338.

——. 1994b. 'Aro Ikeji festival: Toward a historical interpretation of a masquerade festival'. Ann Arbor: ProQuest Dissertations Publishing.

Borgatti, Jean M. 2003. 'The *otsa* festival of Ekperi: Igbo age-grade masquerades on the west bank of the Niger', *African Arts* 36, 4: 40–47, 93–95.

Boston, J.S. 1968. *The Igala kingdom*. Ibadan: Oxford University Press.

Cole, Herbert M., and Chike C. Anakior. 1984. *Igbo arts: Community and cosmos*. Berkeley: Museum of Cultural History.

Gore, Charles. 2008b. '"Burn the Mmonwu": Contradictions and contestations in masquerade performance in Uga, Anambra State in southeastern Nigeria', *African Arts* 41, 4: 60–73.

Imeh, Imo Nse. 2012. *Daughters of seclusion: the revelation of the Ibibio 'fattened bride' as the icon of beauty and power*. New York: Peter Lang.

Kasfir, Sidney L. 2019. 'Igala's royal masks: Borrowed, invented, or stolen?', *African Arts* 52, 1: 62–71.

Nwabueze, Emeka, 1989. 'The masquerade as hero in Igbo traditional society', *Frankfurter afrikanistische Blätter* 1: 95–107.

Okagbue, O. 1997. 'When the dead return: Play and seriousness in African masked performances', *South African Theatre Journal* 11, 1: 69–101.

Okeke, Chika O. 2006. 'At the threshold: Childhood masking in Umuoji and Umahia'. In Simon Ottenberg and David Binkley (eds) *Playful performers. African children's masquerades.* New Brunswick: Transaction publishers, 159–165.

Ottenberg, Simon. 1975. *Masked rituals of Afikpo. The context of an African art.* Washington: Henry Art Gallery.

Sargent, R.A. 1988. 'The Igala of central Nigeria: 1988'. In Sidney L. Kasfir (ed.) *West African masks and cultural systems.* Tervuren: Royal Museum for Central Africa, 17–31.

Vossenaar, T. 1989. *Ziektemaskers uit West Afrika.* Eindhoven: Galerie Tegenbosch.

Jola/Diola

De Jong, Ferdinand. 2007a. *Masquerades of modernity. Power and secrecy in Casamance, Senegal.* Edinburgh: Edinburgh University Press.

——. 2007b. 'A masterpiece of masquerading: Contradictions of conservation'. In Ferdinand de Jong and Michael Rowlands (eds) *Reclaiming heritage. Alternative imagineries of memory in West Africa.* Walnut Creek, CA: Left Coast Press, 161–183.

——. 1999. 'Trajectories of a mask performance: The case of the Senegalese kumpo', *Cahier d'Études africaines* 153, 1: 49–71.

Langeveld, Kirsten. 2003. *Het geheim van het masker.* Amsterdam: Rozenberg Publishing.

Mark, Peter. 1992. *The wild bull and the sacred forest. Form, meaning, and change in Senegambian initiation masks.* Cambridge: Cambridge University Press.

——, Ferdinand de Jong, and Clémence Chupin. 2014. 'Ritual and masking tradition in Jola men's initiation', *African Arts* 31, 1: 36–47, 94–96.

Jos Plateau Nigeria

Chalifoux, Jean-Jacques. 1981. 'Société secrète dodo, thérapie et pouvoirs des cadets chez les Abisi (Piti) du Nigéria (État de Kaduna)', *Anthropologie et Sociétés* 5, 3: 47–63.

Danfulani, Umar. 1999b. 'Exorcising witchcraft: The return of the gods in the new religious movements on the Jos Plateau and the Benue regions of Nigeria', *African affairs: The Journal of the Royal African Society* 98, 391: 167–193.

Isichei, Elizabeth. 1988. 'On masks and audible ghosts: Some secret male cults in Central Nigeria', *Journal of Religion in Africa* 18, 1: 42–70.

Muller, Jean-Claude. 1998. *Jeux de miroirs: Structures politiques du haut plateau nigérian.* Paris: Éditions de l'École des Hautes Études en Sciences Sociales.

——. 1990. 'Transgression, rites de rajeunissement et mort culturelle du roi chez les Jukun et les Rukuba (Nigéria central)', *Systèmes de Pensée en Afrique Noire* 10.

——. 1994. *Le roi bouc émissaire: Pouvoir et rituel chez les Rukuba du Nigéria central.* Québec: S. Fleury.

Sangree, Walter H. 1974. 'The Dodo cult, witchcraft and secondary marriages in Irigwe, Nigeria', *Ethnology* 12, 3: 261–278.

Smith, M.G. 1959. 'Secondary marriages in northern Nigeria', *Africa. Journal of the International African Institute* 22, 3: 298–323.

Jukun

Meek, C.K. 1931. *A Sudanese kingdom: An ethnographic study of Jukunoid-speaking peoples of Nigeria.* London: Kegan Paul, Trech, Trubner and Co.

Rubin, Arnold G. 1982. *The arts of the Jukun speaking peoples of northern Nigeria.* Ann Arbor, MI: University Microfilms.

——. 1974. *Interaction: The art styles of the Benue river valley and eastern Nigeria.* Lafayette, IN: Purdue University.

Kapsiki/Higi

Van Beek, Walter E.A. 2015. *The forge and the funeral. The smith in Kapsiki/Higi culture.* East Lansing: Michigan State University Press.

——. 2012. *The dancing dead. Ritual and religion among the Kapsiki/Higi of North Cameroon and Northeastern Nigeria.* New York: Oxford University Press.

——. 1998. 'Les Kapsiki et leurs bovins'. In Christian Seignobos and Éric Thys (eds) *Des taurins et des hommes, Cameroun, Nigéria.* Paris: Orstom, 15–38.

Kongo

MacGaffey, Wyatt. 2000. *Kongo political culture. The conceptual challenge of the particular.* Bloomington: Indiana University press.

——. 1988. 'Astonishment and power: The visual vocabulary of Kongo minkisi', *Journal of Southern African Studies* 14, 2: 188–203.

——. 1986. *Religion and society in Central Africa.* Chicago: University of Chicago Press.

——. 1983. 'Lineage structure, marriage and the family amongst the central Bantu', *Journal of African History* 24, 2: 173–187.

Kuba/Bushong

Binkley, David A. 2021. *A view from the forest: The power of Southern Kuba initiation rites and masks.* Seattle: Lucia/Marquand

——. 2010. 'Southern Kuba initiation rites: the ephemeral face of power and secrecy', *African Arts* 43, 1, 44–59.

——. 2006. 'From grasshopper to Babende: The socialisation of southern Kuba boys to masquerade'. In Simon Ottenberg and David Binkley (eds) *Playful performers. African children's masquerades.* New Brunswick: Transaction publishers, 105–116.

——. 1987. 'Avatar of power: Southern Kuba masquerades in a funerary context', *Africa: Journal of the International African Institute* 57, 1: 75–97.

Cornet, Joseph. 1982. *Art royal Kuba*. Milan: Sipiel.

Darish, Patricia, and David A. Binkley. 1995. 'Headdresses and title holding among the Kuba'. In Mary-Jo Arnoldi and Christine M. Kreamer (eds) *Crowning achievements.* Los Angeles: Fowler Museum UCLA, 159–169.

Vansina, Jan. 1992c. 'The Kuba kingdom (Zaire)'. In Erna Beumers and Hans-Joachim Koloss (eds) *Kings of Africa. Art and authority in Central Africa.* Berlin: Museum für Völkerkunde, 71–78.

——. 1978. *The children of Woot. A history of the Kuba peoples.* Madison: University of Wisconsin Press.

Verswijver, Gustaaf, Els de Palmenaer, Viviane Baeke, Anne-Marie Bouttiaux-Ndiaye. 1995. *Schatten uit het Afrika Museum Tervuren.* Antwerpen: de Vries-Brouwers.

Kwele, Woyo

Mulinda, Habi. 1995. 'Masks as proverbial language, Woyo, Zaire'. In Luc de Heusch (ed.) *Objects, signs of Africa.* Tervuren: Snoeck-Ducaju & Son, 147–160.

Siroto, Leon. 1972. 'Gon: A mask used in competition for leadership among the Bakwele'. In Douglas Fraser and Herbert Cole (eds) African art and leadership. Madison: University of Wisconsin Press, 57–77.

Lega

Biebuyck, Daniel, 1973. *Lega culture: Art, initiation, and moral philosophy among a Central African people.* Berkeley: University of California.

Limba/Kuranko

Hart, William A. 2019. 'A mask of the Western Kuranko', *African Arts* 52, 3: 28–33.

——. 1988. 'Limba funeral masks', *African Arts* 22, 1: 60–67+99.

——. 1987. 'Masks with metal-strip ornament from Sierra Leone', *African Arts* 20, 3: 68–74, 90.

Ottenberg, Simon. 1988. 'Religion and ethnicity in the art of a Limba chiefdom', *Africa: Journal of the International African Institute* 58, 4: 437–465.

Luba

Nooter, Mary H. 1993. 'Secrecy: African art that conceals and reveals', *African Arts* 26, 1: 54–69, 102.

——. 1992. 'Fragments of forsaken glory: Luba royal culture invented and represented (1883–1992) (Zaire)'. In Erna Beumers and Hans J. Koloss (eds) *Kings of Africa. Art and authority in Central Africa.* Berlin: Museum für Völkerkunde, 79–89.

——, and Allen F. Roberts. 1996. *Memory. Luba art and the making of history*. New York: Prestel, Museum for African Art.

O'Reefe, Thomas. 1981. *The rainbow and the kings. A history of the Luba empire to 1891*. Berkeley: UCLA Press.

Vecsey, Christopher. 1983. 'Facing death, masking death, in Luba myth and art', *Journal of Religion in Africa* 14, 1: 24–45.

Luntu/Bakwa Luntu

Petridis, Constantijn. 2005. 'Bwadi bwa chikwanga: a ram mask of the Bakwa Luntu', *African Arts* 38, 2: 50–59+93–95.

——. 2003. 'Among the Luntu and neighboring peoples of the Democratic Republic of the Congo and Angola'. In Frank Herreman (ed.) *Material differences; art and identity in Africa*. New York: Museum of African Art, 136–141.

——. 1999. 'Luluwa masks', *African Arts* 32, 3: 32–37+91–94.

Luvale

Ellert, Henrik, Ian Murphy, and David Ball. 2004. *The magic of makishi. Masks and traditions in Zambia*. Bath: CBC Publishing.

Sangambo, Mose K., Art Hansen, and J. R. Papstein. 1979. *The history of the Luvale people and their chieftainship*. Los Angeles: Africa Institute for Applied Research.

Wele, Patrick. 1993. *Likumbi lya Mise and other Luvale ceremonies*. Lusaka: Zambia Educational Publishing House.

Makonde

Harries, Lyndon P. 1970 (1944). *The initiation rites of the Makonde tribe*. Lusaka: Institute for Social Research.

Israel, Paolo, 2014. *In step with the times: Mapiko masquerades of Mozambique*. Athens, OH: Ohio University Press.

Mambila

Zeitlyn, David. 2020. *Mambila divination: Framing questions, constructing answers*. Milton: Routledge.

——. 1994a. 'Mambila figurines and masquerades: Problems of interpretation', *African Arts* 27, 4: 38–47+94.

——. 1994b. *Sua in Somié: Aspects of Mambila traditional religion*. Sankt Augustin: Academia Verlag.

Manding/Mandinka/Mande, Wuli

Bravmann, René. 1979. 'Gur and Manding masquerades in Ghana', *African Arts* 13, 1: 44–51, 98.

Weil, Peter. 2005. 'Masking for money: The commodification of Kankurang and Simba mask performances in urban Gambia'. In Stephen Wooter (ed.) *Wari matters: Ethnographic explorations in the Mande World*. Berlin: LIT Verlag, 162–177.

——. 1998. 'Women's masks and the power of gender in Mande history', *African Arts* 31, 2: 28–37, 88–90, 94–9.

——. 1987. 'Fighting fire with fire: The Mandinka *sengko* mask'. In Sidney L. Kasfir (ed.) *West African masks and cultural systems*. Tervuren: Royal Museum of Central Africa, 151–194.

——. 1971. 'The masked figure and social control: The Mandinka case'. *Africa. Journal of the International African Institute* 41, 4: 279–293.

Mende, Kpelle, Temne, Gola

Adams, Marie J. (ed.). 1980. 'Special issue on Sande and Poro Masking', *Ethnologische Zeitschrift*. Zürich/Bern: Verlag H. Lange.

Bellman, Beryl L. 1984. *The language of secrecy. Symbols and metaphors in Poro rituals*. New Brunswick: Rutgers University Press.

——. 1980. 'Masks, societies and secrecy among the Fala Kpelle', *Ethnologische Zeitschrift Zürich* 1: 61–79.

Bledsoe, Caroline. 1984. 'The political use of Sande ideology and symbolism', *American Ethnologist* 11, 3: 455–472.

Blier, Suzanne. 1986. *Radiance from the waters: Ideals of feminine beauty in Mende art*. New Haven: Yale University Press.

Cannizo, Jeanne. 2006. 'The Alikali devils of Sierra Leone: Play, performance, and the social commentary'. In Simon Ottenberg and David Binkley (eds) *Playful performers. African children's masquerades*. New Brunswick: Transaction publishers, 167–180.

D'Azevedo, Warren L. 1994. 'Gola womanhood and the limits of male omnipotence'. In Thomas D. Blakely, Walter E.A. van Beek and Dennis L. Thomson (eds) *Religion in Africa: Experience and expression*. London: Currey and Heinemann, 342–362.

——. 1973. 'Mask makers and myth in western Liberia'. In Anthony Forge (ed.) *Primitive Art and Society*. London: Oxford University Press.

Jedrej, M.C. 1986. 'Dan and Mende masks: a structural comparison', *Africa. Journal of the International African institute* 56, 1: 71–80.

Lamp, Frederick. 2014. 'The master of the rainbow eyes: A prolific carver of the Mende of Sierra Leone', *Yale University Art Gallery Bulletin*, Recent Acquisitions, 47–53.

——. 1988. 'Heavenly bodies, menses, moon, and rituals of licence among the Temne of Sierra Leone'. In Thomas Buckley and Alma Gottlieb (eds) *Blood magic. The anthropology of menstruation*. Berkeley: University of California Press, 210–231.

MacCormack, Carol P. 1979. 'Sande: The public face of a secret society'. In Bennetta Jules-Rosette (ed.) *The new religions of Africa*. Norwood NJ: Ablex Publishing Company, 27–37.

——. 1975. 'Sande women and political power in Sierra Leone', *West African Journal of Social and Political Science* 1, 1: 42–50. Norwood, NJ: Ablex.

Phillips, Ruth. 1995. *Representing woman. Sande masquerades of the Mende of Sierra Leone*. Los Angeles: Fowler Museum of Cultural History UCLA.

——. 1975. 'Masking in Mende Sande society initiation rituals', *Africa. Journal of the International African Institute* 45, 3: 265–277.

Siegmann, William C. 1980. *Spirit manifestation and the Poro society*. Bern: Peter Lang.

Van de Raadt, Steven. 2023. 'Het Sande masker: Een dynamisch verschijnsel', *Tribale Kunst* 11, 1: 61–67.

Minyanka

Jespers, Philippe. 2013. L'ouverture des yeux au Komo. In Anne-Marie Bouttiaux (ed.) *La dynamique des masques en Afrique occidentale*. Tervuren: Royal Museum for Central Africa, 37–66.

——. 2011. Les masques du Komo, figure hybrides comme microcosme. In Paul Marathan (ed.) *Arts d'Afrique. Voir l'invisible*. Bordeaux: Musée d'Aquitanie, 33–39.

——. 1995. Mask and utterance: the analysis of an 'auditory' mask in the initiatory society of the Komo (Minyanka, Mali). In Luc de Heusch (ed.) *Objects, signs of Africa*. Tervuren: Snoeck-Ducaju and Son: 37–56.

Mongo

Bongango, Joseph. 2008. *L'organisation sociale chez les Mongo de Basankusu et sa transformation*. Paris: Éditions Publibook.

Mossi/Kurumba

Baird-Hinckley, Priscilla. 2006. 'The Dodo masquerade of Ougadougou'. In Simon Ottenberg and David Binkley (eds) *Playful performers: African children's masquerades.* New Brunswick: Transaction publishers, 207–220.

Izard, Michel. 2005. *Moogo. L'émergence d'un espace étatique ouest-africain au XVIe sciècle. Étude d'anthropologie historique*. Paris: Karthala.

——. 1992. *L'Odyssée du pouvoir. Un royaume africain: État, société, destin individual*. Paris: EHESS.

——. 1985. *Gens du pouvoir, gens de la terre: Les institutions politiques de l'ancien royaume du Yatenga (Bassin de la Volta Blanche)*. Paris: Cambridge University Press and Maison des sciences de l'homme.

Luning, Sabine. 2010. *Nouvelles choses: Rites et politique dans la chefferie de Maane (Burkina Faso)*. Mande Worlds no. 5. Münster: LIT Verlag.

——. 1991. *Mossi maskers in musea: Dode voorwerpen of levende wezens.* Leiden: Leiden University.

Roy, Christopher. 2003. *African masks: Burkina faso.* DVD.

——. 1979. *Mossi masks and crests.* Dissertation Indiana University.

Schweeger-Hefel, Annemarie. 1980. *Masken und Mythen. Socialstrukturen der Nyonyosi und Sikomse in Ober Volta.* Wien: A. Schendl.

——, and Wilhelm Staude. 1972. *Die Kurumba von Lurum. Monographie eines Volkes aus Obervolta (Westafrika).* Wien: A. Schendl.

Mundang

Adler, Alfred. 1998. 'Des rois et des masques: Essai d'analyse comparative (Moundang du Tchad, Bushong de l'ex-Zaïre)', *L'Homme* 145: 169–203.

——. 1994. 'Levée de deuil et consécration de l'héritier (Moundang, Tchad)', *Systèmes de pensée en Afrique noire* XIII: 89–119.

——. 1989. 'La fillette amoureuse des masques: Le statut de la femme chez les Moundang', *Journal des Africanistes* 59, 1/2: 63–97.

——. 1982. *La mort est le masque du roi: La royauté sacrée des Moundang du Tchad.* Paris: Payot.

Schilder, Kees. 1994. *Quest for self-esteem. State, Islam and Mundang ethnicity in Northern Cameroon.* Leiden: CNWS/African Studies Centre.

Taïno Kari. 2015. *Les Moundang du Cameroun et du Tchad: Onomastique et histoire (XVIIIe–XXe siècle).* Paris: Le Harmattan.

Mumuye

Bovin, Mette. 2011. 'Seen or heard? Masquerades that cry and figures that talk among the Mumuye'. In Marla C. Berns, Richard Fardon and Sidney Littlefield Kasfir (eds) *Central Nigeria unmasked: Arts of the Benue river valley.* Los Angeles: Fowler Museum of Cultural History UCLA, 365–83.

——. 1966. 'Hvadol betyder for Mumuye tamen', *Jordens Folk* 1, 2: 85–91.

Gagliardi, Susan E. 2011. 'Mining the Rubin archive: Mid-twentieth-century documentation of two Mumuye Vabo masquerades'. In Marla C. Berns, Richard Fardon, and Sidney Littlefield Kasfir (eds) *Central Nigeria unmasked: Arts of the Benue river valley.* Los Angeles: Fowler Museum of Cultural History UCLA, 354–363, 576.

Rubin, Arnold. 1985. 'A Mumuye mask'. In Herbert M. Cole (ed.) *I am not myself: The art of African masquerade.* Los Angeles: Museum of Cultural History, 98–99.

Ndembu

Jordán, Manuel. 1993. 'Le masque comme processus ironique: Les makishi du Nord-Ouest de la Zambie', *Anthropologie et Sociétés* 17, 3: 41–61.

Pritchett, James. 2001. *The Lunda-Ndembu: Style, change, and social transformation in South Central Africa.* Madison: University of Wisconsin Press.

Turner, Victor W. 1991 (1969). *The ritual process: Structure and anti-structure*. Ithaca: Cornell University Press.

——. 1974. *Dramas, fields and metaphors: Symbolic action in human society*. Ithaca: Cornell University Press.

——. 1967. *The forest of symbols. Aspects of Ndembu ritual*. Ithaca: Cornell University Press.

Niger Delta

Alagoa, E.J. 1967. 'Delta masquerades', *Nigeria Magazine* 93: 145–155.

Anderson, Martha G. 2002. 'Visual arts of the Niger Delta'. In Martha G. Anderson and Philip M. Peek (eds) *Ways of the rivers: Arts and environment of the Niger Delta*. Los Angeles: UCLA Fowler Museum of Cultural History, 150–165.

Bassey (Engineer). (1998–2001). E*kpe Efik: A theosophical perspective*. Victoria BC: Trafford Publishing.

Carlson, Amanda B. 2019. 'In the spirit and in the flesh: Women, masquerades, and the Cross River', *African Arts* 52, 1: 46–61.

Fenton, Jordan A. 2019. 'Expressive currencies: Artistic transactions and transformations of warrior-inspired masquerades in Calabar', *African Arts* 52: 1: 18–33.

Hlavácová, Anna A. 2006. 'Three points of view of masquerades among the Ijo of Niger river delta'. In Simon Ottenberg and David Binkley (eds) *Playful performers. African children's masquerades*. New Brunswick: Transaction publishers, 151–158.

Horton, Robin. 1963. 'The Kalabari Ekine society: A borderline of religion and art', *Africa: Journal of the International African institute* 33, 2: 94–114.

Miller, Ivor. 2016. 'The Ékpè leopard society of Africa and its Cuban diaspora: A conversation between leaders', *Afro-Hispanic Review* 35, 2: 142–161.

——. 2011. *Voice of the leopard. African secret societies and Cuba*. Jackson: Mississippi University Press.

——. 2005. 'Cuban Abakuá chants: Examining new linguistic and historical evidence for the African diaspora', *African Studies Reviews* 48, 1: 23–58.

——, and Mavew Ojong. 2012. 'Ékpè "leopard" society in Africa and the Americas: Influence and values of an ancient tradition', *Ethnic and Racial Studies*. Special issue on 'Secret or private organisations, race and ethnicity': 1–16.

——, Paul Lovejoy, and D. Imbua (eds). 2017. *Calabar and Cross River: Historical and cultural studies*. Trenton, NJ: Africa World Press.

Nkoya

Van Binsbergen, Wim. 1992. *Tears of rain. Ethnicity and history in Central Western Zambia*. London: Kegan Paul International.

——. 1981. *Religious change in Zambia*. London: Kegan Paul International.

Nupe

Nadel, Siegfried F.S. 1954. *Nupe religion*. London: Routledge and Kegan Paul.
———. 1942. *A black Byzantium: The kingdom of Nupe in Nigeria*. London: Oxford University Press.
———. 1937. 'Gunnu, a fertility cult of the Nupe in Northern Nigeria', *Journal of the Royal Anthropological Institute of Great Britain and Ireland* 67: 91–130.

Pende

Strother, Z.S. 2008. *Pende*. Milan: Cinq Continents.
———. 1998. *Inventing masks: Agency and history in the art of the Central Pende*. Chicago: University of Chicago Press.
———. 1995. 'Invention and reinvention in the traditional arts', *African Arts* 28, 2: 24–33, 90.
———, and Nzomba Dugo Kakema. 2020. 'The role of masks in the Eastern Pende Mukanda'. In Nanina Guyer and Michaela Oberhofer (eds) *Congo as fiction: Art worlds between past and present*. Zürich: Museum Rietberg, 254–272

Salampasu

Cameron, Elisabeth L. 1988. 'Sala Mpasu masks'. *African Arts* 22, 1: 34–43, 98.

Senufo

Förster, Till. 2019. 'The invisible social body: Experience and Poro ritual in Northern Côte d'Ivoire', *African Studies Review*, 62, 1: 99–119.
———. 'Senufo masking and the art of Poro', *African Arts* 26, 1: 30–41, 101.
———. *Die Kunst der Senufo*. Museum Rietberg, Zürich.
Gagliardi, Susan E. 2022. *Seeing the unseen. Arts of power associations on the Senufo-Mande cultural 'frontier'*. Bloomington: Indiana University Press.
———. 2018a. 'Seeing the unseen audience: Women and West African power association masquerades', *Africa. Journal of the International African institute* 88, 4: 744–767.
———. 2018b. 'Art and the individual in African masquerades', *Africa. Journal of the International African institute* 88, 4: 702–717.
———. 2015. *Senufo unbound: Dynamics of art and identity in West Africa*. Milan: 5 Continents Editions.
———. 2010. *Crossing borders, pushing boundaries: Arts of power associations on the Senufo-Mande cultural frontier*. Dissertation UCLA.
Glaze, Anita, 1981. *Art and death in a Senufo village*. Bloomington: Indiana University Press.
———. 1975. 'Woman power and the art in a Senufo village', *African Arts* 8, 3: 24–29, 64–68.

Richter, Dolores. 1979. 'Senufo mask classification', *African Arts* 12, 3: 66–73, 93–94.
Veirman, Anja. 2001. 'Olbrechts en de expedities naar West-Afrika. Cat. Kunst van de Senufo'. In Constantijn Petridis (ed.) *Frans Olbrechts, 1899–1958. Op zoek naar kunst in Afrika*. Antwerpen: Etnografisch Museum, 235–253.

Songye

Hersak, Dunja. 2020. 'Further perspectives on kifwebe masquerades', *African Arts* 53, 1: 6–23.
——. 2012. 'On the concept of prototype in Songye masquerades', *African Arts* 45, 2: 12–2.
——. 2010. 'Reviewing power, process, and statement: The case of Songye figures', *African Arts* 43, 2: 38–51.
Volper, Julien. 2012. *Autour des Songye – Under the influence of the Songye*. Annales des Arts africains no. 1. Montreuil: Gourcuff/Gradenico Publishing.

Tabwa

Roberts, Allen F. 1980. 'Tabwa masks: An old trick of the human race', *African Arts* 23, 2: 36–47+101–103.

Tetela

De Heusch, Luc. 1995. 'Beauty is elsewhere: Returning a verdict on the Tetela masks (Historical and ethnological notes on the Nkutsu)'. In Luc de Heusch (ed.) *Objects, signs of Africa*. Tervuren: Snoeck-Ducaju and Zoon, 175–206.

Tikar

Abega, Séverin C. 2000. *Les choses de la forêt. Les masques des princes Tikar de Nditam*. Yaoundé: Presses de l'UCAC.
Geary, Christraud. 2008. 'Bamum and Tikar: Inspiration and innovation'. In Lorenz Homberger (ed.) *Cameroon. Art and kings*. Zürich: Museum Rietberg, 23–68.
Joseph, Marietta B. 1974. 'Dance masks of Tikar', *African Arts* 7, 3: 46–52, 91.

Tiv

Abuku, Mnena. 2008. 'Masks and symbols in masquerade performances among the Tiv of central Nigeria', *African performance review. Journal of the African Theatre Association* 2, 1: 19–28.
Bohannan, Laura, and Paul Bohannan. 1953. *The Tiv of central Nigeria*. London: International African Institute.

Urhobo

Diakparomre, Abal Mac. 2010. 'Symbolism in Urhobo masks and mask performances', *Journal of Asian and African Studies* 45, 5: 467–484.

Foss, Perkins. 2003. '*Eravwe*: An ephemeral Urhobo water spirit masquerade'. In Frank Herreman (ed.) *Material differences; art and identity in Africa.* New York: Museum of African Art, 132–135.

Wè, Guere

Adams, Monni. 1993. 'Women's art as gender strategy among the Wè of canton Boo', *African Arts* 26, 4: 32–41.

——. 1986. 'Women and masks among the western Wè of Ivory Coast', *African Arts* 19, 2: 46–55, 90.

Guyblehon, Bony. 2013. 'Le masque koui face aux mutations sociales en pays wè'. In Anne-Marie Bouttiaux (ed.) *La dynamique des masques en Afrique occidentale.* Tervuren: Royal Museum for Central Africa, 115–140.

Verger-Fèvre, Marie-Noël. 2005. 'Masks of the Wè in western Côte d'Ivoire', *Tribal Art* 27: 96–119.

Yakö

Forde, Daryll. 1964. *Yakö Studies.* London: Oxford University Press.

Yoruba, Southwest Nigeria

Abiodun, Rowland. 1994. 'Understanding Yoruba art and aesthetics: The concept of ase', *African Arts* 27, 3: 68–78, 102–103.

——, Henry J. Drewal, and John Pemberton III (eds). 1994. *The Yoruba artist: New theoretical perspectives on African arts.* Washington, DC: Smithsonian Institution Press.

Aremu, P.S.O. 1995. 'Egungun masquerades as socio-religious manifestation', *Africana Marburgensia* 28, 1/2: 3–13.

Borgatti, Jean M. 1988. 'Anogiri: Okpella's masked festival heralds'. In Sidney L. Kasfir (ed.) *West African masks and cultural systems.* Tervuren: Royal Museum for Central Africa, 65–84.

Beier, Ulli. 1958. 'Gelede masks', *Odu* 6: 5–23.

Drewal, Henry J. 1974a. 'Efe, voiced power and pageantry', *African Arts* 7, 2: 26–29, 58–66, 82–83.

——. 1974b. 'Gelede masquerade, imagery and motif', *African Arts* 7, 4: 8–19, 95–96, 162–163.

——, and Margaret Thompson Drewal. 1983. *Gelede. Art and female power among the Yoruba.* Bloomington: Indiana University Press.

——, and John Pemberton III with Rowland Abiodun. 1989. *Yoruba. Nine centuries of African art and thought.* New York: Harry N. Abram.

Drewal, Margaret Thompson. 1992. *Yoruba ritual: Performers, play, and agency.* Bloomington: Indiana University press.

——, and Henry J. Drewal. 1978. 'More powerful than each other: An Egbado classification of *egungun*', *African Arts* 11, 3: 28–39, 98–99.

——, and Henry J. Drewal. 1975. 'Gelede dance of the Western Yoruba', *African Arts* 8, 1: 36–45.

Gore, Charles. 2007. *Art, performance and ritual in Benin City.* London: SOAS.

Houlberg, Marilyn. 1978. 'Notes on egungun masquerades among the Oyo Yoruba', *African Arts* 11, 3: 56–71+99.

Lawal, Babatunde. 1996. *The Gelede spectacle: Art, gender, and social harmony in an African culture.* Washington: University of Washington Press.

Lloyd, P.C. 1966. 'Agnatic and cognatic descent among the Yoruba', *Man* 1, 4: 484–500.

Makinde, Taiwo. 2004. 'Motherhood as a source of empowerment of women in Yoruba culture', *Nordic Journal of African Studies* 13, 2: 164–174.

Noret, Joël. 2013. 'La mise en scène du retour des défunts. Les masques egun à Ouidah (Bénin méridional)'. In Anne-Marie Bouttiaux (ed.) *La dynamique des masques en Afrique occidentale.* Tervuren: Royal Museum for Central Africa, 197–213.

Ogundiran, Akinwumi. 2020. *The Yoruba: A new history.* Bloomington: Indiana University Press.

Poynor, Robin. 1976. 'The egungun of Owo', *African Arts* 11, 3: 65–76+100.

Prince, R. 1961. 'The Yoruba image of the witch', *Journal of Mental Science* 107, 449: 795–805.

Schwab, William B. 1958. 'The terminology of kinship and marriage among the Yoruba', *Africa. Journal of the International African Institute* 28, 4: 301–313.

——. 1955. 'Kinship and lineage among the Yoruba', *Africa: Journal of the International African Institute* 25, 4: 352–374.

Smith, Robert. S. 1988. *Kingdoms of the Yoruba.* 3rd edition. London: James Currey.

Willis, John T. 2018. *Masquerading politics. Kinship, gender and ethnicity in a Yoruba town.* Bloomington: Indiana University Press.

——. 2017. 'Bridging the archival-ethnographic divide: Gender, kinship, and seniority in the study of Yoruba masquerade', *History in Africa* 44: 63–100.

Witte, Hans. 2004. *A closer look. Local styles in the Yoruba art collection of the Afrika Museum, Berg en Dal.* Berg en Dal: Afrika Museum.

——. 2002. 'Wereldbeeld en iconografie van de Yoruba'. In Jan-Lodewijk Grootaers and Ineke Eisenburger (ed.) *Vormen van verwondering. De geschiedenis en de collecties van het Afrika Museum, Berg en Dal.* Berg en Dal: Afrika Museum.

Picture Credits

For the pictures in this book we obtained permission from the photographers or owners of the artistic rights, and we are grateful for their enthusiastic support. The captions to the images in the text provide full credit details, this section gives additional information. The authors and publisher are grateful to all the institutions and individuals for permission to reproduce the materials in which they hold copyright. Every effort has been made to trace the copyright holders; apologies are offered for any omission, and the publisher will be pleased to add any necessary acknowledgement in subsequent editions.

Afrikacentrum Cadier en Keer. 6.3. The story of this Yoruba *gelede* headpiece is found in extenso in Leyten 2015, Chapter 1.

Anderson, Martha G. 9.1.

Aniakor, Chike. 9.3. See https://www.facebook.com/103205797759656/posts/ijele-masquaradethe-story-origin-of-ijele-masquaradepreambleijele-masquarade-kno/253426232737611/, consulted 26 April 2023.

Arnaut, Karel. 8.2.

Bay, Edna. 7.1. This picture is on the cover of Drewal and Drewal 1983. Through Henry Drewal.

Borkova, Elena. 9.6. Alamy Stock Photo. Taken during the 2020 FESTIMA in Dedougou, Burkina Faso. See https://www.aljazeera.com/gallery/2016/3/13/in-burkina-faso-festima-a-festival-of-african-masks, consulted 27 April 2022.

Bouttiaux, Anne-Marie. Cover picture: 97-02-13-18, KMMA Tervuren ©. Bouttiaux's work on the dynamics of mask performances and the systematics of masking (Bouttiaux 2009, 2013) lies at the basis of our quest and has been a constant inspiration.

Common source. 7.9. https://www.ancient-origins.net/ancient-places-africa/asante-empire-0016395, consulted 1 May 2023.

Cosentino, Henrietta. 1.4. With thanks to Ruth Phillips for the assistance. Henrietta Cosentino described the mask as presentifying the tutelary spirit of the *sande* associaton.

Dama, Michel. 7.7. With thanks to François Wassouni.

DeClippel, Catherine. 8.1. We thank Jean Colleyn for his assistance.

Denver Art Museum. 8.3b. No. 1942.443.

Drewal, Henry and Margaret Thompson Drewal. 7.2; 11.1. Henry John Drewal and Margaret Thompson Drewal Collection. Eliot Elisofon Photographic Archives, National Museum of African Art, Smithsonian Institution: EEPA

1992-028-01130. The work of the Drewals on Yoruba art is an outstanding example of in-depth understanding of African visual expression.

Dutch National Museum of World Cultures. 10.3. The first author collected this headpiece in Tireli in 2008, as a commission for the Royal Tropical Museum in Amsterdam, at the instigation of the second author, who was its Africa curator at that time. Van Beek had asked his Dogon host for an *èmna anyara*, a mask of a white man, and the smith who carved the mask apparently used him as a model. The headpiece is on show in the permanent exhibition of the Afrika Museum at Berg en Dal, The Netherlands.

Fardon, Richard. 1.2. Fardon's work on the Chamba is is exemplary in bridging anthropology and art studies, a major inspiration for this book.

Fischer, Eberhard. 6.1. The work of the Rietberg Museum group, Hans Himmelheber, Eberhard Fischer, and Lorenz Homberger, has been crucial to our knowledge of West African masking, especially for the Guro and the Dan.

Förster, Till. 2.4a; 5.3; 5.4. The Senufo are a well described group, thanks i.a. to Till Förster, whose work on brass also forms a landmark in African material culture studies.

Frobenius Institut, Frankfurt. 2.5. This classic picture by Leo Frobenius bears the institutional number FoA-04-5289_cFI (002) (002), and is reprinted in Nadel 1954.

Himmelheber, Hans. 3.4; 9.5. Through the Rietberg Museum, Zürich. FHH 437-15. FHH-443-12.

Homberger, Lorenz. 8.5. Through the Rietberg Museum, Zürich. GRK570615

Huet, Michel. 3.3: HQ017897, see Huet 1995: 121; 4.2: HQ0173499; 4.4: 20220506HQ001-001; 6.6: HQ0181982, see Huet 1995: 33, Leyten 2015: 128. The memory of Michel Huet will persist through his photographs, and we are proud to be able to use them.

Isichei, Elizabeth. Drawing 8.4.

Jespers, Philippe. 4.3.

De Jong, Ferdinand. 10.1. De Jong's anthropological analysis of masking in Senegal is crucial for Chapter 10, illustrating the political see-saw between a modern state and a strong masking tradition, as well as the dynamics of mask iconisation.

Knöpfli, Hans. 10.4 Hans Knöpfli and his wife, Heidi, were missionaries in the Grassfields area.

Lamp, Frederick. 2.2: Collection no. 13 500.

Miller, Ivor. 1.3; 4.5; 8.7; 10.5; 10.6. For his broad support for this project, the authors thank Ivor Miller, but especially for his lasting contribution to the understanding of transatlantic cultural connections, and of the creative persistence of cultural heritage.

Muller, Jean-Claude. 2.1. For our understanding of masking in the Northern border area between Nigeria and Cameroon his work has been crucial, and with this picture we honour his memory. Neg. no. 2708 HiRes.

Metropolitan Museum of Art. 2.4b. Part of the Rockefeller collection. © 2023 Image copyright the Metropolitan Museum of Art/Art Resource/Scala, Florence.

Murphy, Ian. 6.9; 7.8. Ian Murphy is a professional photographer with a huge experience in Zambia.

Musée de Neuchatel. 8.3 The photo was taken by Henri Trilles on an expedition to chart the frontier between Gabon and Cameroon near the Atlantic coast between August 1899 and April 1901. This picture, no. P.1903.1.1, is one of twelve photos that the Musée de Neuchatel acquired in 1903; we thank the Museum for its support.

Ottenberg, Simon. 9.2. Ottenberg has enthusiastically supported this project, putting at our disposal a host of visual material from his archives; his work on the Afikpo is fundamental, as an early bridge between art history and anthropology.

Phillips, Ruth. 6.7; Ndoli Sowei and initiates. Bandajuma Kovegbuami, Bo chiefdom, Kenema district.

Roy, Christopher. 2.3. Roy's work on Burkina Faso masking, both in print and through films, has been one of the inspirations for this book, as is his website at the Ohio State Museum. We honour his memory. The archive number is 48 500 001.

Royal Museum for Central Africa, Tervuren. 3.2; 8.6. The museum references to these pictures read: 3.2 'EP.0.0.14742, collectie KMMA Tervuren; photo E.P. Marchal'; 8.6 'AP.0.0.971. collectie KMMA Tervuren'; photo Franz Michel 1898. See Ceyssens 2007: 62, photo 4. This *bwile* headpiece was collected by Charles Lemaire near Pweto, Lake Mweru, DRC, and is now in Tervuren. We thank the Museum for its generous support of our project.

Rubin, Arnold. 3.6 The official capture reads: Figure 2 Unidentified Vaa–Bong masqueraders performing in a funerary ceremony. Photograph by Arnold Rubin, Pantisawa, Nigeria, April 1970. Rubin Archive, Fowler Museum at UCLA, Neg. No. 2708. Image © Fowler Museum at UCLA. Cited in Gagliardi 2018a; see Jones 1985. We thank Marla Berns and the Fowler Museum at UCLA.

Salmons, Jill. 4.6. In memory of Keith Nicklin. The masks people are fleeing from is called *eka ekpo*, the mother of the ghosts, and greatly feared. Information from Jill Salmons.

Strother, Zoë S. 2.6; 3.1; 3.5; 3.8. The latter mask, neg. no. 2708, *thengu ya lukumbi*, is named after the roan antelope, which is notorious for goring hunters who approach it thinking that they have killed it. Strother's work is crucial to our study, bridging the gap between the two disciplines of anthropology and art from the side of art studies.

Thorbecke, Maria. 7.3: VF_17482_2; 7.4: VF_17358. We thank the Museum Völkerkunde Wien for their diligent assistance in this project.

Trilles, Henri. 8.3a. Between August 1899 and April 1901, Henri Trilles was on an expedition to chart the frontier between Gabon and Cameroon near the Atlantic coast. The picture is one of twelve photos bought by the Musée de Neuchatel in 1903.

Turconi, Angelo. 7.5; 7.6; see also Cornet 1982: 247.

Van Beek, Walter. 2.7; 3.7; 4.1; 5.1; 5.5; 5.6, 5.7; 6.2; 6.8; 9.4; 10.2; 11.2, see Van Beek 2012, 2022. Figures 2.7, 5.1, 5.5, 5.6, 5.7, and 11.2 are from the 2008 *dama* in Tireli. As for 4.1, the first author bought this *kanaga* mask from its maker/dancer after the 1989 *dama* in Amani (the picture is taken in The Netherlands, 2019). From the *dama* in Amani in 1989 stem Figures 3.7, 6.2, and 10.2. The description of that last *dama* is in Van Beek 1991a. The photographs in Figures 6.8 and 9.4 were taken during tourist performances in Tireli.

Vink, Nel de. Maps 1, 2, 3, 4, and 5, on resp. pages 9, 10, 11, 12, and 41. The maps are based on information from the authors.

Vogel, Susan Mullin. 6.5. The pioneering work of Susan Vogel on Baule art is important for our analysis of African masking, as a productive cross-over between art history and anthropology.

Index